Key Concepts in
Media and
Communications

Recent volumes include:

Key Concepts in Journalism Studies
by Bob Franklin, Martin Hamer, Mark Hanna, Marie Kinsey, John E Richardson

Key Concepts in Tourist Studies
by Melanie Smith, Nicola MacLeod, Margaret Hart Robertson

Key Concepts in Sport Psychology
by John M D Kremer, Aidan Moran, Cathy Craig, Graham Walker

Key Concepts in Classical Social Theory
Alex Law

The SAGE Key Concepts series provides students with accessible and authoritative knowledge of the essential topics in a variety of disciplines. Cross-referenced throughout, the format encourages critical evaluation through understanding. Written by experienced and respected academics, the books are indispensable study aids and guides to comprehension.

Key Concepts in
Media and
Communications

PAUL JONES AND DAVID HOLMES

Los Angeles | London | New Delhi
Singapore | Washington DC

SAGE Publications Ltd
1 Oliver's Yard
55 City Road
London EC1Y 1SP

SAGE Publications Inc.
2455 Teller Road
Thousand Oaks, California 91320

SAGE Publications India Pvt Ltd
B 1/I 1 Mohan Cooperative Industrial Area
Mathura Road
New Delhi 110 044

SAGE Publications Asia-Pacific Pte Ltd
33 Pekin Street #02-01
Far East Square
Singapore 048763

Library of Congress Control Number: 2011921137

British Library Cataloguing in Publication data

A catalogue record for this book is available from the British Library

ISBN 978-1-4129-2821-2
ISBN 978-1-4129-2822-9 (pbk)

Typeset by C&M Digitals (P) Ltd, Chennai, India
Printed in India at Replika Press Pvt Ltd
Printed on paper from sustainable resources

Contents

V

Our approach to and organization of this book have been strongly informed by a critical engagement with what might be thought of as the 'founding texts' for the key concepts format, the two editions of Raymond Williams' *Keywords* (1976a, 1983b).

For Williams, keywords were a rich public educational resource precisely because they could not be given a single, dictionary-like definition. They were ambiguous because they were still being actively debated. They provided a point of entry for the general reader into conflicts between intellectual traditions. Keywords were the faultlines between the continental plates of fully fledged theories, embedded traditions and popular conventions of usage. Williams was particularly drawn to words that had apparently conflicting academic and popular meanings, such as 'tragedy'.

To overstretch our geological metaphor, some keywords might suddenly erupt into prominence, so becoming a word on everyone's lips that appeared to be borne by subterranean forces of social change, somehow being 'felt' without having yet been fully recognized, analysed or publicly discussed. '**Culture**' was the classic case for Williams. '**Globalization**' might be the most recent example today. Other entries included in this book easily fit this profile – **popular, tabloidization,** for example – but many do not.

Not all key *concepts* have the popular resonance of 'globalization'. They may have been coined and circulated only within academia, often as attempts to provide rigorous clarification of contested keywords. We are also used to thinking of a *concept* as having a greater level of precision than a 'word'. While this could still be argued to be the case, one of the major changes in academic life in the 30 years since Williams first published his *Keywords* is the rising level of uncertainty and scepticism in academic discussion. Even central concepts have not escaped this mounting wave of critical re-examination and reassessment. In short, today, despite the search for rigour, key concepts often have the levels of ambiguity and contestation comparable to Williams' keywords.

A major reason for this uncertainty is the increasing interdisciplinarity in the social sciences and humanities. This is especially the case within the field of media and communications, perhaps the leading example of such interdisciplinarity in the last 30 years. Accordingly, we have sought to provide, where possible, accounts of the disciplinary sources of some taken-for-granted entries, such as **influence**.

Our first principle of selection has been the centrality of the concepts to the field of media and communications studies. Here we felt one of our chief tasks was to strike a balance between 'old' and 'new' concepts, as well as 'old' and 'new' media.

Not far behind for us, however, is our second selection criterion, which is that *the concepts provide a useful entry point for discussion of central concerns because of their contested status.* Such contestation might also arise when there is a choice between two related concepts. Should we speak, for example, of the media coverage

of the **discourse** or **ideology** of neoliberalism? Alternatively, the contestation may arise because one concept is the site of differing usage claims – for example, **medium, articulation**.

Intellectual traditions and media theories are mainly addressed by elaborations of their key concepts rather than looking at them in their own right. We do not have entries on structuralism or political economy, but we do for **sign** and **capitalism**. The exceptions to this tendency – for example, **postmodernism** and **deconstruction** – have been included because they have effectively become keywords in Williams' sense. That is, they have managed to reach a much broader audience and are probably already familiar to many students and general readers.

Of course, Williams not only provided us with a 'key concepts' template in *Keywords*, he also made major contributions to the fields of communications and media studies. In fact, these two dimensions are closely linked. *Keywords*' historical semantic 'method' was critically engaged with the linguistic and cultural 'turns' that have featured prominently in all fields of humanities and social sciences scholarship, particularly media and communications. We were disappointed to see that a recent 'updating' of *Keywords*, despite being conducted in evident good faith, had itself curiously set aside this most crucial dimension of the project and so diminished the significance of Williams' own theoretical achievements (Bennett et al., 2005; Jones, 2006). So, we tried to keep that perspective in play, not only in terms of how we have framed the presentation of the entries but also in our accounts of Williams' contribution to concepts relevant to the linguistic and cultural turns, as seen, for example, with **sign, culture** or **cultural form**.

We have discovered two forms of Williams' influence on media and communications that are notable in this context. First, *Keywords* itself and related texts were often used by others as a source for relevant concepts – **culture, popular** or **hegemony**, for example. Second, in a pattern that echoed his broader reception, his early work, explicitly focused on media and communications, was respected, but his later work, explicitly communications-orientated or not, was underutilized.

This was partly a product of Williams' own way of addressing interdisciplinarity in his written output. As Nicholas Garnham (1990: 20) once remarked of one of Williams' key late statements on means of communication, '[it] is hidden in a book of literary theory'. Thus, some of Williams' most important insights for media and communications had to be critically teased out from his broader writings or relatively unknown texts that have not been republished. This need has also shaped some of our concept choices, such as **cultural form**.

In the case of other media and communications concepts to which Williams contributed – for example, **hegemony, popular** – we were delighted to discover that this tendency towards critical rediscovery and recovery was also evident in the media and communications literature itself. It is recognized that key figures in the field, such as Stuart Hall, Marshall McLuhan, James Carey and Jürgen Habermas, all drew on Williams' work. More recently, however, as some of the older debates in the field have settled, his work has been more explicitly employed. The 2009

International Communication Association Conference, for example, took 'Keywords in Communication' as its organizing theme. Similarly, current work on popular culture and tabloidization now makes use of some of his previously underutilized texts.

We could say something similar of another major emphasis in this book – the work of the Frankfurt School and, more broadly, critical social theory. Here we join with David Hesmondhalgh and Jason Toynbee (2008) in arguing that media and communications would benefit strongly from greater interaction with social theoretical traditions.

Williams acknowledged that *Keywords* did have a precursor: the 1956 *Aspects of Sociology* (Frankfurt Institute for Social Research, 1973). Indeed, of all the available models, he drew closest parallels with this book, in which its authors 'combine analysis of key words or key terms with key concepts' (Williams, 1976a: 22). We have already suggested that such a mixture is what is required today. Moreover, as it happens, Theodor Adorno and his colleagues presented this combination in a format not unlike that of the Sage *Key Concepts* series – that is, a set of long-form essays rather than multiple short entries. Like us, they found the need for an index of subcategories that may well have qualified as key concepts themselves. It is in their index that one finds 'administrative research', for example, rather than in the listed conceptual entries. We have followed a similar course. So, it is in our index, rather than the contents pages, that you will find affordance, genre, semiotic and so on.

In terms of 'content', this emphasis does not manifest as a bias in concept selection, but shows how some of the relations between the words form what Williams called *key clusters*. For example, we were especially struck by how the Frankfurt understandings of 'critique' and 'ideology' have received little exegesis in media and communications, while one of the supreme applications of these understandings, Habermas' 'public sphere', has become central to the field. While our contents listing and index are necessarily alphabetical, we have done our best to guide you to such clusters with the internal cross-referencing systems.

Needless to say, Williams and the Frankfurt School are not our only foci. Rather, in this preface, we wanted to draw attention to the contribution of these intellectuals to the design of this book.

Omissions, of course, are a necessary part of this process. We already have our own list of absences and oversights. So, again in the spirit of Williams' texts, we welcome suggestions for putative later editions.

HOW TO USE THIS BOOK

ix

In keeping with the series' format, this book is based on long-form essays. Thus, not every term you wish to explore will be listed in the contents pages, so *it is very important that you check the index* as this may be your best guide to finding what you need in particular cases.

Each entry provides an account of the meaning(s), sources, role and influence of the term within the field of media and communications.

The Related concepts text under each title provides a guide to other relevant concepts in this book. Cross-references to other concepts, often highlighted, are also given within the text of each entry.

Finally, each entry contains a Further reading section that provides suggestions for following up aspects of the key concept, usually with readings beyond those already cited in the entry. All such references are detailed in the References section at the end of the book.

Our thanks to Chris Rojek for commissioning this book and also to his colleagues at Sage, Jai Seaman and Katie Forsythe. Special thanks to Diana Barnes for sterling and rigorous editorial support in meeting publication timelines, as well as indexing, and to Ben Manning for his research assistance on the final draft.

Paul Jones: Many entries I drafted benefited from discussions with colleagues, most often of related materials and papers rather than the drafts themselves, sometimes over many years. None of course bear any liability for what follows. Thus, I'd like to thank Georgina Born (regulation); Michael Chesterman (freedom of communication); John Corner (cultural form, culture); Chas Critcher (moral panic); James Curran (regulation, public sphere); Andrew Goodwin (popular/populist; cultural form); Nicholas Garnham (capitalism; information society; public sphere); Pauline Johnson (public sphere, critique); Sonia Livingstone (influence); György Márkus (culture, ideology and critique); Stuart Rosewarne (capitalism); Michael Symonds (culture industry, modern, critique); Rod Tiffen (populism) and Judy Wajcman (technological determinism, mobile privatization). Student feedback over many years has been invaluable. This project also benefited from UNSW sabbaticals.

My contribution wouldn't have been possible without the affection, care and support of my partner, Catherine Waldby.

David Holmes: My contributions to this volume have been enriched by teaching communications and media at Monash University for the past eight years. Many of my entries were originally prepared for the lecture theatre and have been put through their paces in the Honours seminar. Of the colleagues who have provided feedback, I would like to thank Eduardo de la Fuente and Andrew Padgett for their constructive insights. Past discussions with colleagues from the US-based Media Ecology Association and the Australia and New Zealand Communication Association have been most beneficial in addressing some of the challenges of new media analysis. I am also grateful to the Faculty of Arts at Monash for providing sabbatical leave to write-up a great many of the concepts that were assigned to me.

Lastly, I would like to thank my daughters Elena and Georgia, for their patience, and my partner Vasilka for her encouragement, love, and forbearance.

Paul Jones and David Holmes, May 2011

List of abbreviations

ANT Actor Network Theory

AOL America Online

AT&T American Telephone and Telegrah

BBC British Broadcasting Corporation

CBS Columbia Broadcasting Service

CCCS Centre for Contemporary Cultural Studies (Birmingham)

CDA critical discourse analysis

CMC computer-mediated communication

CNN Cable News Network

DVD digital video disc

FCC United States Federal Communication Commission

FTA Free Trade Agreement

GUI graphic user interface

G3 Europe, Japan and the USA

HBO Home Box Office

HTML hypertext markup language

ICQ I seek you

ICT information and communication technology

IMF International Monetary Fund

ISA Ideological State Apparatus (Louis Althusser)

ITN Independent Television News (UK)

ITV Independent Television (UK)

MIT Massachussets Institute of Technology

MNC multinational corporation

MNTS major new technology systems

NWICO a new world information (and communication) order

OSN online social networking

PC personal computer

PDA personal digital assistant

PSB public service broadcaster/broadcasting

r.a.t.s. rec.arts.tv.soaps

R&D research and development

SEC Signature, Event, Context (Jacques Derrida)

SMS short messaging service, text

STPS Jürgen Habermas' *The Structural Transformation of the Public Sphere* (1962, 1991)

STS science and technology studies

TD technological determinism

TD2 technological determinism of the second order

UNESCO United Nations Scientific and Cultural Organization

URL universal resource locator, Web address

WTO World Trade Organization

WWW World Wide Web

9/11 September 11 2001

> **Related concepts:** *capitalism, criticism/critique, culture, encoding/decoding, hegemony, ideology, technological determinism.*

'Articulation' might be thought of as a conceptual 'Holy Grail' in media studies. It is one of the most difficult and elusive terms addressed by this book. This entry relies more than others on familiarity with some of the other key concepts. As the concept has also been much misunderstood, we have dealt with it in greater detail.

Variants of its usage share a common broad purpose: to account for the relationship between '**media**' and their social context without reducing one to the other. There have been two linked 'waves' of application of the term in media and communications:

- in the work of Stuart Hall and Birmingham cultural studies (and its revival within critical **discourse** analysis)
- in the more recent British 'domestication school'.

The shift between these two is indicative of shifts of emphasis within media studies. Broadly, the first addresses mediated **cultural forms**, the second new media technologies.

INFORMING FRENCH DEVELOPMENTS

As with many other relatively recently developed concepts in media and communication studies, articulation was borrowed from work in structuralist linguistics. In its first application to non-linguistic phenomena – in anthropology – it goes under another name, 'homology'. The structuralist anthropologist Claude Lévi-Strauss applied techniques developed by Roman Jakobson in Prague for the analysis of language to kinship systems and myths. Lévi-Strauss 'decoded' myths held by indigenous peoples by finding patterns of repetition of key elements. Crucially, he looked to these recurrent structures or forms rather than the 'content' of the myths. From these he derived two sets of binary oppositions (or 'differences'). For example, in Lévi-Strauss' (1973: 149) interpretation of the resemblance by association the Nuer people recognize between twins and birds, he says, 'It is not the resemblances but the differences which resemble each other'. That is, the resemblance is not to be found superficially in the semantic *content* of 'twins' or 'birds' but in the *form* – in the system of differentiation within which 'twins' and 'birds' are positioned (Lévi-Strauss, 1973: 153):

> Twins 'are birds', not because they are confused with them or because they look like them, but because twins, in relation to other men, are as 'persons of the above' are to 'persons of the below', as 'birds of the below' are to 'birds of the above'.

1

Such analyses of homologous relations were usually represented diagrammatically with colons thus:

Birds of the below : birds of the above :: persons of the below : persons of the above

Lévi-Strauss offered this model as a solution to the Marxian dilemma of 'vulgar reflectionist' accounts of the relationship between ideas and their social sources (the base and superstructure metaphor – see **capitalism**). Rather than look at content, as many Marxist analysts had, they should look at 'the structure', that people thought through such structural relations, rather than overt content, Lévi-Strauss suggested. This form of relationship is variously known as 'structural', 'homologous', 'formal correspondence' or, eventually, 'articulation'. Many disputed Lévi-Strauss' extraction of these binary oppositions from the myths. This was in part because an evident power relation existed between researcher and those researched. Lévi-Strauss deemed the believers of myth incapable of consciously changing it, just as Ferdinand de Saussure deemed users of language (see **sign**). Rather, for both Saussure and Lévi-Strauss, changes in the structure were effected by the collective weight of usage/mythmaking. Crucially, for Lévi-Strauss, each myth was a 'bricolage' or assemblage of elements of previous myths that were changed in response to the need for an account of changed social circumstances, such as a loss of territory to another group. This implicitly political relationship between researcher/researched was central to Stuart Hall's adoption of the model.

While Roland Barthes took up the term mythology for his **sign**-based early analysis of **ideology**, Pierre Bourdieu and Louis Althusser took up Lévi-Strauss' implication that homologous analysis could be extended to modern societies. Althusser made a tentative step towards resolving the base-and-superstructure impasse from a structuralist perspective by altering the topography of the metaphor to one of 'levels'. He introduced 'articulation' when applying the classic structural linguistic model of a combination of linguistic elements formed from synchronic and diachronic axes to a whole society ('social formation') instead of a language. A given society is thus 'structured like a language' in that it is the product of the combination/articulation of different levels – economic, political, ideological – that are 'relatively autonomous' from one another, with the economic level determining all 'in the last instance'. Althusser found a warrant for this position in one of Karl Marx's methodological texts on production and consumption, a position that initially drew Hall to the concept (Althusser, 1982; Hall, 1974a; Marx, 1973b). Any gains Althusser made for media analysis, however, were undermined by the reductive formulation of **ideologies** as 'ideological state apparatuses' or ISAs (Althusser, 1971).

Althusser's colleague, Nicos Poulantzas, developed this use of articulation further in relation to 'the political' level, coupling it with a closer reading of Antonio Gramsci. It is Poulantzas who is usually credited with renaming Gramsci's 'historical bloc' – the combination of classes and class-fractions who 'rule' and so dominate the state and seek **hegemony** within civil society – as a 'power bloc' (Poulantzas, 1976: 296ff.), a term picked up by both Hall and Fiske as well as many others in cultural studies.

2

Pierre Bourdieu set his strongly class-based sociology of education and culture against the structuralist project – and especially semiology – but, nonetheless, developed his own form of homologous analysis that owed much to Lévi-Strauss (Bourdieu, 1991). Where Lévi-Strauss had established his first pair of binary oppositions speculatively, Bourdieu usually took institutionally given binaries – such as two-party political systems – as his starting point. Later, he expanded this model into what has become known as his theory of *fields*. Fields are understood as realms of relatively autonomous political or intellectual practice. Bourdieu's homologies posit resemblances between distributions of power – 'the rules of the game' – usually across two distinct and otherwise discrete fields and often in the form of binary oppositions. Bourdieu (2005) conducted most of his own research on fields of 'cultural production' and, towards the end of his life, applied this model directly to 'the journalistic field'.

HALL AND LACLAU

Hall, too, had sought a solution to the problem of base and superstructure and, like Gramsci, had been drawn to Marx's 'The Eighteenth Brumaire of Louis Bonaparte' (1950b) as a possible solution.

Like Raymond Williams, Hall identified in Marx's own practice an important variant of the use of the base and superstructure metaphor that did not merely reduce the political and ideological to the economic, as orthodox Marxism had done, but recognized something approaching 'relative autonomy' within the superstructures. In brief, Marx argues that political and literary 'representatives' of social classes work within different 'theatres' but, nonetheless, reproduce the 'limits in thought' of the classes they represent (see **ideology** and **hegemony**). In a series of essays, Hall (1977a, 1977b, 1977c) tracked this issue from Marx to Gramsci and Althusser and, finally, to Bourdieu's field model (Hall, 1978).

Significantly, in these methodological papers, Hall (1977b: 45) identifies Marx's method in 'The Brumaire' with homology and generally holds on to this term until he discusses Bourdieu's 'mutual articulation of two discontinuous fields' (1978: 29). What is common to both of these uses for Hall (1977b: 58) is the notion of 'double movement' or, as Bourdieu (1991: 169) calls it, 'double determination'. In Hall's routine usage, this expression becomes famously 'double articulation'.

By now, hopefully, the intent of all these models is becoming clearer and the need for Hall's 'double' qualification more evident. If one realm of practice – for our purposes, say, journalism – is to be linked *systemically* with another – say, politics – then the 'rules' of each 'game' need to be comprehended first. The 'players' operate according to the logic of their respective 'fields' – and, yet, so the argument goes, these fields tend to reproduce similarly *structured* internal power dynamics. Moreover, the consequences of such homologies/articulations have implications beyond the immediate fields – indeed, for the distribution of power within the whole society. As Hall

3

(1978: 29) paraphrases Bourdieu's conception of 'symbolic power' in relation to 'the field of class relations':

> Symbolic relations are not disguised metaphors for class relations. It is *because* they do symbolic work of a certain kind, that they can function as the articulation of another field – the field of class relations: and hence do the work of power and domination.

Characteristically, Hall had been working with such a model 'in practice' before he fully theorized it. As early as his 1972 essay on news photographs, he had argued for a 'double articulation' of two levels of analysis – in that instance, between 'neutral' **news values** and the connotative resonances of news photos (Hall, 1972: 75). In 1976, however, he (and colleagues) conducted a very Bourdieu-like analysis of the professional **encoding** of the BBC's flagship current affairs programme *Panorama*. Here, two 'discontinuous fields', in Bourdieu's sense, were painstakingly analysed: the parliamentary theatre of party politics and the 'rules' of BBC current affairs, especially interviewing, as retrieved – consistent with the **encoding/decoding model** – by semiotic analysis. Broadcast current affairs is shown to be *not* susceptible to conspiratorial charges of 'bias'. Rather, it is precisely its limited autonomy – including its norms of balance and objectivity – that demonstrates the homologous relation Hall proposes. This can be characterized by the following 'Lévi-Straussian' model:

> State : political sphere :: political sphere : media.

Thus:

> Some such interpretation suggests that the relationship of the media to the political is remarkably *homologous* to the *general* relationship between politics and the State itself, in which politics (party practices) accords to the State (the institutions of power such as Parliament and the Courts) a certain measure of independence and neutrality, because this appearance is, ultimately, the most effective way in which politics can use or make itself effective *through* the State, without appearing directly to do so in the defense of narrow or short-term |c|lass or Party advantage … This is the sense in which both Gramsci and Poulantzas speak of the State as necessarily a 'relatively independent' structure. It is by the displacement of class power through the 'neutral and independent' structures of the State, that the State comes to provide the critical function, for the dominant classes, of securing power and interest at the same time as it wins legitimacy and consent. It is, in Gramsci's terms, the 'organizer of hegemony'. If, then, we consider the media in homologous terms, we can see that they, too, do some service to maintenance of hegemony, precisely by providing a 'relatively independent' and neutral sphere … And this reproduction is accomplished, not in spite of the rules of objectivity (i.e. by 'covert or overt bias') but precisely by holding fast to the communicative forms of objectivity, neutrality, impartiality and balance. (Hall et al., 1976: 88)

It was this dimension of Hall's work that shared common ground with that of the political theorist Ernesto Laclau, who had provided the most significant contribution to the advancement of the concept of articulation, initially within Poulantzas' framework. Laclau did not, however, write about media and communications directly. His primary interest was in political regimes such as fascism and, especially, in the political phenomenon of **populism** – a theme later picked up by Hall in his work on authoritarian **populism**.

Laclau explicitly proposed articulation as an alternative to economic reductivism to account for the relationship between social classes, politics and ideologies. Like Hall, Laclau drew heavily on Gramsci's conception of **hegemony**. In particular, he elaborated the mechanisms involved in the development of the ideology of a ruling bloc that seeks to become hegemonic. So, rather than reduction, Laclau developed Gramsci's key hegemonic mechanism of *incorporation* in effect, *as* (primarily linguistic/ideological) *articulation*. Laclau argued that incorporation required the articulation of elements outside the organic ideology of the dominant bloc into a new combination.

His primary example of incorporation was the modifications that liberalism had to make to its commitment to free market principles in the nineteenth century in the wake of open class struggles over wage rates and child labour (Laclau, 1977: 161–2). However, the reorganization of free market principles towards regulatory ones in the wake of the 2008 'meltdown' of financial markets would serve just as well. In each case, the central ideological task is to incorporate elements of critics' and opponents' arguments so that fundamental contradictions – as basic as whether or not child labour or financial market regulation should be a feature of capitalism – are presented as mere differences and so ideological continuity is maintained. Crucially for Laclau, it is this new articulation – as in 'it is crucial to maintain financial market stability at all costs so that people do not lose jobs', for example – that seeks to ideologically interpellate not only the general population but also members of the power bloc itself.

To put this in purely theoretical language, ideologies are thought of as consisting of separable 'elements' that can be recombined in different ways into, for the later Laclau, **discourses**.

Laclau's emphasis on hegemonic success being dependent on the articulation of dispersed elements joined neatly with Hall's established fascination with Gramsci's reflections on *common sense*. Common sense gives us a more familiar formulation of just what it is that is being 'articulated'. We all have a ready understanding of the term – which appears to have an equivalent in most languages – usually because someone in authority has told us we lack it. This very familiar experience is perhaps the most ubiquitous act of 'interpellation'. Most of us have been 'hailed' by the invocation that in lacking common sense, we lack an adequate everyday understanding of the way the world 'really is'. This is what Laclau would later call an 'empty signifier', completely amenable to all forms of (re)articulation.

If we start, as Hall often does (1985a, 1996b, for example), with Gramsci's metaphor of 'an infinity of traces without … an inventory' (Gramsci, 1976: 324), then we can think of common sense as a repository of elements that have no internal coherence, something like the way all proverbs seem to have contradicting partners. *This* dimension of articulation for Hall refers to the combination and linking of elements of common sense with a particular ideological element.

Crucially, Hall follows Laclau's specification that the internal relationship between these elements is not 'logical' but 'connotative' (Laclau, 1977: 10) – such articulatory combinations operate as chains of association rather than 'rational argument'.

The role of the media from this perspective, then, is primarily framed, for Hall (1977a), by the process of articulation of the dominant ideology in the power bloc's quest for hegemony. It is, however, only framed – not 'determined' – as the whole purpose in developing this concept is the avoidance of economic reductivism.

So what has happened to the 'double movement'? In a now famous metaphor provided in a 1986 interview, Hall compared his understanding of mediated ideological articulation with the ambiguity in the British use of the term articulation to mean both 'to utter' and to connect – as in 'articulated lorry', which is a truck consisting of a driver's cabin and separable trailer: 'Either the cabin or trailer can exist separately – they don't necessarily have to go together' (1996c: 140). This articulation is, thus, still 'double', as it was for Hall in 1972. It refers to both (in its 'utter' sense) the contingent constitution of an ideological discourse from dispersed elements (including common sense) *and* the linkage that 'matters' for Hall (1996c: 141), 'between that articulated discourse and the social forces with which it can, under certain historical conditions, but need not necessarily, be connected'.

Later, Hall and Laclau differed significantly, following Laclau's shift towards a Foucaultian conception of **discourse**, which was not easily compatible with Hall's 'lorry' version of articulation (Hall, 1996c: 147–8; Laclau and Mouffe, 1985). Instead, Hall, like some later critical **discourse** analysts, developed his model of **discourse** from Vološinov's emphasis on semiotic contestation (Hall, 1982: 79–83, 1985a; see **sign**).

Laclau's 'logical/connotative' distinction also echoes the primary distinction Barthes makes between denotation and connotation in his definition of code (see **sign**). So this conceptual repertoire is remarkably similar to the one Hall had already developed in his work on **encoding/decoding**. In effect, if we accept the Althusserian model of 'levels' – as Hall and Laclau usually do – then the media need to be seen as a fourth 'level' with their own conditions of relative autonomy (contra Althusser's ISAs but closer to Bourdieu's fields).

THE DOMESTICATION SCHOOL AND ITS 'DOUBLE ARTICULATION'

The version of 'double articulation' developed by Roger Silverstone and his colleagues dates from a later period in media studies: broadly the mid-1990s to the present (Livingstone, 2007a). The simplest contrast with a Hall/Laclau usage would be to suggest that its starting assumption is the centrality of the media and mediation in everyday life, rather than a politically focused Gramscian political agenda. By the 1990s, the research focus had shifted from politics and ideology to consumption and meaning. This shift should not be overemphasized, however.

Yet, within cultural studies itself, articulation was reformulated within a revised **encoding/decoding** model of a circuit of cultural production and meaning that was the conceptual centrepiece of an influential series of Open University textbooks (du Gay et al., 1997). The career of David Morley is indicative here. While his early work was central to the empirical application of the **encoding/decoding** analyses of mediated meaning within the wider frame of Hall's conception of articulation, his subsequent research has increasingly addressed the 'domestication' of new media technologies themselves. As Morley and Silverstone put it in an early version of this position, media are considered both 'texts and technologies', the meanings of which are emergent properties located within, but not determined by, micro-social environments in which their use is 'domesticated' – most notably within households. Crucially, for Morley and Silverstone (1990: 33), 'acts of consumption (of both texts and technologies) provide the articulating dimension'. In this sense, the domestication school's use of the same phrase, (double) articulation, actually addresses an issue related to but distinct from Hall's earlier formulation – that is, the interplay between media as technologies and media as cultural forms played out in other conceptual contests covered in this book (**medium, cultural form**). To connect the domestication school's understanding with Laclau/Hall's concern with politics and economy may well require a 'triple' (Hartmann, 2006) or even 'quadruple' articulation – or a multilayered Bourdieuian field approach.

FURTHER READING

The key texts by Hall and Bourdieu are cited within this entry. A more recent application of Hall's 'double articulation', mixed with the domestication school approach, can be found in Shaun Moores (2000). Laclau's project on developing a general theory of populism – from much the same conceptual framework as his earlier work – has continued (Laclau, 2005, for example). David Morley (2000) is indicative of his later work on domestication (especially Chapter 5). Robin Mansell and Roger Silverstone (1996) is a representative collection of the domestication approach included within a range of studies of information and communication technologies (ICT). Thomas Berker et al. (2006) provides a recent 'updating' of the domestication framework.

Audience

Related concepts: broadcasting, culture industry, image, influence, mass, media effects, modern, popular, public sphere.

The sense of the term 'audience' that has traditionally concerned communications and media studies is that of the **mass** audience.

At a minimum, the mass audience is typically defined as the indeterminate group(s) to which mass communications are addressed. The membership of such groups is delimited to those who are within range of a media performance. Here a question arises as to whether the audience is defined as those who are actually listening or viewing or those who are within range of it. Marshall McLuhan's claim that electronic **media** (be they visual or sonic) are consumed according to an 'aural' logic rather than a visual one is significant here, as it becomes impossible to escape media that envelop the senses. They are ubiquitous and, in a sense, cannot be turned off. From this standpoint, to live in **modern** society is to be automatically part of an audience. The orthodox way in which media industries think of an audience, however, is in terms of a 'target audience'. Such a sense of audience is proscribed by the transmission paradigm of communications, where the point of a media performance is to 'reach' its target audience and 'get the message across'.

Much of the difficulty with the concept of audience lies in the tension between conceptions of mass audience and target audience. The mass audience is often imprecisely defined as the available audience, whereas the target audience is a fictional device invented by advertisers and marketing executives. The difficulty in identifying the mass audience is its low visibility, compared to the mass audiences of antiquity. Indeed, early administrative research on broadcast audiences was largely concerned with mapping this new invisibility. The theatres of ancient Mediterranean Turkey, Greece and Rome in Athens, Thebes, Ephesus, Miletus and Priene, held from 20,000 spectators to the 160,000 accommodated at Rome's Circus Maximus. These audiences were distinguished by the fact that they were physical assemblies in space and time. Modern mass audiences are segregated in time and space, either as a readership or an electronic assembly. The electronic assembly is the dominant form of mass audience today, in which audiences are segregated in space, but integrated by simultaneous event reception. Conversely, readerships are separated in space and time because the media product can be consumed over time, rather than ephemerally. The unity of these readerships is nevertheless defined and organized around particular texts: the broadsheet, the tabloid or the novel.

In the 1940s, the Leavisite and Frankfurt schools anticipated that electronic **mediums** would overtake readerships, as popular culture overtook literary traditions. This trend even extends to popular culture making literature over in its own image, with the development of the easily digestible – Mills and Boon and 'pulp fiction' – novel in an attempt to convert electronic audiences back to readerships.

The nature of the electronic audience has changed substantially since the 1930s and 1940s, however. The vertical integration of the large movie studios (which had a monopoly over cinema content) in the 1940s was soon to be challenged by television broadcasters bringing 'programmed' audio-visual content into people's homes. Instead of movie patrons packing cinemas to see a relatively small selection of movies, considered compulsory viewing, regardless of genre, television made possible an entire day of viewing diverse content and the programming of the day into different genres, such as breakfast, soaps, movies, sport, news and so on.

The diversity of **cultural forms** within the one medium of television made possible audience segmentation according to programme content. (In print culture, this segmentation became mirrored by the proliferation of magazines.) The loyalty of viewers to a small number of broadcasters operating when television was first introduced was transformed by the 'fragmentation' of the mass audience across a large number of channels afforded by cable delivery systems. Of course, like early cinema, such services were characterized by a national concentration of ownership, but, unlike cinema, they could deliver a bewildering array of content that has proliferated over the following decades of production.

The mass audience is only possible when there is a high degree of concentration of broadcast ownership and content delivery. Such audiences survive today, in spite of forces of fragmentation, in relation to mega events, such as the Olympic Games, or spectacle disasters or new **genres,** such as reality television.

While audience fragmentation leads to a remarkably high degree of solidarity within 'audience communities' (see below), all audiences suffer from the problem of low visibility between members. Low visibility helps account for the fact that, from the earliest propaganda models of media influence onwards, audiences were frequently regarded as passive receptacles, inert masses, vulnerable to manipulation and persuasion.

Although there were earlier exceptions, the most influential break away from this 'passive' model developed from the work of the Birmingham Centre for Contemporary Cultural Studies (CCCS) and, later, in 'active audience' studies. Beginning with Stuart Hall's **encoding/decoding** framework, a trajectory in cultural studies, from David Morley to John Fiske, argued that audiences decode media texts in a range of ways that may differ from how these texts are encoded. The key shift within this trajectory was Morley's empirically based qualification of Hall's assumption that such 'aberrant' or 'resistant' decodings were rare because of the dominance of a preferred reading, consciously or unconsciously encoded by programme producers. By the time we reach John Fiske's work, however, we have reached the opposite of Hall's position: the thesis that popular audiences had a general capacity to resist, negotiate and self-empower in their use of media texts. This tension remains controversial in cultural studies and beyond.

Central to these reformulations was a wave of feminist studies of cultural forms popular among female audiences, from magazines and romance novels to, especially, television soaps. The key texts cited are usually Ien Ang (1985) and Janice Radway (1984; see also Geraghty, 1991). These studies are generally more nuanced than Fiske's (1987) account of them (see **popular/populist**). Ang's early work, for example, drew attention to the specificity of the cultural forms in question – that is, the narrative form of soaps, for example, led them to be more polysemous and so capable of sustaining a greater degree of resistant decodings than Hall envisaged in his work on news programmes.

The study of gender in television audience formation not only looks at media texts and their discursive role in the construction of gender but also the fact that much programming is specifically targeted in gender terms (D'Acci, 2004a; Joyrich, 1996). In societies with a heightened sexual division of labour, the daily cycle of television content was historically highly structured around gender, with daytime soap operas and talk shows traditionally viewed by women, family viewing placed either side of the evening meal and male-orientated sports shows scheduled in the evening.

9

Later, work in the sociology of media and interactivity addressed the problem of the 'invisibility' of the audience (Dayan, 2001; Thompson, 1995) and looked at ways in which audiences reclaimed such visibility by media-related practices, such as fan clubs (Hills, 2001), media pilgrimages (see **ritual**) and, through such practices, formed 'audience communities' (Baym, 2000).

Typically, such audience communities lack the direct means to share their experiences of texts, other than the specular ontology of the television or cinema screen (Meyrowitz, 1990). An attraction of such media is the deferred or anticipated sociability that may result. Broadcast texts allows audience members to form an opinion with which to engage in everyday conversation. This is what Pasquier calls 'serial-induced sociability' (cited in Dayan, 2001: 752), which occurs in the face-to-face lifeworld, yet such sociability has much smaller boundaries than the electronic ones that define the television audience. Today, invariably, the imagined community of a television audience has national or global potential and its specularity contains a global power, which can never be consummated by local forms of sociability. In other words, whereas a broadcast generates an instant 'international context' of social connection, there are few ways in which individuals can achieve meaningful *interactions* that make tangible, or do justice to, those global connections.

THE CYBER-AUDIENCE

Some studies that specifically address how mass audiences began to 'double' themselves online (Baym, 2000; Hills, 2001; Schultz, 2000) show how the Internet has become a medium by which audience communities are able to reassemble and become remediated. They also show how strong these communities are, independently of the Internet.

In her work on rec.arts.tv.soaps (r.a.t.s.), one of Usenet's first and most popular sites for fan culture chat, Nancy Baym (2000) points out that, hitherto, analyses of audiences have been confined to analysing texts in terms of how they attract a certain audience profile. This is because 'audience communities are diffuse. All members of audience communities are members of other communities as well. Therefore it has been both theoretically and empirically difficult to separate out the audience component of the community without relying heavily on the text' (Baym, 2000: 19). Baym claims that the Internet radically changes this because it is an environment that allows diffuse audience members who are already, in a sense, 'communicating' with each other via the screen to locate each other directly.

The significance of computer-mediated communication (CMC) is that, while it may not touch as many individual lives as broadcasts do, it, nevertheless, provides the possibility for more 'electronic interaction' between people constituted by broadcast integration. Quoting Ien Ang, Baym points out that audiences rarely 'represent and organize themselves as "we, the audience", and on rare occasions when that happens, they are generally not taken very seriously ... The Internet has changed that, in part by making audience communities more visible and, also, by enabling their proliferation' (Baym, 2000: 19).

Baym's exploration of r.a.t.s. is not representative of fan groups in general, but it gives a concrete and very novel illustration of how the social dimensions take over from the textual ones as an audience becomes a community. Her study revealed that, while soap opera and television viewing provides the initial drawing together of an audience community online, that community follows its own path, without simply taking its reference from particular soap operas.

Through their connection to soap opera in texts, r.a.t.s. built a range of practices that function to pool information and collaboratively interpret the content. In this sense, r.a.t.s. is clearly an audience. Although connection to the text is essential, it offers us an inadequate understanding of what it means to be an audience community. Out of these textually oriented practices, r.a.t.s. also developed interpersonal practices and connections that came to be equally (and sometimes more) important to its participants (Baym, 2000: 209).

The value of Baym's work is that it illuminates the social bond that already exists in audience communities with the help of a newer medium. When refracted through another medium, the nature of this bond and its 'rituals' are *practically* revealed.

THE WEB 2.0 AUDIENCE

While, by making mass media their content, early Internet users reinforced the importance of the mass audience, some theorists argue that Web 2.0 has reversed this trend and fragmented mass audiences by opening the flow of media across so many platforms on a global and technical scale. Henry Jenkins argues that audience members can actively intervene in the circulation of content, be it corporately or individually produced. According to Jenkins (2006b), anybody can be a producer of media and the way in which producer and consumer interact is becoming increasingly unpredictable. There are no 'end users' of convergent social media in Jenkins' view. Rather, the blogosphere, the wikisphere, Flickr, YouTube and social networking sites and microblogging, all become vast repositories of content that can be drawn on, mashed up, collaged, pastiched and uploaded to myriad sites and platforms. In this way, what is seen as the collective passivity of mass media audiences becomes a collective intelligence, in which each participant is afforded a moment of creativity.

Jenkins' vision of the supplanting of mass media by participatory media has been challenged by the popularity of mobile devices that actually limit participation in the Web 2.0 forms of publishing Jenkins describes. Facebook and Twitter on mobile phones, iPads and other PC tablets, signal a return to the Web 1.0 page metaphor of information retrieval. These interfaces privilege a return to the user generating text only, rather than experimentation with multimedia production. Moreover, many of the most popular 2.0 mediums indicate a return to simply reacting to broadcast media, which Baym had described in the 1990s.

The microblogging site Twitter, for example, is less about exchanging the content of popular culture than it is a form of 'presencing' to redress the inequality inherent in the architecture of broadcast. Twitter reasserts the demotic, the banal

11

or the domain of everyday life and is, therefore, a social media counterpart to reality television. Unlike other social media, where other participants are often known from external contexts, Twitter typically uses programmed forms of mass media as its main context, leading to what Alice Marwick and danah boyd (2010) see as engagement with an imagined audience. 'A variety of imagined audiences stems from the diverse ways Twitter is used: as a broadcast medium, marketing channel, diary, social platform, and news source' (Marwick and boyd, 2010: 122). This leads to what they call 'context collapse' as, unlike social networking sites, Twitter is anonymous and provides very few external contexts that can be used to verify audience identity. 'Privacy settings alone do not address this; even with private accounts that only certain people can read, participants must contend with groups of people they do not normally bring together, such as acquaintances, friends, co-workers, and family' (Marwick and boyd, 2010: 122). As long as the audience remains indeterminable, Twitter users have a sense of being watched by others. This necessitates 'self-presentation strategies' , self-censorship, and some-times a 'lowest common denominator effect, as individuals only post things they believe their broadest group of acquaintances will find non-offensive' (Marwick and boyd, 2010: 122).

So, the reversal of visibility that the champions of interactive new media had long promised for audiences is attenuated by the lack of an 'identity context' beyond participation in the medium itself.

This example supports our final point about the emergence of a post-television audience environment that is worth emphasizing. The routine use of 'interactive' and 'interactivity' in reference to Internet-based communications may seem to completely replace the older debates about **influence** and active audiences. That is, the question of whether audiences routinely or only occasionally 'actively decode' may seem superseded by an environment of 'permanent interactivity'. Such a view is mistaken. While interactive media have rendered this situation more complex, we can still make the primary distinction between media tech-nologies and media texts embedded within mediated **cultural forms**. That is, what-ever the technical infrastructure, issues of decoding remain to be resolved in the interpretation of mediated cultural forms, even if we prefer to regard the 'audi-ence' of Internet-based communication systems as *users* with *encoding* options largely unavailable to broadcast audiences.

FURTHER READING

The field of audience studies has been formalized as a branch of media studies, with many key texts being compiled in readers such as Will Brooker and Deborah Jermyn (2003). It is comprised of extracts of classic works on the audience includ-ing one of Paul F. Lazarsfeld's voting studies and, among other 'active audience' selections, one from David Morley's *The 'Nationwide' Audience* on the varied reception of a popular current affairs programme in the UK (Morley, 1980; Morley and Brunsdon, 1997). The Pertti Alasuutari (1999) collection offers a very useful set of retrospective and prospective reflections on this tradition, including an interesting contribution from Morley. See also the set of readings and accompanying volume by Virginia Nightingale and Karen Ross (2003) (Ross and Nightingale, 2003 is the companion volume). Later work on audiences in relation to the Internet has looked at how online culture makes broadcast audiences more visible than they would otherwise be, as fan cultures meet online to discuss popular culture (Baym, 2000). Sonia Livingstone's work (1998a, 1998b, 2005, 2007b) provides excellent overviews and interventions in broadcast audience studies and transitions to new media environments.

Broadcasting

> **Related concepts**: audience, culture industry, image, mass, modern, popular, public sphere.

An institution and an architecture, broadcasting emerged as the most powerful form of *central* media in the twentieth century. It continues to provide a powerful basis for social integration today, despite prophecies about its demise by Internet utopians in the 1990s.

Of the foremost theorists of broadcasting, Raymond Williams provides a definitive social history of broadcasting in *Television: Technology and cultural form* (1974a). Rather than simply studying media effects, Williams provides a broad frame for the analysis of the reasons for broadcasting's emergence as well as an account of its extension of consumerism and consumer culture.

ORIGINS OF BROADCASTING

In *Television: Technology and cultural form*, Williams argues that, although broadcasting is generally assumed to be an innovation, it has been carefully developed to satisfy consumer demand. Thus, in fact, it is an unintended consequence of an unconnected history of military and economic events.

In the early twentieth century, improvements to communication technology served 'operational' military and economic needs. The use of telephony, telegraphy and radio was one-to-one, 'person to person, operator and operative to operator and operative, within established specific structures' (Williams, 1974a: 20). By contrast, *broadcasting* emerged as 'a technology of specific messages to specific persons … complemented, but only relatively late, by a technology of varied messages to a general public' (Williams, 1974a: 20). Broadcasting had precedent, however, in 'specific institutions of [the] kind of communication which involves or is predicated on social teaching and control: churches, schools, assemblies and

13

proclamations, direction in places of work. All these interacted with forms of communication within the family' (Williams, 1974a: 21).

The press is one of the earliest examples of this response to the development of extended state administrations and their limits on communication. As Williams explains, through 'the transmission or news and background – the whole orienting, predictive and updating process', the press met the demands for greater involvement in participatory democracy (Williams, 1974a: 21).

The development of electronic means of broadcasting, however, coincided with, and to a large extent responded to, urban consumerism and the increasing separation between the private household and public life. This is in particularly true of television, but the process began even earlier. Radio could easily have been diffused as point-to-point communication, as its military form was, but it was decisively shaped by this redetermination of public–private relations.

THE ARCHITECTURE OF BROADCASTING

The twentieth century saw broadcasting develop into a strong social institution, but its main function is as a social architecture that has existed for thousands of years. The earliest civilizations produced icons on a **mass** scale and circulated them on coins and tablets.

Broadcasting does not have to be electronic; it can have a mechanical quality, as in the press, or be a feature of an embodied assembly, such as a speech or lecture. Nor does broadcasting have to correspond to a specific technology, but is, rather, a quality of many communications technologies. For example, it is commonplace to think of the Internet as a host for network communication, but it also enables individuals to broadcast information by e-mail or microblogging. Likewise, Carolyn Marvin (1988) has discussed the early use of the telephone as a form of broadcasting.

For Williams (1981), the primary difference between modern and premodern systems of broadcasting is that today's audiences assemble in a wider range of combinations, rather than the '**mass**ing' of earlier audiences:

> we have at once to notice that there are radical differences between, for example, the very large television audience – millions of people watching a single programme, but mainly in small unconnected groups in family homes; the very large cinema public – millions of people seeing a single film, but in audiences of varying sizes, in public places, on a string of occasions; and the very large actual crowds, at certain kinds of event, who are indeed (but only in this case) physically massed. (Williams, 1981: 15)

As a social rather than a technical architecture, what is common to all broadcasting is that the communication *events* it enables are characterized by unequal relations between senders and receivers of messages. This is true whether it is in real time, as in a news service, or in stored time, as in the products of the culture industry generally. Moreover, a broadcasting event may be asynchronous but have high visibility, such as is the case with magazines and billboards. They tend to have a regular but not very immediate visibility. The impact of the content of such forms tends to build up over time. Other kinds of broadcast 'mega-events', like the Olympic

Games or the funeral of an international iconic personality, exhibit high concentrations of visibility and 'liveness'. Michael Real (1984: 222) describes the Olympic games as the most 'widely shared regular event in human history'.

THE END OF BROADCASTING?

As a social architecture, broadcasting has become the subject of much reassessment in the wake of the 'second media age' thesis in communication theory. This thesis sees broadcasting in decline. Broadcasting is regarded as uni-linear, one way, 'top-down' and predisposed to political control. This is in contrast with network communication, which is seen to be 'interactive', 'two-way', decentred, non-hierarchical and 'grass roots'. Thus, the second media age thesis rests on a strong conception of broadcasting as an oppressive communication medium from which network communication provides emancipation.

This thesis persists today in much of the literature on media '**convergence**', particularly in the argument that 'grass roots' media, such as YouTube, appropriate the **genres** and content of mass media and thereby subvert its authority (Jenkins, 2006a).

On the other hand, there are arguments that traditional broadcasting **audiences** become remediated by new sources of media content as they find alternative, but much more fragmented, ways to consume the same content. The latter arguments rest on a technical rather than an architectural conception of broadcasting – the idea that broadcasting can only occur in mediums specifically developed for that purpose. The Internet, however, provides a platform that can also accommodate limited forms of broadcasting, such as spam, broadcasting e-mails and mirror-broadcasting. Likewise, broadcasting can be transformed by its demassification and personalization via new delivery means, such as cable. David Marc (2000: 631) has argued that cable has resulted in a trend away from mass delivery and a collapse of its 'transdemographic' possibilities and, ultimately, broadcasting will be relegated to a 'biblical era of mass communications' in which great events and famous people will have become entombed.

Most technicist conceptions of broadcasting rest on a heightened *historical* conception of the difference between broadcasting and **network** communications. The periodization of the contemporary era as a 'digital', interactive' or 'Internet age' contrasted with a bygone age of broadcast media has become something of an orthodoxy. It is in relation to broadcasting that 'New Media' has become a fetish, although Marshall McLuhan (2003) was using the term over 50 years ago in relation to print.

There are a number of problems with distinguishing between broadcast and network communication on historical grounds alone. First, while an analytic distinction between broadcast and network is useful, there are continuities between these forms that are overlooked at the expense of the adherence to historicism. Both television and the Internet facilitate similar logics of urbanization, consumerism and **mobile privatization**.

A second problem is that it does not sufficiently distinguish between the social structure of communication environments (decentred, centred, one to many, many to many) and the technical organization in which such social forms are realized. Distinguishing between the social structure of communication environments and their technical organization would reveal that broadcasting is possible within 'new media' just as **interactivity** is possible within broadcast. Nevertheless, an accentuated 'isomorphism' exists between communication mediums and the social qualities attributed to them.

At an analytic level, these continuities can be contrasted with specific qualities of broadcasting that are not apparent within the architecture of network communication. As David Holmes (2005) argues, these include liveness, performativity and interpellation. In all its forms, broadcasting is the only media architecture capable of 'liveness', beginning with the live intensity of electronic forms, but also exhibited in the daily ritual of newspaper consumption. In relation to television, Patricia Mellencamp (1998) argues it is not the 'nowness' of television that gives it liveness, but the fact television programming is simultaneous with other programmes as well as with itself. Relatedly, broadcasting is the only truly performative medium able to extend speech acts to an almost unlimited synchronous audience that recognizes itself as the addressee of such an event. In this medium, any utterance, regardless of whether it is true or false, constitutes a communicative act with an authority deriving from the simultaneity of that act for the audience. This simultaneity, in turn, constitutes a mass audience, itself constituted by radial transmission through which each audience member is interpellated (see **identity**).

FURTHER READING

Williams' *Television: Technology and cultural form* (1974a: 9–31), remains a definitive chapter in the social history of *broadcasting*, but see Briggs and Burke (2009) for a more recent attempt at a fuller social history and Roger Silverstone's (1994) 'suburbanization' of Williams' argument. A discussion of pre-electronic forms of broadcasting can be found in Garth S. Jowett (1981). For analysis of the challenge of new media to broadcasting, see David Marc (2000), Jostein Gripsrud (2004) and Jeanette Steemers (1999). For an examination of the interrelationship between broadcast and network media, see David Holmes (2005: 83–121).

16

Capitalism

Related concepts: criticism/critique, culture industry, globalization, hegemony, ideology, tabloidization.

We have included this concept because it is foundational to many other concepts in this book and it has also become increasingly acceptable in general parlance. For a long time, it was considered 'too critical' a term and so was confined mainly to

Marxian usage and, within media studies, political economy-based approaches (see below). All that changed with the fall of European communism. Occasionally, capitalism has even been openly declared to be 'cool' (McGuigan, 2009). Its public use in phrases like 'the future of capitalism' has also been very noticeable since the 2008 financial crisis.

ORTHODOX ACCOUNTS

The avoidance of an everyday use of 'capitalism' relied heavily on the viability of substitute terms that acted as euphemisms for – or even idealizations of – social relations within capitalism. Chief among these was 'free market(s)' or 'market society'. The circulation of these terms owed much to the rebuilding of the discipline of economics in response to the devastating critiques of the inequities of nineteenth-century capitalism put forward by the classical political economists and Karl Marx. The resulting *neoclassical* approach within economics remains enormously influential and underpins much of contemporary neoliberalism and at least some versions of the **information society** thesis (Mosco, 2009).

THE MARXIAN CRITIQUE OF CAPITALISM

Most crucially for Marx's understanding of capitalism is his thesis that it is an historically specific 'mode of production' – that is, a particular combination of certain types of productive forces and social relations in production.

Informing Marx's emphasis on production is a philosophically derived assumption that the starting point in any analysis should be the identification of how humans solve problems of 'basic needs'. By productive force, Marx means technical resources – including knowledge – brought to bear in production processes. So, productive forces include, but are more than, our usual understanding of 'technology'. Social relations of production include all those systems of social organization that control how production is organized. Such systems organize people into economic social classes.

In co-emphasizing social relations in this way, the Marxian analysis is quite different from a **technologically determinist** position, even though Marx was enormously impressed by capitalism's capacity to harness technology. Similarly, he attributed neither capitalism's dynamism nor the profits earned by capital investment merely to its 'technological superiority' or 'efficiency' but, rather, to the combination of technical innovation and exploitative social relations involved in production.

Plainly, Marx's conception of capitalism was based on its nineteenth-century form. So his model of an advanced economy is mid-nineteenth-century industrial Britain typified by steel mills and textile production. In extending that analysis, as leading **information society** theorists such as Daniel Bell and Manuel Castells claim to do, we need to take into account the many factors that have changed since his time.

Marx conceived the exploitative character of capitalism to be both economic and 'cultural'. He was convinced that wage labour systematically exploited the productive labour of humans. He often argued that capitalism could only lead

17

to greater *immiseration* of the working class. He did not anticipate the rise of the modern consumer society and 'Fordism' in some nations (see **mobile privatization**). He also argued, however, that something fundamental was lost in capitalist social relations involved in production where a worker could not identify with the product of his or her own labour. By this, he means more than the common observation today that 'our work gives our life meaning'. There is a strong tendency within his theory of *alienation* to privilege *artisanal production* – that is, the relatively self-organized relations of production of craft workers and the related Romantic ideal of the artist. Much of Marx's account of capitalism in *Capital* concerns the destruction of artisanal relations of production by factory-based methods. From this normative position, Marx argued that capitalism was itself an alienated social system. Marx also argued that capitalism was organized not to produce useful products but commodities – the specific 'end product' of the capitalist production process. A similar loss was involved here as commodities' exchange value was privileged over the products' potential 'use value'. Both these perspectives were developed further by Theodor Adorno in his **culture industry** thesis and later theorists within this field.

THE PROBLEM WITH 'BOURGEOIS'

Marx employed the French terms *proletariat* and *bourgeoisie* – instead of working class and capitalist respectively – when analysing political developments because he considered contemporary French politics more 'advanced' than those elsewhere. One effect of this usage – continued by most intellectual followers and commentators – is the considerable confusion English-language readers have with *bourgeois*. A simple translation of it from a French–English dictionary renders it as 'middle class'. Crucially, Marx did not locate the bourgeoisie/capitalists at the middle of the social pyramid but, instead, at the very 'top' – that is, the economically *dominant* or *ruling* class. Unlike the situation in Britain and other European cases, the French Revolution had ruthlessly 'eliminated' the former ruling class, the aristocracy. Marx tended to use the term *petit bourgeois* for the classic middle-class occupations based on self-employment, such as professionals and shopkeepers. The modern corporation – and the somewhat impersonal 'capitalist' it represents – was only just beginning to emerge in Marx's time, so some contemporary analysts use the term 'grand bourgeoisie' to cover such entities.

One interesting exception to the subsequent trend towards 'faceless' corporations is the long-standing persistence of the 'newspaper mogul' or 'media mogul' who emerged from a dynastic family and has survived into the present day. Although Rupert Murdoch, for example, now heads a modern global corporation, due to his very conspicuousness, for many, he embodies the 'ugly face of capitalism'.

From the perspective of immanent **critique**, however, bourgeois also refers to the bourgeoisie's development of central components of democracy and the role of the media within democracy. It is in this sense that Jürgen Habermas, for example, refers to the **public sphere** as 'a category of bourgeois society'.

THE PROBLEM WITH 'BASE AND SUPERSTRUCTURE'

In the academy, 'post-Marxist' positions proliferated in the 1990s. These were, in part, a reaction to the fall of East European communism and, soon afterwards, the movement on which many Marxist intellectuals had pinned their hopes, 'Eurocommunism'. This Gramsci-inspired strategy popularized his concept of **hegemony** and centred on the possible and actual role of the French and Italian communist parties in the 'historic compromise' of coalition governments.

Eurocommunism also coincided with attempts to rethink the relationship between traditional class politics and new social movements, especially feminism. Theoretically, however, the *bête noire* variously known as 'vulgar Marxism', 'reflectionism', 'reductivism' or, especially, 'class reductivism', continued to haunt this tradition. In brief, this failing refers to the tendency to reduce non-economic phenomena – such as media content – to economic ones, most often social class. Ironically, at least the most obvious versions of this problem had been addressed by Marx himself, the Frankfurt School, Gramsci, Williams and others. The continuing influence from the 1970s of the reductive postulations of Althusser's structuralist appropriation of Gramsci (see **ideology**), however, came for many to stand for Marxian analysis itself. Similarly, for those unfamiliar with the complexities of the Marxian tradition, intellectual doubts about Marxian work on **culture** and **ideology** rest on the understanding of a single metaphor Marx used on just a few occasions. Such texts circulated more widely than others, mainly because of their use by communist parties as teaching/propaganda tools. So, summary texts were often presented as 'the whole story'. Here is part of such a passage from Marx's 1859 'Preface':

> In the social production of their life, men [sic] enter into definite relations which are indispensable and independent of their will, relations of production which correspond to a definite stage of development of their material productive forces. The sum total of these relations of production constitutes the economic structure of society, the real foundation, on which rises a legal and political superstructure and to which corresponds definite forms of social consciousness. The mode of production of material life conditions the social, political and intellectual life process in general. It is not the consciousness of men [sic] that determines their being but, on the contrary, their social being that determines their consciousness. At a certain stage of their development, the material productive forces of society come in conflict with the existing relations of production or – what is but a legal expression for the same thing – with the property relations within which they have been at work hitherto. … With the change of the economic foundation the entire immense superstructure is more or less rapidly transformed. In considering such transformations a distinction should always be made between the material transformation of the economic conditions of production, which can be determined with the precision of natural science, and the legal, political, religious, aesthetic or philosophic – in short, ideological – forms in which men [sic] become conscious of this conflict and fight it out. (Marx, 1950a: 328–9)

The summary character of this account implies a reductivism not in keeping with Marx's extended historical analyses. The beginning of the passage is consistent with the account above of Marx's broad view of modes of production, of which capitalism is one example. Marx understands all the elements of the superstructure to refer to their elaborated 'professional' forms rather than, say, everyday personal philosophies or aesthetic preferences. So the 'superstructure' is necessarily a set of state institutions and elaborated intellectual 'forms'. In an earlier usage of the same metaphor in *The Eighteenth Brumaire of Louis Bonaparte* (1950b), Marx makes it plain that he has a 'division of intellectual labour' in mind where some specialize in politics and intellectual matters while most do not. The opposition he establishes between a 'material' base and 'ideological' superstructure used throughout the early unpublished manuscript, *The German Ideology* (Marx and Engels, 1976), however, is highly problematic and also sets up a series of dilemmas for subsequent adherents to this model.

Nonetheless, it is important to redress here a conflation that has developed within media studies, probably traceable to Stuart Hall's popularization of the term 'classical Marxism' (1996a, for example). Hall uses this term to cover *both* the 'summary' works of Marx and the later 'orthodox', 'vulgar' or 'reflectionist' tradition that commences with Engels' publications after Marx's death and goes on through the activities of the twentieth-century communist parties. As the above indicates, Marx's position was at times ambiguous, but he did not always – and arguably never did – reduce the superstructural to 'the economic'. (Nor, for that matter, was his work compatible with the totalitarian practices of the communist parties.) Accordingly, this book uses the terms 'vulgar', 'orthodox', 'reflectionist' and so on rather than 'classical', to refer to the post-Engels tradition rather than to Marx.

POLITICAL ECONOMY OF MEDIA AND COMMUNICATIONS

Another terminological ambiguity exists here as media and communications approaches to political economy have tended to be dominantly Marxian rather than, as their name would suggest, directly influenced by the nineteenth-century classical political economists (whom Marx criticized; see Table 1). The more important point is that contemporary political economy approaches to media are, without fail, *critical* above all of:

- capitalism's inequities
- approaches to the media that might overlook such inequities.

In one of their several influential manifesto-like formulations, Peter Golding and Graham Murdock (1991: 17) distinguish a 'critical political economy' as holistic, historical, concerned with the balance between private corporations and public intervention and, finally, unlike most orthodox economics, driven by moral imperatives of justice, equity and the public good.

Table 1 (Very) simplified map of dominant theories in 'economics'

1800s –	Classical political economy (challenged in mid-1800s by radical critiques such as Marx's)
1890s –	Rise of neoclassical economic theory – restoration of eighteenth-century model of 'free market'
1930s – 1970s –	Great Depression of 1930s 'answered' by Keynesian economics' recognition (again) of capitalism's failings – role for State enhanced in policy – era of welfare state begins from 1940s – 'embedded liberalism' of constrained capital
1970/1980s – September/ October 2008 –	Keynesian policies enter crises in 1970s (although how dominant Keynesian thought was is debated); *neoliberal* return to (eighteenth-century) neoclassical premises of market – era of privatization, deregulation of finance markets, welfare state and much related media regulation – constraints on capital movement progressively removed until crash of 2008
2008 –	Re-regulation of finance sector mooted – neoliberal era increasingly declared over – but this remains much debated. Increasing evidence that poorest will carry burden of repaying the State debt that was used to 'save' the banks.

Accordingly, political economists have been major contributors to debates about media **regulation** in the media/communications policy field and the related concerns of critical political communication. Indeed, Habermas' public sphere thesis was introduced to English-language media studies via an essay by a leading political economist, Nicholas Garnham (1986), in a collection on political communication. The implication of Habermas' thesis as a form of *immanent* **critique**, however, has tended to be downplayed within the critical political economy literatures. Rather, an unmasking conception of ideology critique (see **ideology**) has tended to inform its notion of critical practice. The chief targets here have been liberal, liberal–pluralist and neoliberal market-based models of media organization and policymaking.

These themes came together in what remains perhaps critical political economy's most important conceptual legacy – the concept of *cultural imperialism* (CI). Economic imperialism was a concept developed by early twentieth-century Marxists to account for the increasing internationalization of capital. In a sense, it is a critical precursor of **globalization**.

In brief, the CI thesis asserted that dominant economic powers within such a world trade system – most notably the USA – exerted comparable cultural dominance via the circulation of cultural commodities. Hollywood was the classic instance usually cited after the important case of international news agencies. Table 2 follows Colin Sparks' account of the CI thesis' formation and transformations from its critique of a variant of modernization theory through to arguments about globalization. It thus usefully situates the concept among others in this book.

Table 2 Development, imperialism and globalization: the implications of the paradigm shifts in international communication (adapted from Sparks, 2001a)

Key element	Phase I: Developments in communication 1950s–1960s	Phase II: Cultural imperialism 1970s–1980s	Phase III: Globalization 1990s–?	
Central concept	Modernization (techno-economic)	Independence (for subjugated peoples)	Globalization a **contested** concept	
Geopolitical emphasis	Decolonization (and Cold War)	Imperialism (and Cold War)	**(Sceptics)**	**('Cultural globalists')**
			Globalization as continuation of cultural imperialism	Globalization as qualitatively new situation
Indicative academic titles (following Sparks)	Lerner, *The Passing of Traditional Society* (1958)	Schiller, *Mass Communication and American Empire* (1971)	Herman and McChesney, *Global Media: New Missionarie of Corporate Capitalism* (1997)	Featherstone, *Undoing Culture* (1995)
Model of 'audience'	Vulnerable peasantry – dying local culture – potential citizens	(Mis)informed citizens	(Mis)informed citizens and poorly served cultural consumers	Creatively resistant consumers and/ or local/national cultures
'Media' content focus	'Information' (often propaganda)	News	News still emphasized over 'culture'	'Culture'
Role of 'markets'	Strongly Advocated	Strongly Criticized	Strongly Criticized	Ambivalent
Key 'media'	Radio	*News agencies	(Satellite) TV and information and communication technologies (ICT)	
Forum	UNESCO	UNESCO	*UNESCO and WTO*	

Of most note is the changing model of the **audience**. Once active audience models were imported into this debate and combined with an affirmative version of globalization, the CI thesis came under considerable pressure and was widely regarded as obsolete by many who followed a 'post-Marxist' course. Even for its critics, however, much remains retrievable. Sassoon's more broadly historically pitched 2002 model of international cultural markets – that is, markets in exclusively cultural ('content') commodities, such as film rather than 'hardware' – delineates a subtypology that avoids the possible oversimplifications of a 'first world v. third world' binary (see Table 3).

Table 3 Five types of states in cultural markets (based on Sassoon, 2002)

Culturally dominant	Abundant local production supports strong domestic market as well as abroad – high export, low import	USA since 1945 Britain/France in 19th century
Extreme protectionist	Strong domestic cultural market, but unable to export; prevents imports	USSR (until 1989)
'Balanced protectionist'	Strong protected domestic cultural market capable of significant export; allows imports	Contemporary UK
Partial protectionist/ mixed (partly dominated?)	Substantial domestic market – some or no local subsidization – minor export market	Japan, India
Culturally dominated	Cultural consumption originates mainly from abroad	Bulgaria, Belgium

A NOTE ON RECENT CAPITALISM

As Tables 1 and 2 suggest, the analysis of twentieth-century capitalism underwent many conceptual reassessments in response to actual changes as well as different critical perspectives. The development of the arguments around Fordism and post-Fordism, for example, recognized that the gendered division of labour was part of the 'stablization' of class relations in a situation beyond immiseration and open class warfare in advanced capitalist societies.

Neoliberalism has tended to be used as a descriptor for the most recent phase of capitalism, even though it more accurately concerns a cluster of economic and political philosophies and policy settings. Harvey's (2005) useful 'brief history' situates neoliberalism very plausibly as a form of **hegemony** as per the description in Table 1. Unlike classical liberalism, which generated many of the normative principles relevant to the media such as freedom of speech (see **freedom of communication**), neoliberalism has seemed to have few redeeming features that would render it susceptible to immanent **critique** – that is, an appeal to its guiding utopian principles – as it celebrates little but the virtue of 'market forces' (but, for another view, see Plant, 2009).

FURTHER READING

Vincent Mosco (2009) provides a history of critical political economy and an account of the political economy of communication. Mosco is representative of both Canadian concerns and a broader North American political economy tradition that would also include Robert McChesney (2007, 2008) and Dan Schiller (1996, 1999, 2007). Canadian research is connected to an important Francophone

23

political economy tradition (Lacroix and Tremblay, 1997; Miège, 1989, for example). The UK tradition is most associated with the work of Nicholas Garnham (1990, for instance) and Peter Golding and Graham Murdock (such as 1991), but see also Colin Sparks (2007). Andrew Calabrese and Colin Sparks' *festschrift* for Garnham (Calabrese and Sparks, 2004) includes James Curran's history of 'the Westminster School' (of which Garnham was a founder). To a considerable degree, this field overlaps with the critical political communication one, especially strong in the USA (Bennett, 2008, for example). For a powerful reassertion of the relevance of both Marx and the media/cultural imperialism thesis respectively, see Christian Fuchs (2010a, 2010b).

Communication(s)

> **Related concepts**: broadcasting, criticism, culture, influence, mass, media effects, media/medium, network (society), ritual.

Communica*tion* and communica*tions* are so often conflated as objects of study, but they are historically distinguished methodologically and disciplinarily. That separation is hard to discern today, however.

The study of communica*tion* was often confined to interpersonal, organizational or linguistic forms of interaction, whereas communica*tions* opened more explicitly onto a vast field of means of communication, technologies, mediums and their architectures, as well as the relationship between a communication medium and the messages that circulate within it. Consequently, communication research faced the risk of being framed as administrative research (see **media effects**; **criticism/critique**) whereas communica*tions* tended to more readily open up critical cultural and sociological research into media technologies, environments, policies and institutions.

Often allied to reductive psychological models, administrative research proliferated so that there was a wide array of positivist studies into human communication, each guided by instrumental aims. These strongly informed the US tradition of **media effects** research. That is, they were interested in improving communication processes, producing 'successful' communication or identifying the right methods for communicating. Therefore, communication studies was much more aligned with the fields of marketing, public relations and advertising. Especially in its applied forms, it was less a critical discipline and more one that serviced others by facilitating conflict resolution (servicing the workplace and capitalist society at large), cross-cultural communication (servicing the contradictions of cultural globalization), organizational communication (servicing the power of management in enhancing the efficiency of large organizations).

Communication studies typically understood communication processes to be divided between 'interpersonal' and 'mass' communication. On the other hand, communications looked at the abstract and impersonal systems and means of communication that make possible realities not visible within interpersonal communication, such as the 'audience', ideology, cyberculture, hegemony, mass, the 'popular', public sphere, and network society.

Ontologically, the two fields of study have less to do with each other than is commonly thought, although they do overlap in terms of the relationship they identify between mediums and messages – that is, the way that mediums shape or permit messages. Increasingly, the rise of digital personal and social media has challenged the communication/communications distinction. For some time now, that division has been breaking down. The US-based *Journal of Communication*, for example, has long published articles based in both communication and communications perspectives.

Perhaps the greatest overlap between the study of communication and communications came from the intersection between the traditional communication concern with speech and rhetoric and the rise of structuralist linguistics across the humanities and social sciences. In something like the contradictory role played by the Leavisites in informing the British tradition (see **culture**; **mass**), studies of rhetoric in the USA were quite capable of forming critiques of advertising that anticipated, say, the work of Roland Barthes. Jürgen Habermas' early work on speech acts was also influential in the USA, as was his later work on communicative or **discourse** ethics. More broadly, Ferdinand de Saussure's structuralist linguistics was the decisive influence. His overturning of philology and the subsequent establishment of formalist semiotics and structuralism in anthropology and communication studies has endured. In 'mass communication' studies, semiotics and the study of the **sign** have profoundly influenced branches of media studies, including film theory, television studies and visual communication in general. The argument that each of these mediums develops its own code and system of signs specific to it is well established, suggesting that complex communications systems develop their own 'language' with characteristics quite different from natural languages.

Raymond Williams' 1962 book *Communications* (1976b) was one of the first to challenge the communication/communications distinction, especially in its 'interpersonal communication' v. 'mass communications' form. Too much unnecessary academic territorialization rested, Williams (1974b: 17) thought, on 'that significant plural'. His initial, later disappointed, hope for the then emergent (British) cultural studies was that it might provide the means for transcending this distinction. He was unsympathetic, however, to the *formalist* character of the subsequent influence on cultural studies of structuralism and medium theory, as he understood them (see **cultural form**). Instead, he deliberately developed an alternative conceptual basis for bridging the communication/communications distinction, one he regarded as building on the foundational sociological work of Karl Marx and Max Weber. This alternative involved the concept of *means of communication* developed from the Marxian means of production (Williams, 1980a, 1995; see **Capitalism**).

25

COMMUNICATION(S) AS MEANS OF EXPRESSION AND MEANS OF COMMUNICATION

For the Williams of *Keywords* (1983b: 72–3), there is, thus, an 'unresolved range' in the noun 'communication' – especially in relation to its implications for communication theory – between transmission on the one hand and 'common or mutual process' on the other. Williams' coinage of the term 'means of communication' in this period is plainly his attempt to 'resolve' that range and this concept becomes his alternative to McLuhan's 'media' in his later work. It singularizes 'communications' but, in its full range of usage, includes practices formerly associated with 'communication'. When combined with the related concept of means of cultural production, it ranges from embodied means of communication, such as gesture, through to sign systems and the most sophisticated technologies (Williams, 1995; see Table 4).

A central strategy of *Communications* (1976b) was to insist on the inadequacy of *transmission models* for democratic conceptions of communication. 'Transmission' here is similar to the instrumental sense of communication beloved of early administrative research (see **ritual** and **media effects**). Unusually for Williams – and unnoticed in most accounts of the rise of cultural studies – his vision of a democratic system of communication is articulated in terms of basic rights, notably a reciprocal notion of freedom of expression:

> There are two related considerations: the right to transmit and the right to receive. It must be the basis of any democratic culture … that these are basic rights …

> On the right to transmit, the basic principle of democracy is that all are full members of society, all have the right to speak as they wish or find. This is not an individual right but a social need, since democracy depends on the active participation and the free contribution of all its members. The right to receive is complementary to this: it is the means of participation and of common discussion.

Table 4 **'Human and non-human' means of communication/cultural production (based on Williams, 1995, as developed in Jones, 2004)**

Human resource/means of production	Examples
Inherent (bodily) resources	Dance, song, speech
Combination of inherent and related separated objects	Masks, body paint and so on
Instruments of performance	Musical instruments
Separable objects that carry cultural significance	Use of clay, metal, stone and pigment in sculpture and painting
Separable material systems of signification	Writing
Complex amplificatory, extending and reproductive technical systems	Subjection of any of the above to amplification, extension or reproduction by 'means of communication'

The principle [of a new kind of democratic institution] should be that active contributors have control over their own means of expression. (Williams, 1976b: 120–1)

So it was democratic institutional innovation that could resolve *in practice* the tension in 'communication' for Williams, at least in the UK policy environment of the 1960s and 1970s. 'Community' is his shorthand for such participatory democratization, rather than a nostalgia for lost 'ways of life' for which his usage is often mistaken. Thus, means of communication is understood as not merely means of transmission but also means of democratic expression and dialogical participatory discussion. For Williams, this new category is thus normative rather than instrumental.

This conception also provides the foundation for Williams' understanding of debates about mass/minority and high/low culture. Those he would later call 'cultural producers' also play the role of responsible controllers of their own means of expression in a democratic culture. Underpinning both these positions is a proto-Marxian Romanticism that wishes to redress the (commercial) alienation of the means of production of expression and culture and return them to the producers by means of media policy innovation and regulation. It is, thus, quite compatible with contemporary discussions of digitalization and increased portability/accessibility of new means of communication.

The US communications scholar James Carey was similarly attentive to the historical semantics of communication, specifically for the US case. He argued against the limitations of a transmission model of communication (Carey, 2008: 13). Significantly, both Williams and Carey regarded the conceptual linkage of communication with **culture** as the best means of redressing the instrumentalism of the transmission focus. They considered that this linkage with culture, understood in either its aesthetic or 'way of life' senses, necessitated a more dialogical and implicitly democratic conception of the role of communication (see **culture; ritual**).

FURTHER READING

In the USA, Paul F. Lazarsfeld's foundational text 'Remarks on administrative and critical communications research' (1941) serves as a point of origin for the one-time great divide within the discipline of communication(s). See the further reading for **criticism/critique** for more references on this history. In the USA, the departmentalization of communications (organizational, interpersonal, mass, computer-mediated and so on) is more developed than elsewhere. By contrast, in Europe, the anthropological, social and political dimensions of communication(s) are explored much more within the legacies of critical social theory. For example, John B. Thompson's *The Media and Modernity: A social theory of the media* (1995) charts the integral role of media in the transition to modern societies, Raymond Willams' edited volume *Contact: Human communication and its history* (1981) delves into 'when old communications systems were new' to demonstrate the constancy of human communications as a trans-historical force in social life. See also John Durham Peters' *Speaking into the Air: A history of the idea of communication* (1999).

Convergence

> **Related concepts**: *capitalism, digital, information society, interactivity, network (society), technological determinism.*

Convergence, like 'interactivity', has become a buzzword in both popular understandings of media and in communications and media studies. For the everyday consumer, convergence is largely understood as an outcome of miniaturization or the introduction of the computer management of consumer appliances, where form, function and capability are enhanced by combining technologies.

While convergence may be observed in a wide range of industries, in communications and media it is seen to occur between the three areas of computerization, media and telecommunications (Van Dijk, 1999a: 9). Any innovation in one of these areas may increase the convergence between the three domains. For example, an increase in the processing power of PCs has made possible the hosting of video streaming. Conversely, as telecommunications corporations make available broader bandwidth, PC manufacturers scramble to add new features, such as video calling. At the level of consumer technologies, there is also a strong drive towards the *personalization* of these technologies. Hand-held technologies – that can play music and video, mobile phones that can take photos and browse the Web – are examples of convergences that require massive capital investment.

CORPORATE AND TECHNOLOGICAL CONVERGENCE

Convergence is much more than combining consumer electronics within one device, however. Theorists of convergence identify two broad forms of convergence: technological and industrial. Technological convergence refers to:

- infrastructure – transmission links between optic fibre, cable, microwave and satellite, for example
- new ways of combining content – sound, text, data and images
- transportation – content being transported in a new way (such as the Internet on TV, TV on phones, entertainment on the Internet) (Van Dijk, 1999a).

Corporate convergence refers to mergers, partnerships, takeovers or bartering between the three different sectors of media, telecommunications and computing.

Such convergence represents something more than the familiar economic behaviour of 'horizontal integration' where two or more of the same kind of industry merge (newspapers, TV and radio, for example). This is because the aims of such a merger are not just related to economies of scale or functionality but also to the fact that the particular 'industry' may be redefined by changes in technological convergence. Thus, the opportunities involved in corporate convergence are primarily based on the ability to sell more content in different mediums that are otherwise closed. Van Dijk (1999a: 9) gives the example of 'a cable company that exploits telephone lines and a telephone company that exploits cable television'. The cable company uses telephone lines to deliver more television content in greater bandwidth, while the telephone company advertises itself on cable television.

One of the largest mergers to enable cooperation between online service providers and traditional broadcast industry models was the $207 billion merger of US America Online and Time Warner in 2001 (Devereux, 2003: 38–9). In 2001, AOL owned such enterprises as AOL Service, AOL Anywhere, AOL International AOL@School, CompuServe, Digital City, DMS, ICQ, iPlanet, Mapquest, Moviefone, Netscape and AOL Music, while Time Warner listed 227 corporate ventures, including 6 cable companies, 1 telecommunications company, 4 book publishing companies, 1 audio book company, 30 ventures in its home box office business, 15 cable entertainment channels, 2 network television channels, 10 CNN news services, 15 CNN websites worldwide, 6 subsidiaries of New Line Cinema, 15 subsidiaries of Warner Brothers movies, a further 15 subsidiaries of Warner Brothers music and 58 magazines published under the Time Inc. label.

The significance of such a merger cannot be attributed simply to horizontal or vertical integration (extending ownership up or down the line of production). Rather, the new conglomerate has had the capacity to cross-sell, cross-promote and create entirely new needs and markets for media consumers. The Time Warner side of the merger already had powerful distribution industries, but its strength in the provision of content across platforms became unparalleled with the addition of AOL.

The relationship between the convergence of platforms and corporate convergence is dynamic. Corporate convergence gives rise to new combinations of mediums, technological innovation and content delivery, while technological innovation creates the compulsion for new kinds of corporate convergence.

Paradoxically, this merger, which, at the time, was the largest in US history, collapsed nine years later and the two companies separated. Judgements about the inevitability of technological convergence were confounded by the fact that the two companies operated with entirely different corporate cultures: the aggressive marketing and deal-making practices of AOL executives versus the content production-focused work ethic of Time Warner. Another problem with the merger was that because the two businesses did not duplicate any services between them, there were no cost savings. On the technological side, there was the problem that most of AOL's 22 million customers were still on dial-up in 2000, so selling them high bandwidth content just did not work. It was a case of the ideology of convergence running ahead of the actual technical compatibilities of two different mediums.

This latter impulse can often be overstated as a technologically determinist logic. Brian Winston (2005: 377) has argued that, in recent years, technological convergence has become a rhetorical justification for further deregulation in the communications and media industries that 'downplays the usual logic of capital concentration as a cause'. That is, mergers and takeovers aren't just about plundering technological opportunities but are also driven by the exhaustion of monopolization in one industry or even a tendency for the rate of profit to fall in one industry. When there is little room to increase profitability, diversification becomes very attractive.

Another argument against some of the more hubristic accounts of convergence is that technological convergence is not at all new. Most of the recent analysis of media convergence highlights the importance of **digitization** in opening up media flows between platforms and technologies, but, as Winston (2005: 379) has also argued, it is not *required* for convergence. Rather, there have been other sufficient means of convergence based on analogue signals that have allowed interchangeability between medium functions for many years. These are largely centred on the convergence between wired and wireless. For example, radio was first used for point-to-point communication and the telephone was used as a form of network broadcasting in its early years. So today, Winston scoffs:

> That people can listen to their radio over their digital television – so what? That they can make telephone calls on their computers – so what? The reality is that the change over to digital is far more comparable to the move from analogue amplitude modulation to analogue frequency modulation in radio 40 years ago than it is, say, to the slightly earlier post-war shift from radio to television. (Winston, 2005: 377–8)

Certainly, however, digitization has eroded the distinction between wireless and wired communication technologies, which tended to be aligned with electronic broadcast and electronic network communications respectively. Broadcast media, including free-to-air TV, cinema, radio and the press, are 'wireless' forms of media. By contrast, wired media is dominated by interactive communications networks, the telegraph, telephony interactive cable TV, and the Internet. The digitization of broadcasting signals, however, has resulted in the delivery of wider bandwidth and the potential for new forms of complex interactivity.

Older forms of network technology have also become remediated by a **digital** version of the older media (Bolter and Grusin, 1999; Callanan, 2004), which enable wider bandwidth, but not necessarily greater speed or interactivity. Rather, these latter capabilities have demanded the emergence of technologies that are 'born' digital, such as the Internet, and mobile phones that can send text and images, for example. In turn, the complexity of communicating in a 'multimedia' way demands larger and larger forms of bandwidth and the compression of data into signals that can be sent via satellite, microwave or cable (see Table 5).

Henry Jenkins (2006b: 2) claims that digitization has democratized the means of broadcast as it has enabled a 'flow of content across multiple media platforms' and the 'flow of media audiences across these same platforms'. The most significant intersection for him is that between so-called 'grass roots' and corporate media. He gives the example of Dino Ignacio, a Philippine-American schoolboy who put together an image of Osama Bin Laden and the character 'Bert' from *Sesame Street* using the PC application Adobe Photoshop and then posted it on his Web page. Soon after September 11, the image was screenprinted in Bangladesh and found its way on to anti-US placards used in street marches in the Middle East that were televised by CNN. Jenkins (2006b: 2) comments, 'from his bedroom, Ignacio sparked an international controversy. His images crisscrossed the world,

Table 5 Digital convergence

	Broadcast (wireless and wired)	Network (wireless and wired)
Technology	'Older' media being remade in accordance with digital technologies and their mediums, such as digital TV, radio online, Newstext online, DVDs	Older network technology 'digital enabled', such as ISDN, mobile telephony, from analogue to digital Altogether newly 'born digital' technologies, such as the Internet, mobile text, mobile data, mobile video text, networked PDAs, and new services, such as online shopping, banking, gambling, searchable databases
Mediums	Radiowaves, satellite, microwave, cable	Satellite, microwave, cable
Policy	Broadcasters pressure governments to relax policies, because 'everyone' can be a broadcaster	Networking makes provision of information and entertainment that is otherwise commodified by broadcasters and telcos free, in the form of MP3s, movies and news, which dilutes the 'user pays' dimension of media

sometimes on the backs of commercial media, sometimes via grassroots media. And, in the end, he inspired his own cult following'. The ease with which content can flow across multimedia platforms means 'anybody' can be a producer of media, but that 'media producer and the power of the consumer interact in unpredictable ways' (Jenkins, 2006b: 2).

For Jenkins, convergence provides much more active participation in media. He argues that whereas old consumers of media were isolated individuals, new consumers of convergent media are 'more socially connected' because they can upload their own content and choose from a much wider array of fragmented information, including both corporate and grass roots media.

Jenkins' main assumption here is that the distinction between corporate and grass roots media is levelled by convergence culture. If this were the case, however, corporate media would no longer have a need for its professional codes as it could simply lift the vision and sounds it needed from amateur content. The production values that corporate media adhere to, then, according to genre, quality and content expectations are not influenced by the existence of 'alternative media'. The Ignacio-inspired cult following was only made possible by the CNN mass audience broadcast and the publication of his story in a book about convergent media.

FURTHER READING

Jenkins' (2006a, 2006b) declarations on convergence culture portray an emerging tension between what he calls 'grass roots media' and 'corporate media'. As a framework for understanding new forms of media flow, his *Convergence Culture* provides useful coordinates, but neglects the political economy of these processes. A counterpoint to the presentism of convergence theory is given in two of Brian Winston's major texts – *Media, Technology and Society* (1998) and *Messages* (2005). He surveys numerous examples of convergence over the past 100 years and the political and economic forces that brought them about, thereby highlighting the hubristic tenor of recent analysis. For a recent rethinking of these questions, see Klaus Bruhn Jensen's *Media Convergence: The three degrees of network, mass and interpersonal communication* (2010).

Criticism/critique

> **Related concepts**: *audience, cultural form, culture, culture industry, ideology, news values, popular, public sphere, regulation, tabloidization.*

'Criticism' and 'critique' are two terms encapsulating taken-for-granted assumptions that communications and media studies inherited from their informing disciplines and related debates. Contenders for a list of these informing fields would be literary criticism (now more commonly called literary studies), the debate over whether or not any of the social sciences could be critical as well as 'objective' and understandings of critique from philosophy. In short, the terms' history has been shaped by continuing debates about the relationship between the *methods* used to research aspects of media and communications and the *judgement* of those aspects.

A good measure of the tremendous shifts these words have undergone in English is the increasing academic usage, over the last 30 years or so, of the verb 'to critique'. Formerly, 'to criticize' would have been the standard verb form for both the nouns criticism and critique. This, we'd suggest, is because 'to criticize' had become too strongly associated with making arbitrary judgements from a position of assumed social or cultural superiority.

'Criticism', of course, has a related commonsense meaning, of nitpicking or similar pedantic attention to minutiae rather than the larger picture. Essay assessment, for example, should entail more than making spelling corrections. So what is at stake here?

THE CASE OF *MEDIAWATCH*

A good example of the dilemma is provided by regular programmes, columns and blogs that 'criticize' the media, especially journalism. These programmes are now ubiquitous in many nations in broadcast or online form. They often take the name 'media watch'. An ongoing Australian television programme, *MediaWatch*, is a case in point. Now an Australian public service broadcasting institution, it provides a 13-minute weekly review of mainstream media coverage of the previous week, as well as matters of media policy. Its founding presenter, Stuart Littlemore, had a background in both television journalism and law. The programme became famous for exposing journalistic errors and malpractice, including plagiarism, errors of fact, 'chequebook journalism' and the use of inappropriate, even faked, visual footage. Initially, however, Littlemore's acerbic tone meant that it achieved more notoriety for his (usually humorous) schoolmasterly correction of punctuation and spelling errors.

Littlemore's perceived arrogance hit a raw public nerve that at first might seem to be attributable to a peculiarly Australian egalitarian ethic. As suggested above and discussed further below, however, 'criticism' itself has attained a similarly strong association with an elitist, indeed schoolmasterly, perspective. Ironically, in 1989 in a prospective description of the programme's 'method', Littlemore described himself as moving away from standard 'lay' cultural criticism:

> It will be very personal, my view of how the media worked that week. However, I will also be using objective criteria … My beef with critics, particularly of film and TV, is that they don't know what they're talking about. It's all done from the point of view of an intelligent lay criticism. Now, while I'm sure there is a place for that, it does nothing for the industry. It doesn't say to them: 'Look, we know you cut corners here, we know you could have done this – but you didn't bother.' *Media Watch* will be done from the point of view of someone who really knows the medium from the inside. (Littlemore, 1996: 167)

Littlemore's equation of 'objective criteria' and 'from the inside' may seem odd. In practice, what he meant was what Stuart Hall had named the 'professional code' of the '**encoding**' – that is, in this case, journalistic ethics and the routine means by which ethical principles, such as 'balanced news reporting', are put into practice (see **news values**). In this sense, his criticism was not an arbitrary 'uninformed opinion' but an immanent, informed one. Here, 'immanent' means literally 'from within' or 'internal to'. More than this, the immanence of *MediaWatch*'s mode of critique is to hold journalists to account *according to their own 'internal' professional criteria* rather than make accusations according to quite arbitrary 'external' criteria. While professional codes are internal to a profession, they also provide objective criteria against which each professional individual can assess him- or herself. 'Criticism', in contrast, tends now to be associated with arbitrary external criteria.

THE TROUBLE WITH 'CRITICISM'

In principle, the same could be said of aesthetic judgements (that is, those relating to art). Philosophical aesthetics, for example, is premised on the assumption that taste judgements are more than arbitrary subjective opinions. Criteria of judgement can be extracted from what may appear merely subjective reactions articulated as matters for discussion. For example, a difference of opinion between two people who have both seen a film or concert should, in principle, be able to move beyond, 'Well, we are each entitled to our own opinion' to an examination of the differences in criteria of judgement (qualities of acting/singing, script, narrative resolution and so on).

The sense of 'criticism' bequeathed to media and communication studies by literary criticism, however, seemed immune to such dialogical discussion. F.R. Leavis (1965) – who did much to push literary criticism towards the analysis of **popular culture** – famously refused to describe his 'method' as anything other than the accumulation of the individual critic's experience.

Such a perspective was easy prey for those within the social sciences who wished to label all qualitative (that is, non-quantitative) approaches 'unscientific' and, thereby, expose their apparently arbitrary subjective judgement. Within the philosophy of the social sciences, such insistence on modelling methods of analysis on those of the physical sciences is known as *positivism* (see **modernity/modernism**). Its historical opponent was *hermeneutics* – a term applied initially to disciplined forms of textual analysis and, later, to all forms of social analysis that seek to reconstruct and understand, rather than explain, meaningful social actions. Prior to the rise of structuralism and poststructuralist analyses of **ideology** and **discourse**, hermeneutic techniques were the chief methodological alternative available to critical analysts. Some **discourse** analysts would join their work with the hermeneutic tradition (Howarth, 2000b). At its extreme, the positivist conception of media content would reduce it to a 'message' devoid of any ambiguity and so assessable solely by quantitative methods. Much of the later shape of media and communications was determined by responses to the positivist challenge.

CRITICISM AND CULTURE

Part of the problem here was that 'qualitative' techniques borrowed from literary studies and similar arts-based disciplines had been developed in relation to a radically delimited range of objects of analysis within 'high culture'. Literary studies, for example, had famously worked with selective traditions or canons of 'great works'. The expansion of the range of admissible work to *all* 'popular culture' or 'popular arts' available via the popular media first confronted the analyst as a problem of sheer scale. Hence the potential attractions offered by quantitative solutions.

An alternative set of approaches to subjectivist ones like Leavis' – and to positivist quantification – soon emerged. The most immediately influential of these alternatives was Roland Barthes' (1967) semiology based in Saussurean linguistics, later more commonly called semiotics (see **sign**). Barthes initially saw his approach as scientific, too. What Barthes' approach shared with contemporaries such as the early Marshall McLuhan was an attention to the *formal* properties of the material under analysis as opposed to their content (see **cultural form**; **genre**). This shift was fundamental: it broke with content-based hermeneutic approaches as well. It was a shift from *what* the cultural object 'meant' (via its content) to *how* meaning was formed and circulated (via its form). The chief formal properties Barthes and other semioticians pursued were **signs** and codes.

The form/content distinction is itself far from absolute. In practice, it is a matter of emphasis. So, it shouldn't surprise us that formalist approaches were already known within the arts-based disciplines. The study of **genre**, most obviously, attended to the enduring **cultural forms** within which aesthetic works were consciously composed, or later classified, by critics. It has proven especially fruitful in television studies, for example. What has remained at stake in this distinction, however, is the degree to which concerns more associated with 'content' can remain 'in play' in a given formalist analysis.

CRITICAL V. ADMINISTRATIVE RESEARCH

So far, this discussion has focused on media 'content'. The reconciliation of empirical methods and normative orientation that marked the positivism/hermeneutics dispute also surfaced spectacularly within early mass communication studies of **audiences** and **media effects**. Theodor Adorno and Paul F. Lazarsfeld clashed over the models of intellectual practice embodied in Adorno's goals for critique, on the one hand, and those of externally funded empirical research on the other. For Adorno, there could be no easy reconciliation. Perhaps more significantly, Lazarsfeld's characterization of the terms of the debate – critical versus administrative research – set a framework for discussion that was maintained well into the 1980s and resurfaced with the rise of cultural policy studies in the 1990s (Jones, 1994; McGuigan, 2004; see **regulation**).

As Hanno Hardt (1992: 111) has noted, Lazarsfeld's use of the term 'critical', however, did not attempt to encompass the sophistication of the Frankfurt Critical Theory tradition, of which Adorno was perhaps the supreme exponent. This ambiguity in such usages of 'critical' (capitalized or not) has continued in and beyond media studies. 'Critical theory' today would most likely connote a broader field that might include cultural studies and postmodernist and poststructuralist literatures. Similarly, political economists of media usually attach 'critical' as a forename to their field to distinguish it from classical political economy (see **capitalism**). Other key figures affiliated with the Frankfurt tradition (most rendered *émigrés* to the USA by Nazism) were Herbert Marcuse, Max Horkheimer, Leo Löwenthal and Walter Benjamin (whose attempt to escape Nazism tragically failed). The most famous second-generation Frankfurt figure is Jürgen Habermas.

CRITICISM/CRITIQUE AND THE PUBLIC SPHERE

The immanent v. external criticism/critique distinction overlaps strongly with discussions of **ideology**. Indeed, depending on one's views about using the term 'ideology', 'ideology critique' and 'critique' are almost interchangeable terms here. So, both ideology critique and critique are open to the external/immanent distinction. Habermas' public sphere thesis, in its earliest form at least, is an extended 'emancipatory ideology critique' in the sense understood by Adorno (see **public sphere**; **ideology**).

While the public sphere thesis is well known today as the basis of a normative account of the role of the media, the pivotal part played by the emergence of aesthetic criticism has only recently attracted growing attention in communication and media studies. Habermas regards early literary criticism as the first form of modern deliberation. Since he regards it as proto-political, however, he tends to assume that this function was either destroyed by the culture industry or replaced by the role of social movements.

More recently, feminists and other scholars have seen the literary public sphere model's potential for thinking through the relations between culture and the public sphere (Jacobs, 2006; Jones, 2007; Lara, 1998; McGuigan, 2005). McGuigan, Jones and Jacobs have all drawn attention to the function of *contemporary* aesthetic/cultural criticism to such debates. There is little popular culture, for instance, that does not have its own immanent forms of criticism, such as popular music criticism, and this is often constituted in something like the mode of Habermas' literary public sphere. This suggests that the links between aesthetic criticism and media are not only to be found in histories of intellectual traditions but also in contemporary social institutions of public debate.

FURTHER READING

Adorno's essay 'Cultural criticism and society' (1984) is difficult but highly pertinent to this topic. Adorno (1969) provides his later account of the conflict with Lazarsfeld. The definitive account of the formation of the Frankfurt School remains Martin Jay (1996). Jay (1984) also provides an excellent introduction to Adorno. For a more recent set of assessments of the Frankfurt School directly related to media and communications, see Jeffrey T. Nealon and Carren Irr (2002). Hardt (1992) provides an excellent overview of the intersections between critical theory and other research traditions in the development of critical tendencies in US communications studies. John A. Lent (1995) is similarly useful. Slavko Splichal (2008) gives a superb overview of these literatures. See also Clifford G. Christians et al. (2009). For an attempted 'updating' of critical media approaches, see Paul A. Taylor and Jan L. Harris (2008). For a rare feminist entrant into these literatures, see Sue C. Jansen (2002).

Cultural form

> *Related concepts*: communication, criticism/critique, culture, culture industry, encoding/decoding, genre, mass, media/medium, popular, sign.

'Cultural form' covers a highly contested field central to several key concepts that border each other and even overlap. It might once have been headed **genre** or narrative. We have, however, taken our guiding concept from Raymond Williams' distinction between cultural form and means of **communication** because it entails a broader range of approaches than most contemporary accounts of genre and narrative analysis (Lacey, 2000, for example). It could include, for instance, **encoding/decoding**. Moreover, Williams' distinction was designed to capture the dynamic *reconstitution* of cultural forms within new means of communication, without then succumbing to **technological determinism**.

The classic instance of this distinction for Williams (1974a) is the one between television 'technology' and television 'programming'. In that sense, cultural form and Williams' related conception of flow speak to the future as well as the past and present. This is quite significant as we have reached a point in digital reconstitution of the means of communication where some commentators have begun to announce the possible end of the usefulness of genre classification (Casey et al., 2002: 111, for example). Since at least the development of cinema, distinguishing between 'technological' means of communication and genre-like cultural forms has been a controversial issue.

CULTURAL FORM/TECHNOLOGY TO CULTURAL TECHNOLOGY?

There is, for instance, no generally agreed terminology for the means of communication/cultural form distinction or even whether such a distinction is needed in all cases of mediated communication. It is probably fair to say that the more theorists and analysts are concerned with the 'internal workings' of cultural forms, the less concerned they are about the 'social shaping' (see **technological determinism**) of either cultural forms or their enabling means of communication. Likewise, the more analysts are concerned with matters ostensibly external to cultural forms, the less likely they are to take into account the social consequences of meaning-making systems such as narrative.

For example, Nick Lacey (2000: 225ff.) makes the connection between genres and their popularity with audiences via the concept of a 'generic cycle' that shifts with audience tastes and the sudden rise of 'new genres', such as reality TV. A key moment here is the replication/imitation of a generic innovation resulting in the proliferation of particular genre types and the displacement of others – the revival of sci-fi from the late 1970s in cinema and television, for instance. Genre analysts tend to see such developments as a property of genres themselves. Political economists, in contrast, would regard the same phenomena as near direct consequences of the organization of the particular **culture industry** and the relative production costs of particular genres. Free-to-air advertising-funded television markets, for example, were notorious for this 'copycat' phenomenon economists call Hotelling's Effect (see **tabloidization**).

The legacy of the ambiguities within Marshall McLuhan's **media/medium** is here considerable for it is often impossible to distinguish which 'side' of Williams' distinction McLuhan is addressing when he refers to 'media'. McLuhan treats both means of communication and cultural forms – notably television – as 'media', largely in the sense derived from the older usage of 'medium' as artists' material means of expression and composition (the painter's medium of oils, for example), but also a sense of 'medium' extended to genres. Moreover, McLuhan's reason for this aesthetic derivation is fairly clearly related to his sympathy for **modernist** avant-gardes. Many early twentieth-century avant-gardes across all the arts held a similar view of the socially transformative potential of technological innovation (Poggioli, 1968). To some extent, the tension between McLuhan and Williams over media as form v. media as technology is similar to that between Walter Benjamin and Theodor Adorno over art and 'technological reproducibility' (see **culture industry**).

In Williams, the category is most visible in the subtitle of his book, *Television: Technology and cultural form* (1974a). Its purpose seems fairly plain: to distinguish between two dimensions often conflated in McLuhan's 'medium', the technology that constitutes television as a medium and the cultural forms that that medium-as-technology bears as programming. Typically, Williams employs the phrase 'means of **communication**' to refer to medium-as-technology and rarely employs the term 'media'. His *Television* book is perhaps best known for its opening critique of **technological determinism** and its subsequent application of that critique to the work of McLuhan. Williams also accuses McLuhan of *formalism*, however — a charge he was to repeat several times against others in following years, including, initially, Ferdinand de Saussure and semiotics and, later, the work of the Birmingham Centre for Contemporary Cultural Studies (CCCS; see **sign, genre** and below; Williams, 1986).

Williams' distinction works relatively well for cases where the means of communication and cultural form are relatively discrete and even 'visible'. Television 'sets' and associated production and transmission hardware – and, indeed, the socially shaped institutional configuration of broadcasting – are easy to distinguish from programming content. Cinema is less transparently so, even though the concept of genre thrives in cinema studies. Williams' use of cultural form plainly derives from the aesthetic sense of the concept of **culture**, but it can be expanded to refer to televised programme forms and the increasingly hybridized (intermixed) genres that television has generated (comedic drama and so on). If we continue with the case of television, for example, we can lay out some of the competing terminologies in Table 6.

We might even add to Table 6 the common industry term 'platform'. Like McLuhan's 'medium', it tends not to recognize the distinctions above. Williams' distinction, more or less echoed by Thompson, can be extended to digital media. Thus, we might think of the Internet as a specific, socially constructed form of digitalized convergence in the same way that broadcasting was a specific social configuration of certain technical developments in the formation of radio and television. Likewise, we might think of the Internet as supporting a series of cultural forms – e-mails, websites, streamed programming and so on – though these are perhaps more accurately considered forms of mediated interaction than aesthetic forms. What forms of mediated interaction and aesthetic forms share, however, are social conventions of appropriate interaction, whether between 'users' or between artists (and other cultural producers) and audiences/publics.

Lury's (2008) discussion of the concept of cultural technologies is very representative of some current trends within the field, at least in relation to the first column in Table 6. Its formulation is plainly *not* technologically determinist and, indeed, it takes Williams' critique of **technological determinism** – and his conflict with McLuhan – as one of its starting points. At its most basic, it seeks to specify

Table 6 Competing terminologies

Theorist	Television 'technology'	Television 'programme'
McLuhan	Medium	Medium
Williams	Means of communication AKA ('socially shaped') technology	Cultural form
Thompson (*The Media and Modernity*, 1995)	Technical medium	Symbolic form
Lury	Cultural technology	Cultural technology?

the usage of the technologies in question – that is, cultural technologies as opposed to mining technologies and so on. It, thus, moves in tandem with usages such as 'creative industries' (see **culture industry**), which seek to specify the 'productivity' of these industries for economies and so recognize that aesthetic/intellectual cultural production today is no longer a handicraft form of labour.

Beyond these points, Lury draws on Foucault's expansion of the use of the category of technology, which, like his comparable reconceptualization of **discourse**, moves us well beyond its usual referent of mechanical and similar devices (technologies of power, subjectivity and so on). Foucault frames this analysis in much the same pessimistic critical mode as Adorno's portrayal of the **culture industry** serving a broader project of social administration. Thus, in this expansive sense, cultural technologies also refer to the bureaucratic and other means by which 'culture' is organized and administered.

The distance 'cultural technology' takes us from Williams' distinction is thus considerable. In fusing 'technology' and 'culture' it:

- moves away from the conceptual separation of aesthetic practices and their enabling technics
- increasingly relies on the 'way of life' as well as aesthetic senses of **culture**
- is difficult to reconnect with social shaping approaches.

Athough 'cultural technology' seems to be speaking to the technology side of Williams' distinction, curiously the issue of form remains central, as it does in McLuhan's 'media'. This is because many of the approaches thus employed are, like McLuhan's, *formalist* ones.

'FORMALIST' MODELS AND THEIR LIMITS

Both McLuhan's and Williams' first discipline was literary studies. Within that field, the study of genres had become especially highly developed prior to the rise of media and cinema studies. McLuhan was particularly influenced by the cyclical literary genre theory of fellow Canadian Northrop Frye (1957).

Two resulting issues, which are directly relevant to much contemporary analysis of communications technologies and cultural forms, have therefore become confused.

- Formalism, like **technological determinism**, is prone to a reductive avoidance of a 'social shaping' dimension. 'Artistic devices' were often conceptualized as automated self-sustaining mechanisms rather than socially agreed *conventions* of aesthetic practice. Conventions, for example, more obviously entail an implicit negotiation between artist and audience/public as a literary public sphere might require. This line of disagreement emerged even within the Russian and Prague Formalists (Dimitry Medvedev, Mikhail Bakhtin, Valentin Vološinov, Jan Mukarovsky – see **sign**). Williams christened this group and their successors – including himself – 'social formalists' (Jones, 2004: 94–5).
- The hybridization (intermixing) of some technologies and cultural forms (such as in cinema) has led to *a methodological hybridization* in media analysis *that is rarely acknowledged as such*. The key moment is McLuhan's use of aesthetic formalist techniques to analyse technologies *as well as* cultural forms, but the increasingly popular importation of Bruno Latour's formalist work within science studies is a more recent case in point (see **technological determinism**; Jones, 2010).

SEQUENCE AND FLOW

Williams conceded the impossibility of separating technology and cultural form in the case of television in one important instance – his much discussed concept of flow (Williams, 1974a: 78–118). It provides a good example of his 'social formalism' in action. The analysis remains textually based (significantly, with quantitative components as well). Williams could already see the inadequacy of traditional genre categories – including those developed *within* popular culture, such as vaudeville's 'miscellany' and 'variety' – to capture how television 'reworks' cultural forms. His primary task is thus to establish *new* categories of textual analysis that can adequately construct what Stuart Hall was already calling the decoding options of a viewer. Even Hall's famous **encoding/decoding** diagrams, however, continued to represent the coded television text as a singular 'programme as meaningful discourse'. Williams instead tended to assiduously avoid the categories of formalist semiotics and even **sign**.

Sequence and flow, then, are alternative modes of 'programming'. Flow is usually defined as the non-discrete sequencing of televisual programming, as in the flow of an evening's viewing of one channel's programming. A sequence, in contrast, is more discernibly a series of clearly demarcated 'programmes', each of which would conform to a recognizable genre category (news, drama, variety and so on). Williams correctly regarded the conventional linear broadcasting sequence as a 'residual' form and flow to be moving from an emergent to dominant role (see **hegemony**).

All this only makes sense if we appreciate the aesthetic-normative position Williams tended to assume in 1974 – the integrity of the 'unity' of a television programme, especially drama. Flow was developed to account for US television's (now almost globally ubiquitous) alternating/interruptive programming of advertising, promotions and 'actual programmes'.

Unlike more formalist categories, such as McLuhan's medium, flow points towards extra-textual production as well as reception. Indeed, Williams (1974a: 92) insisted that the commercial variant especially was truly *planned* flow, an 'irresponsible flow of images and feelings'. For Williams in 1974, the signified border between sequence and flow was the use of 'interval signals', such as channel identification symbols (the BBC's then famous turning globe), with *complementary* voiceovers that located the viewer in the evening schedule of the sequence. The more recent practice of replacing closing program credits (themselves now often miniaturized) with promotional voiceovers is a more contemporary example, also indicative of the dominance of planned flow.

Such social formalist analysis enabled Williams to think of televisual analysis and 'production' analysis together and so regulation environments could be drawn into formal analysis in a way never possible for McLuhan. All this sounds a little quaint if we consider the ways in which the interruptive ad flow has insinuated itself into so many formerly ad-free systems, not to mention that Williams was writing before the dominance of remote controls. The broader social shaping context of this argument, however, was that this 'irresponsible' destruction of the integrity of programmes had potentially contradictory social implications, especially if audiences were able to engage with an alternative form of distribution. Consider, for example, the rise and rise of the DVD boxed set as a new mode of distribution of television programming that, by eliminating advertising, remarkably restores the traditional form of the (PSB) broadcast 'sequence' based on programmes' integrity.

FURTHER READING

John Corner's (1999) chapter on flow is easily the best overview of the concept and subsequent debates; see also Paul Jones (2004). Teresa Rizzo's (2007) is an innovative application of Williams' conception of flow to the contemporary phenomenon of the playlist. Derek Kompare (2006) provides a detailed case study of the DVD boxed set as flow. He states that it relies on Bernard Miège's quite different sense of flow, but Miège (1989) is closer to Williams than Kompare suggests. See also Klaus Brun Jensen's (1995) placement of flow within his social semiotics.

Culture

41

> *Related concepts*: capitalism, communication, criticism/critique, cultural form, culture industry, mass, modern, popular, ritual.

This term is probably now most directly associated with media and communications studies via the field of *cultural studies*. The initially British formation of cultural studies is usually dated from the 1950s and followed by the Birmingham Centre for

Contemporary Cultural Studies (CCCS), founded in 1964. Contemporaneous US debates about mass communication, however, overlapped with those about **mass culture** and were heavily dependent on the role of *émigré* European intellectuals (Bennett, 1982; Bramson, 1967). Similarly, both US and British developments owed much to prior debates in literary studies that would be grouped *together* by literary theorists and literary historians as 'new criticism'. So, culture and **criticism/critique** are also linked.

Indeed, in the case of (British) cultural studies, the shift in meaning of 'culture' *from* that used within literary studies – a shift usually attributed to Raymond Williams – is often presented as foundational for the field. That shift, in turn, is usually presented as one from an 'elite' confinement to a great tradition or canon of 'great works' to a more 'anthropological' or 'whole way of life' sense. The shorthand for this account tends to be 'high culture versus low or popular culture'. In fact, both Williams' position and the whole history is more complex and it is important to keep the narrative more 'open' than this simple account would suggest.

The earlier 'literary' understandings of culture tended to share (even with some anthropology) a common Romantic conception of culture, one that developed as a critical response to the Enlightenment (see **modern**). The Enlightenment's usage principally signified the progressive process of secular human self-development or 'self-making'. It was to find its fullest articulation in the development of philosophical aesthetics in works such as those of Friedrich Schiller and Georg W.F. Hegel, a tradition to which members of the Frankfurt School also contributed. It was thus closely related to the central Enlightenment category of *reason* informing conceptions of public opinion and the **public sphere**.

One useful summation of this conception of culture is the following: 'culture is the process of developing and ennobling the human faculties, a process facilitated by the assimilation of works of scholarship and art and linked to the progressive character of the modern era' (Thompson, 1990: 126). This sense was central to many models of humanist education.

While not necessarily hostile to such a humanist characterization, the Romantic sense of culture was more open to the realms of human emotion and 'other cultures'. The key strand of this reformulation for modern media and communications was the Romantics' development of *folkloricism*, a concern with the fate of cultural forms of European lower classes (primarily) and of 'other' peoples. European folk cultures especially were deemed to be at risk from the effects of industrial capitalism and so 'cultural conservation' was the Romantics' strategy. Key Romantic theorists such as Johann Gottfried von Herder were also collectors of folksong. This practice went into one of its most active phases in the early years of audio-recording technology where phonograph recordings of folk music were undertaken in remote communities.

F.R. Leavis' much-criticized canonical conception of 'the great tradition' – against which cultural studies is often positioned – owed much to this folkloric phase. Particularly important was a crucial collection of notated folk songs by Cecil Sharp, *English Folk Songs from the Southern Appalachian Mountains*, first published in 1917. It demonstrated the remarkable maintenance of the English and Scottish folk song traditions among the Appalachian communities of the USA. Sharp (1966) goes to great lengths in his introduction to stress the uniqueness of the Appalachians' 'way of life', especially their apparent prioritization of leisure time and singing over material comforts.

For Leavis (1965: 190), the survival of folk song traditions demonstrated the necessary integration of 'authentic' folk culture within an organic community, a '"way of life" (in our democratic parlance) that was truly an art of social living'. Its negation was the 'mass civilization' of contemporary England. For Leavis, modern 'civilization' was 'technologico-Benthamite' – his term for industrial capitalism. Leavis insisted that such a civilization necessarily denied the popular classes access to an integrated 'way of life'. Popular creativity was thus deemed to be dead. Against this stood a 'minority culture' of educators bearing what Leavis saw as the contemporary embodiment of Matthew Arnold's conception of 'the best that has been thought and known in the world' (1960: 70), the great tradition of English literature.

Crucially, Leavis' critical perspective on culture as a 'way of life' led not to elitist withdrawal but, rather, critical analysis of mediated popular cultural forms and, notably, popular education. He influenced Marshall McLuhan, Raymond Williams and Richard Hoggart (founder of the CCCS). In contrast, T.S. Eliot's openly anti-democratic 1948 text, *Notes Towards the Definition of Culture*, claimed to employ the 'anthropological' 'whole way of life' sense of culture. It advocated a quite simplistic re-establishment of a quasi-feudal class and taste hierarchy.

It was this book, not Leavis' work, that drove Williams to formulate an alternative conception of the 'whole way of life' sense of culture. This alternative saw culture as the product of a modern democratic society rather than the anthropological positioning of a particular social group. Williams' famous 1958 *Culture and Society* (1990) recognized a (British) Romantic tradition of cultural critique of capitalism, which included Leavis.

Williams later recognized the parallels and direct connections between this British Romantic tradition and a Germanic one, from which members of the Frankfurt School drew, in part, their practice of immanent **critique** (Williams, 1969). The contrast between 'high' and 'low' culture was too simplistic for Williams because it presumed a reduction of aesthetic culture to, usually, class. Rather, the Romantics had insisted on the necessary autonomy of aesthetic culture. In the confusingly titled 1958 'Culture is Ordinary', Williams puts the issue this way:

> We use the word culture in these two senses: to mean a whole way of life – the common meanings; to mean the arts and learning – the special processes of discovery and creative effort. Some writers reserve the word for one or other of these senses; I insist on both, and on the significance of their conjunction. (Williams, 1989d: 4)

Williams could not endorse a wholesale shift to a 'whole way of life' sense as it removed from view the achievement of the realm of autonomous aesthetic culture. The price of such a 'democratization' was, for him, too high. Rather, he insisted on – and for many years practised in adult education – a radicalization of the Leavisite project in which aesthetic skills were more widely distributed.

Where Leavis had aimed for a popular education programme that fostered well-trained consumers of 'the best', Williams wanted one that fostered a wider social base of cultural *producers*. It was, however, Richard Hoggart's 'left-Leavisite' position, not Williams', that prevailed in the institutionalization of cultural studies. This model, announced in his *The Uses of Literacy* (Hoggart, 1976) and related writings, broadly continued the extension of literary critical analysis of commercial popular culture begun by the Leavisites but coupled it with quasi-literary reflections on the working-class milieu of Hoggart's early life. Williams' published critical reviews of *The Uses of Literacy* (1957, for example) made plain his differences from this programme.

At the heart of Williams' insistence on maintaining a place for the achievements of 'high culture' is the *social* role of culture Williams reconstructed from the Romantic poet Samuel Taylor Coleridge – a 'court of appeal' against which the failings of a social order could be judged. From this, Williams constructed his own model of immanent **critique**, instead of taking the more conservative Arnoldian route followed by Leavis and Hoggart. Williams' position overlapped significantly with Marx's conception of alienation but it also anticipates the role of a literary **public sphere** (Jones, 2007). Moreover, the logic of Williams' position led directly to a concern for the role of media **regulation** in adequate distribution of 'communicative means of production' (see **communication**). This, in turn, led to significant differences between Williams and Hoggart over cultural policy (Jones, 1994).

In subsequent developments in cultural studies, the Hoggart/Williams tension has replayed itself, especially with issues related to **popular** culture and **tabloidization**. The widespread adoption of dominantly formalist semiotic methods of textual analysis tended to encourage an 'external' form of textual criticism in which criteria of judgement – Marxist, anti-racist, feminist and so on – are brought to bear on the text in question (see **criticism** and **cultural form**). Culture as 'whole way of life' legitimated the application of such methods to many practices beyond high cultural forms and their commercial 'mediated' correlates, such as popular television programming – the full panoply of popular practices opened up by Roland Barthes' *Mythologies* (1972) and beyond. Semiotic analysis of the codes of youth subcultures, for example, was both an extension and radicalization of Hoggart's agenda for the Birmingham CCCS (Hall and Jefferson, 1976). Stuart Hall's dominant/negotiated/resistant typology of **encoding/decoding** was employed here, too, and so subcultural research laid some of the foundations for later 'active **audience**' research. This is not to deny the enormous gains these methods made, but they did come at a considerable cost to the immanent hermeneutic project formerly associated with 'culture' (see **criticism/critique**).

CULTURE AND COMMUNICATION

Within US sociology, there is a long tradition of examining culture in its 'way of life' sense that has anthropological roots not dissimilar from the folkloric idea of culture that informed Leavisite British literary studies. The work of the Chicago School of Sociology from the 1920s is usually positioned as the historical embodiment of this tradition and is regarded as a major alternative to the East Coast traditions dominated by either theoretical functionalism or positivist/ 'administrative'/quantitative sociology and related communications research.

Chicago School sociologists developed important quasi-anthropological qualitative fieldwork methods, such as participant observation. They practised forms of community-based research in the 'social laboratory' of a city that embodied many of the major social and cultural contradictions of not only the contemporary USA but also contemporary capitalism – from street-corner youth subcultures to architectural **modernism**. Howard Becker's later work (1963) on moral entrepreneurship and the 'labelling' of 'outsiders', for example, is classic Chicago School sociology and directly informed Stan Cohen's conception of **moral panic** in the UK and the Birmingham CCCS.

The relationship between Chicago sociology and journalism is especially notable. Not only did it generate major sociological studies of journalism by the ex-journalist Robert Park but also sociology itself was seen to have much in common with the public intellectual role of journalism, especially in the new urban USA. This mix of 'cultural' qualitative sociological methods and commitments directly informed later major US participant observation studies of journalists such as Gaye Tuchman's (1978: 3–4).

Nonetheless, James Carey (2008: 15–16) was likely correct in observing in 1989 that the concept of culture had still not been successfully conceptually or methodologically integrated into the US tradition of communication studies. He regarded the Chicago School as the chief source for a US tradition of cultural studies, traceable to the earlier work of pragmatist John Dewey. Significantly, however, Carey (2008: 73) regarded Chicago's qualification as deriving from its having 'transplanted Weberian sociology in American soil'.

Weber's sociology was strongly associated with a hermeneutic understanding (*verstehen*) approach to culture (see **criticism/critique**; **modern**). Weber's formulations were important to German critiques of positivism in social science and later for the *émigré* Frankfurt School. Accordingly, the term *geistwissenschaften*, or, 'cultural sciences' was used to distinguish approaches that did not follow the positivist emulation of the methods of the natural sciences. Williams had come to the same conclusion as Carey in the 1970s and early 1980s. He even offered 'cultural studies' as a better translation of *geistwissenschaften*, as Carey had done in the USA (Grossberg and Carey, 2006; Williams, 1974b).

Despite the insights of these key figures, this Weberian legacy does not characterize cultural studies today. The tradition identified by Carey and Williams is discernible at work more indirectly, however. Carey points, for example, to the work of anthropologist Glifford Geertz, whose deliberate borrowings from literary criticism go some way to redressing Williams' critique of '(mass) communications'. In particular, Geertz's suggestion that the 'thick description' of ethnographic research resembles literary criticism's 'interpretation of interpretations' certainly echoes the hermeneutic resonance of Weberian *verstehen*.

Carey, however, is notably cautious about Geertz's (1973: 452) proposition in his famous 'reading' of the Balinese cockfight that:

> [t]he culture of a people is an ensemble of texts, themselves ensembles which the anthropologist strains to read over the shoulders of those to whom they properly belong.

Even though Geertz is far more generous about the authorship/ownership of such cultural practices than the average structuralist, Carey (2008: 45–6) is wary of Geertz's effective reduction of cultures to ensembles of texts, preferring Weber's emphasis on the mutuality of 'action'. Again, the parallel with Williams is strong – Williams railed against such 'textualization' and advocated using the term 'practice' instead.

Yet, when Carey's hope that Geertzian 'thick description' would enter media analysis was realized, it came from outside the field of communication studies – from anthropologists operating on 'the new terrain' (Ginsburg et al., 2002) of formerly discrete cultures increasingly subject to – and of – global and local mediation (Abu-Lughod, 1997). Carey certainly anticipated one related strain of such thinking, however, in marking as **ritual** the US culturalist alternative to transmission-based conceptions of **communication**. Indeed, it is perhaps the growing field of media anthropology that is the strongest contemporary indicator of the continuing dynamism Williams and Carey advocated between culture and communication.

FURTHER READING

See Paul Jones (2004) for further discussion of many of the issues raised in this entry. One early exchange concerning the fate of the 'intrinsic' in 'culture' in the context of UK media/literary–cultural studies is that between John Hartley and Terence Hawkes (1977) and Tony Bennett and Graham Martin (1977), which remains useful. A good overview of the prestructuralist accounts of culture and their fate in cultural studies can be found in Goodall (1995). Terry Eagleton (2000) is also very good on the literary tradition. See also Mulhern (2000). The standard account of British cultural studies is Graeme Turner's (2003) but see also Chris Rojek (2007) and Chris Barker (2000). For a more literary-focused account of the emergence of the US tradition than Carey's, see Patrick Brantlinger (1990). Faye D. Ginsburg et al.'s collection (2002) is a good indicator of the range of anthropological studies of mediated cultures. On just how broad this range can be, see the collection by Kelly M. Askew and Richard R. Wilk (2002) (which opens with classic pieces by McLuhan and Williams) and the collection by S. Elizabeth Bird (2010) on the anthropology of journalism. Barbie Zelizer's (2004) account of 'cultural analysis and journalism' is also very useful here and relevant to the above account. Eric Michaels' (1986, 1987) now classic 1980s study of the Warlpiri Media Association and its 'invention of Aboriginal television' anticipates these anthropological developments. For an excellent example of an anthropologist bringing ethnographic thick description to bear on the major media institution of the former imperial metropolitan centre, see Georgina Born's (2004) study of the BBC in transition.

> **Related concepts**: *criticism/critique, culture, mass, modern, popular, postmodern-ism, tabloidization.*

Perhaps no concept has undergone greater transformation since it was coined than 'culture industry'. Its dominant meaning has shifted dramatically in its *normative* orientation, from a resolutely critical one to a contemporary meaning that is normatively neutral, if not completely affirmative, when it is reworked as cultural industr*ies* and 'creative industries'.

CULTURE INDUSTRY FOR THE FRANKFURT SCHOOL AND RAYMOND WILLIAMS

Theodor Adorno developed the concept of culture industry in the 1930s and 1940s in his famous debate with Walter Benjamin about the consequences of 'technological reproducibility' for works of art (below).

For Adorno, the very words 'culture industry' were meant to convey a 'shock effect' similar to that many **modern**ist avant-gardes strived to achieve through their art, which was to awaken the recipient to a process of which they were apparently oblivious. For Adorno, the mere juxtaposition of the two terms should have been sufficient to achieve this 'shock'. Clearly, for him, 'culture' – explicitly understood in its aesthetic sense – and 'industry' were irreconcilable opposites. The term was also adopted as an explicit alternative to 'mass culture' to avoid any possible implication of such popular culture being 'of the people' (volk/folk) (Adorno, 1991a: 85).

For many years, initial familiarity with Adorno's argument for those in (Anglophone) media studies came via the abridged version of a chapter extracted from his and Max Horkheimer's *Dialectic of Enlightenment* (1979). As more recent collections have made plain, however, the *Dialectic of Enlightenment* version is perhaps the least clear – yet most polemical – source available.

At base, Adorno's position is a relatively straightforward, if unusually sophisticated, Marxian sociology of art perspective asserting that the conditions of production of artworks are no longer compatible with the goals of aesthetic autonomy as celebrated in Western philosophical aesthetics. That is, art no longer fulfils the Kantian ideal of 'purposelessness' and so can no longer play a critical social role. At least for the case of Western 'fine' music, Adorno identifies *artisanal* relations of cultural production (see below) as the key means of securing aesthetic autonomy. He notes that the composer J.S. Bach, for instance, identified as an artisan (1945: 211). In a remarkably sympathetic elaboration of the same premise designed to apply across the arts, Raymond Williams provided the typology presented in Table 7.

47

Table 7 Williams' typology of forms of relationship between cultural producers and socio-cultural institutions (based on Williams, 1995, as developed in Jones, 2004)

Societal-institutional form	(Sub-) Type of relationship	Chief characteristics
1. Instituted artists (socially embedded)	Nil	A *social stratum* that is part of central social organization rather than differentiated as 'artist' (such as Celtic bards)
2. Patronage	(i) Institution to patron	Transitional role between institutionalized order and dependency on patronage
	(ii) Retainer and commission	Individual artists retained or commissioned by aristocratic households or the Church
	(iii) Protection and support	'Milder' form of social support not necessarily involving economic exchange relations (such as theatrical companies of Elizabethan England)
	(iv) Sponsorship/ commercial sponsorship	First form of patronage that takes market for artworks as given, so patronage primarily monetary where formerly more commonly hospitality or social introduction and so on; commercial sponsorship is survival of this form of patronage into present era of full market dominance, but some forms of corporate sponsorship are of subtype (ii) and others are more overt forms of self-promotion
	(v) The public as 'patron'	Replacement of patron with taxation-sourced revenue; potential contradiction in that power relation in earlier forms of patronage is difficult to reconcile with public accountability; considerable confusion about which historical form of patronage is being emulated
3. Market	(i) Artisanal	Producer wholly dependent on immediate market but retains ownership of work until sale
	(ii) Post-artisanal	'Next phase' of commodity production with two stages:
		(a) *distributive*: work sold by artist to distributive intermediary who then usually becomes effective employer of artist
		(b) *productive*: intermediary productive and invests in work for purposes of profit[1] and here 'typically capitalist social relations' begin to be instituted
	(iii) Market professional	Further development of productive post-artisanal relations, pioneered by publishing where means of replication develop first. Copyright struggles ensure general ownership of artwork remains with authors, hence rise of negotiated contract and royalty as 'newly typical relationship', but this draws authors more fully into the 'organized professional market'

(Continued)

Societal-institutional form	(Sub-) Type of relationship	Chief characteristics
	(iv) Corporate professional	Productive post-artisanal organization now a modern corporation with strong tendency to reduce role of artist to salaried professional but still compatible with market professional relationship (as in book publishing). Increases tendency to produce for market. 'New' (post-book) media most strongly corporate and so became dominant and typical in late 1900s. In this context, advertising has arisen as a new form of cultural production
4. Post-market	(i) Modern patronal and intermediate	Modern patronal institutions are non-governmental institutions of public patronage (e.g. foundations) of arts that cannot self-sustain within market relations (cf. 2[v]) above). Intermediate institutions (like BBC) depend on public revenue but also 'direct their own production'. Employment modes range from patronal to corporate
	(ii) Governmental	The cultural institution as 'department of state' in some capitalist societies.

Williams' artisan-centred typology (developed in 1981) is more finely detailed than Adorno's typical accounts, but it shares Adorno's concern that the chief negative consequence for artistic autonomy is the increasing consolidation of capitalist relations of cultural production and the formulaic standardization of the cultural commodity. With Hollywood especially in mind, as Adorno developed his arguments while living in California, he could see that much art was being produced 'industrially'. Moreover, for Adorno, mid-twentieth-century art needed to conform increasingly to the utilitarian criteria of *commodities* in an 'administered' capitalism; in Marxian terms, the rules of use-value and exchange-value.

Such standardization and commodification, however, does not only refer to the process by which much *popular* culture is 'manufactured' on production lines like 'Aunt Jemima's ready-mix for pancakes' (Adorno, 1945: 211). Crucially, for both Adorno and Williams, these features apply to both 'high' *and* popular culture. Neither was merely defending 'high culture' against an encroaching popular culture. Adorno pointed to the rising cult of the conductor and 'popular classics' programmes within fine music performances and their radio broadcasts as evidence of culture industry developments within high culture. In his correspondence with Benjamin (Adorno, 1977: 123), he famously commented that contemporary high and popular culture were 'torn halves of an integral freedom, to which, however, they do not add up'. Similarly, Williams sourced the very formulation of 'minority' and 'mass' in the British tradition – which fed directly into twentieth-century British media and cultural studies – to the early nineteenth-century reactions of the Romantic poets to the collapse of the patronage

Table 8 Williams' assessment of institutional relations of exemplary contemporary (1981) cultural forms (based on Williams, 1995, as developed in Jones, 2004)

Cultural form	Institutional relations
Painting	Patronal relations still strong (such as commissioned portraiture), but distributive, post-artisanal relations common in gallery system
(Fine) music	Patronal relations in commissioned works; distributive post-artisanal in orchestral works and traditional sheet music
Popular music	Productive post-artisanal phase long established, plus major moves to later phases (market professional and corporate) of market relations
Literature	Still some artisanal and distributive post-artisanal but long dominance of distributive post-artisanal and signs of later phases of market relations

system. Nonetheless, as Williams' 1981 assessment suggests (Table 8), these tendencies continued to operate *unevenly* across the fields of high and popular culture.

REDRESSING ABSENCES IN THE CULTURE INDUSTRY THESIS

Williams' supplementation of Adorno's work goes some way to teasing out the limits of the initial thesis. From a Marxian perspective, Adorno and Williams – and, more reluctantly, Benjamin – want to apply the model of forces and relations of production to 'culture' (partly in order to redress the reductivism of the base and superstructure metaphor – see **capitalism**). In their attachment to the artisanal norm of artistic autonomy, however, neither is hostile to 'the market' as such. Rather, as Williams' microformulations make clearer than much of Adorno's polemic, artistic autonomy was historically most secure for individual artists/artisans when they could act as self-employed small producers, their work being circulated within a relatively small, appreciative market. As with the fate of small presses in the history of newspapers (see **news values**), however, technological innovation facilitated increasing capitalization of production. Greater circulation required larger capital investments in, most obviously, mechanized presses – and, of course, the pursuit of larger, increasingly anonymous, markets of cultural 'consumers'. The situation of the cultural producer (artist, journalist and so on) changed according to the rhythm of development of these changes across different arenas of cultural production – as Williams' assessment in Table 8 also suggests.

Media – especially reproduction technologies – thus function, from this perspective, as *forces of cultural production*. (Importantly, Adorno and Williams also want to regard *cultural forms* as forces of cultural production.) Where artisanal *relations of cultural production* are superseded, they see aesthetic autonomy to be at risk. What this perspective tends to downplay – even in Table 8 – is the possibility that modern media technologies might be compatible with artisanal relations of cultural production and, similarly, artisanal relations (or their equivalent) might be reconstituted, even within Adorno's 'administered' capitalism.

Quasi-artisanal relations of autonomy needn't mean working in an eighteenth- or nineteenth-century garret with eighteenth- or nineteenth-century aesthetic means of cultural production, such as paper, pens and easels. Williams' distributive post-artisanal relations plainly fit this twentieth-century role of preserving relative autonomy for cultural producers.

Here, Benjamin's famous 'The Work of Art in the Age of its Technological Reproducibility' (2008) has become crucial in the reception and discussion of these arguments. Adorno tends to assume that 'technological reproducibility' primarily encourages factory-like conditions – hence, 'culture industry'. Benjamin, however, drawing on the views of the Surrealist avant-garde, welcomes technological reproducibility as enabling new means of artistic expression (photography and cinema, for example) and the destruction of the 'aura' that attaches to great works of art.

Adorno and Benjamin (and Williams at times) render this as a distinction between (industrial) *technology* and (aesthetic) *technique*. There is a strong parallel here between Benjamin's 'technique' and McLuhan's **medium** (although McLuhan has no conceptual means of distinguishing medium as technique from medium as technology). Cinema was the specific case study Adorno and Benjamin used in their contestation of each other's approaches. Benjamin considered its potential for radical editing techniques facilitated the aesthetic **modern**ist practice of montage as inherently revolutionary. Adorno, maintaining his view of cinema as an industrial technology, in effect simply pointed to Hollywood.

It is not so well known that the later Adorno (1991b) revised his views about the culture industry generally and cinema specifically. The rise of what is now routinely called 'the arthouse film' demonstrated – finally, to Adorno's satisfaction – that it is possible to regard cinematic filmmaking as an aesthetic technique that enables aesthetic autonomy. Adorno's concession is compatible with Williams' view that quasi-artisanal relations of cultural production are achievable in modern capitalism. Certainly, for Williams, the establishment of such autonomy should be a major goal of media and cultural policy. As sociologists of popular music were perhaps the first to recognize, however, what Williams calls 'market asymmetry' might also produce such quasi-artisanal conditions independently of state policy. Market asymmetry might be thought of as Williams' 'mid-position' within the Adorno/Benjamin polarity (Jones, 2004: 153–6). It simply reminds us that the fit between forces and relations of cultural production need not be as neat as Adorno assumes, but is instead more contingent. In such conditions, artisanal spaces – now routinely described as 'independent/indie' across all the arts – could also result more spontaneously from contradictions within the capitalist organization of cultural production, as in, for example, conflicts between recording companies and broadcasters over the role of new technologies and copyright. Indeed, some have argued that the enormously dramatic changes that overtook modern popular music in the 1950s were largely enabled by such conflicts.

REFORMULATIONS OF THE CULTURAL INDUSTRY THESIS

For many years, arts and cultural policy, as Williams' typology in Table 8 implies, attempted to compensate for the decline of the patronage system by making the state or 'public' (via taxes) a patron, especially in nations such as Australia where traditions of private philanthropy were weak. Arts policies that provided stipends for artists thus complemented European and similar media **regulation** that protected spaces for artistic production and journalism from 'market forces' and, in the case of the BBC, explicitly pursued an Arnoldian project of aesthetic 'improvement'. The twin pressures of neoliberalism and revolutions in means of communication have, however, shifted such policies from the centre of what is now routinely called cultural policy. Even Williams' assumption in Table 8 of large-scale inhouse production of programming by public service broadcasters such as the BBC is now largely obsolete (journalism excepted). Moreover, the (then) profitability of the recording industries began to be recognized by those concerned with the realm of 'industry policy' (hitherto separate). Adorno's 'cultural industry' was reborn as the more neutral 'cultural industries'. Arts policy became cultural policy and increasingly merged with state policies premised on the emergence of an information or digital economy.

'*Creative* industries' is a more recent and unquestionably affirmative (endorsing) version of this culture industries argument. Its advocates argue that it is more digitally focused and globally relevant than the former cultural (arts) industries policy discourses of nation states (Cunningham, 2005: 285). They also make their industrial case for creative industries primarily by pointing to statistical evidence of shifts in sectoral contributions in 'the new economy' (Flew, 2005, for example). This approach has much in common with Daniel Bell's post-industrial and **information society** theses and its dependence on demonstrating a transition to a service economy (McGuigan, 2004: 96).

Both post-industrial and creative industries approaches practise a kind of hyperbolic overestimation of the significance of discrete changes in the forces and relations of (cultural) production. Conspicuously absent from these formulations are concerns for the fate of artistic autonomy and social critique that motivated Adorno's initial formulation. It seems likely that Adorno would have dismissed the creative industries push as 'administrative research'; moreover, the transparent repositioning of university arts faculties as trainers of creative labour for creative industries today would merely demonstrate that, from Adorno's perspective, universities and academic cultural producers too have become part of the contemporary cultural industry in an administered capitalism.

Is such a polarization between pessimistic critical theory and administrative/affirmative research in this field inevitable?

Adorno's 'epochal' pessimism was challenged by no less a figure than his student, Jürgen Habermas. Anticipating Adorno's own revisions to the culture industry thesis, Habermas' formulation of his account of the **public sphere** was premised on a suspicion that Adorno had pushed Max Weber's thesis of endlessly rationalizing administration in modern capitalism too far (see **modern**).

Weber's assumption of an increasing means–ends technical rationality shares much with a **technologically determinist** position (Feenberg, 1992). Such an emphasis underestimates what Weber called expert 'value spheres', such as cultural criticism relating to the arts. These have continued to be developed, as in Habermas' identification of a literary public sphere. Although Habermas' initial formulation of his public sphere thesis was equally pessimistic in its contemporary (1962) assessment, the logic of his argument did not render these conditions inevitable. Thus, it shares much with critical political economy and critical sociology of art approaches and recent work concerning aesthetic/cultural public spheres.

David Hesmondhalgh's *The Cultural Industries* (2007) is the best recent example of a critical approach that avoids both (early) Adornian absolutist pessimism and the uncritical affirmation of the creative industries push. He productively builds on Williams' typology above and adapts it to twenty-first-century conditions (Hesmondhalgh, 2007: 53–4ff.). Hesmondhalgh re-renders Williams' 'corporate professional' as 'complex professional' – a stage that emerged in the twentieth century. Hesmondhalgh argues that the key features of the complex professional 'era' (from the early twentieth century to the 1970s) were loose corporate control of creative input from cultural producers, coupled with tighter control of technical reproduction and circulation (Hesmondhalgh, 2007: 69). Subsequent neoliberal developments have tightened this relative looseness of control of cultural production, but have also rendered increasingly precarious the employment conditions of cultural producers for all but an elite of 'superstars' (Hesmondhalgh, 2007: 197–201).

It is Benjamin's essay, however, that has tended to be the template for the more optimistic rethinking, within Frankfurt School terms, of each subsequent wave of revolutions in means of communication, not least that of digitization. There is now a plethora of papers that mimic Benjamin's title by such devices as adding a different affix to 'The Work of Art in the Age of ...' (Blythe, 2002; Dornsife, 2006; Goodwin, 1988, 1992, 2004; Mitchell, 2003). In most cases (with the notable exception of Goodwin), the promise tends to be that new developments will be sufficiently potent to alter the contradictory balance between forces and relations of cultural production – that is, Benjamin's optimism about revolutionary possibilities in aesthetic technique will prevail over Adorno's pessimistic rejoinder that their incorporation as technologies within capitalist industrial production is inevitable.

FURTHER READING

Beyond the works cited in the last section of this entry, for a relatively recent German reconsideration of the original culture industry thesis from a contemporary media perspective, see Heinz Steinert (2003). Keith Negus (1997) provides arguably the most 'user-friendly' guide to Adorno's thesis yet produced. For a more radical and challenging reworking that, nonetheless, argues 'Adorno's worst nightmares have come true', see Scott Lash and Celia Lury (2007). Hesmondhalgh (2008) provides an excellent discussion of culture industry and creative industries debates. Garnham (2005b) also critically tracks the transition from Adorno through to creative industries policy. See also the Further reading suggestions for the Criticism/critique entry.

Cyberculture

> **Related concepts**: digital, interactivity, technoculture, time–space compression.

Used interchangeably with 'Internet culture', 'cyberculture' is a term that attained its greatest popularity in the 1990s, at the height of the diffusion and domestication of the Internet in technologically developed nations. Since that time, it has tended to broaden out to a range of interactive interfaces (Robinson, 2006) and competes with the now more established term 'new media'. This latter term has a longer history and does not carry a time stamp wherever it goes. Marshall McLuhan was speaking of 'new media' back in the 1950s, whereas 'cyberculture' is easy to periodize, to the point where it has its own evolutionary history, in which defining periods of 'cyberstudies' are carefully identified (Silver, 2000, 2006).

In the 1990s, Silver distinguished between three periods of cyberculture scholarship:

- popular cyberculture
- cyberculture studies
- critical cyberculture studies.

Silver's geneaology is useful, but its historical linearity is not so easily argued for. The proliferation of 'popular cyberculture' journalism in the early 1990s persists today, with every innovation in new media receiving descriptive forms of civic introduction by IT journalists. Silver's (2000: 19) stage two 'focuses largely on virtual communities and online identities, and benefits from an influx of academic scholars'. The third stage, of critical cyberstudies, expands the notion of cyberculture to include four areas of study as follows (Silver, 2000: 19):

- online interactions
- digital discourses
- the social, cultural, political and economic factors enabling or impeding access to the Internet
- the interface design of cyberspace.

Since marking out this typology, Silver has argued that critical cyberstudies addresses the fact that cyberculture is well established in everyday life, which includes how it is represented in old media. As Silver explains (2006: 7):

> early adopters of the Net took pleasure in knowing that most people had no knowledge of what would soon be called cyberspace, let alone more 'tangible' elements like e-mail, ftp, and unix commands. Today, of course, cyberculture is everywhere,

especially in the West – in sit-coms and sci-fi, in political campaigns and political mobilizations, in *Wired* and *Women's World*, in URLs printed on public billboards and scrawled on bathroom walls.

Following this typology, then, cyberculture denotes both a popular movement away from traditional media and new media environments.

CYBERCULTURE AS MOVEMENT

As a popular movement that rebuffs traditional media, cyberculture is heralded as an emancipation from **broadcasting** and the rise of **interactivity** with electronic media. Any form of new media that reduces dependence on broadcast or mass media can qualify as a form of cyberculture. Thus, cyberculture cannot just be confined to the Internet, but also embraces those new media that empower users with the opportunity to actively produce texts and images and exchange them dialogically. Being able to feed images to a website from a mobile phone, having time-shifting capabilities in a television or gaming culture, be it online, on a television or a portable device, are all examples of ways in which very common communications devices allow users greater control than ever before.

The technologies of cyberculture fulfil Norbert Weiner's (1961) vision of cybernetics at a domestic level – where control over information flow is built into the communication network. In this way, the cybernetic or 'steering' experience becomes generalized by cyberculture. As a personal computing experience, this was greatly enhanced by the development of the graphic user interface (GUI). The ability to click on text in a non-linear way, which is today the basis of hypertext on the Web, has enhanced the PC interface enormously. Advertised as 'user-friendly', it is a seductive and addictive illusion of control over a simulated reality.

SPACES OF CYBERCULTURE

Cyberspace was one of the first descriptors to mark out a new kind of media space in the 1990s. At first, the term was used interchangeably with 'virtual reality', a legacy of which, is the description of online communities as 'virtual communities'. Virtual reality (see **embodiment**), however, relates much more to the interface between an individual's senses and a media environment, whereas cyberspace denotes a space in which people *meet* in a computer-mediated environment. Today, the term online communities is used much more widely than virtual community, but the most popular and delineated submedia of the Internet, namely blogs and networking sites, have the status of spatial media, so we have the blogosphere and online social networking such as MySpace and Facebook.

One way to explain the attractions cyberculture spaces hold for users is in terms of the increasing physical separation of public and private domains in social life. The urban subdivision of populations into self-enclosed worlds of sovereign privacy results in a dephysicalization of interaction. The more time is spent interacting via

55

telecommunications mediums, the less people feel the need for physical interaction. The less physical interaction experienced, the greater the need to connect with others online via Facebook and so on. Cyberculture can be viewed as a heightened form of this trend, and of **mobile privatization**.

In *Life on the Screen* (1995), Sherry Turkle claims that the high street, shopping centre and café have been replaced by virtual online substitutes. In the USA, she says (1995: 235), 'We seem to be in the process of retreating further into our homes, shopping for merchandise in catalogues or on television channels, shopping for companionship via personal ads'.

Micro-urbanization and personalization – the portability of communications devices, mobile phones, laptops and personal digital assistants (PDAs) – make it possible to inhabit a media cocoon, which remains familiar regardless of where you are physically. Arthur and Marilouise Kroker (1996: 75) describe this as a space in which the 'electronic self' immunizes itself 'against the worst effects of public life by bunkering in'. 'Bunkering' describes the sheltering of the 'beleaguered self in a techno-bubble'.

Cyberculture provides the bunker[ed] self with 'immediate, universal access to a global community without people: electronic communication without social contact, being digital without being human, going on-line without leaving the safety of the electronic bunker' (Kroker and Kroker, 1996: 77).

Moreover, in the conditions of large-scale social integration, cyberculture personalizes everyday spaces by affording new kinds of control over interaction. As Craig Calhoun (1992, 1998) theorized in a suite of articles, computer-mediated communication can be used to avoid accidental contact with strangers. While in its early years the Internet involved anonymous communication, Web 2.0 apps such as blogging and OSN are used for precisely this purpose. Blogging facilitates self-publication and enhanced control over how individuals choose to present themselves online compared to the serendipitous encounters people have in face-to-face life. Online social networking establishes relationships on an invitation-only basis. These forms of belonging in cyberspace mimic the formation of offline groups.

THE PREHISTORY OF CYBERCULTURE

If cyberculture is viewed as a heightened form of mobile privatization, it is possible to theorize a number of simulated physical realities that prefigure networked cyberculture.

A central feature of mobile privatization is that it contracts everyday environments down to a space in which control, or the illusion of control, becomes a key element, be it by means of a remote control, mouse or steering wheel. Typically, this involves substituting an outside world with a distracting world of simulation. Thus, the idea of cyberculture provides a lens for categorizing proto-cyber realities, which may be architectural (the theme park, road/dashboard relationship or shopping centre), electronic (the MP3 player, PDA or mobile phone) or audiovisually enclosed or semi-enclosed (the cinema or video game).

In the entry on **time–space compression**, the telegraph is discussed as the first kind of 'cyberspace' because it contracts the world down to a technologically closed network of shared interaction and substitutes global realities for parochial ones. Similarly, cinema is a technology of substitution. Cinema bursts the 'prison world of the metropolis asunder', as Benjamin (1969: 236) once remarked, 'so that, in the midst of its far flung ruins and debris, we calmly and adventurously go travelling'. Like the WWW of the twenty-first century, the attraction of early cinema lay not in entertainment, but in the ability to travel without risk and in a manner impossible in physical reality. Cinema, the zograscope, diorama and panoramas of the world fairs shared the desire to achieve an 'integral realism … a recreation of the world in its own image, an image unburdened by the freedom of interpretation of the artist or the irreversibility of time' (Bazin, 1974: 21).

The distinctive nature of cinema and telegraph in their early years illuminates the changing nature of the observer that resulted from the speeding up of everyday life and the end of the *longue durée*. The stability of everyday life was broken up by industrialization and urbanization, requiring a radical change in consciousness and perception, as well as an increased tolerance for speed and abstract relationships.

FURTHER READING

A primary early text on cyberculture is Michael Benedikt's *Cyberspace: First Steps* (1992), in which he distinguishes cyberspace from the then popular discourses on 'virtual reality'. In the mid-1990s, Arturo Escobar attempted an 'anthropology of cyberspace' (1994) and, in the late 1990s, a succession of edited compilations were published dealing with questions of identity, corporeality and communication in cyberspace (see Featherstone and Burrows, 1995; Holmes, 1997; Jones, 1995; Shields, 1996). David Silver (2000, 2006) provides the best attempt at a genealogy of cyberculture and cyberculture studies.

Deconstruction

57

> *Related concepts*: criticism, postmodernism, sign.

'Deconstruction' is a term that entered everyday usage with remarkable speed. It was first used by the French philosopher Jacques Derrida in the 1960s and later taken up by feminist critic Gayatri C. Spivak and US literary critics such as Paul De Man and Geoffrey Hartmann.

In communication, social and cultural theory, the term is used to characterize Derrida's work as a project and a methodology, while, in everyday use, it is loosely taken to be a highbrow way of saying '**critique**'. Either way, the term does not actually meet with the approval of its author. In his essay 'The time of a thesis: punctuations', Derrida (1983: 44) claims that he has never approved of the word: 'I use the word for the sake of rapid convenience, though it is a word I have never liked and one whose fortune has disagreeably surprised me'. In the *Ear of the Other*, he complains of deconstruction being associated with an architectural model as a practice of conceptual dismantling:

> personally I don't subscribe to this model of deconstruction ... That is why the word deconstruction has always bothered me. I had the impression that it was a word among many others, a secondary word in the text which would fade or which in any case would assume a non-dominant place in a system. (Derrida, 1985: 85–6)

A PRACTICE OF READING

In Derrida's work, deconstruction is a practice of reading that undermines the historical legacy of what he calls 'logocentrism'.

Logocentrism involves a hermeneutic or 'religious' theory of reading, which defines reading as interpretation or exegesis, a powerful desire for self-presence through signification. Logocentrism looks for an *arche*, an origin, or a *telos*, a purpose, to texts in which the Logos (word as spirit) and the mythology of the Book dominate. Logocentrism is a metaphysic of presence, a belief that, 'beneath' every signifier, there is a privileged signified that must be found by a correct reading in order for successful communication to occur.

By example, as an actual practice of reading, rather than an argument that takes a 'position', deconstruction menaces the idea of a 'one-to-one' correspondence between a signifier and signified. As discussed below, it is not just the case that the same signifier can mean many different things (polysemia), but it can also exceed any attempt to list a fixed set of signifieds (dissemination).

Signifiers are made up of other signifiers at a graphematic level (what Derrida calls the trace or the gram – groups of letters that obtain their force from the relationality that they have regarding other traces and other contexts of signification). It is at the level of the trace (which, Derrida claims, also makes up the unconscious of the text) that conceptuality operates, rather than through signifiers as self-identical units as the Saussurian, semiotic argument posits.

According to Derrida, logocentrism is also extremely hierarchical in the way in which it orders signifiers into binary pairs in Western culture. Within these binaries there is always a privileged term that Derrida, throughout his work, wants to show is linked to culturally constructed prejudices about race, gender, ethnicity and nature. These prejudices are so internalized by Western discourse that they create immense cultural anxieties about the same and the other, the closure of self-identity through the construction of an 'other' and a need to decide quickly who is friend and who is foe.

Derrida argues that logocentrism is so entrenched in the texts of Western culture that it is not simply a matter of mounting an argument against it, since arriving at a critical position is simply to reproduce a form of closure – one of the hallmarks of logocentrism. Rather, deconstruction operates by persistently intervening in the particularity of texts, turning them against themselves in a way that disturbs the hierarchy of values.

Derrida's general strategy of reading that courses through nearly all of his works – particularly the early texts *Of Grammatology* (1976), *Writing and Difference* (1978), *Dissemination* (1981) and *Margins of Philosophy* (1982a, b) – cannot be regarded as hermeneutical or critique in the normative sense. Rather

> an opposition of metaphysical concepts (for example speech/writing, presence/absence, etc.) is never the face-to-face of two terms, but a hierarchy and an order of subordination. Deconstruction cannot limit itself or proceed immediately to a neutralization: it must, by means of a double gesture, a double science, a double writing, practice an *overturning* of the classical opposition *and* a general *displacement* of the system. It is only on this condition that deconstruction will provide itself the means with which to *intervene* in the field of oppositions that it criticizes … Deconstruction does not consist in passing from one concept to another, but in overturning and displacing a conceptual order, as well as the non-conceptual order with which the conceptual order is articulated. (Derrida, 1982a: 329)

To read a text, therefore, is not to interpret it but actively negotiate with it, such that it can 'deconstruct' itself and new 'concepts' become a kind of self-knowledge of its incoherence. The contradictions Derrida seeks to specify in texts are not to be thought of as visible logical errors, but the 'unconscious' of the text and its protocols of reading. In other words, a writing is interested in itself and also enables us to read philosophemes – and consequently all the texts of our culture, as kinds of symptoms of something that could not be presented in the history of philosophy and, moreover, is *nowhere present*. Further, in 'White mythology: metaphor in the text', Derrida (1982b: 213) writes of the repressive nature of metaphysics: 'White mythology – metaphysics has erased within itself the fabulous scene that has produced it, the scene that nevertheless remains active and stirring, inscribed in white ink, an invisible design covered over in the palimpsest'. Therefore, when Derrida reads, one of his tactics is to focus on the supposedly innocent and trivial, incidental and anecdotal, to reveal the strategies that devastate the visible logic of the text.

THE CHALLENGE TO LOGOCENTRIC MODELS OF COMMUNICATION

59

One of the most important claims that Derrida makes about his practice of reading is that it reveals the nature of *language-as-writing* and, therefore, also the conditions of possibility of communication. In several texts, Derrida offers a theory of communication that is opposed to the 'logocentric' theory of communication, which involves 'a *transmission charged with making pass, from one subject to another, the identity* of a *signified object*' (1979: 23, italics in original).

This conception borrows from the value of presence involved in 'auto-affection', where the temporal and spatial are united to guarantee that a message will reach its destination, a situation in which the speaker hears herself speak at the same moment as the hearer does. In this model of communication, subjects are posited as the self-present symmetrical poles of an intersubjective process. The other value central to logocentrism, as we have seen, is that there exists an inventory of fixed signifieds that precede, and are anterior to, the speaking subject – they are merely drawn on in order to communicate meaning and make present a common reality.

Derrida is critical of the metaphysics of language that subscribes to the idea that meaning can be sourced from an original and homogenous context. With **media effects** analysis, for example, messages are regarded as the stable product of an homogenous context of production which will impact upon its receiver just as it impacts upon the original context.

Derrida's argument that *writing*, rather than self-presence, should be taken as the model for all language is an attempt to redefine the context of the production of meaning in all cases as resting on the force of texts. In *Limited Inc* (1988: 8), he writes: 'To be what it is, all writing … must … be capable of functioning in the radical absence of every empirically determined receiver'. In other words, for Derrida, the text has a materiality that is not confined to intentionality, nor to assumptions about a likely reader. For him, writing does not 'stand in' as a representation of an absent presence, the absence of original intentions of subjects or a referent. The sense of writing, which Derrida calls 'phonetic', is commonly determined as secondary to speech, a kind of speech by other means.

To clarify, however, 'writing' is not simply opposed to speech in Derrida's work. Rather, what he means by *language-as-writing* is a force of language that characterizes all forms of signification – the repeatability, or 'iterability', of the grapheme, word or part-word is a part of its identity. The grapheme gains its positivity from the way it differs from other graphemes, in terms of its spatial juxtaposition and iterations separated by time. Derrida uses the word *differance* to explain this – a term in which the 'a' is phonetically silent, but differs enough from the French *difference* – to indicate the kind of relationality involved in signification. Consequently, the grapheme can never be sutured or totalized as a term that stands for a signified concept. Its repeatability means that there can never be two identical readings as there is always a surplus, a dissemination of meaning.

In this regard, Derrida discusses telecommunications as an extension of the force of writing. Both writing and telecommunications introduce the 'always open' potential for a signifier to be abstracted from its original context. In other words, when a signifier is repeated, it is not as a self-identical meaning. It therefore makes no sense to speak of either an 'original context' or a 'later context'.

For Derrida, the possibility of reproducing a self-identical meaning (which, in the 'media effects' tradition, is the goal of communication) is undermined by the practice of repeating the signifier. The more the signifier is mass reproduced, the possibility that an original meaning is *also* repeated diminishes. While it can be considered *de jure* as a technology for the reproduction of meaning, writing is also the medium that *de facto* undermines the ideal of self-identical meaning. Derrida's argument can be crudely illustrated whenever public figures complain that their words have been 'taken out of context'. Often, the words have been uttered in a 'controlled' studio situation and were carefully prepared. No matter how controlled and seemingly closed the context is, however, the speaker has no control over how such utterances may circulate, typically in ways that are cut off from the 'original' context.

POLYSEMIA AND DISSEMINATION

It is important to clarify the distinction between polysemia and dissemination. In 'Signature Event Context' (SEC), Derrida speaks of:

> the necessity of, in a way, separating the concept of polysemia from the concept I have elsewhere named dissemination, which is also the concept of writing. (1982a: 316)

> The semantic horizon which habitually governs the notion of communication is exceeded or punctured the intervention of writing, that is of *dissemination* which cannot be reduced to a *polysemia*. Writing is read, and 'in the last analysis' does not give rise to a hermeneutic deciphering, to the decoding of a meaning or a truth. (1982a: 329)

Thus, the difference between dissemination and polysemia inheres in the latter being determined by, and functioning within, some notion of homogenous context. Within this context, the task of interpretation is still to recapture the possible meanings of the text. Commentaries on Derrida's work claiming that deconstruction is a method for revealing the 'multiple meanings' within a text are therefore misguided. There are *always* many possible interpretations of a text, yet such interpretations are always situational since possible meanings can never be fixed within a given text.

Dissemination can be defined as one of the sides (or effects) of the iterability (repeatability) of the mark, the side on which the mark fails to reproduce a signified content. The ability of a mark to reproduce a signified content can be reduced to polysemia – that is, the production of a range of possible meaning-effects resulting from contextual chains in which the mark can be associated with other marks in a horizontal fashion.

Modern telecommunications heightens the incidence of dissemination, thereby challenging logocentric culture. This is the opposite of the ideology of telecommunications, which celebrates the advent of a 'global village'. There is not a strengthening of the 'communication of consciousnesses' but the establishment of the force of writing subordinates the logocentric 'system of speech, consciousness, meaning, presence, truth, etc.' (Derrida, 1982a: 329).

FURTHER READING

A good starting point for understanding deconstruction is the collection of interviews with Derrida in *Positions* (1979). Derrida's most developed analysis of deconstruction's relationship to 'communication' can be found in his essay 'Signature, event, context' (1982a) and *Limited Inc* (1988). Useful introductions and commentaries on Derrida's work that attempt to define deconstruction can be found in Liz Grosz (1986), David Holmes (1989), Christopher Norris (1987) and Julian Wolfreys (1998).

> **Related concepts**: convergence, cyberculture, technoculture, time–space compression.

The idea that we live in a 'digital age' is frequently asserted and rarely contested, reflecting the epochalism to which communications technologies are so often tied. Digital formats for the storage and circulation of information have quickly become the basic standard across computing, media and telecommunications. Some argue that digitalization is the basis for media **convergence**, while others see the digital platform as the basis for interoperability between discrete kinds of media, by enabling a common language (Jenkins, 2006a, 2006b; Kittler, 1997).

Unlike analogue information, which is based on an analogy corresponding to the world (such as when light falls on film), digital data exists in a parallel binary language that always needs to be converted from and to aurally and visually consumable content.

0S AND 1S

Indeed, digital information finds its greatest contrast with analogue in its 'reducibility' to binary mathematical combinations of 0 and 1. These mathematical matrices are manifested in the microelectronic medium of the microchip as sequences of silicon 'switches' that are either 'on' or 'off'. For example, the absence or presence of a pixel on a screen corresponds to such switches. The configuration of strings of such switches on a microchip provide sufficient pixels for a character, a word or an entire book on a screen. The same switches can be reconfigured to produce images on the same screen or digitally encoded sound. Such information can also be digitally encrypted on other hardware, such as optical or magnetic hard disks or plastic discs that can be read by lasers. With ephemeral media such as sound and video, the product is not continuous as each bit samples only a minute fraction of a second of sound and moving image: 'in an audio CD for example, the sound has been sampled 44.1 thousand times a second. The audio wave form … is recorded as discrete numbers (themselves turned into bits). Those bit strings, when played back 44.1 thousand times a second, provide a continuous-sounding rendition of the original music' (Negroponte, 1995: 14). These bit strings are so close together in time that the ear experiences them as a continuous sound.

The digital basis of such media is, therefore, largely invisible, except where there is some malfunction in the equipment. Just as digital switches are either on or off, there are no degrees of quality with binary logic: the corresponding image, sound or text generated by each switch is either there or not there. The transmission of analogue media, of course, may suffer a loss in signal, but this usually means an attenuation of quality only. Similarly, analogue and digital differ in their reproducibility. Analogue media degenerates the more it is copied, whereas digital media may be copied infinitely without loss.

The reducibility of digital information to binary packets of information makes it good for blending with other digital information, heralding the term 'multimedia'. Such binary digits, or 'bits', of information, can also find a home within many different kinds of devices designed for the storage and transmission of images, sound and texts. Moreover, while the language to which the data has to conform is programmed by computer programmers, the data is easily accessible by users and, increasingly, we are given the tools to reprogramme such information.

DIGITAL AESTHETICS

The fact that, technically, there is no analogue relationship between binary code and the real meant that early advocates of the digital arts saw this as an opportunity for a radical departure from expressive realism and its variations. Moreover, digital media were seen to be capable of a unified aesthetic and it was assumed that all art would no longer be tied to a referent but a new world of creativity would open up. For example, in cinema, digitally produced 'special effects' remove the boundaries of physics to produce images in which human fantasy could flourish as never before. Similarly, the multimedia capabilities of personal computers for montage and the digital manipulation of photos, texts and digital recordings expand the boundaries of media production.

As Sean Cubitt suggests:

> Several authors have attempted to use such effects as distinguishing factors in describing a single, universal digital aesthetic. However, in the early years of the 21st century, it became apparent not only that older aesthetic principles still hold good in such areas as digitally animated films and digitally generated dance music, but that many modes of software have evolved their own specific aesthetic properties and practices. (2006: 250)

In other words, while digital technology may be moving into more and more areas of life, thus far it has not threatened the metaphysics of analogue representation, as digital art is mainly concerned with mimicking the analogue and even improving on it.

DIGITAL PROLIFERATION

Just as, in the arts, digital media have not seen the emergence of a unified aesthetic, neither have they produced a monoculture of media platforms. At the level of consumer electronics, devices and incompatibilities appear to be proliferating as new technologies are enabled and older analogue technologies are frequently remediated into more than one form. The immense variety of ports into and out

63

of a digital television is evidence that we are not moving towards standardization but diversity, as each producer seeks to get an edge regarding what the consumer will want most. It is not just the devices but also the delivery 'platforms' for communications, information and entertainment that are proliferating. Digital technology has made it possible to receive television on PCs, high-definition and large-screen TVs and mobile phones. Conversely, video can be recorded on camcorders, PCs, cameras and mobile phones in a multiplicity of ways.

Lastly, the activities enabled by digital technology have diversified within each of these devices. So many applications can be introduced to the mobile phone that it has become a 'digital assistant', handling e-mails, street navigation, video games, diary, address book, YouTube viewing, weather guidance and Web browsing.

So, together, the expansion of activities on single devices and the multiplication of devices that can perform the same activities produces complexity and uncertainty as to the future of media **rituals** and the marketing of media related to such rituals.

According to Leopoldina Fortunati (2005), the paradox of new media is that the more media are unified by digitization, the more heterogeneous they become at the level of the 'interface'.

THE TELOS OF DIGITAL CULTURE

Poised against the proliferation thesis is the argument that digital ontology will eventually erase the distinction between mediums. For now there is uncertainty and, therefore, a great degree of technological experimentation related to the transition from analogue ICTs.

Friedrich A. Kittler, however, a contemporary philosopher of the 'digital', argues that the most profound transition involved in the shift to digital media is not from analogue media but the restoration of a function once fulfilled by written texts. For Kittler, written texts, unified by the institution of the library, once functioned as the universal archive for the storage of cultural data. In 'Gramophone, film, typewriter', Kittler (1997) posits that the written text had conferred romantic and spiritual power on language until its monopoly was destroyed by cinema and the phonograph. While film and the phonograph record images and sounds, the typewriter usurps writing's dependence on the eye's control of the hand.

For Kittler (1997: 44), 'the historical synchronicity of film, phonography and typewriter separated the data flows of optics, acoustics and writing and rendered them autonomous'. For him, this state of separation has been awaiting the kind of reunification afforded by digital code since the introduction of Turing's encoder through to the microchip and now thoroughly embedded in everyday life. The interoperable nature of calculations performed on microprocessors is leading all technology towards digital mediation, such that 'current electronic technologies are bringing them back together; in the future a total connection of all media on a digital base erases the notion of medium itself. In the meantime we live among "partially connected media systems"' (Kittler, 1997: 32).

In turn, digital technology is relocating the place of the observer. For Jonathon Crary (1990: 1), computer-generated imagery, and its 'fabricated visual analogical "spaces", [are] radically different from the mimetic capacities of film, photography, and television'. Digitally derived imagery provides techniques that are 'relocating vision to a plane severed from a human observer' (Crary, 1990: 1). Increasingly, 'visuality will be situated on a cybernetic and electromagnetic terrain where abstract visual and linguistic elements coincide and are consumed, circulated, and exchanged globally' (Crary, 1990: 2).

THE DIGITAL SUBLIME OR DIGITAL DIVIDE?

The transformations associated with digital technology are the subject of a number of hubristic discourses about the promise of digital culture, a form of determinism that postulates a 'digital sublime'. As Vincent Mosco (2004: 2–3), one of its critics, puts it, 'Powered by computer communication, we would, according to the myths, experience an epochal transformation in human experience that would transcend time (the end of history), space (the end of geography), and power (the end of politics)'.

Instead, for many critics like Mosco, the more pressing concern is equity of access to digital technology's more modest but, nonetheless, potent capacities. Thus, nations and even the world as a whole can be divided into digital 'haves' and 'have nots' or differing qualitative levels of access. 'Digital divide' is the usual term invoked here, but it has been a much-debated concept (see Compaine, 2001, for example).

For some writers, the digital sublime is ultimately about liberation from the flesh – from **embodiment** and the constraints of the physical body. The digital sublime is a decidedly **postmodern** worldview of technology, premised on the idea that reality can be broken down into the smallest possible components, then reconstituted, replacing the otherwise given forces of nature. Here, the digital is continuous with nanotechnology, DNA and nuclear technologies, which, like digital code, are invisible, but from which what Jean François Lyotard has called 'new nature' can be built.

FURTHER READING

Director of the MIT Media Lab, Nicholas Negroponte's *Being Digital* (1995) is an advertorial celebration of the digital over analogue forms of media. A sustained critique of the emancipatory potential of a digital ontology can be found in Mosco (2003). Kittler is the most philosophical historian of the digital and, in a dense, but useful introduction, he traces its ontology back to Turing (see the essays collected and edited by John Johnston, 1997). Jim Macnamara (2010) provides a useful overview of the digital divide debate, suggesting that the term covers three distinct social phenomena: technological access, social and cultural access and digital media literacy.

Discourse

> **Related concepts**: articulation, criticism/critique, deconstruction, hegemony, ideology, modern, sign.

Discourse occurs in two major forms, with consequences for media and communications:

- its strongly philosophical and theoretical usage by Jürgen Habermas and post-structuralist 'post-Marxist' thinkers such as Michel Foucault, Ernesto Laclau and Chantal Mouffe (for the latter especially, it is seen as a replacement for, or revision to, the concepts of **ideology** and **hegemony**)
- the separate but related development of the field of *discourse analysis* – usually traced to functional linguistics – that has been applied directly to the media.

Poststructuralist versions of the first form given above have had a significant influence within cultural studies approaches to media and communication, most notably in the work of John Fiske. More recently, critical discourse analysis (CDA) has consolidated from the second form listed. While still dominantly applied to the media, CDA has increasingly provided a powerful conceptual critique of post-Marxian work and the broader role of the concept of discourse within social theory.

FROM IDEOLOGY TO (POST-MARXIST) DISCOURSE?

The limitations of the vulgar conception of **ideology** provoked a need for more adequate critical accounts of the relationship between systems of thought – and, indeed, languages – and their 'contexts', especially social relations of power. Moreover, the vulgar Marxian tradition's obsession with a poorly specified 'economic' and 'class' determinacy (see **capitalism**) said little to those trying to analyse the relationship between social power and other forms of dominance, notably those based in gender, race and sexual identity.

Foucault's initiatives readily appealed to such constituencies. His work has a complex relationship with the linguistic turn that dominanted French thought from the 1960s (see **sign**). His conception of discourse, however, is neither limited to the analysis of language nor the use of a structural linguistic model. Yet Foucault was a student of the structuralist Marxist Louis Althusser – who denied his affiliation with structuralism – and his writing gives the impression that he is mapping an alternative to Althusser's highly scientistic conception of **ideology**, itself an attempt to redress failings in vulgar Marxism. Indeed, it is the Marxism of the (communist) party that Foucault most often rejects, rather than Marx per se, and many of his formulations read like Althusser minus his economic determinism and scientism.

Foucault's 'capillary' model of micropower, for example, was more subtly configured than a vulgar economic determinism. Where Althusser's style can seem almost mechanistic, Foucault's is famously 'writerly'. Adherents see this as one of his strengths, while his critics regard it as the source of evasion and self-contradiction.

At stake here is Foucault's conception of discourse. For Foucault, discourses, discursive formations and discursive fields tend, ironically, to share with Marx's own conception of ideology and Antonio Gramsci's expansive conception of intellectuals, a self-delimitation to intellectual/professional practices and their broader social location. For Foucault, these are constituted by a complex array of discursive regularities and irregularities – revealed by historical research – that he calls 'dispersions'. (Althusser developed a somewhat similar practice of reading theories for absences called 'symptomatic reading'.) Foucault traces these dispersions to capillaries of power (or 'power/knowledge'). It might be useful to think of the post-Marxian conceptual vocabulary Foucault develops as, like his writing style, a form of aesthetic **modernist** defamiliarization of previously taken-for-granted practices, such as 'medicine'. It is a wholesale shift in vocabulary geared to facilitate critical distance. Indeed, Foucault's choice of the discourses he analysed – madness, prisons, sexuality – is closely related to his interest in displacing the heroic narrative of Enlightenment **modernity** and focusing instead on the practices of *exclusion* that the Enlightenment's celebration of human reason fostered.

Methodologically, advocates of such a conception of discourse stress its independence from positivist conceptions of social research and some even emphasize its proximity to hermeneutics (see **modernity/modernism**; **criticism/critique**). It is worth noting that the French poststructuralist tradition developed its conception of discourse largely in ignorance (or avoidance) of the emancipatory sense of **ideology**.

Indeed, from a media perspective, a logical extension of Foucault's hermeneutics of suspicion would be to interrogate the Enlightenment ideals relating to **freedom of speech** and their reconstruction within Habermas' **public sphere** thesis. Although Foucault did not conduct this research himself, others have subsequently moved in this direction (Rose, 1999).

Foucault's conception of discourse was directly adopted by Laclau and Mouffe (1985: 105–6) in their highly influential and avowedly post-Marxian reconstruction of Gramsci's conception of **hegemony**. Subsequently, Habermas set this line of thinking against the *discourse ethics* he developed and integrated within his **public sphere** thesis (Butler et al., 2000: 3).

The discourse ethics overlap with the **public sphere** thesis' emphasis on the importance of procedures of communicative dialogue in a democracy. Habermas also uses this perspective to ground his philosophical and social theory – that is, to provide a set of assumptions that he believes follow *necessarily* from the human requirement to engage in 'speech acts' and so contain implicit rules for the ethical conduct of dialogue. Thus, Habermas' chief starting point is not the individual rational thinking human subject of the Enlightenment tradition, but humans *in dialogue*. Nonetheless, Foucault (1991: 120–2) sees the Frankfurt tradition, of which Habermas is part, as promoting a 'quite traditional' philosophical conception of the subject.

67

Likewise, Laclau and Mouffe reject such 'humanist' and 'extra discursive' assumptions and adopt Foucault's dispersion model of discourse instead. Accordingly, their use of 'discourse' remains especially confusing to the initiate as it raises epistemological and ontological issues similar to those implied by Ferdinand de Saussure's signifier/signified binary division of the **sign** – that is, is there a 'real' referent 'outside' discourse?

In a lucid reply to one of their critics, Laclau and Mouffe (1987) made it plain that they understand discourse to include what commonsensically might seem to be 'non-discursive' actions within a discursive totality. Their intent in so doing, they explain, was to stress that all objects and actions have a discursive – meaningful – dimension and, consistent with structuralist linguistics, we only fully apprehend an external 'reality' via language or, in the case of theoretical work, from within theoretical models or paradigms (Howarth, 2000a). This may be so, but plainly the formulation is more provocative than clarifying to the initiate. Raymond Williams (1995: 208–9) made the same point some years earlier with the more readily comprehensible suggestion that, while signification was a component of every practice, it existed in 'different degrees of solution' in different practices/objects. This is closer to the understanding of the relationship between meaning, action and techniques of analysis advocated in hermeneutics. The onus in such forms of analysis is then on the social analyst to account for distinctions between 'objects' and 'meanings'.

Fiske (1996a) directly appropriated (his understanding of) Foucault's model of discourse in his *Media Matters: Race and gender in US politics*. He described his own method of discourse analysis as (in part), 'analyzing what statements were made and therefore what were not, who made them and who did not, and with studying the role of the technological media by which they were circulated' (1996a: 3).

Significantly, Fiske (1996a: 4) felt that he 'needed to go beyond Foucault's theorizing', not only because the USA presented greater degrees of historical complexity (in his view) than those cases examined by Foucault but also because, '[f]or Foucault … discourse was a technique of inequality, but it was not a terrain of struggle'. This is undoubtedly contestable. Foucaultians might retort that Foucault always coupled his discussions of power with a necessary resistance.

Significantly, Fiske felt the need to add to his use of Foucault an account of contested *signification* that owed much to Stuart Hall's (1977a) largely Gramscian/Vološinovian account of the role of accented **sign**s and signification in **hegemony** and **articulation**. It is also consistent with Fiske's (1996b: 216–18) contemporaneous suggestion that Hall should develop a dialogue between the work of Gramsci and Foucault. It is this Vološinovian perspective that has partly informed critical discourse analysis (CDA).

CRITICAL DISCOURSE ANALYSIS (CDA)

The trajectory of CDA is much more firmly grounded in linguistics than the above poststructuralist reflections on the political and intellectual legacy of the orthodox Marxian tradition. So, for these thinkers, discourse tends to be linguistically focused and is thus closer to a commonsense understanding of the term. CDA has resolved more overtly the ontological ambiguities raised by the poststructuralists' expansive conception of discourse (in which 'discourse' appears to embrace all forms of social action). Ironically – or perhaps necessarily – this led CDA to recover (or maintain) some of the very same Marxian concepts – most notably ideology (Van Dijk, 1998) – that the poststructuralist conception of discourse aimed to radically revise or abandon.

Although CDA includes a diverse group of practitioners, Lilie Chouliaraki and Norman Fairclough's *Discourse in Late Modernity* (1999) – a major intervention within the field of CDA – provides succinct indications of some core shared principles. Their account of discourse employs the work of Valentin Vološinov to develop a *dialectical* perspective that combines elements of both structuralist and 'constructivist' (social shaping) approaches and so locates discourse within *and as* a social *practice*. Social practices are defined as forms of social interaction. Crucially, '*Not all interaction is discursive* – people can interact for instance by tidying a house together – but most interaction substantively and centrally involves discourse' (Chouliaraki and Fairclough, 1999: 38, emphasis added). Thus:

> Discourse therefore figures in two ways within practices: practices are partly discursive (talking, writing etc. is one way of acting), but they are also discursively represented. In so far as such representations help sustain relations of domination within the practice, they are ideological. Networks of practices and particular practices within networks constitute particular relations which can be conceptualized in terms of the concept of hegemony – as struggles for closure which can never totally succeed, which always give rise to resistance.

> … Discourse therefore includes language (written and spoken in combination with other semiotics, for example, with music in singing), non-verbal communication (facial expressions, body movements, gestures etc.) and visual images (for instance, photographs, film). (Chouliaraki and Fairclough, 1999: 37–8)

Significantly, Chouliaraki and Fairclough also resort to the concept of **articulation** to define the forms of relationship between such discursive and non-discursive elements within social practice.

The methods CDA employs vary widely, but could be thought of as following from the above programmatic statements. Thus, Fairclough's (1995: 32–4) *Media Discourse*, for example, sets out a list of 'desiderata' for critical analysis of media discourse that includes genre analysis, semiotics, conversation analysis and so on. It is important to stress that these techniques are not applied in isolation but, rather, within overarching conceptual frameworks, such as the one described above. Notably, such discourse analyses provide a broader set of techniques than the more limited range bequeathed to the analysis of media and communications by the formalist–structuralist tradition (primarily semiotics and formalist narrative analysis; see **genre**; **cultural form**).

Although it has its own set of specific antecedents and broader fields of application than media and communications, CDA's role in media analysis has constituted

69

a recovery and development of Stuart Hall's initiatives of the late 1970s. Teun A. van Dijk's work *Racism and the Press* (1991) in particular was highly significant here and provided an even more elaborated analysis of dimensions of the relationship between racism and journalistic practices than Hall and the CCCS were able to achieve in the 1970s. Beyond this, CDA has staked a significant claim to being the leading form of discourse analysis of mediated communication, most notably journalism.

FURTHER READING

Foucault's 1970 inaugural lecture, 'Orders of discourse' (1971), is often cited as a foundational moment for his conception of discourse. A good secondary account of the poststructuralist tradition can be found in David Howarth (2000a). Although he was initially critical of Foucault (see **articulation**), Stuart Hall (1997) later provided an account of 'The work of representation' that presented Foucaultian discourse analysis as a final theoretical step following a more standard cultural studies recapitulation of the work of Saussure and Roland Barthes (see **sign**). Hall's earlier interest in Gramsci and Vološinov receives no mention there, nor does CDA. Anabela Carvalho (2008) provides a good overview of the relationship between CDA and journalism studies. Allan Bell and P. Garrett (1998) is an excellent compilation of media-related discourse analyses. Nick Crossley (2005) provides a good account of Habermas' discourse ethics in a companion volume in this series. Chouliaraki (2008) includes Habermas in her recent broad-ranging survey of this field.

Embodiment

> *Related concepts*: cyberculture, identity, mobile privatization, technoculture, time–space compression.

When you are out on the phone or on the air, you have no body. (Marshall McLuhan, 2008)

The status of the body and embodiment in relation to media has been problematized by the challenge cyberspace presents to the experience of physical space. The proposition that cyberspace affords environments of immersion which substitute and displace physical spaces has become something of an orthodoxy in the literature.

Such a thesis is often confined to the 'digital' or interactive features of 'new media' rather than extended to all electronic media. Yet, ten years prior to the domestication of the Internet, Joshua Meyrowitz (1985) was already exploring the nature of place and space in relation to electronic media in *No Sense of Place*. For Meyrowitz, electronic media make possible arbitrary relations between a concrete space and a sense of place. By undermining 'the traditional relationship between physical setting and social situation', the constraints of embodiment, such as being in one place at the one time, disappear (Meyrowitz, 1985: 7).

The value of this analysis lies in its anticipation of what has only been attributed to 'cyberspace', that the mobility attributed to the Internet is characteristic of all electronic media. The mobility enabled by electronic media has challenged the ontologies of embodiment, sense of place and movement in a range of ways.

VIRTUAL TRAVEL

Mobility in electronic spaces is a practice whereby travel becomes dephysicalized. As Anne Friedberg (1993: 169) suggests, 'in the age of the easily replayable, accessible time-shifting' visual culture, individuals have become temporarily mobile 'time-tourists'.

In turn, such tropes challenge conventional ways of thinking about travel. It becomes possible to travel without bodily movement as we visit other worlds in a simulated way, which eventually annuls the need to travel with our bodies. Media, not just electronic, expose individuals to so many other worlds. Literature takes us to other places, television and cinema bombard our senses with images from afar and we can search online to confront difference or what Dean MacCannell (1999: 5) calls 'the absolute other'. What is the nature of 'visitation' when the 'local' construction of place is framed by the global reach of the Internet? What happens to the physical confrontation of 'difference' and otherness when we arrive at a destination to find that we have already visited such a place?

Interestingly, even though virtual travel is the most common form of mobility in media societies, the metaphors of virtual travel still follow those of physical movement. 'Surfing the Net', 'riding the information superhighway' and 'Where do you want to go today?' are appeals to being immersed in virtual experiences on the Internet that are heavily laden with the metaphorics of travel. In other words, virtual travel is still experienced as a question of getting to a destination, as travel, defined as 'away' in relation to a metaphysics of the home.

Theorists of the **network society**, however, think about mobility differently. In so far as the network itself is our home, distinctions between origin and destination are attenuated. One way of thinking about this can be found in Castells' (2004a) argument that media consumers and citydwellers increasingly live in spaces of flow rather than the space of place. Just as travel is dephysicalized, individuals remain stationary while the surrounding world moves around them.

Such mobility can also be seen to follow the phenomenon of **mobile privatization**. Public space is increasingly accessed from the home or, as McLuhan (1971) once argued referring to media-saturated North American society, in media-saturated societies, we go outside to be alone and stay inside to be connected to the spaces of 'communication at light speed'. Since McLuhan's writing on the contraction of the lifeworld to the 'central nervous system' simultaneous with its expansion to a 'global village', media technologies have become intimately personalized. The mobility possible within the private architectures of the car, office and home has been dramatically extended by a range of information and communication technologies. Mobile computing and telecommunications enable us to step into global spaces of flow.

Whereas the mobility of groups has historically been seen as a threat to nation states, from the Romanies and Jews of Europe to the modern 'asylum seeker', individual mobility is a highly valued status marker for the 'international middle class' (MacCannell, 1999: 13). Zygmunt Bauman has pointed out that individual social mobility is heavily divided along class lines. On-the-move elites, privileged by the relationship to the circulation of capital, experience a much more borderless world than wage-labourers. The latter class, who, in the nineteenth century, were assisted to move to countries with labour shortages, today live with the space-bound conditions imposed by protectionist economies. For Bauman, those with such limited access to *physical* mobility are nevertheless able to *consume* mobility by purchasing the virtual means of travel, channel surfing or surfing online. Both forms of individual mobility provide forms of cultural capital, but with completely opposite ways of valuing time and space. The physically mobile are time poor and, for them, space is easily collapsed, while the virtually mobile do not move from their screens, but are immersed in an activity in which they kill time, rather than space (Bauman, 1998).

THE RISE OF 'NON-PLACES'

With the rise of virtual travel, experience of the physicality of the built environment changes (Boyer, 1996; de Certeau, 1988; Featherstone, 1998: 912). Here it is argued that, as travel increasingly becomes dephysicalized, our relationship with the physical world becomes derealized and the fact of embodiment irrelevant.

Thus, the much-heralded 'hyperreality' of postmodern physical spaces – the airport, motorway, shopping centre and theme park – come to represent the new culture of flow. Most of these spaces are familiar as globally standardized spaces, but they are also extremely disorientating at a personal, physical level. They are worlds of immersion, in which the body becomes subject to a perpetual present, decontextualized in time and space. Like cities themselves, such spaces are nodal points for the circulation of bodies and commodities.

Non-places are the architectural equivalent of the dephysicalization of travel, achieved by heightened scales of visual consumption. They are typically places dominated by the image, which have no place-based history and therefore little that can be related to at a physical level (Auge, 1995: 77–8). As architectural analogues of the image, however, these places are extremely familiar as non-places are made up of a generalized urbanism where what they may lack in stylistic singularity they more than make up for in their global repetition.

FURTHER READING

For an attempt at making 'mobility' a defining condition of modern life, see Urry (2007), including an exegesis of the 'mobilities' paradigm. This follows on from Urry's work in the sociology of tourism and global complexity. Zygmunt Bauman's *Liquid Modernity* (2000) suggests an historical trend that has problematized the body and established the new ontology of mobility. The disappearance of parochial settings of everyday life and the liquid uncertainty of the lifeworld make mobility itself a constant. Similarly, Pico Iyer's *The Global Soul* (2000) looks at international 'spaces of flow' as analogues of future senses of place, something that Joshua Meyrowitz first began to explore in *No Sense of Place: The impact of electronic media on social behaviour* (1985; see also Meyrowitz, 1999).

Encoding/decoding

> *Related concepts*: articulation, audience, discourse, hegemony, identity, ideology, popular, sign.

Few concepts could have achieved as much fame as Stuart Hall's 'encoding/decoding' on the basis of such a slim and openly provisional formulation. It is usually cited as a primary influence on the rise of ethnographic and related active **audience** research, a general shift in media content analysis towards semiotic approaches and, moreover, the **populist** turn in 1980s cultural studies.

As Hall has more recently insisted, however, encoding/decoding was framed within the broader CCCS project of investigating semiotics, ideology and hegemony and, crucially, related political commitments (MacCabe, 2008: 29). Indeed, it was also tied to other applied work at Birmingham outside media and communication studies (Hall and Jefferson, 1976). The seminal text is Hall's (1973a) 'Encoding and decoding in the television discourse'. Prepared for a colloquium in 1973, it was one of many stencilled working papers produced by the CCCS. This source has tended to mean that, in the main, it has been discussed as if it were only ever meant to apply to the case of television, but most of its core formulations had been used by Hall in a 1972 article on the semiotics of news photographs and by 1977 Hall had included the encoding/decoding model as part of an account of the ideological role of the media in general (Hall, 1972, 1977a).

The better-known version is entitled 'Encoding/decoding' and first appeared in a 1980 collection of republished CCCS papers (Hall, 1980a). An explanatory note describes the 1980 version as an edited extract from the stencilled paper, but it is, in fact, a substantial reworking of it. In the opening of the first version, Hall situates encoding/decoding in opposition to the then very influential 'uses and gratifications' model of audience 'effects' research. As Hall elaborated in another paper the same year, however, he primarily wished the encoding/decoding model to challenge the assumption of a de facto 'transparency' in all communication practices that so displayed many features of liberal–pluralist political theory (Hall, 1973b).

The role of power in ideologically distorting such forms of communication initially articulated by Hall in terms of Habermas' 'systematically distorted communication' (1973a: 1, 1973b: 2) was crucial, as he later argued in extensive detail (1982). Accordingly, although much of the text is identical, the later version of the 'Encoding/decoding' essay is newly framed by a brief account of Marx's model of the circuit of production and consumption that had significantly contributed to Hall's understanding of **ideology** and **articulation**.

The notion of a 'circuit' is pivotal for Hall and formed the basis of a revised version of this model – and that of **articulation** – within a 'circuit of culture' in his collaborative work at the Open University in the late 1990s.

Part of the subsequent confusion in discussion of the 'Encoding/decoding' essay derives from their accompanying diagram(s). As Hall (1994: 260) put it, 'I make a mistake by drawing that bloody diagram with only the top half'. The 'top half' was indeed all that was visible in the 1980 version (see Figure 1), but the more roughly sketched 1973 version (see Figure 2) indeed makes it clear that Hall had always intended a circuitous journey to describe the production, encoding and decoding of mediated 'meaningful discourses'. Note, too, that the 'extra arrows' in the 1973 version indicate an attempt to address directly the relationship between 'structures of production' and the circuit of meaning. This emphasis returns in a slightly

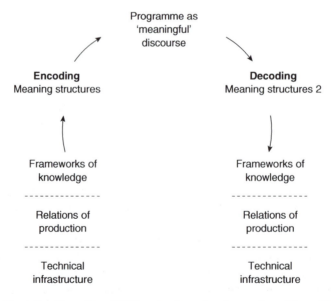

Figure 1   Encoding/decoding, 1980 revised version (reproduced from Hall, 1980a)

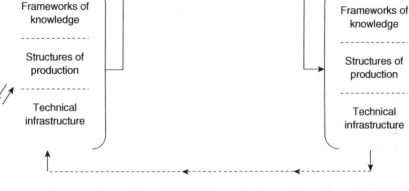

Figure 2 Encoding/decoding, 1973 initial version (reproduced from Hall, 1973a: 4)

altered form within later cultural studies' treatments of **articulation**. In 1973, however, Hall (1973a: 1) certainly had the role of institutional structures of media organizations as the 'production elites' of 'meaning producers'– the concerns of a 'political economy' of media – clearly in his sights. In both versions of the paper, Hall (1980a: 129) echoes Marx, making it plain that 'in one sense the circuit begins here' – that is, with production.

Hall's own major case studies using encoding/decoding focused on the encoding of television and photographic journalism (Hall, 1972, 1974b; Hall et al., 1976). The original 'Encoding/decoding' paper (only), however, also includes a discussion of a popular television genre: the Western. This discussion draws on some of Hall's earliest work on the **popular** arts and from the CCCS's little-known, but very substantial, attempt to contribute to a contemporary enquiry into television violence via a study of crime drama (Shuttleworth et al., 1975).

Hall uses his Western example to introduce the concept of *polysemy* – the semiotic phenomenon whereby a sign may bear more than one meaning. To read Westerns as mere denotative displays of violence, Hall points out, is to miss the connotative resonance of the hero as a model of good conduct. A 'behavioural' or 'instrumental' reading of the moral of '*hero draws his gun, faster than anyone else (he seems to have always known how) and shoots the villain with bull's eye aim*' would interpret it to mean: 'when challenged, shoot to kill without question' (1973a: 9). By contrast, a 'connotative' reading that takes into account the code of the genre conventions of the Western, Hall speculates, might be: 'to be a certain kind of man (hero) means the ability to master all contingencies by the demonstration of a practised and professional "cool"' (Hall, 1973a: 10).

The denotative/connotative binary – and, of course, the concept of code – derive from the work of Roland Barthes (see **sign**). Like the Barthes of *Mythologies* (1972), Hall located his semiological analyses primarily within an 'unmasking' conception of **ideology critique**, where the principal function of the ideology is understood to be such 'naturalizing' legitimations of an existing order. Hall extended to news(paper) photographs Barthes' semiological work on the immanent *formal* delimitation of the possible ways in which photo advertisements are interpreted by their viewers. Crucial to these for Barthes is the practice of *anchorage* of the polysemy of the visual image by the linguistic message (such as an advertisement's linguistic text).

Hall pooled the insights of Barthes and his own reflections on popular forms to develop the most famous feature of the encoding/decoding model. In parallel with Williams' typology of the possible relationships between a **hegemonic** order and cultural forms, Hall established a triple ideal-type typology of reception – dominant, negotiated and oppositional decodings. Crucially, in parallel with the role of 'anchorage' in the photo analyses, Hall also argued for a fourth code, within which media texts were produced and 'structured in dominance' to produce a difficult to avoid 'preferred reading'. This was a professional *encoding* that, while relatively independent of the dominant decoding, still operated within its **hegemony** by means of such practices as the achievement of apparent 'transparency of communication' and the overaccessing of *élite* sources in news story production (Hall, 1973a: 16).

In what remained a controversial dimension of this model, however, the professional code evidently could not manifest itself as plainly as the linguistic component of Barthes' photo advertisement. Only formal–semiotic analysis of programmes could reveal the 'hidden' professional 'preferred encoding' (Hall et al., 1976: 67–8). Thus, such analysis also revealed the 'preferred reading' or dominant *decoding*. This professional encoding dimension has tended to be overlooked in many subsequent discussions of the encoding/decoding model. Note, too, that none of this complex four-code typologization was specified in either version of the diagram.

ACTIVELY DECODING AUDIENCES?

Although the model was developed in tandem with the early CCCS audience research by David Morley, a plain implication of Hall's typologization was that such empirical research was not absolutely essential. Like that of Ernesto Laclau, Hall's conceptual framework lent itself readily to *formal* analyses of mediated **cultural forms** that required no 'fieldwork' component.

Here we need to remind ourselves of Hall's more recent insistence that this work was located within his overtly political research, especially his assessment of the balance of forces in contemporary hegemony. The supreme example of this work, *Policing the Crisis* (Hall et al., 1978), makes a series of claims about public opinion and popular beliefs based solely on formally derived evidence. Similarly,

Hall's other elaborations of the role of encoding/decoding outside the two famous papers located the model within his further reflections on the concepts of ideology, hegemony, articulation and semiotic contestation (Hall, 1977a, 1982).

A very large body of empirical work proliferated in the 1980s, which developed the 'decoding' side of the process Hall had outlined. It became known as 'active **audience**' research. It is important to restress here that Hall had first offered the model as a critique of one school of 'effects' research, so, to a large degree, the active audience research was positioned, at least retrospectively, against an assumed orthodoxy that imputed a 'passive' audience. The degree to which such orthodoxies were unfairly cast as 'straw figures', however, remains an issue (see **influence**).

David Morley's seminal *The Nationwide Audience* (1980) opened with a powerful and well-informed critique of orthodox empirical audience research traditions, but later references to these by 'active audience' researchers were less complete. For example, John Fiske – a key figure in active audience formulations (although not empirical audience research) – set aside all such 'empirical' research in his *Introduction to Communication Studies* (1991: 135) in favour of semiotic methods.

Increasingly, within later cultural studies, the encoding/decoding model was recast as a 'circuit of culture', first in the work of Richard Johnson (1986; see also Figure 3) and later in the work of Hall and colleagues at the Open University (du Gay et al., 1997; see also Figure 4).

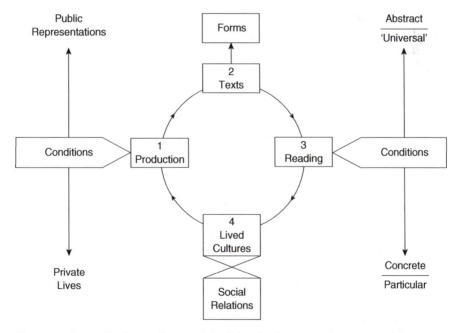

Figure 3   Encoding/decoding and the 'circuit of culture' (reproduced from Johnson, 1986)

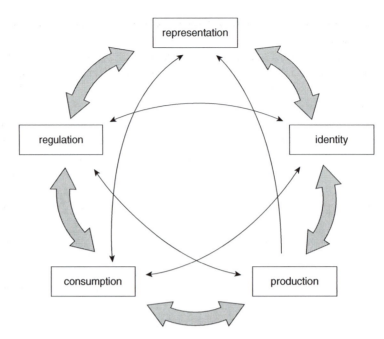

Figure 4   The circuit of culture (reproduced from du Gay et al., 1997)

Like Hall, Johnson was keen to maintain a broad Marxian framework. Each moment of the circuit is, for him, one of transformation and the perspective obtained by a participant in the circuit at any given moment is unlikely to reveal its full configuration. Structural asymmetries of power and resources, as well as misreadings and misunderstandings, are assumed to be pervasive but still contingent (Johnson, 1986: 47). Johnson, however, also commenced a practice of recasting the 'meaningful discourse' as 'cultural products' (in his article rather than the diagram) and thus encouraged such tendencies in both **culture industry** theory and the domestication school's conception of **articulation**.

Although Johnson's model was well-theorized, both circuit models were of a more introductory bent than Hall's earlier exploratory theoretical work, while the Open University version uneasily coexisted with a Foucaultian conception of **discourse** rather than Hall's earlier focus on **hegemony**. One effect of the Open University version is that it has further deprivileged the broader socio-political frame of Hall's earlier work, often reducing it to a somewhat anodyne notion of 'context'. For the earlier, more Althusserian, Stuart Hall, such a circuit was primarily a circuit of **ideology** – that is, media and culture provided the means of reproducing ideologies and sustaining a social order as a result by reproducing popular consent to a contested **hegemony**. Likewise, Hall's initial grounding of his circuit in production (as per Marx) was explicitly deprivileged (du Gay et al., 1997: 3).

Lawrence Grossberg (1993: 92) has strongly criticized this shift within cultural studies towards a 'communicational' configuration that projected the encoding/decoding model on all practice and so lost sight of the Marxian inspiration for Hall's circuit and the related concept of **articulation**. His complaint is similar to those who point to cultural **populist** tendencies within cultural studies' increasing focus on cultural consumption. Yet, as noted above, in the case of encoding/decoding Hall conceded that a partially drawn diagram can have widespread implications for conceptual (mis)understanding – and clearly he did see the encoding/decoding model as applying to all media within a larger conceptual schema.

One way to resolve this dilemma might be a diagram like our Figure 5, illustrating a double circuit according to Hall's 'double **articulation**' principle in his work on **hegemony**, **ideology** and encoding/decoding. This means that the two circuits meet in a zone of contestations that could be broadly labelled civil society or the civil sphere (Alexander, 2006). In so doing, we lose some of the gains of Johnson's model (notably his addition of public/private, which provided a clearer link to feminist critiques and research, as well as the **public sphere** that inspired it). Figure 5 is best understood when considered in conjunction with the related key concepts listed in the box above.

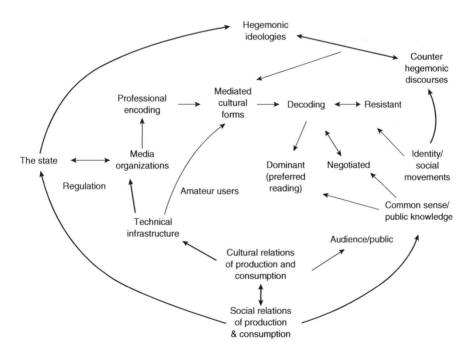

Figure 5   Encoding/decoding within 'doubly articulated' circuits

FURTHER READING

Beyond the texts cited above, on the broader conception of 'code' and its relation to communication theory, see John Corner's 'Codes and cultural analysis' (1998). Justin Lewis (1983, 1991, 1996) has provided some of the most clearly articulated assessments of the encoding/decoding model (he was one of Hall's interviewers in his 1994 discussion). On the model's wider influence in media and especially television studies, see Sonia Livingstone (1998b), Virginia Nightingale (1996) and Nick Stevenson (2002). For its use as a tool for media research in a 'new media' environment, see Livingstone (2004, 2007b). For a review and proposed revision of both encoding/decoding and the circuit of culture models for media analysis, see Julie D'Acci (2004b).

Freedom of communication

Related concepts: capitalism, communication, criticism/critique, ideology, modern, news values, public sphere, regulation.

This entry is headed 'freedom of communication' but ranges across its variants, freedom of speech and freedom of the press.

Freedom of speech is routinely thought to mean 'freedom from censorship', most notably as stated in the USA's First Amendment to the Constitution (1791):

> Congress shall make no law respecting an establishment of religion, or prohibiting the free exercise thereof; or abridging the freedom of speech, or of the press; or the right of the people peaceably to assemble, and to petition the Government for a redress of grievances.

Certainly this freedom does speak directly to the usual understanding of the democratic right to individual free expression. This formulation also expands the right explicitly beyond 'speech' to include 'the press'. To this extent, it speaks to a long European and US history in which independent 'publisher presses' had been used to expand **public spheres.** Publisher presses struggled to succeed due to attempts to suppress and limit them by means of censorship – often by taxes or onerous defamation laws – imposed by European monarchs, courts, early parliaments and state-established religions. Indeed, Jürgen Habermas (1996a: 368) regards the struggle for such fundamental rights as a precondition of modern public spheres. Of course, those struggles continue in many emergent democracies today.

Especially in its subsequent judicial interpretation and emulation elsewhere, however, this freedom plainly also speaks forwards in time to a more modern sense of 'the press' in its 'normal' quasi-institutional role in fully formed democracies that newspapers and professional journalists across all media play – holding public figures and governments to account.

Freedom of the press thus tends to draw us away from questions concerning individual liberty from governmental restrictions on individuals' conduct and access to restricted materials (such as debates about anti-terrorism legislation, Internet filtering and pornography) and towards discussion of the role of the media in a democracy as *quasi-institutionalized watchdog*.

Free speech discourse provides a sounder basis for the discussion of this role than its rival, the archaic term 'fourth estate', which alludes to 'the estates', the predemocratic institutions, usually three in number, consulted by some European monarchs (Conboy, 2004: 109–27; Jones, 2000b). 'Fourth estate' is also sometimes confusingly (and erroneously) glossed as the 'fourth branch of government'. This version alludes to the constitutional separation of powers in many modern democracies between legislature, executive and judiciary. Part of the very freedom of 'the press', however, is due precisely to the fact that it does *not* have this formal legal existence as a 'branch of government'. As much as legislatures and judiciaries can also play that watchdog role sporadically, it was felt that 'the press' needed to maintain greater autonomy from the state in order to be that watchdog, especially on a routine day-to-day basis.

Just how that autonomy can be established and maintained has remained a key issue in debates about **regulation** that, in turn, become matters for judicial decisions by courts, especially constitutional 'supreme' courts. To this extent, the situation of 'the press' and its autonomy resembles that of the **culture industries** generally.

Hopefully, it is clear by now that such references to 'the press' are not reducible to the technology of printing. Yet, plainly, the available means of communication do alter the informing understanding of the freedom. Face-to-face-based assumptions about 'speech' are plainly insufficient in a modern democracy. Moreover, the intellectual temptation has been to make the **technologically determinist** speculation that 'new media' will not only enhance freedom of speech but also render questions of social equity in its mediation irrelevant by making us *all* publishers or 'speakers'. Such arguments have proliferated since at least de Sola Pool's *Technologies of Freedom* (1983).

As with all technologically determinist arguments, such utopian projections overlook the social relations of production and consumption of such means of communication. The liberal tradition of political theory, which did much to elaborate notions of freedom of speech, was characteristically blind to such social preconditions of mediated freedoms. Lichtenberg (1990), for example, pinpoints a typical ambiguity in J.S. Mill's 1859 *On Liberty* (1991). Mill opens the famous second chapter, 'On the Liberty of Thought and Discussion', with the de facto assumption that there were no contemporary differences between free speech among sovereign individuals and the operation of a diversity of free presses.

In fact, at the time of Mill's writing in 1859, that distinction was already crucial in Britain. The diversity of small presses that had successfully campaigned for expansions to suffrage was already under challenge from the newer capitalized (and more mechanized) presses directed at broader markets that eventually lost the battle to survive. It was those larger organizations – such as *The*

Times – that instituted the division of labour between publisher/owners, editors and journalists. Indeed, *The Times* declared itself 'the fourth estate' (Conboy, 2004). Unquestionably, this was a complex and contradictory process, one of the outcomes of which was the establishment of modern 'professional' journalism (see **news/values**). In practice, however, this division of labour still poses the difficult question of which 'layer' of 'the press' should enjoy 'press freedom' – owners or journalists (Barendt, 1991; Gibbons, 1992)?

Curran's (1979; Curran and Seaton, 2009) thesis that 'press freedom' became 'a property right' carries much weight here. Indeed, in more recent years, many corporations have increasingly sought the right to be regarded as 'persons' in law. 'Corporate freedom' to take over another company, for example, can be represented as a form of 'press freedom' or even the freedom of speech of an owner/ publisher (in the case of privately owned corporations).

While new media environments are undoubtedly altering this balance of forces in various unpredictable ways, there is no prospect of a miraculous digital recreation of eighteenth-century 'handicraft' publishing conditions extended to all citizens. For that to occur, the dominance of modern corporations in news production and circulation would have to be removed completely. Instead, corporations are very likely to remain key components of any future role for 'freedom of the press'. A 'digital divide' is thus likely to continue to exist within the citizenry of the old democracies and more notably between nations and supranational groupings.

Yet the freedom is also increasingly recognized as susceptible to immanent **critique** and even widespread social movement mobilization in favour of forms of state regulation of corporate power. The renewed interest by US political economists in the freedom and the related highly successful 'Freepress.net' Media Reform social movement is especially noteworthy (McChesney, 2007).

BINARY NO 1: NEGATIVE V. POSITIVE

In short, freedom of speech/press is a contradictory discourse. To help clarify these conundrums, free speech scholars and legal practitioners usually employ a distinction between a *negative* 'freedom from' sense and a complementary, *positive* – 'freedom to' sense. So the negative sense characterizes the familiar *freedom from* state excesses, such as censorship and other restrictions of civil liberties. In effect, it requires the state to desist from acting. In contrast, the positive sense places an obligation *on the state to act* positively to provide a suitable set of circumstances for informed public debate. In the case of the media, the positive action envisaged involves the provision of the resources and circumstances suited to establishing *informed citizenship*.

Accordingly, the positive sense also invokes citizens' *freedom to* access resources such as reliable and diverse sources of information and opinion. Indeed, 'diversity of opinion' or, more vaguely, 'diversity' is frequently invoked in such discussions.

The negative sense of freedom of expression has come to predominate not only because it is much better known, but also, historically, it seemed sufficient for the period of the rise of the free press. Gradually, a powerful assumption was added: that the free press' independence from the state was guaranteed by 'the market'. John Stuart Mill's metaphor of 'a marketplace of ideas' tended to be thought of as a policy requirement rather than an analogy. Of course, 'the market' envisaged initially here – as in much early social thinking – was that of a small market town. Images of early town meetings, especially in the US tradition, have remained part of the free speech imaginary, despite the absorption of market towns into the realities of contemporary capitalism. Accordingly, the positive case often seems at odds with the 'obviousness' of the marketized ideal of the negative freedom. In this field, a marketized reduction of diversity of opinion and information sources to 'diversity of ownership' has frequently functioned as a policy compromise.

BINARY NO 2: STRUCTURAL V. CONTENT REGULATION

When it comes to media regulation as such, structural v. content regulation, another broadly complementary binary, is used (Lichtenberg, 1990: 127).

Content regulation is more readily rejected by the negative freedom perspective than the positive because it more clearly imposes what free speech theorists call 'a burden' on 'speech'. By 'rejected' we mean the likelihood that an appeal to a court based on freedom of speech principles might result in striking down the regulatory legislation. The Fairness Doctrine of the United States Federal Communication Commission (FCC), for example, prevailed in the USA from 1949 and was progressively weakened from 1987. It was increasingly thought to be at risk of such a challenge. Such content regulation usually requires little more than the adherence of mediated journalism to the norms espoused in codes of ethics and editorial guidelines (see **news values**). The UK system practised content monitoring of such regulations by the independent regulator for many years. More typically, content regulations have become complaint-based systems where individuals lodge complaints concerning violations of content regulations. Many of these regulatory regimes now include coverage of Internet content, especially regarding issues such as hate speech.

The requirements depicted in Table 9 were largely fostered in the era of broadcast media dominance, where spectrum scarcity permitted a legitimate role for state regulation (see **regulation**). A key feature of these modern regimes has been the exemption of newspaper 'content' from such legislated regulation. Indeed, newspapers usually only became implicated in structural regulation when their proprietors owned both newspapers and broadcasting licences. The subsequent neoliberal deregulation facilitated by digital convergence and 'channel abundance' has undermined both the rationale for structural regulation and the feasibility of monitoring-based content regulation (Internet filtering notwithstanding).

The resulting shorthand for the neoliberal regulatory regime was 'light touch'. All media were thought to be entitled to newspapers' exemption from 'red tape'. As the neoliberal promise of a digital utopia of infinite diversity of published opinion has failed to emerge, however, the case for positive reregulation has strengthened. Accordingly, content regulation has tended to survive in the form of complaint-based systems and/or its former role has been replaced by more informal media monitoring by citizens' initiatives. Comparative free speech analysts increasingly conceptualize the positive case as something akin to the **public sphere** model (Hitchens, 2006).

Within the realm of 'moral regulation' and media, the 'individual liberty' sense of freedom of speech has been played out most notably in the realm of pornography,

83

Table 9   Negative and positive freedom and modes of regulation (as developed in Jones, 2001)

	Negative free speech perspective	Positive free speech perspective
(Non-censorial) content regulation	Nil or, at most, self-regulatory initiatives on model of press councils	Positive programme requirements, especially for provision of fairness and diversity in news and current affairs established by regulations modelled on professional journalists' codes of ethics (such as former US Fairness Doctrine and European impartiality codes), administered by independent regulators
Structural regulation (of 'mode of communication')	'Fit and proper person' provisions for commercial licensees	State-initiated 'public service' institutional monopoly (such as the early BBC) or viable alternative presence
	'Ownership and control' provisions that foster institutional diversity (tolerated as they do not directly address content)	State-initiated subsidy, cross-subsidy and 'economic incentive' strategies *for professional journalism*
		Separation of 'media ownership' from journalistic programme production (Britain's early ITV/ITN relationship, continued with Channel 4)

erotica and erotic or sexualized content of mainstream media. While conservative interests have chiefly dominated the moral regulation of broadcasting and cinema, feminist analysts and activists have a long history of engagement with magazine-based pornography and erotica and the use of sexualized imagery in advertising across all media.

One of the most famous texts in this tradition, by Andrea Dworkin (1985), took the form of draft legislation banning pornography in the public interest. Dworkin took particular care in her argument to distinguish her proposed regulation of pornography from censorship. Of course, the obvious counter-argument remains a libertarian 'freedom of individual choice'. Dworkin's text remains a valuable exercise in demonstrating the distinction between a reasoned case for regulation of sexually explicit materials and one based in **moral panic**.

Nadine Strossen's *Defending Pornography: Free speech, sex, and the fight for women's rights* (2000) has been seen as the definitive 'civil rights' feminist response to Dworkin. Other recent feminist work influenced by the cultural turn and post-modernism has tended to shift from the view that *all* pornography constitutes violence against women towards greater emphasis on the distinction between erotica and exploitative pornography – a distinction fraught with difficulties (Arthurs, 2004). We can expect all these arguments to resurface as campaigns for Internet filtering increase in the near future, especially in nation states without well-established traditions of debate about free speech rights.

Similarly, democratic hopes for new media continue to come up against the ethical dilemmas that the free speech/press tradition renders explicit for us. Most notable here is the enthusiasm for blogging, citizen journalism and participatory online journalism. Habermas' (1996a: 379ff.) distinction between a public sphere in crisis and 'public sphere at rest', where the latter means relatively 'normal' democratic circumstances, is pertinent. If the former constitutes a kind of vast online expansion of the op-ed page for the public sphere at rest, the latter is usually typified by the immediacy of uploaded and recirculated amateur mobile phone photos and video 'reportage' from domestic crises, such as Hurricane Katrina (Allan, 2006: 143–68). This form, however, is also well-suited to external reporting of more overtly political crises from within relatively 'closed' nation states, such as Iran, and within nations that have undergone democratic transitions, such as South Korea (Woo-Young, 2009). As ever, though, we need to be wary about extrapolating from these instances a major revision of the professional norms of reportage, especially for 'the public sphere at rest'. As Jay Rosen (2003) has eloquently noted at his blogsite, our very use of 'media' in such contexts risks losing sight of the professional ethical and social conventions embedded in freedom of *the press* (see **news values**).

FURTHER READING

The literature here is vast. A good starting point from a media perspective is Clifford G. Christians et al. (2009). Frederick Schauer (1982) is a much-cited modern classic on freedom of speech. Merrill (1974) is an equally classic discussion of journalism in a similar vein. A key comparative legal text that highlights the differing 'European' and 'US' traditions and their implications for media practices is Eric Barendt (1993), but see also Barendt (2005). Hutchison (1999) provides a good account of the relationship between freedom of speech principles and media policy (with a focus on the UK). For the USA, David Croteau and William Hoynes (2003: especially Chapter 3) cover well the relationship between 'the first freedom' and media regulation, including The Fairness Doctrine. C. Edwin Baker (2002, 2007) brings an extremely sophisticated critique of orthodox economic theory to these questions. See also the Further reading sections for **regulation** and **news values**.

Genre

85

Related concepts: *criticism/critique, culture, culture industry, encoding/decoding, mass, popular, sign.*

EVERYDAY USAGE

A 'genre film' today is accepted industry parlance for the most routine formulaic products of that **culture industry**. The genre categories used are similar to those in programme guides, DVD shops and popular cultural criticism – romantic comedy, action, thriller and so on. Thus, audience members are routinely educated in the use of these terms. Even at this level, there is a kind of understanding between producers and audiences about the formal conventions that constitute such genres. From this quite conservative aesthetic perspective, violation of genre conventions risks audience disappointment or incomprehension. Commercial film producers now infamously test screen films in order to anticipate such communicative breakdowns.

The role of **criticism** and **critique** in this set of social and cultural relations is quite pivotal for the circulation of genre categories. Film reviews that operate as little more than promotional endorsements of the latest 'product' will simply recirculate the producer's genre categorization and perhaps the marketing department's 'hype' by tying it to the personality of stars – 'Tom Cruise's latest adventure', for example.

More independent critics are likely to contest such genre categories either by adding pejorative labelling (such as hackneyed, banal, clichéd) or by using alternative genre classifications that imply a lesser achievement. To counter-categorize a new film or television 'drama' as 'melodrama', for example, may diminish the directors'/producers' claims that their work is a fine example of the dramatic genre. (Although feminist analysts have revealed that such forms of genre hierarchization are highly gendered, they are employed nonetheless.) Such counter-classification depends on a more elaborated and nuanced genre vocabulary that includes subgenres. It relies on a critical vocabulary that goes beyond the usual limits of everyday knowledge. Here popular criticism and key concepts overlap.

Finally, both popular criticism and conceptually based genre analysis have recognized the increasing hybridity of genres, most notably in their commercial form of mixed-genre films that appeal to multiple audience segments. For example, there is a tendency in digitally animated children's fantasies to include elements of satire that can be recognized by accompanying parents/adults.

GENRE AS CONCEPT

Genre loosely translates as 'type'. The genre classification of artistic practices can be traced to Plato and Aristotle and has tended to shadow the history of aesthetic movements. Indeed, typologies of major aesthetic genres/narratives often look identical to those of the major aesthetic movements of cultural modernity (see Table 14 accompanying the entry for **modern**; see also Lacey, 2000: Chapter 2).

One key issue of great relevance to media studies emerged in modern genre studies: the 'enduring' dimensions of genres. Plato and Aristotle, for instance, recognized drama as a type. While classical drama differs in many respects from modern drama (however defined), the commonality between ancient and modern dramatic forms – and, indeed, such genres' existence across many traditional and modern cultures – begs questions of social, cultural and historical determinacy.

One way to frame the ancient/modern relation within European understandings was via deference to the 'classical' work of the ancients. Neoclassical rules required that certain laws of composition be followed. The nineteenth-century Romantic avant-gardes rebelled against such formal rules, seeking inspiration instead from folk cultural forms. This rebellious tendency remains alive as a dynamic within popular musical innovation, although today the challenged rules are the formulae for the 'genre' products of the culture industry.

Another commonly offered explanation for genre endurance is that some genres address 'universal' human themes (such as death) and, thus, have a transhistorical quality. Tragedy is often cited as such a genre, for example. Rather, as Raymond Williams (1979) and more recently Terry Eagleton (2003) have argued, while the same genre type may be in use, the social meaning of an enacted narrative shifts with different sociohistorical contexts. 'Tragic', for example, no longer applies exclusively to the fictive actions of heroic leaders and similar archetypal figures within hierarchical societies. Today, it applies to the most everyday forms of death, as in the routine news reportage of deaths in car accidents as 'tragic'.

Three broad implications follow for media studies:

- certain media, notably television and cinema, can be seen to 'bear' the contemporary legacy of the performance traditions of genres such as drama in their hybridized reworking – television genres, for example
- this begs the question of the social relations of genre change and continuity: the literary/aesthetic debates assumed a relatively slow pace of genre change and gave great weight to traditions and canons
- genre analysis can be fruitfully extended beyond the obvious 'fiction' modes to reveal previously underrecognized embedded quasi-aesthetic conventions in, for example, the melodramatic character of much news reportage.

NARRATIVE: THE FORMALIST LEGACY

Partly in response to universalist theories of genre, twentieth-century genre analysis was increasingly informed by the same intellectual currents that led to the structuralist revolutions (see **sign**) and their critics. The common 'source' intellectual movement here was Russian (and later Prague) formalism. The Formalists were closely linked to one of the modernist avant-gardes, the (Russian) Futurists (see **modern**).

The Formalists' key innovation moved from a premise shared with many avant-gardes: that the *techniques* of aesthetic practice should be rendered transparent and not cloaked in simulation and artifice. They sought to conceptually isolate and specify the distinctiveness of aesthetic practices – what they increasingly referred to as aesthetic techniques and *devices* (Shklovsky, 1965), even production, that rendered certain uses of language, for example, poetic and others not.

Even more than the Romantics, the modernist avant-gardes usually sought to break with overarching traditions, so the 'historical weight' of genre theory tends to be set aside for the Formalists' preferred term, narrative. (Such avant-gardist impatience with 'laws' and 'genre' also informs Derrida's influential essay, 'The law of genre', 1980.)

Thus, Vladmir Propp's 1927 *Morphology of the Folktale* (1968) laid out a somewhat mechanical model of the 'deep form' of the *functions* of *narrative* that

87

directly informed the work of Roland Barthes (1977c) and has remained almost standard in studies of mediated narratives ever since (Lacey, 2000: 46ff.). Propp's technique rested on isolating the constituent elements/functions of narrative into the smallest component units, morphemes. Tzvetan Todorov's (1981) more simplified multimorphemic account is commonly used today (see Table 10).

While this is enormously useful in analysis, especially of forms of popular narrative, like all formalist criticism, it leaves little room for an immanent normative **critique** that would seek to distinguish elements of the 'content' (which are so radically set aside here). If we think of the form as the skeleton of a narrative, then the content might be thought of as 'the flesh'. So, while the model in Table 10 delineates key skeletal features to be found in *all* narratives (arguably), it would be insufficient to analyse the 'flesh' on *particular* skeletons that make those bodies distinctive – that is, the differences in content between, say, the narrative of a highly formulaic television programme and one breaking with the formula, such as the differences between *Law & Order* and *The Wire*. One of the functions of critique is, precisely, to delineate what distinguishes television narratives of the likes of *The Wire*, *The Sopranos* and so on as 'special'. Significantly, this 'new golden age' of US television is often celebrated via the use of comparisons with tragic and realist genres.

LAW & ORDER V. THE WIRE

We can go a certain distance with the above formalist model. Common forms of narrative analysis would focus on the form of narrative 'resolution'. *Law & Order* offers a highly mechanical predictability in its very compressed narratives. The first half of each episode focuses on the policework involved in apprehending a suspect and the second half on the role of the judicial system in trying that suspect. Thus, one of the hallmarks of the programme is its tendency to present the apprehension of a suspect as a difficult but straightforward narrative process, while the judicial system often seems to frustrate the completion of this narrative when suspects appear to 'escape justice' via legal manoeuvres.

In contrast, while arguably just as concerned with crime and its punishment, *The Wire*'s narrative form is quite different. Each narrative unfolds over an entire

Table 10   Todorov's model of narrative (based on Todorov, 1981: 51)

Stage 1	A state of equilibrium is defined
Stage 2	There is a disruption to the equilibrium by some action or crisis
Stage 3	The character(s) recognizes that there has been a disruption, sets goals to resolve problem
Stage 4	The character(s) attempts to repair the disruption, obstacles need to be overcome to restore order
Stage 5	Reinstatement of the equilibrium, situation resolved, conclusion announced

season (at least). Shorter narratives are developed and often resolved within each episode, but these contribute as much to character development as the larger narrative. *The Wire*'s admirers, including a *New York Times* editorial, have compared it with a nineteenth-century realist novel – that is, a very long narrative, by contemporary standards, conveying the rich complexity of the social milieu of the lives of all its characters. Moreover, such novels – notably those of Charles Dickens – often conveyed an account of a social milieu unfamiliar to readers. *The Wire*, whose core audience were subscribers to the US HBO cable network, likewise portrays in considerable detail the very different world of street-corner drug dealing within the underclass of US cities. There are few instrumental characters who merely embody 'the bad guy'. The programme dramatizes the struggles within law enforcement and political elites by focusing on both easily solvable small-scale crime, thus generating 'good stats', and the more expensive, time-consuming task of tracking dealers and their corrupt networks of influence.

So, a purely narrative-based analysis does point to the analytic significance of narrative resolution in this short case study, but, inevitably, we need to go to elements of 'content' as well to assess such differences. More significantly, we would need to draw on other concepts in addition, such as ideology or discourse, to more fully situate the two programmes' very different articulation of the relationship between crime and key social institutions.

Genre analysis lends itself quite readily to that broad scope. It is highly pertinent that *The Wire*'s own creator, David Simon, and his appreciative critics pointed to the need for a genre analogy to account for the distinctiveness of the programme. Simons' preferred analogy was with ancient Greek tragedy rather than the Shakespearian forms he regarded as dominating other critically acclaimed series such as *The Sopranos* and *Deadwood* or, indeed, the nineteenth-century novels with which *The Wire* has been compared (Bowden, 2008).

Nonetheless, social realism was long regarded by critical television scholars as the ideal genre for conveying such necessary complexity of social life. It fell out of critical favour, however, during the rise of postmodernism. Williams (1977b) usefully contrasted (social) realism with the related genre of naturalism. For Williams, while naturalism meets realism's standards in some levels of complexity, such as character portrayal, it does not situate these characters' social milieux with the same level of sophistication, settling instead for a more surface account that 'naturalizes' what is often a narrower social perspective. *Law & Order* easily meets that definition of naturalism.

FURTHER READING

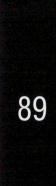

The entry for **cultural form** follows up several central concerns of this key concept. Introductory works and websites on genre and narrative analysis are ubiquitous. Nick Lacey (2000) covers the field very well and has a good guide to the literature, but see also Horace Newcomb (2004). A very clear analysis of the relevant literary theories can be found in Selden and Widdowson (1993). One classic collection worth revisiting is Robert C. Allen (1987) (especially the essay

89

on televisual genre analysis by Jane Feuer). For a more recent fine collection of feminist interventions and reappraisals of television genres and related criticism, see Charlotte Brunsdon and Lynn Spigel (2008). On narrative and television, see John Corner (2000: Chapter 5).

Globalization

Related concepts: *capitalism, convergence, culture industry, time–space compression.*

Globalization is an outcome of **time–space compression** that is over 500 years old, yet it only recently became the *fin-de-siècle* zeitgeist that it is now for journalists and much of the social sciences. At its most hubristic, from the early 1990s until 9/11 2001, globalization had become the subject of a new kind of **moral panic**, according to which a 'postmodern' or postindustrial market had cut loose from state or supra-state control.

During this time, some argued that globalization became an ideology of late capitalism – globalism (Steger, 2009), a confused admixture of utopian belief in the 'global village' or a triumphalist celebration of liberal capitalism as the final form of social evolution (Fukuyama, 1992) versus more apocalyptic narratives about the break-up of nation states and the end of the national polity (Greider, 1997; Martin, 1997 ; Ohmae, 1995). To this extent it might be considered an affirmative account of processes previously understood as cultural imperialism (see **capitalism**).

Marxist political economists Paul Q. Hirst and Grahame Thompson (1996) argue that negative ideologies of the threat globalization poses to the nation state have been used as a convenient justification for governmental restructurings of finance policy. The source of these ideologies can also be located in the 'antiglobalization' protests of the 1990s, largely reported as attacks on global development rather than global inequality, however.

As an objective process rather than an ideology, Roland Robertson (1992: 8) describes globalization as 'both ... the compression of the world and the intensification of consciousness of the world as a whole ... both concrete global interdependence and consciousness of the global whole in the twentieth century'.

TWO KINDS OF GLOBALIZATION

This two-fold definition of globalization, as both a movement of interdependence *and* a new awareness of a global culture, corresponds to economic and cultural globalization. Economic globalization refers to the way in which the production, circulation and consumption of goods increasingly becomes subject to an international division of labour (production) and consumption. This entails the possibility of corporate entities wielding more economic power than states, but also gives rise to global regulatory bodies, such as the World Bank and International Monetary Fund (IMF).

For media and communication studies, however, the most important forms of globalization are cultural. The most orthodox sense of cultural globalization is as an increasing inmixing and intermingling of centres of cultural diversity – in language, religion, customs, music, cuisine, international trade, migration, global media, tourism and telecommunications. Liberals often argue that this is a means of eroding prejudice between groups and allowing the individual to emerge as the basic social unit.

A second thesis on cultural globalization is that the globalization is not of 'cultures' ethnically defined, but of capitalism itself as an entity with its own culture. Karl Marx and Fredrick Engels (1967: 83–4) put forward this thesis almost 150 years ago as follows:

> The need of a constantly expanding market for its products chases the bourgeoisie over the whole surface of the globe. It must nestle everywhere, settle everywhere, establish connections everywhere. ... In place of the old local and national seclusion and self-sufficiency, we have intercourse in every direction, universal inter-dependence of nations ... National one-sidedness and narrow-mindedness becomes more and more impossible, and from the numerous national and local literatures, there arises a world literature.

GLOBALIZATION AND COMMODIFICATION

The strongest arguments for the globalization of capitalist culture today, however, are the non-Marxist ones put forward by George Ritzer (1993) and Alan Bryman (1999). In their texts, the globalization of capitalism is driven by the rationalization of production and consumption in ways that extend the commodification of culture known respectively as McDonaldization and McDisneyization. Drawing on the concept of rationalization developed by the early sociologist Max Weber, McDonaldization refers to the way in which consumer goods are produced, not to satisfy given demands, but according to the producer's need to cut costs by rationalizing production, including the conditions of consumption.

McDisneyization refers to a narrowing range of cultural themes by way of the 'Disneyfication' of consumption (Bryman, 1999). Disposable commodities, assemble-it-yourself furniture, showhome conformity and the architectural homogeneity of motorway design and shopping centres create the conditions in which the act of consumption becomes dedifferentiated (Bryman, 1999: 33–6).

Both these theses thus share much with Theodor Adorno's **culture industry** thesis (see **culture industry**). With the globalization of capitalist culture, the ethnically derived diversity of cultural expressions such as food, music and aesthetics are reduced to a small number of styles. Everywhere, kitsch and the massification of art genres for private consumption replaces the public appreciation of art in

91

galleries. Instead, as one postmodern thinker has suggested (Lyotard, 1992: 17), in the face of globalism, individuals become randomly eclectic – indifferent to the localized contexts of different styles:

> Eclecticism is the degree zero of contemporary general culture: you listen to reggae, you watch a Western, you eat at McDonalds at midday and local cuisines at night, you wear Paris perfume in Tokyo and dress retro in Hong Kong, knowledge is the stuff of TV game shows.

The aesthetic loses its depth in consumer culture, forcing individuals to turn to the mass market of images in acquiring an identity. Here, selection is made from the mass-produced styles offered by the 'culture industries' of advertising, tourism and retail culture (Jameson, 1991).

While it is possible to think of cultural globalization as bringing together many cultures and, thus, enhancing the appreciation of regional difference and diversity, it is also a process that displaces 'culture' in its ethnically framed, regional or national sense. The agents of cultural globalization are means of exchange, but they are also cultures unto themselves that bring about their own 'spaces'. As Holmes (2001) argues, the screen – television or computer – airport, shopping centre, motorway, tourist attraction, theme park, resort and modern city itself are all expressions and outcomes of this effect of cultural globalization.

Whether travelling virtually online or trekking a path described by a tourist guide, familiarity overcomes the differences we might perceive:

> the Oberoi in Katmandu, the Taj in Delhi, the Ramada in Amsterdam, the Hyatt in Washington, are virtually indistinguishable, as are the historic structures converted to festive malls. Even Bohemian milieus seem imitative of one another – the Left Bank in Paris, New York's East Village, London's Camden Locks – all boast similar cafés, galleries and street vendors. Cities seemingly would gain by distinguishing themselves from their competitors, but their civic leaders and their tourism entrepreneurs either fear to break the mould that resulted in apparent success elsewhere or cannot envision anything different. (Fainstein and Judd, 1999: 13)

THE 'PRESENTISM' OF THEORIES OF GLOBALIZATION

Some argue that the role of communication, consumerist and tourist cultures in the establishment of a global consciousness and interconnectedness is a more important force of global transformation than economic globalization (Crang et al., 1998; Eade, 1997; Holmes, 2001; Rojek and Urry, 1997, for example).

While some phenomena, such as McDonaldization, McDisneyization and post-modern consumption, might be considered very recent, much of the 'presentism' of the globalization discourses of the 1990s has been ridiculed by a variety of theorists. They argue not only that globalization is a good deal older than the 'globalism' ideologists would have us believe, but also that the world was more globalized between 1880 and the First World War than it is today.

At the height of the globalism hubris of the 1990s, Hirst and Thompson (1996) argued that 'globalization' has today become a somewhat mesmerizing discourse for sociologists and journalists alike and such a discourse harbours myths and pretensions that are unjustifiable in light of contemporary international relations. In *Globalisation in Question: The international economy and the possibilities of governance* (1996: 2–3), they argue, as summarized here, that:

1) The current international economy is in many respects less globalized than in 1870–1914 (note Wallerstein [1999] concurs that 1850–1900 was the high point of incorporation of all nations into a global division of labour), a time when the Gold Standard, *pax Britanica*, and the inter-continental telegraph system provided the minimum conditions for a truly globalized (as opposed to internationalized) economic system.

2) Genuine trans-national corporations are relatively rare. Whilst 'trade' is multinational, corporate structure is centred on a National base, far more than extreme globalists care to represent.

3) The third world remains largely marginal to Foreign Direct Investment.

4) Trade, investment and financial flows are concentrated in the G3 of Europe, Japan and the USA.

5) A policy co-ordinated G3 can substantially steer global trends contra the thesis of the extreme globalists that global markets or a 'postmodern economy' is beyond regulation and control.

Hirst and Thompson's analysis suggests that, at the time Marx and Engels were writing the *Communist Manifesto*, the conditions for economic globalization were much more favourable than they are today and economic globalization was a precondition for the forms of cultural globalization we find are much more systemic today.

If this longer view of globalization is accepted, it leads back to the question of the ideological function of globalism as a discourse. Why did this discourse command such ascendancy at the end of the millenium? Does globalism today simply promote a condition it purports to describe?

FURTHER READING

Roland Robertson's *Globalization* (1992) is an influential early classic, while 2010 saw the publication of a third edition of Hirst and Thompson's cogent political critique of the 'tidal wave' thesis on economic globalization, *Globalisation in Question* (1996). On media globalization specifically, see the useful overview in David Croteau and William Hoynes (2003). The work of Terhi Rantanen is of particular note here as it develops from studies of the history of global news agencies (Boyd-Barrett and Rantanen, 1998) to the broader analysis of media globalization and cosmopolitanism (Rantanen, 2005). See also the important journal edited by Rantanen, *Global Media and Communication*, and the references in Table 2 in the **capitalism** entry.

93

Hegemony

Related concepts: articulation, capitalism, criticism/critique, culture industry, ideology, popular, tabloidization.

Hegemony is perhaps the most enduring of the concepts contributed to media studies by the Marxian tradition, having survived the 'post-Marxist' intellectual fashions of the 1990s surprisingly well. Ironically, it also has the most 'communist' pedigree of those concepts. It was developed within the scattered *Prison Notebooks* of Antonio Gramsci (1976), an Italian communist party leader, former party newspaper editor and communist member of parliament. Following the seizure of power by Mussolini's fascists in the early 1920s, Gramsci was imprisoned for many years. The notebooks were not published until the late 1940s and not fully translated into English until the 1970s, when they immediately began to be actively used in media research. In this sense, hegemony is a recently developed concept.

The shorthand definition of hegemony is usually given as something like 'rule by consent rather than coercion'. Gramsci introduces the role of consent in order to correct the still widely used understanding of the term as simply 'domination', especially in relation to global politics, as in 'US hegemony under threat by rise of China'. Even Gramsci's corrective, as we shall see, does not capture the sophistication of his approach.

Within the Marxian tradition, hegemony is usually seen as an improvement on the reductive understandings of the concept of **ideology**. The fate of the two concepts has been closely intertwined. Althusser's theory of **ideology** is heavily dependent on Gramsci's conception of hegemony and Stuart Hall, the most influential 'Gramscian' within media studies, uses the concept of hegemony to distance his work from Althusser's failings.

HEGEMONY IN GRAMSCI

The prevalence of the term hegemony in academic writing owes much to Gramsci's being one of the first Marxists, and certainly the first leader of a communist party, to demonstrate any continuing analytic interest in, and a kind of respect for, 'bourgeois' democracy – that is, broadly Western parliamentary representative models of democracy. Prior to his work on hegemony, the usual assumption of communist strategists was that democracies – and the 'bourgeois presses' – manipulatively tricked the proletariat into voting for 'non-revolutionary' parties. The intoxicating influence of the Russian revolutionary success in 1917 – after only the briefest imaginable phase of bourgeois democracy – also suggested to them that such a form of democracy was an aberration. In contrast to this revolutionary impatience, Gramsci appreciated that the populations of the Western democracies were increasingly becoming what we'd now call 'stakeholders' in the capitalist democracies, in part because of transformations in workplaces and social life that he characterized as 'Fordism' (see **mobile privatization**). Karl Marx's immiseration thesis was becoming increasingly irrelevant in those societies (see **capitalism**).

Gramsci's prison musings on such matters arose because of the massive defeat of his political hopes by the fascists and their establishment of the first of the European 'totalitarian societies' of the twentieth century. This gives a first indication of the distinctiveness of hegemonic rule for Gramsci, which is that totalitarian rule lacks a hegemonic dimension because it requires no (active) consent. It is, simply, coercive domination or, at most, a 'balance of forces' where consent plays a minor role. Equally, however, Gramsci was under no illusion that consent was the only means by which democracies were ruled. So, in capitalist democracies, hegemonic consent is usually 'protected by the armour of coercion' (Gramsci, 1976: 263).

Gramsci, himself a political journalist/propagandist, drew heavily on a most remarkable piece of political journalism: *The Eighteenth Brumaire of Louis Bonaparte*, Marx's (1950b) reflective account of the defeat of the 1848 revolution and the rise of the dictatorial Louis Napoleon. Like Marx, Gramsci was interested in forensically assessing the social and political forces that had led to an unanticipated 'counter-revolutionary' defeat. Gramsci borrowed from Marx the principle that the analysis of any given situation – what the Althusserians would later call a 'conjuncture' – required finely tuned 'micro-level' concepts to assess 'the balance of forces'. Social class, for example, was fine-tuned to be subdivided into the smaller-scale 'class fractions' (Marx and Gramsci talk of the internal class divisions between finance capitalists (bankers) and manufacturers, for example).

Of most interest to us is how Gramsci's analysis connects with the media. His major improvement on Marx's *Brumaire* model was to expand the political role of *intellectuals* as 'class representatives'. Describing what in many ways were early forms of party 'machine politics' and 'spin doctors', now routinely dramatized on programmes such as *The West Wing*, 'The Brumaire' advanced the thesis that social class fractions had intellectual as well as political representatives. For Gramsci, however, 'intellectual' refers to those who elaborate the taken-for-granted assumptions of non-intellectuals within a class. Each social grouping has its own such 'organic' intellectuals. For Gramsci (1976: 5–23), it is primarily the intellectuals of the dominant bloc who organize social and cultural hegemony by such 'intellectual leadership', but the subordinate or subaltern classes also have their own organic intellectuals.

Gramsci's (1976: 9) much-quoted preliminary definition of intellectuals is 'All men [sic] are intellectuals ... but not all men have in society the function of intellectuals'. Its implicit democratization of intellectual capacity anticipates debates about elitism in **culture** within media and cultural studies. The prime intellectual function for Gramsci within a given hegemony, however, is not merely thinking but, rather, *the organization of consent*.

To what end is consent being organized, though? Just capitalism? Here *The Brumaire*/Gramsci model of power comes into play. For Marx and Gramsci, 'a ruling class' is not simply 'the capitalists'. The different fractions of a capitalist class – and potentially other social class fractions – form competing and exclusive *alliances* of interests that, in turn, require parliamentary party or coalition representation (blocs). Bankers and mining companies might be at odds with manufacturers and farmers, for example, over matters today as varied as broadband policy, immigration and exchange rates. Gramsci calls such a complex set of alliances an 'historical bloc', but, in media studies, the terms 'dominant bloc' and 'power bloc' are usually substituted. Crucially for Gramsci, this bloc needs to develop an ideology that 'represents' its coalition of forces but also seeks to become hegemonic. The subaltern (subordinate) and their organic intellectuals may undertake counterhegemonic actions and sections of those subaltern groups may enter into new historical blocs and thus become *incorporated* (see **articulation**).

Gramsci's (1978) most likely early model for intellectual leadership in Catholic Italy was the local priest, not least because of his then near-monopoly position in 'broadcasting' from the pulpit. Plainly anyone who has similar skills of rhetoric and persuasion could fulfil the same 'function', most obviously editorialists and their descendents in news production, but also, in principle, many more media practitioners, such as public relations consultants today.

For Gramsci, intellectuals successfully organize consent when they accurately address 'common sense' – those taken-for-granted assumptions that even the most uneducated person might recognize as 'obvious'. These include resorts to the 'national popular', appeals to a broader folkloric knowledge – increasingly tied to notions of national identity – and would today include fragments of information obtained from the media (see **articulation**).

HEGEMONY IN MEDIA STUDIES

For media, communications and cultural studies, the term 'hegemony' offered a ready means of situating the field of **culture** in relation to power, especially the power wielded by the state. It was also clearly designed to avoid the errors of reductivism in 'orthodox Marxism'. Thus, it played an especially prominent role in the work of the CCCS. Gramsci's emphasis on the need for popular consent to be pursued and 'won' also appeared less deterministic than much contemporary **audience** theory and other Marxian models of **ideology**, including Althusser's. The Althusserian reduction of hegemony to 'ideological state apparatus' had set back such arguments considerably.

The CCCS initially drew on the explicit connection Raymond Williams made between hegemony and his already highly influential work on **culture**. Williams had proposed three historical positions for socio**cultural forms** in relation to hegemony:

- dominant
- residual
- emergent.

Residual and emergent forms could play an incorporated, alternative or oppositional role in relation to the dominant forms. The purpose of this schema was to underpin, against the Althusserian interpretation, Gramsci's own stress on the contingency of any given hegemonic dominance (Williams, 1977a, 1980b; see also Jones, 2004). The Birmingham research on emergent counterhegemonic youth subcultures and their hegemonic incorporation explicitly employed this model (Clarke et al., 1977), as Stuart Hall (1977a: 331–2) did in his initial theorization of the media's role in hegemony.

The Birmingham researchers also sought a more satisfactory reconciliation between Marxian and structuralist semiotics (see **sign**) than that facilitated by the Althusserian experiment, however. Hall opened up analysis of the role of the media within hegemony with his influential **encoding/decoding** model and especially his conception of **articulation**. Hall (1988) became famous as a political–cultural analyst and strategist of the transformation of the major Western democracies by Thatcherist neoliberalism and, later, for his work on subaltern identity. Perhaps Hall's most lasting legacy in this context is his transformation of deviance and **moral panic** theory into the frame of hegemony. The key moment here for Hall (et al., 1978) is the ideological construction of a general interest understood as societal consensus, especially concerning crime.

THE DISCURSIVE TURN AND HEGEMONY

Ernesto Laclau and Chantal Mouffe's (1985) 'post-Marxist' rethinking of the concept of hegemony coincided with the tendency to replace the concept of ideology with Michel Foucault's **discourse** and, for many in cultural studies, Gramsci's hegemony with Foucault's *governmentality*. For Foucault especially, the avoidance of economic reductivism was at the heart of the terminological and conceptual shift towards 'discourse'. As noted in the entry on **ideology**, however, the failings in question were traceable to orthodox 'Marxism' and Althusser's scientism rather than to Marx or the Frankfurt tradition of studies of ideology ranging from Theodor Adorno to Jürgen Habermas. Both Laclau and Foucault's conceptions of power focus far less on the economy, social class and the state than those of Gramsci or the 'orthodox' Marxist tradition. Such dispersed models of power have thus often been seen to be more readily suited to the analysis of power relations – and media representations – related to gender and race, for example.

RECENT WORK

Gramsci's conception of organic intellectuals rested on the assumption of an equally organic political agency that was receptive to those intellectuals: the communist party. For very good reasons of preserving intellectual autonomy, such an assumption was usually unsustainable when the concept of hegemony was adopted within the academy. Like many other Marxian categories, it was employed as a term of critical analysis of features of capitalism and not necessarily connected to a particular political position. The most notable exceptions were in France and Italy, where large communist parties enjoyed popular electoral support and

Marxist intellectuals such as Althusser sought to democratically reform those parties from within. By the time Williams adopted the concept, he had long since lost respect for such parties, even though he had a classic 'organic' working-class background. Evidently for Hall, the organic intellectual model spoke equally to the subaltern Afro-Caribbean background he shared with the 'folk devils' of the 1970s mugging **moral panic**.

These complex issues of intellectual politics have strongly influenced the fate of the concept in media and communications in recent years.

The model of the subaltern intellectual has appealed to those who feel an obligation to bring to recognition the specific interests of their background. This has especially been the case with those whose subaltern identities relate to race, ethnicity or national identities based in the former Third World as intellectual fields are themselves now highly globalized. As Joke Hermes (2004) has argued, however, basing one's approach entirely in terms of a subaltern **identity** tends to lead to a tension between 'advocacy' and 'autobiography', at least among those whose media studies research is entirely grounded in cultural studies. Valid self-doubts about the legitimacy of one's capacity to speak for those who share the subaltern identity – but who do not enjoy the privileges of an intellectual – tend to arise. Accordingly, Gramsci's concept of hegemony – which defines organic intellectuals as such leaders/representatives of counterhegemonic practice – also becomes problematic.

One alternative embraced by many within cultural studies was to adapt part of the work of Althusser's student Michel Foucault on governmentality. Foucault's work appealed especially to this constituency because it was felt to break completely with the risks of economic/class reductivism. Governmentality focuses attention on institutions and expertise as forms of governing others. Foucault shifted away from Gramsci's apparent focus on the state as the major instrument of social power in society. As the neoliberal reduction and privatization of many state services accelerated, this attention to 'poststatist' governance assumed greater relevance. Increasingly, (cultural) citizenship and consumerism were brought into alignment.

As Foucault later admitted (1991: 116–18), the logic of his governmentality position was anticipated by the Frankfurt School (see **criticism/critique**), especially in their work on 'instrumental reason'. By this they meant the 'technologizing' of artistic, intellectual and other potentially critical dimensions of social life. Administrative research was the embodiment of this trend for Adorno, best exemplified by the rise of market research and its influence on early media research. Similarly, opinion polling has come to embody for many this denial of critical autonomy as in, for example, Pierre Bourdieu's (1993) writings on public opinion and Habermas' early work on the **public sphere**. Such a view of opinion polling – and, by implication, all such technologizing models – has been challenged by Justin Lewis (2001). Lewis argues persuasively that opinion polls are **cultural forms** conducive to the hegemonic organization of consent yet nonetheless contestable. Thus, Lewis' work demonstrates that the concept of hegemony can be used effectively to address 'post-State' forms of governance.

There are at least three other critical intellectual positions compatible with maintaining the concept of hegemony.

- Within the study of international relations, hegemony is being rethought beyond Gramsci's nation state framework as part of more critical approaches to **globalization** and neoliberalism (Harvey, 2005). Power blocs, for example, are obviously no longer limited to single nation states. This perspective is starting to influence approaches to media and cultural globalization (Artz and Kamalipour, 2003). It has much in common with a critical political economy approach to the media that relies on an 'unmasking' **critique**.
- **Public sphere** theorists turned to the concept of hegemony to redress absences in Habermas' original model. Nancy Fraser's (1993) influential reworking of the **public sphere** thesis relies explicitly on the concept of hegemony for its development of a multiple publics model based in 'subaltern counterpublics'. This in turn indicates that immanent **critique** is one alternative critical intellectual position available to the subaltern (Buck-Morss, 2003).
- There has been a revival of work on **populism** akin to Hall's (1980b, 1985b) Gramscian authoritarian populism thesis related to his work on Thatcherism. This new work has been stimulated by the rise of right-wing neopopulist parties and movements in Europe and elsewhere during the last 15 years. The quasi-hegemonic role of media in this process is attracting attention (Mazzoleni et al., 2003).

Like **capitalism**, however, hegemony is a concept designed to be employed in critical opposition. Unlike **public sphere**, it has no obvious alternative conception of democracy built 'within' it. 'Counterhegemony' is at best an implicit demand for a more socially inclusive democracy. Gramsci's own obvious preparedness to subordinate civil society to a battle between contesting hegemonies leaves little space for a civil or public sphere or, indeed, media autonomy. The continuing survival of the concept – despite the proverbial premature obituaries in recent years – testifies to the continuing need for such a critical unmasking concept, but one that should be used with caution.

FURTHER READING

Recent exegeses of Gramsci and hegemony have tended not to focus on media and communications, but Peter Ives (2004) does so via the central issue of hegemony and its relationship with language. The authoritarian 'risks' carried within the concept of hegemony have been detailed in political theory by Jean Cohen and Andrew Arato (1992). A similar, more media-related, perspective informs Jeffrey C. Alexander's *The Civil Sphere* (2006). Stuart Allan (1998) represents a powerful case study demonstration of the relevance of Hall's hegemony/encoding framework to contemporary discourse analysis. US media studies texts that employed the concept of hegemony include important works by Todd Gitlin (1980, 1994, 2000) on news reportage and the 'hegemonic commodification of prime time television', as well as Kellner (1990) and Hallin (1994). Lewis (1999) partly informs his more recent work cited above. John Fiske's work (1987, for example) is indicative of the progressive replacement of the critical dimensions of Hall and Laclau's work with more 'cultural populist' approaches within much of cultural studies. Although not directly concerned with media and communications, Michelle Barrett (1991) captures very well the moment of the post-Marxist turn to Foucault. For a recent application of the governmentality approach in media studies, see Laurie Ouellette and James Hay (2008).

Ideology

Related concepts: articulation, capitalism, criticism/critique, culture, deconstruction, discourse, hegemony, public sphere.

Few concepts have left such a contested legacy as 'ideology'. As critical Marxian terminology is again coming back into vogue after the 'post-Marxisms' of the 1980s and 1990s, it is important to recover its meanings with some care. There is considerable confusion surrounding this term so precision is important.

In brief, most of the 'Marxism' that many rejected in the 1980s and 1990s had little to do with Marx, just as much of what we understand as 'communism' can be separated from Marx's actual writings and political practice. Rather, what was rejected was a 'Marxism' constructed inside the communist movement, including, to a large extent, the highly influential work of the French communist Marxist Louis Althusser. This is not to suggest that Marx's own work is immune from criticism; rather it is to suggest that perhaps more than bathwater was thrown away in much post-Marxism.

PRE-/NON-MARXIAN USAGE

For most of its history, ideology has had a pejorative connotation, but it is the negative sense first attributed to Bonaparte that is pervasive. The routine reference in much journalistic use is similar to Bonaparte's, an impatience with those who are insufficiently 'flexible' and 'pragmatic'. In this everyday sense, an ideologist is a dogmatist who refuses to alter his or her presuppositions even if they are contradicted by 'the facts' or significantly altered circumstances. An example would be those who advocated the invasion of Iraq despite the lack of evidence of weapons of mass destruction. There are similar everyday descriptive uses that roughly translate as 'a set of beliefs'.

What Marx's conception of ideology shares with everyday parlance is a focus on intellectuals and ideas. Most references to the concept in Marx occur in conjunction with his views on ideolog*ists* rather than as separate discussions of ideolog*ies* or ideolog*y*. The distinction is an important one.

Broadly speaking, for Marx, then, an ideologist is an intellectual, so an ideology is an articulated intellectual theory, not the everyday thoughts of someone who is not a (quasi-) professional intellectual. A typical ideology for Marx is Ricardo's theory of political economy as opposed to the off-the-cuff views of a person in a café. As Gyorgy Márkus (1983, 1995) has established, unlike many 'Marxists', Marx does not use the term to refer to the ideologically distorted views of every-day people or their 'false consciousness' (a term never used by Marx). This is an important point to remember in the context of subsequent 'theories of ideology' and positions attributed to 'Marxism'.

If we follow Antonio Gramsci in broadening our understanding of professional intellectuals to include such figures as, say, priests and journalists (see **hegemony**), then ideologies are more properly understood as sets of beliefs that the rest of the population may or may not accept. Today, the role of the media in such circulation is pivotal. Marx's polemics against those suffering from ideological misconceptions are, likewise, aimed at (particular) intellectuals rather than the general population.

It is worth noting that the above account of ideology follows the position of Marxian scholars such as Márkus rather than a key figure in media studies, Stuart Hall. Although our account overlaps with his, Hall (1996a: 27) insists that Marx regarded ideology as including everyday consciousness. Hall's position is closer to that of Althusser, despite his being one of Althusser's most careful critics. In effect, Hall wishes to include all 'common sense' within ideology (see **hegemony**; **articulation**). This may seem an arcane distinction, but it does have real conse-quences for how we conceptualize the social role of media. It still leaves open the question of whether or not everyday consciousness may involve the routine mis-recognition of forms of social power, such as everyday racist assumptions. The Gramscian tradition at least would consider these as the receptive ground (within 'common sense') for racist interpellations/articulations.

For Marx, then, the key mechanism of an ideologist is *not* manipulation (in its psychological sense), but the subtler process of representing a specific interest as a general interest – representing an unpopular war as for 'the common good', 'love of nation' and so on, for example (Hall, 1977a: 338). This may take place deliberately or inadvertently. For Marx, intellectuals, artists and, especially, politicians are the specialists in this practice. It should be added that not all intellectual thought, art or even political debate is 'ideological' for him, nor are all appeals to a common good.

The key text here is Marx's *The Eighteenth Brumaire of Louis Bonaparte* (1950b), which profoundly influenced Gramsci's conception of **hegemony**. For Marx, the 'political and intellectual representative' of a class reproduces *the lim-its of thought* – the horizon of the possible – of a social class. His classic example here is the contradictory location of the petit bourgeois (for instance, shopkeepers) whose sense of being squeezed between organized labour and capital, Marx felt, was detectable in certain political parties' versions of the national interest. There need not be any direct linkage between shopkeepers and 'representative' political parties, however, as what 'corresponds' is the 'limits of thought'. Hall (1977b: 56–7) applied this model directly in one of his earliest analyses of Thatcherism. Similarly, Gramsci's conception of the role of intellectuals in shaping and maintaining **hegemony** is very much an elaboration of this aspect of Marx's portrayal of the ideologist.

IDEOLOGY AND CRITIQUE: TWO TYPES

Marx's exposure of the particular 'interest' or 'class character' behind an ideology's claimed general interest could be called a **critique** of that ideology. Indeed, the phrase 'ideology critique' is routinely used across the humanities and social sciences today to refer to such a practice. There are actually two kinds of ideology critique, however.

First, the *'Brumaire'*-like revelation of interests 'behind' an ideology can be seen, following Márkus (1995), as an *unmasking* ideology critique. For example, some of the **technologically determinist** arguments about the 'inevitable' consequences of ICT convergence were revealed by Vincent Mosco (2003) to be masking the corporate interests of some telecommunications companies. Advocates of such positions could be described legitimately as ideologists. Marx's own concrete analyses, such as the *'Brumaire'* example above, seek to respect the different domains of what he elsewhere called the base and superstructure (see **capitalism**) in something like the manner of Bourdieu's 'fields' (see **articulation**). In clumsier hands, however, notably Engels', such an unmasking argument reduced the ideological to the economic.

Second, the other, more complex, kind of ideology critique, is 'immanent' or 'emancipatory'. As immanent means loosely 'from within', it contrasts with the external interests brought to bear in an unmasking critique. Here 'critique' corresponds closely with the sense elaborated under the entry for **criticism/critique**. The commonality of these roles for immanent critique is the necessary complexity of the ideology or work of art. Such phenomena cannot be explained away as mere masks for external vested interests. Instead of 'limits of thought', we are speaking here of highly elaborated and rich discourses. Critique of them often reveals a redeemable, even emancipatory, dimension. Within Marx's own work, immanent ideology critiques include those he undertook of elaborated theories, such as political economy. His goal there was reconstruction rather than exposure or dismissal.

In media studies, Habermas' **public sphere** thesis represents such an immanent critique; one that, in Habermas' own words, 'moved totally within the circle of a classical Marxian ideology critique, at least as it was understood in the Frankfurt environment' (1993b: 463). This dimension of his analysis goes a long way towards explaining the tension in the public sphere thesis between empirical description and utopian promise. The public sphere is the emancipatory promise of democracy.

Its immanent critique reveals the limits of the success of that promise, but also seeks to reconstruct the ideology, such that its emancipatory promise can be kept in sight and prospects for its realization improved or fulfilled.

IDEOLOGY IN ADORNO

Adorno's use of the term ideology is consistent with Marx's and, if anything, even more stringent in its delimitation of what constitutes an ideology. It also accounts for 'the Frankfurt environment', to which Habermas refers above. In 1956, following the return to Germany (from the USA) of key Frankfurt School figures, an important set of essays was published under the name of the Frankfurt Institute. It now looks very much like the first 'key concepts' book (Frankfurt Institute for Social Research, 1973). In a section now attributed to Adorno (Jay, 1984: 180), the distinction between unmasking and immanent ideology critique is drawn especially clearly in an assessment of what remains a major reference point for such discussions, the Nazi Germany from which Adorno himself had had to flee:

> Accordingly, the critique of ideology, as the confrontation of ideology with its own truth, is only possible insofar as the ideology contains a rational element with which the critique can deal. That applies to ideas such as those of liberalism, individualism … But whoever would want to criticize, for instance, the so-called ideology of National Socialism would find himself victim of an impotent naiveté. Not only is the intellectual level of the authors Hitler and Rosenberg beneath all criticism. The lack of any such level, the triumph over which must be counted among the most modest of pleasures, is the symptom of a state, to which the concept of ideology, is no longer directly relevant … rather it is a manipulative contrivance, a mere instrument of power, which actually no one, not even those who used it themselves, expected to be taken seriously. With a sly wink they point to their power: try using your reason against that, and you will see where you end up … Where ideologies are replaced by approved views decreed from above, the critique of ideology must be replaced by *cui bono* – in whose interest? (Frankfurt Institute for Social Research, 1973: 190)

According to Adorno, the contrast here between immanent and unmasking critique is very plain. Nazism fails as an ideology 'worthy' of immanent analysis because it lacks a redeemable 'truth content'. It is mere 'manipulative contrivance', motivated by vested interests that are easily unmasked. Adorno's *'cui bono'* in effect passes the analytic baton back to Marx's *Brumaire* and that other famous analyst of fascism, Gramsci. Yet, as noted in the entry on **hegemony**, Gramsci is also inclined to set fascism aside as a special case: it is non-hegemonic, for him, as its balance between coercion and consent is massively weighted in favour of the former. Adorno's characterization of fascism as a 'manipulative contrivance' would probably have been endorsed by Gramsci. Like Marx, they both would have seen it as reproducing key features of Louis Bonaparte's regime – a particular interest misrepresented as a general interest. Gramsci's reservations aside, that general interest nevertheless included appeals to a spurious 'national interest' that, in much milder form, continues to be deployed by advocates of war and **moral panics** in contemporary democracies. This is very much the terrain of Hall's conception of **articulation**.

IDEOLOGY IN ALTHUSSER

It is ironic, then, that Althusser, the figure whose work is most routinely cited as a 'Marxist theorist of ideology' in media and communications studies, owes least to the dominant understanding of ideology in Marx. Although an internal critic of the French Communist Party, Althusser's conception of ideology is nonetheless that of the party strategist. His intellectual debt on this topic is more to Lenin than Marx or Gramsci. It is Althusser who pushes hardest the view that all ideologies (or, in his terms, 'ideology in general') are 'unscientific' and some form of specialist intellectual knowledge is required to move 'beyond' ideology. Where 'truth' for Adorno means a redeemable, perhaps utopian, dimension within an ideology or cultural form, Althusser regards something like 'scientific truth' as the polar opposite of ideology. It is this strong association of the concept of ideology with both party and 'truth-as-science' (scientism) that was explicitly rejected by Althusser's student Foucault and replaced in his own work by **discourse**.

Althusser claimed that his model was a development of Gramsci's conception of **hegemony**, but the subtlety of the Gramscian model's emphasis on social production and, thus, the contingency of hegemonic ideologies was largely set aside. Althusser attempted to reconcile Gramsci's conception with structuralist linguistics, which tends to ignore questions of social production (see **sign**). Althusser's starting point was not the contingency of any hegemonic order but, like the givenness of language for Saussure, the objective necessity of the 'reproduction of the relations of production', such as the reproduction of capitalism. Inevitably, then, social institutions were seen as 'apparatuses' that merely functioned as conduits for the reproduction of an ideology and, thus, also the relations of production. This failing in the Althusserian model is usually referred to as 'functionalism'.

Gramsci had suggested that, like intellectuals, the state could be understood in narrow and expansive senses. The expansive conception of intellectuals enabled him to identify the 'organizers of consent' as a broader social group than professional intellectuals, notably including journalists. Similarly, in a more fateful formulation, an expansive conception of the state enabled Gramsci to define the field of non-coercive hegemonic power as the arena of the organization of consent. Crucially, Gramsci always maintained both the narrow *and* expansive senses of these terms.

Althusser collapsed the nuance of Gramsci's narrow/expansive thought experiment into the phrase 'ideological state apparatus' (ISA). Perhaps also framed by the French experience of state intervention in the administration of broadcasting, the media were thus situated as an ISA. Despite the routine declaration that all levels of the Althusserian system are 'relatively autonomous', this model leaves no room for any kind of autonomous practice within the media. Althusser eventually conceded the failings of this model and the conception of 'ideology in general' in his lesser-known _Essays in Self-criticism_ (1976), but the original formulation nonetheless continues to be circulated within media studies (O'Shaughnessy and Stadler, 2005).

It is also worth adding that Gramsci's expansive conception of the state was hardly innocent. Critics such as Jean Cohen and Andrew Arato (1992) and Jeffrey C. Alexander (2006) have rightly pointed out that it strongly suggests that Gramsci's own Leninism rendered any space for civil society – the arena of constitutional and civil rights and, of course, media freedoms – highly vulnerable to state control.

Althusser's 'ISA essay' was published in English with another article embedded in the same text. A central feature was its framing of ideology within the context of a circuit, not the 'circuit of culture' (see **encoding/decoding**) but, in effect, Marx's circuit of capital. Thus, Althusser positioned ideology as a key means of reproducing capitalism and capitalist social relations. The embedded essay provided a more lasting legacy for Althusser's conception of ideology: the important proposition, derived from Lacanian psychoanalysis, that ideologies succeed by 'interpellating individuals as subjects'. This has come to be understood as a formal property of such ideologies and discourses – that, like Barthes' codes (see **sign**), they offer subject positions which 'hail' their addressees with proffered forms of identification in which they might 'live within' the terms set by an ideology. Althusser provides the probably autobiographical example of Catholicism. Hall (1985a: 108–9) provided the striking case of the _multiple_ ways he had been addressed as 'coloured' and 'black' in Jamaica and the UK. Althusser's interpellation proposition was quite crucial to the more elaborated concept of **articulation**, but, at a more basic level, it spoke directly to media practices such as tabloid headlines that routinely interpellate their audiences with the use of vernacular language, such as the infamous 'Gotcha!' headline used by _The Sun_ newspaper in the UK during the Falklands war to refer to the sinking of an Argentinian battleship.

As clumsy and openly provisional as it was, Althusser's work introduced to media studies a question never seriously broached by Marx – but, as we have seen, often wrongly attributed to him – the influence-like 'effects' of an ideology on a general population.

IDEOLOGY IN MEDIA STUDIES

Hall (1982) famously called the rise of the use of the concept of ideology in media studies from the 1970s – in broadly its unmasking sense – 'the return of the repressed'. By this he meant the return of issues of _power_ to a media sociology research agenda regarding **media effects** that had, in his view, forsaken such critical questions, assuming that a lasting societal consensus had emerged. Todd Gitlin's (1978) landmark critique of Lazarsfeldian **audience** research similarly argued that its central concept of **influence** also repressed questions of power. For Hall and early Birmingham cultural studies, then, the concept of ideology was central to analytic models such as the **encoding/decoding** one. Exposing racist ideologies, for example, was central to the Birmingham project. This tradition has been renewed and maintained within critical **discourse** analysis (CDA).

The role of democracy is often at stake in these disputations. The earlier phase of dominantly US media research took the rise and expansion of representative democracy as a given. Its concerns were narrowly focused on processes of public communication in voting studies. It also, however, paid attention to microprocesses of communication that the ideology studies tended to neglect. The unmasking conception of ideology critique, however – and the conception of **discourse** developed by Foucault – tended to be suspicious of such democratic claims. Perhaps it is not surprising that the practice of emancipatory ideology **critique** associated with the **public sphere** thesis has more easily reconnected with the earlier phase of the study of communication in democracies in media and communications.

FURTHER READING

This entry has followed Márkus' scholarship on Marx's conception of ideology, which is at odds with – and, in our view, superior to – the work of Jorge Larrain (1979), whose account of Marx is frequently cited in media and cultural studies and, indeed, much 'post-Marxism'. Márkus and Larrain (Larrain, 1984; Márkus, 1983, 1987) had an important debate in the 1980s over these differences. Most Anglophone overview texts on ideology tend not to cover the unmasking/emancipatory distinction, but John B. Thompson (1990) is a good source, with links to media studies. John Corner (2001) valuably assesses Thompson's and others' attempts in the 1990s to reconstruct the concept. John Downey (2008) provides an important response to Corner that builds on the more recent Frankfurt critical theorist of recognition, Axel Honneth. Nicholas Garnham's (2004, 2005a) critiques of the information society thesis provide good examples of an unmasking ideology critique of a theory.

Identity

Related concepts: embodiment, ideology, image.

The question of identity in communications and media studies is delimited by several conflicting theoretical approaches, in relation to which the status of the individual/subject can be problematized.

Moreover, the place of identity in relation to media varies according to the social and architectural aspects of media. For example, with broadcast communications, questions of language and ideology come to the fore, while, with network communications, the concepts of anonymity, a 'second self' or avatar arise.

For the process model of communication, the nature of identity in communication processes is relatively untheorized. Just as this model separates information content from the means of its carriage, the status of the sender and receiver is largely irrelevant, be they human, animal or machine. The external contexts of the subjects involved in communication processes are not important in assessing communication events. In fact, as long as there is no 'signal noise' in a given transmission, all subjects are considered to be given the same opportunity for observation. The guiding principle of the process model is that meanings attributed to objects, subjects and events can be faithfully reproduced between senders and receivers, as long as the medium or channel is transparent and noise-free.

A CHALLENGE TO THE PROCESS MODEL

In the 1970s, Stuart Hall challenged this model of communication as a form of naïve empiricism in a paper first delivered at the University of Leicester, one of the few university communications departments teaching the process model in the UK (see Cruz and Lewis, 1994). His essay 'Encoding/decoding' became a key text in demarcating the American mass communications traditions from a new linguistics-derived approach to cultural studies (Hall, 1973a, 1980a).

Hall's paper, heavily influenced by Louis Althusser's (1971) work on ideology and identity formation, expanded the moments of 'message-making' that the process model prescribed to include four stages:

- production
- circulation
- use
- reproduction.

The stages of 'circulation' and 'use' intervene to produce multiple variations in the message between encoding and decoding. (For a fuller account of this paper, see the entry on **encoding/decoding**.) This 'intervention' imposes further limitations on the range of possible meanings that can be decoded, but does not dictate them.

Hall regards the fact that a text might be decoded in the same way as it is encoded – the test of successful communication for the process model – as contingent on a number of conditions coinciding. The sites of production and consumption of messages are influenced by specific frameworks of knowledge, relations of production and technical infrastructure that are seldom symmetrical and, in turn, mediated by a more general inventory of ideologies which structures the process of encoding and decoding.

This model assumes that the meaning of a message or signifier cannot be considered independently of the subject position of the sender and receivers. Hall specifies three kinds of subject positions involved in both encoding and decoding:

- dominant hegemonic coding – when the viewer decodes a message in terms of the reference code in which it has been encoded, they are operating inside the dominant code

- negotiated coding involves a number of contradictory subject positions, a mixture of adaptive and oppositional elements
- oppositional coding detotalizes the message and retotalizes it in terms of an alternative frame of reference.

Hall (1980a: 135) observes that 'more often broadcasters are concerned that the audience has failed to take the meaning as they – the broadcasters – ... intended'. What they really mean to say is that viewers are not operating within the 'dominant' or 'preferred' code. Their ideal is 'perfectly transparent communication'. Thus, in his critique of the process model, Hall effectively invokes the anti-essentialist, anti-humanist view of the subject found in the work of Althusser. Individuals are never the authors of ideology and meaning so much as they are inscribed in them. The linearity of the process model is overturned by the idea that an audience is both source *and* receiver of messages, but, as such, they may occupy contradictory subject positions.

THE SUBJECT OF IDEOLOGY

Althusser's theory of **ideology** is unorthodox, in so far as it does not simply look at how ideas are generated and whose interests they serve. Rather, Althusser is concerned with the process of the constitution of individuals necessary for various forms of social practice. For Althusser, individuals are not given subjects with an experience of the real, but, via ideology, they experience themselves as being at the centre of meaning and action. For Althusser (1971), individuals (subjects) are never essential but are constituted (an 'effect' of ideology).

Althusser's view escapes the (essentialist) idea of 'personality', attributing some kind of unique individuality to people that is somehow seen to typify their character. For Althusser, individuals are what they are as a result of the ideologies they produce and by which, in turn, they are produced (the anti-essentialist position). Consequently, individuals continually find themselves in contradictory positions, particularly in relation to complex ideological state apparatuses, where there are so many sources of interpellation. Each individual is divisible into many possible subjects, who are bearers of 'politically correct', racist, sexist or other discriminatory discourses. Althusser's point is that neither disposition (what is called a 'subject position') represents the 'real' person; they are each just discursive positions.

IDENTITY, GENDER, IDEOLOGY

There are few discursive positions that illustrate the work of ideology in mass media more effectively than the category of gender. Historically, in societies where there is a strong sexual division of labour, sex and gender have been seen to be inextricable. Ideology typically supports such a division of labour by encouraging subjects to experience gender as 'natural', appealing to a parallelism – that masculinity is self-identical with men and femininity with women. This rigid correlation of gender (ideologically constructed attributes) with sex (biologically evident at birth) has been challenged in developed nations in the past 40 years by large numbers of women entering the workforce, the rise of casualized labour and success of women's movements demanding social equality across all areas of life.

Socialist feminists in the 1970s took up the concept of ideology to explain women's oppression in relation to class analysis. Socialist feminists point out that, while social class is constituted by, and is constitutive of, capital, the *social* division of gender (to be distinct from sex) has no essential mechanism of constitution (at least one that is open to theoretical analysis) and, yet, historically, it has persisted in the form of a sexual division of labour for as long as the history of class society (Barrett, 1988). For Michelle Barrett, it is the materiality of ideology that is decisive here in the historical reproduction of the sexual division of labour, sexism itself and gender inequality.

Analyses of the construction of gender in mass media have sought to monitor the equity of representations of gender in mass media and television in particular – including the numerical representations of men and women, representations of gender roles, formation of gender-differentiated audiences and the heterosexist framework that determines most assumptions about a likely viewer according to sex stereotypes. Feminism has had a profound influence here on the conceptual and methodological reformulation of research on **audiences** and the **popular** (D'Acci, 2004a; Jansen, 2002; Joyrich, 1996).

FROM IDEOLOGY TO DISCOURSE

A student of Althusser, philosopher and historian Michel Foucault has also been influential in rethinking identity in relation to media and institutions. Continuous with Althusser, Foucault replaces the notion of the individual with that of subjects who are inserted into certain institutions of discursive practice where knowledge is produced within **discourse.** The subject is not the individual; in fact, an individual can be many subjects at once – a bearer or unwitting supporter of many different discursive practices, be they patriarchal, classist, ethnocentric, elitist and so on. Foucault's view also gets away from the idea of 'personality'. For Foucault, people are what they are as a result of the discourses they produce, which, in turn, produce them.

Following from the notion that individuality is itself formed via power relations, Foucault argues that power cannot be possessed (by the control of an apparatus or the possession of knowledge). Rather, power is one of the conditions for the legitimization of knowledge. Knowledge is never a reflection of power relations: 'power and knowledge directly imply one another, there is no power relation without the correlative constitution of a field of knowledge, nor any knowledge that does not presuppose and constitute at the same time power relations' (Foucault, 1979: 27).

ONLINE IDENTITY

While the work of Althusser and Foucault has been central to analysing identity formation in relation to broadcast media, they have little to offer in the analysis of online identity.

There are two main traditions in the study of online identity:

- users and groups who have a relationship outside of their computer-mediated communication (CMC) relationship
- relationships that are formed solely online in the domain of the avatar.

Each form of study has its own methodology, with 'user' research often employing, overtly or otherwise, a 'cues filtered out' approach and avatar research favouring the psychological analysis of being online, questions of anonymity, intensity and 'feeling' among avatars (Riva and Galimberti, 1998; Suler, 1996; Whitty, 2002; Whitty and Gavin, 2001).

AVATAR RESEARCH

Avatar research is an early area of the study of online interaction. It involves inter-actions that have no direct external context. Rather, avatar identities acquire a history that is entirely internal to computer-mediated communication. Identity is entirely generated by what can be typed or posted in images and text. Avatar enthusiasts see this as an entirely neutral space of interaction that gives partici-pants a new-found freedom without the constraints of embodiment, such as sex, class, ethnicity and age. Participants can change their real-life (RL) gender or have no gender and thereby explore the degree to which their gender shapes the way others relate to them.

Psychologists see the study of the avatar as potentially invaluable research. Understanding the interactions of communicants who purportedly have no inhibi-tions, can furnish insights into behaviours that are not restricted by social norms and, thus, provide some kind of direct link to 'human nature' (Riva and Galimberti, 1998; Turkle, 1995; Whitty, 2002; Whitty and Gavin, 2001).

Interest in avatar research has declined, however, and is of little significance to the Net generation, who do not see anything original about being on Second Life or in any kind of avatar environment. Susan Herring (2004: 33) has argued that this generation does not relate well to the 'utopian and dystopian speculations of earlier decades, and find the debates of the 1990s about online democracy, identity and virtuality hyped and vaguely silly'. Rather, avatar research might be of interest to digital migrants, especially the first groups to move online, drawn from middle-class educated elites, but for those who are digital natives and grew up with online media, being online has become just as important a context as life offline.

USER RESEARCH

User research explores how CMC mediates or extends face-to-face and institu-tional forms of relationship. In this approach, CMC is measured against the rich contextual information afforded by face-to-face communication. User research looks at how the cues involved in face-to-face communication become attenu-ated or 'filtered out' in the online environment and, in addition, compensative communication is offered in its place, such as emotions and gestures formed by typing, such as smiling, winking, a sad face and so on (emoticons). Arguably, there is also a higher sense of etiquette, or 'Netiquette', online to counter the fact that the new medium developed without readymade norms of behaviour and interaction.

Nancy Baym (2000: 139–40) argues that, without the rich non-verbal contextual information offered by face-to-face communication, interactants need to 'put back in' contextual cues to render the interaction more meaningful. For Baym (2000: 141), 'All interaction, including CMC, is simultaneously situated in multiple external contexts' (such as language, or city), affordances of the network (such as speed, interface, synchronous/asynchronous) and the social background of the participants. Much effort goes into bringing these external contexts into the content of interaction.

USER RESEARCH OF SOCIAL MEDIA

Online social networking (OSN) has emerged as an extremely popular form of networking and 'identity performance' in recent years. OSN is distinguished by a familiar 'external context' in which participation is by invitation only. Therefore, all OSN identities are brought in from an offline context. Consequently, OSN is a way of continuing offline social networks in an extended electronic way. There is potential for an increase in daily interactions in OSN as well as an 'efficiency' that allows participants to be part of a larger group than they would otherwise be part of offline. This efficiency may translate into raising social expectations to participate (in 2010, Facebook had 500 million users worldwide). Studies show that OSN can also be very time-consuming, managing what is posted up, checking groups and attending to privacy settings.

The extra time the users spend on OSN is related to the fact that it is a Web 2.0 read-write medium. OSN moves on from the page metaphor of Web 1.0 in allowing for 'produserly' user-generated content. Users of OSN can post up materials drawn from other forms of media in order to create an 'identity performance' that is experienced as unique and personalized, but group-orientated. In Web 2.0, information and presentation are increasingly separated, so content can be reused from one platform (YouTube, blogs, flickr, music sites and so on) to another. The production of the personal profile page is a key characteristic, enabling users to become visible to others within the online space, while others, in turn, make themselves visible to users – a space where appearance constitutes existence. As an 18-year-old teenager said to her mum, 'If you're not on MySpace, you don't exist' (boyd, 2007: 119).

Such identity performances need to be considered in relation to the saturation of mass media occuring in the background. Nicholas Abercrombie and Brian Longhurst (1998) claim that mass media audiences typically use the narcissism and spectacle endemic in media texts to guide their own identity performances. Mass media is an important resource from which individuals can model everyday practices and transform life into a 'constant performance' (Abercrombie and Longhurst, 1998: 73).

As an Internet counterpart to karaoke, OSN facilitates online performances that are exhibitionist in nature, where identity is a staged performance to be gazed at or possessed. Like other Web 2.0 platforms, such as YouTube and Twitter (Marwick and boyd, 2010), OSN allows people to reveal themselves using the materials of popular culture. They are not so much social media as they are forms of self-promotion that mimic, satirize or worship the media-saturated environment, which emerges as the most important external context beyond friendship.

FURTHER READING

The centrality of mediated interaction over face-to-face communication in modern life corresponds with symptomatic generalizations about modern individuality, such as 'the schizoid subject' (Jameson, 1991) and the saturated self (Gergen, 1991). Such generalizations ignore the way in which mediated identity formation can vary according to different cultural forms and communication mediums. McLuhanist analysis is useful for understanding the differences between print and electronic forms of identity. Central to understanding the mass-mediated subject, however, are the traditions of **ideology** and **discourse** analysis (Hall et al., 1980; Thompson, 1990). For a useful introduction to the sociological and psychoanalytic conditions of online identity, see Sherry Turkle (1995).

Image

> *Related concepts*: encoding/decoding, identity, mass, popular, sign, simulacra.

The concept of the image became central to European traditions in media studies in the 1960s, as 'the image' assumed an ontological status in theories of mass media. In some of these traditions, 'the image' is not necessarily visual, but refers to the kind of media power that derives from the circulation of signs, be they aural, visual or written (for the analysis of mediated images as visual signs, see **sign**).

Thus, the importance of the image in media studies coincides with the rise of publicity, advertising and 'public relations'. Typically, this involves a 'brand', celebrity or political image that takes on a life of its own, a life that is carefully controlled, through marketing and advertising agencies or 'image consultants', for example, which separates it from the actual referent.

In large part, twentieth-century theories of the image were informed by Marxist theories of commodification. Marx's description of 'commodity fetishism' in *Capital*, Volume 1 (1976: 166), as the expression of 'direct social relations between persons in their work' as 'material relations between persons and social relations between things', foreshadows a theory of the image, via the Lukacsian theory of 'reification'. Georg Lukács' theory found its way into much modern thinking on media signification. In literature and painting, the image loses its sense of 'imitation' and takes on a power that is closely integrated with the exchange of commodities.

DEBORD AND BAUDRILLARD

Two French media thinkers who pursued this approach in the 1960s are Guy Debord and the early Jean Baudrillard. Debord's *Society of the Spectacle* (1977) and Baudrillard's *Consumer Society* (1998) are key texts here.

Among a series of epigrams, Debord's central thesis is that the culture of late capitalism is reduced to a vast domain of spectacle, in which 'social relations among people [become] mediated by images' (epigram 4, Debord, 1977: 32). Spectacle 'concentrates all gazing and all consciousness' (epigram 3, Debord, 1977: 32). Like the commodity in Marx, individuals are both separated and connected by the image. The image is most powerful when it is privately consumed and audience members have no recourse to challenge the fact of the image or its content. In these circumstances, only the image can unify consciousness. 'What binds the spectators together is no more than an irreversible relation at the very center which maintains their isolation. The spectacle re-unites the separate, but re-unites it as *separate*' (aphorism 29, Debord, 1977: 40).

Baudrillard's account of the image echoes many of Debord's formulations, although, as William Merrin (2005: 21) argues, it is less the case that Baudrillard followed Debord, than that both thinkers inherited a radical Durkheimian tradition in which the image was conceived as an alienated and anomic form of gift exchange, which, in tribal society, is known as the potlatch. Baudrillard makes the transition from the symbolic to the semiotic a basis for communication in which the image or **simulacra** becomes dominant.

The semiotic is a domain in which consumer objects get their meaning not from the use value of objects but from a system of signs, what he calls a 'code' in which objects are located. Baudrillard's work in *The System of Objects* (1996) and *Consumer Society* (1998) applies Saussurian linguistics to consumerism and suggests the limitations of economic and Marxist analysis. For the early Baudrillard, however, the theory of the semiotic is necessary to explain the continued reproduction of the capitalist mode of production and how such reproduction is increasingly reliant on the expansion of consumption and the production of 'new' needs:

> The image is seen to be central to this phase of capitalism, or as Marx explains: production not only supplies a material for the need, but it also supplies a need for the material ... The need which consumption feels for the object is created by the perception of it. ... Thus production, produces consumption 1) by creating the material for it; 2) by determining the manner of consumption; and 3) by creating the products, initially posited by it as objects, in the form of a need felt by the consumer. (Marx, 1973a: 92)

113

To Marx's central concepts of use value and exchange value, Baudrillard adds sign value, meaning the way an image expresses social power, status and style. Whereas commodities were once bought for their use value and their ability to satisfy a need, increasingly this value is usurped by sign value, due to the need to obtain an image through the act of consumption itself.

THE 'IMAGE' IN THE USA

In the United States, attempts to theorize the image have been related to the excessive consumerism associated with American culture, as in Daniel Boorstin's *The Image* (1961) and Todd Gitlin's exploration of image saturation in *Media Unlimited* (2002).

In his classic work *The Image*, Boorstin argues that the overconsumption of screen-generated images alienates everyday experience and the appreciation of time. In so far as images do not refer beyond themselves, Boorstin (1961: 231–2) writes:

> With movies and television, today can become yesterday; and we can be everywhere, while we are still here. In fact it is easier to be there (say on the floor of the national political convention) when we are here (at home or in our hotel room before our television screen) than when we are there.

Thus, the image provides a world of substitution, where political and cultural expression is homogenized and pressed into the demands of publicity and image management. Thus, for example, public opinion is no longer seen as the expression of public sentiment, but 'an image into which the public fits its expression'. Where access to social reality must increasingly pass *through* the image, the relationship between action and belief becomes a self-fulfilling prophecy.

Boorstin's thesis, which saw media at the centre of a shallow consumer society, has a modern equivalent in Gitlin's analysis of what he calls 'super-saturation' and the 'speed of the media torrent'. In *Media Unlimited: How the torrent of images and sounds overwhelms our lives* (2002), Gitlin argues that overexposure to images leads to disposable emotions. The act of consuming images is a more acute form of commodity consumption, in that it induces '"limited liability feelings" on demand – feelings that do not bind and sensations that feel like, and pass for, feelings' (Gitlin, 2002: 41).

Gitlin's argument extends George Simmel's account of the blasé attitude in modern society, a condition most prevalent in the metropolis. It is in the nineteenth-century city where the 'clamouring confusion of posters had become a commonplace' and, at night, 'had become a spectacle unto itself, for the streets were now electrified with the lamps and signs and bright displays' that were an early version of what e-business jargon today would be described as 'push technology … These images entered your perceptual field whether you wanted them around or not – powered, in a sense, by your own legs' (Gitlin, 2002: 47).

Today, screens occupy our perceptual field. They populate public spaces, but, more importantly, become central to our daily routines of consumption, whether we have a television on in the background (ambient television) or an appointment with it each evening (programmed television).

The speed of the media torrent of images has precursors in modernity. Train travel, for example, resulted in a mechanization of perception, by which the travellers' gaze lost sight of the foreground, but, at the same time, cultivated a tolerance for rapid changes in sensorial impressions.

As Wolfgang Schivelbusch argues in *The Railway Journey* (1987: 60):

> Increased velocity calls forth a greater number of visual impressions for the sense of sight to deal with. This multiplication of visual impressions is an aspect of the process peculiar to modern times that Georg Simmel has called the development of urban perception.

This argument is exemplified by the essay Schivelbusch refers to here, Simmel's 'The metropolis and mental life' (1971). In the metropolis, the sensitive person will be overpowered and feel disorientated by what Simmel (cited in Gitlin, 2002: 45) describes as 'the crowding together of heterogenous impressions'. In response to the rapidly changing sensorium of the city, 'The metropolitan type of person … develops a (faculty) protecting him against the threatening current and discrepancies of his external environment which would uproot him. He reacts with his head instead of his heart' (Simmel, 1950: 410).

The tolerance of changes in impression lies at the root of the blasé attitude or 'neurasthenia' now regularized in the channel-hopping, Web-surfing 'click' interface with modern media. Instead of the body travelling past a torrent of images, the viewer of late modernity, in a sense, 'travels' via the screen.

FURTHER READING

In the Marxist tradition, the concept of the image has precursors in theories of alientation and Georg Lukács' (1971) concept of 'reification'. The influence of Debord and the situationist movement of the 1960s on a politics centred on the image is traced in a number of later histories and appraisals, including Anselm Jappe's *Debord* (1993) and Sadie Plant (1992). Naomi Klein's influential critique of corporate marketing, *No Logo* (2000), charts the rise of the 'brand' in media-consumer culture.

Influence

115

> *Related concepts*: capitalism, criticism/critique, discourse, media effects, news values, public sphere, regulation, tabloidization.

'Influence' might be considered the key concept linking **audience** and **media effects** with **news values** and the related ideals of informed citizenship and the **public sphere**. 'Influence' might at first be thought of as a variant of 'effects'. As this entry details, however, its origins and use are actually wider than, crudely, the 'content' of the 'impact' on media effects research.

INFLUENCE AND AUDIENCE RESEARCH

As John Corner warns in his invaluable typologization of the research traditions related to this concept, any overview of 'influence' risks becoming an account of decades of arguably inconsequential research results from the many empirical programmes that have sought to investigate it. It is, Corner argues, perhaps the most 'method-driven' area of media research. Corner (2000) is one of the few within media studies who have sought to place influence research within a broader social theoretical context.

Those empirical evidence-based traditions of media and communications research that are of most relevance to this concept are covered under **media effects**. While **media effects** definitely includes studies of the effects of media representations of violence and the role of the media in the socialization of children, influence studies tend to concentrate on news and information and, by implication at least, adult citizens in democracies. Violence, like the earlier studies of propaganda, was conceived as having 'effects', but 'normal' news and information understood as political communication was considered to achieve 'influence' more benignly, perhaps even as a modest variation of informed citizenship. Even this is not a hard and fast rule, however. Corner (2000: 394) is surely correct in saying that the earliest research assumptions about influence assumed a 'hard' causality (probably derived initially from assumptions about propaganda). Moreover, one authoritative survey from within political communication (Blumler and Gurevitch, 1982), for example, chose to mix influence and effects by addressing 'the political effects of mass communication'.

The field of influence research grew fairly directly out of 1940s 'voting studies' within the Lazarsfeld project examining the relationship between media and opinion formation. Moreover, as both Corner (2000) and Sonia Livingstone (1996) emphasize in their respective overviews of the influence and effects fields, the research of the 1940s was informed chiefly by two disciplines: sociology and social psychology. Paul F. Lazarsfeld's research programmes combined both and, on the question of influence, shifted strongly towards social psychology in his major final study in the series with Elihu Katz, *Personal Influence: The part played by people in the flow of mass communication* (Katz and Lazarsfeld, 1955). The implication of this research was a decentering of the role of the media. The initially revised model was a 'two-step flow' involving 'opinion leaders' – that is, individuals who remained informed and influenced others. This model, and related small-group research methods developed by Lazarsfeld's team, both remain mainstays in contemporary 'administrative' polling research conducted for political parties. *Personal Influence* attributed increasing significance to small group communication, placing its social role on a par with that of 'mass communication' and the individual citizen's engagement with democratic processes.

To this extent, as Livingstone has powerfully argued in a series of interventions (1998a, 1998c, 2006), these empirical research programmes anticipated the shift towards 'active audiences' usually attributed to the legacy of the **encoding/decoding** model, which has become the dominant narrative of the development of **audience** studies. Livingstone notes that, in his contribution to *Personal Influence*, Elihu Katz, in particular, laid the groundwork for his path-breaking later work on media events as **media ritual**. One might add that *Personal Influence* also anticipates the dramatic reordering of the significance of small group communication that has developed around recent studies of **mobility** and, especially, the mobile phone.

The reception of *Personal Influence* remains an important watershed in the development of the concept of influence. In a much-cited essay, 'Media Sociology: The dominant paradigm', Todd Gitlin (1978) rejects the Lazarsfeld/Katz research, especially *Personal Influence*, as it seems to set aside all prospects of a conception of influence that was compatible with an unmasking conception of **ideology**. He advocated, instead, the growing Birmingham CCCS-based research then focused on the concepts of **hegemony** and **encoding/decoding**.

In contrast, David Morley's overview of audience research paradigms in *The Nationwide Audience* more respectfully acknowledges Katz's key insights (1980: 4–5), but sets his work aside as allied to the 'uses and gratifications' paradigm, against which early Birmingham CCCS media research was defined. Ironically, Morley finds the chief failing of the uses and gratifications tradition to be an overly 'open' conception of the interpretive powers of audiences, the very position that later became dominant within active **audience** models (Morley, 1980: 12).

There are a number of interrelated concerns at stake in these academic debates, namely:

- the relationship between media institutions and power
- related normative perspectives in media research
- the relationship between 'influence' and 'culture'.

These are addressed below.

INFLUENCE, POWER AND CULTURE

In many ways, both Katz's empirical identification of the significance of the 'primary group' in the flow of influence and the more recent assertion of something very similar within **mobility** studies are compatible with long-held positions about socialization and influence within social theory.

Cooley distinguished *primary* groups – such as the family and close friends – from weaker *secondary* 'indirect' ones, in part by their different communicative capacities. In turn, Katz's empirical evidence refutes more pessimistic social theories which assert that the destruction of such forms of social association follow inevitably from urbanization and '**mass** society'. Following Joshua Meyrowitz, John B. Thompson (1995) and Craig Calhoun (1992) have explicitly expanded such a conception of 'indirectness' to communications media (see **interactivity**) as a feature of **modernity**.

In these terms, the continuing point of debate about influence remains to this day more concerned with the durability of the weaker secondary associations, including democratic institutions, than the primary ones. Williams' **mobile privatization**, for example, postulates a weakening of ties of cooperative 'horizontal' social solidarity – such as trade unions and other 'voluntary associations' – in the wake of the complicity of broadcast media's social configuration in the consumer culture and Fordist reorganization of workplaces and domestic life (suburbanization). In Cooley's terms, such voluntary secondary groupings become progressively more indirect and have less and less of the face-to-face character of primary groups. Of course, Williams was thinking in terms of broadcasting rather than (mobile) telephony's capacity to build solidarity 'indirectly' within primary groups. The mobile phone can also be used to reassert vertical hierarchies of employer/employee, however, especially in today's 'flexible labour markets', such as the common expectation that casual employees leave their mobiles turned on and are permanently 'on call'.

In such contemporary instances, the early concerns of influence researchers still remain very plausible, even if the concept of 'influence' is used less readily. One enduring use of the term that reveals this lies within media **regulation**. References to 'influential media' need not indicate media consumption practices of audiences – or their 'effects' – but can be a code for the influential practices of press/media barons and 'moguls' *within* the most powerful sectors of a society. Regulatory practices, such as cross-media ownership regulation, were designed to limit the capacity of such moguls to exercise influence over the political process itself – by, for example, brokering secretive deals with incoming governments – rather than merely altering audiences'/citizens' likely voting preferences. Sociologists and comparative political communication analysts refer to such networks of influence within central systems of societal power as 'clientelist'; Berlusconi's Italy is a common contemporary example (Hallin and Mancini, 2004).

There has been increasing recognition from a number of sources, however, that the see-sawing conflict between models of influence based on institutions and ideologies and those based on interpersonal communication within primary groups (and/or active audiences) is at cross-purposes. Overcoming this dilemma is very much a conceptual/theoretical task as the vast numbers of empirical studies have not really resolved the issue. The easy answer, as is often the case with much contemporary analysis, is to increase the recognition of the role of 'culture'. Plainly, Katz's legacy in the study of media **ritual** suggests advantages in 'anthropologizing' our understandings of the 'influence' of contemporary media events. In a sense, this strategy extends the model of the primary group to encompass the entire society. Yet this option would appear to leave unresolved the place of democratic and other institutions chiefly associated with **modernity** – that is, societies in which the primary group is no longer unchallenged as a dominant social institution.

The US social theorist and cultural sociologist Jeffrey Alexander has pursued this matter more consistently perhaps than any other theorist. Drawing on Talcott Parson's conception of influence, Alexander's (1981: 43) work embarks from the premise that the primary group v. media institutional influence debate is unproductive. He argues that these elements need to be located within the sociological distinction between embedded and *differentiated* social practices.

Much social theory holds that modern societies have tended to increasingly 'disembed' activities previously embedded in traditional social orders and, thus, elaborate them as autonomous, or at least distinct, institutions (see **modern**). This process is known as *differentiation*. Markets are the most famous example of this process, while others include aesthetic **culture** (art) and media systems. Differentiation does not destroy traditional forms of social association, however; rather, it coexists with the old. Thus, while an autonomous media system is often differentiated in tandem with democratization – a '**free press**', for example – traditional forms of social association and belief survive, and even flourish, often as 'norms' (what is usually referred to in media studies as 'culture' or the 'moral' in **moral panics**).

Thus, Alexander shares doubts raised by many in media studies about the overly 'rational' and 'cognitive' expectations of many **modern** norms applied to the media, such as the cognitively driven rational citizen. He does not wish to abandon or radically revise the emancipatory norms of modernity but, rather, contextualize them within the framework of older social and cultural norms. The formation of public opinion – and, thus, of influence – is necessarily entangled in **cultural forms**, both 'aesthetic' and 'anthropological'. Most recently, Alexander elaborated this insight in *The Civil Sphere* (2006), which can be read as a 'cultural' alternative to Habermasian models of the **public sphere**.

One consequence of this social theoretical rethinking of influence is the possibility of a more elaborate typology of modes of influence. Livingstone partly followed Alexander's theoretical lead by recasting the institution v. primary group distinction in the more familiar sociological shorthand of 'macro v. micro'. She proposed that the very notion of audience might address *both* macro and micro dimensions. Thus, she recast the classic problems in audience/influence theory detailed above within the terms of the following illuminating but quite challenging paradox. Some familiarity with the other concepts listed in the box above may be necessary to appreciate the full significance of Livingstone's (1998a: 206) insight here:

> In integrating these levels, it may emerge that the active appropriation of meanings by individuals or households (that is, drawing a new consumption object into existing, divergent, meaningful practices) operates, at the economic level, as a kind of conservatism. In other words, unless the micro is discriminated from the macro, the following paradox arises: resistance at the micro-level may mean no change (that is, resistance to new meanings) while conformity may mean change (that is, adaptation of everyday practices to prevailing or incoming norms); but, at macro level, resistance implies change while no change implies conservativism. If analytic coherence across level[s] is not sought, one is left with a kind of either/or analysis, in which the audience is conceptualized either at the macro level, as a market or public, or at a micro level, in terms of family interactions, peer relations, even parasocial interaction with the screen.

Although now over ten years old, this remains a profoundly suggestive observation that speaks to many conflicts among different traditions, all claiming a 'stake' in influence research – active audience theory, medium theory, political economy, cultural studies and so on.

To oversimplify Livingstone's thesis, what may seem to have conservatively 'influenced' audience/user practice from a macro context – for example, a rise in the popularity of melodrama – may seem the opposite from a micro context and vice versa.

The direct impetus of Livingstone's argument has become most evident in Alexander's major work (2006) and some of Livingstone's later work (Couldry et al., 2007) on political communication. It has coincided with an increase in work in Europe on media and *citizenship*, another concept employed to bridge the culture/public distinction. Livingstone's insight is equally compatible with the Marxian legacy of work on **hegemony** and **populism**.

FURTHER READING

Livingstone's (1996) and Corner's (2000) overview papers are the best starting points for further reading about this tradition, but see also McDonald (2004) and the more recent history by David Park and Jeff Pooley (2008). Livingstone (2006) (and the other essays in the same volume) provide an excellent insight into the revaluation of the links between *Personal Influence* and more recent audience research (Simonson, 2006). See also the Further reading section for **media effects**.

Information society

> **Related concepts**: *capitalism, modern, network (society), postmodernism, public sphere, technological determinism.*

Variants of the information society thesis have been in development since the 1950s and have come to figure in theories of governmentality, **postmodernism** and the **culture industry**. Initially taking the form of Daniel Bell's 'post-industrial' society thesis, the rise in information technology and digitally convergent technologies encouraged a shift in the central term of reference from 'post-industrial' to 'information'. In Bell's initial formulation, 'knowledge workers' were the new characteristic feature of the post-industrial era.

The success of these terms is analogous to McLuhan's 'media', in that their circulation extends well beyond the academy and has entered business, administrative and political policymaking parlance. 'Information economy', for example, is a phrase used within the (re)naming of many government ministries also responsible for communiciations and culture. The meaning of the central term shifts according to the immediate need of the author. Webster (2007: 274, note 1) explains Bell's later adoption of 'information':

> Bell (1979) distinguishes the terms conceptually as follows: information means 'data processing in the broadest sense'; knowledge means 'an organised set of statements of fact or ideas, presenting a reasoned judgement or an experimental result, which is transmitted to others through some communication medium in some systematic form' (Bell, 1979: 168). In practice he often uses the two terms interchangeably when discussing post-industrial society, though often … his theorising depends on a particular meaning of the term 'knowledge'.

INFORMATION V. KNOWLEDGE

The key conceptual shift for the more sophisticated theorists of the information society tends to be *from* knowledge *to* information. Information, very often understood as mere 'data' rather than knowledge, is seen to be important for the regulation of large-scale social systems, bureaucracies and corporations. Information is impersonal, easily detached from its moment of production; it is transmittable and portable. It can be stored and retrieved. Knowledge, when viewed unsympathetically from such a perspective, can be seen as very personal (a result of experience and wisdom) or, where it is abstract, confined to and controlled by an elite group of 'experts'.

In contrast, knowledge (or, indeed, information) understood as informed public deliberation is the core of Enlightenment models of informed citizenship and the **public sphere** within **modernity**. So, the rising tide of fascination with instrumental 'information' for its own sake appears from this perspective to be uncritical, even ideological. Critical self-reflective knowledge remains a core value among many competing comparable theories, even the 'posts'.

Webster notes, however, that the information/knowledge distinction, while perhaps the most convincing, is one of many different features information theorists have identified as 'epochal' or similarly significant in effecting an information society. As Webster (2007: 8) also notes, many move from the assumption that the existence of an information society today is simply self-evident: 'It seems so obvious to them that we live in an information society that they blithely presume it is not necessary to clarify precisely what they mean by the concept'. Perhaps it is unsurprising, then, that easily the most pervasive rationale for an information society tends to be the equally blithe and pervasive usage of technologically determinist arguments.

DANIEL BELL: UNCOUPLING FORCES AND RELATIONS OF PRODUCTION

As noted in the entry on **technological determinism** (TD), TD assumptions can also be projected into *de facto* social theories as a kind of second-order TD (TD2). When Raymond Williams (1974a: 13) characterizes TD, he notes its capacity to generate views such as 'technology ... has made the modern condition'. At least at the level of popular journalism, we might find one template for information society thinking – that is, the projection of a linear 'timeline' conception of history and futures that simply marks off technological innovations and speculates about new ones and their wide-ranging social 'effects'.

In contrast, classical social theory – a major source of our conceptions of 'modernity' and 'society' – always acknowledged technical innovation, but usually located this major force *within* an account of other social and cultural developments. For Max Weber, technical innovation was indicative of an increasingly instrumentalizing ethic that reduced all human reason to means–ends practical thinking or calculative rationality. In Weber's view, the prospects were grim that such a process of rationalization could be altered and he pessimistically anticipated all other ethics being subsumed by its 'iron cage'. Karl Marx deliberately coupled (largely technological) forces of production with social relations of production and placed them in a dialectical tension understood as a mode of production (see **capitalism**).

Daniel Bell's *The Coming of Post-industrial Society* (1973) is almost always touted as the primary text on the information society. In it and *The Cultural Contradictions of Capitalism* (1996), Bell aimed to develop a synthetic and analytic means of accounting for the major transformations of the twentieth and twenty-first centuries in the mode of the classical social theorists. Crucially, however, he had already rejected all emancipatory/utopian normative thinking (Bell, 1962) and adopted a more or less positivist confidence in 'social forecasting' (see **modern**). His title, *The Coming of Post-industrial Society*, indicates part of the popular appeal of his logic. It plays on the familiar notion of an (eighteenth- or nineteenth-century) industrial society/revolution in Europe and, implicitly, the related TD belief that 'machines made the industrial revolution' in the transformation from an agricultural economy to an industrial one. The most cited feature of the book is Table 11, in which Bell simply projects this logic 'forwards' to an imminent post-industrial future/present.

Bell later (1999) rejected (the numerous) charges of TD. On media specifically, he had already practised the kind of linear technological determinism McLuhan had avoided (1989). The core insight Bell elaborated and defended in his 1999 defence of *The Coming* against the TD charge is the most revealing and most relevant to media and communications. Under 'methodology', Bell correctly notes that, since the nineteenth century, technological innovation has become increasingly organized and systematic. 'Tinkering' and individual experimentation (as in even the popular culture image of rogue scientists working in their own basements or garages) has been replaced by highly complex corporate research and development laboratories. As the entries on 'transforming resource', 'strategic resource' and 'mode of work' all suggest (see Table 11), however, Bell's blindspot was the social organization of this corporatization of technical innovation.

It is easy to acknowledge Bell's more recent qualification (1999: xiv–xv), that the scale of technical innovation now includes whole *systemic* changes which have profound consequences for social organization. Paschal Preston (2001) has elaborated a similar (TD-free) argument within the social shaping perspective (see **technological determinism**).

Table 11 Bell's 'march through the sectors' (reproduced from Bell, 1999: lxxxv)

	Pre-Industrial	Industrial	Post-Industrial
Mode of Production	Extractive	Fabrication	Processing, information
Economic sector	*Primary* Agriculture Mining Fishing Timber Oil and gas	*Secondary* Good producing Manufacturing Durables Non-durables Heavy construction	*Series* *Tertiary* Transportation Utilities *Quarternary* Trade Finance Insurance Real estate *Quimary* Health, education Research, government Recreation, entertainment
Transforming resource	Natural power, wind, water, draft, animal, human muscle	Created energy, oil, gas, nuclear power	Information and knowledge: programming and algorithms, computer and data transmission
Strategic resource	Raw materials	Finance capital	Human capital
Technology	Craft	Machine technology	Intellectual technology
Skilled base	Artisan, manual worker, farmer	Engineer, semi-skilled worker	Scientist; technical and professional occupations
Mode of work	Physical labour	Division of labour	Networking
Methodology	Common sense, trial and error, experience	Empiricism experimentation	Models, simulations, decision theory, systems analysis
Time perspective	Orientation to the past	Ad-hoc adaptiveness, experimentation	Future orientation: forecasting and planning
Design	Game against nature	Game against fabricated nature	Game between persons
Axial principle	Traditionalism	Productivity	Codification of theoretical knowledge

Information society

123

However, Bell (1999: xviii) also reiterated that he had simply 'decoupled' Marx's forces and relations of production and treated them as 'independent variables' (see **capitalism**). There could not be a much surer conceptual formula for the above table and its related TD formulations than, for example, replacing Marx's complex model of 'mode of production' with mere technical industrial processes. By, in effect, eliminating capital and capitalism, Bell's information society becomes a fantasy world in which, for example, universities – as concentrations of knowledge/information – would become the pre-eminently powerful institutions in society. 'Information' thus replaces not only 'heavy industry' but also (finance) capital.

Somewhat hidden here is Bell's enthusiasm for technocracy or leadership by technical experts. Similarly, Bell imagined that the dominant form of labour would become 'servicework', characterized not by 'Macjobs' but knowledge and information. In a sense, Bell practises – but does not make transparent – the same kind of blind optimism that once fuelled predictions the Internet would make capitalism irrelevant.

Indeed, it is for precisely such reasons that Nicholas Garnham, among others, has posed the very legitimate question of whether the information society is a theory at all or perhaps an ideology (in the sense of legitimizing existent power relations). As Garnham notes, for example, the specific ideological form the information society thesis took in the late 1990s operated to legitimate corporate **convergence** of 'old' and 'new' media companies. It also legitimated the establishment of a new sector in financial markets that grouped technology, media and communications stocks on the fallacious assumption that they operated according to the same economic dynamics. Thus, the seeds of failure for the 'dotcom boom' were laid (Garnham, 2005a).

So one ideological function of the information society thesis is to group the components of corporate convergence into a plausible but shifting signifier that retains an aura of 'inevitability'. Thus, neoliberal demands for **deregulation** are still articulated in this form. Moreover, as Garnham notes ironically, one of the curious effects of Bell's 'decoupling' of Marx's conception of contradictory socioeconomic relations and productive forces is that the information society thesis also tends to reduce society to economy more vulgarly than any vulgar Marxist!

The slipperiness of information society/economy – and its mutations into e-society and so on – is its apparently endless capacity for reinvention as 'the next big thing'. For all its considerable sophisticated elaboration, Manuel Castells' **network society** thesis is certainly vulnerable to this charge. Most recently, as Garnham points out, information society theorization has converged with the creative industries end of **culture industry** thinking.

As with the critique of technological determinism, it is important to reiterate that TD2 theories are not pure fictions. They do contain partial truths – for example, dirty nineteenth-century manufacturing industries did become less visible in Europe and the USA, partly because some changed but often because they had moved offshore. Thus, many people did move from dirty industrial jobs to 'clean' servicework. 'Servicework', however, entails both 'white-collar factories', such as call centres, *and* self-employed software designers. To cite both as evidence of a growing 'information' (or creative) workforce would be misleading.

So, TD2 theories do draw our attention to real technical and related changes and speculate about their consequences. Unfortunately, their speculations are rarely admitted to be such. They should perhaps be considered in the same vein as 'early adopters' of new media: a little overenthusiastic and not necessarily the most reliable guides in the larger context. We have adapted the following from Garnham's (2005a: 301) very useful critical checklist:

- Which version of the information society thesis is being mobilized (Webster, 2007)?
- Ask what theory of social change is being advanced and what are its main drivers.
- Then ask what empirical evidence, if any, is being used to support such claims.
- Assess whether that evidence is either appropriate or adequate.
- How does it define any policy problems?
- Whose interests may be served by the form of its proposed solutions?

FURTHER READING

Webster (2007, and previous editions) remains the definitive overview – likewise the Webster-edited reader of primary sources (2004). Both include sections on Castells. While Castells' *The Rise of the Network Society* (2000a) is the obvious successor to Bell, the most elaborate and sustained Marxian/political economy of communication alternative to Bell (and perhaps Castells) would be the work of Dan Schiller (1996, 1999, 2007). For sociological critiques of the information society thesis, see Craig Calhoun (1992) and Krishnan Kumar (1995). On the nexus with the culture industries, see Jean-Guy Lacroix and Gaetan Tremblay (1997) and David Hesmondhalgh (2007). On the role of the information society thesis in higher education and beyond, see Fuller (2002: 125ff.).

Interactivity

Related concepts: communication(s), cyberculture, embodiment, media/medium, network (society).

Interactivity has almost turned into a dull buzzword. The term is so inflated now that one begins to suspect that there is much less to it than some people want to make it appear. No company would fail to claim that it is keen on feedback. No leader would fail to praise the arrival of a new communication era. Apparently interactivity has hardly any threatening meaning for the elites. (Schultz, 2000: 205)

Typically defined simply as 'two-way' communication, 'interactivity' has recently appeared as both a buzzword and a fraught concept within communication theory. For early information theorists (such as Shannon and Weaver, 1949), interactivity denoted two-way communication between humans, animals or machines, but, today, it has become exclusively hardwired to the telecommunications and computing sectors. In information theory, the content of communication is separated from the means of **communication**, and the aim of communication is to control the reproduction of a 'message' in any **medium** or means of communication. Today, then, the term 'interactivity' is reserved only for those communication events that are electronically extended in space and time.

The term 'interactivity' has been rapidly conscripted into the discourses of a 'new media age' (see **cyberculture, network (society)**). Interactivity is central to a cluster of terms that preoccupy the study of cyberculture. Around it are assembled so many of the binary terms of new media theorizing: active/passive, one-way/two-way, linear/nonlinear, synchronous/asynchonous, mediated/face-to-face and so on.

The strongest proponents of the importance of interactivity are the 'second media age' theorists (George Gilder (1994), Mark Poster (1995), Howard Rheingold (1994)). They bestow it with emancipatory meanings in contrast to the one-way architecture of the first media age of 'broadcast' media (see **broadcasting**). Traditional media of newspapers, radio, television and cinema are viewed as repressive, controlling, subordinating and attacking individuality itself. By contrast, new media are seen to place the control of meaning making back into the hands of the individual viewer, to the extent that they enable interactivity. Indeed, for Poster, interactivity is elevated to the status of a 'mechanism' of modern media:

> Subject constitution in the second media age occurs through the mechanism of interactivity. ... interactivity has become, by dint of the advertising campaigns of telecommunication corporations, desirable as an end in itself, so that its usage can float and be applied in countless contexts having little to do with telecommunications. Yet the phenomenon of communicating at a distance through one's computer, of sending and receiving digitally encoded messages, of being 'interactive', has been the most popular application of the Internet. Far more than making purchases or obtaining information electronically, communicating by computer claims the intense interest of countless thousands. (Poster, 1995: 33)

Manuel Castells, in his influential *The Internet Galaxy* (2001: 374), takes the concept further, with the term 'interactive society', which he defines as the 'digitized, networked integration of multiple communication modes' (see **network**). He claims that communication outside of such networked spheres (face-to face communication, say) increasingly becomes marginalized (see **public sphere**): 'From society's perspective, *electronically-based communication (typographic, audiovisual, or computer-mediated) is communication*' (Castells, 2001: 374).

What is clear in these accounts of 'interactivity' is that it is only computer-mediated or tele-mediated *interaction* that is significant. Embodied forms of 'interaction' (see **embodiment**) do not figure at all in the contemporary conception of 'interactivity'. For this reason, Roger Silverstone, like Tanjev Schultz, situates the concept as an **ideology** of contemporary disembodied consumerism:

> The new ideology of interactivity … [is] one which stresses our capacity to extend our reach and range and to control, through our own choices, what to consume, both when and how … . It is hailed to undo a century of one-to-many broadcasting and the progressive infantilization of an increasingly passive audience. It is an expression of a new millenialism. These are the utopian thoughts of the new age in which power is believed to have been given, at last, to the people: to the people, that is, who have access to, and can control, the mouse and the keyboard. (Silverstone, 1999: 95)

An antidote to the inflated uses of interactivity in recent communication theory can be found in John Thompson's typology of 'interaction', which reclaims face-to-face communication as a substantive component of communicative interaction and as important as extended forms of interaction.

Thompson distinguishes between three types of interaction:

- face-to-face interaction
- mediated interaction
- mediated quasi-interaction

which are analytically distinguishable by their spatio-temporal potential (see Table 12). Face-to-face interaction occurs in a context of mutual presence; it is interpersonal and dialogical. Mediated interaction (writing, telephoning) is also dialogical, but its spatio-temporal context is extended rather than mutual. Lastly, mediated quasi-interaction (books, radio, newspapers) is also extended in space and time, but is monological or 'one-way'. Thompson points out, however, that senders and receivers within this kind of interaction nevertheless form bonds that transcend the fact of their interactions.

What courses through all of these form types is the progressive filtering out of communication cues. Where face-to-face interaction provides a high degree of contextual information (such as body language and gestures), the mediated forms substitute such information with narrower contexts (letterhead, signature, time announcement on the radio, station promotion and so on).

The value of Thompson's typology is in its insistence that all three modes of interaction may co-exist within a particular communication event. Drawing on Erving Goffman and Joshua Meyrowitz, he shows how a television talk show may involve layers of face-to-face communication (in the studio and between viewers watching the programme at home), as well as the mediated quasi-interaction of the programme's 'fans', linked by feedback systems where viewers' comments might be aired on the show.

Thompson is also interested in the fact that even traditional broadcast media carry forms of interaction and reciprocity overlooked by new media theorists. There are letters to the editor, talkback and talk shows, but there is also the fact that readers, listeners and viewers 'quasi-interact' in the act of simultaneous reception of the event.

127

Table 12 Thompson's types of interaction (adapted from Thompson, 1995: 85, Table 3, as developed in Jones, 2000a)

Interactional characteristics	Face-to-face interaction	Mediated interaction	Mediated quasi-interaction
Space–time compression	Context of embodied co-presence; shared spatio-temporal reference system	Separation of contexts; extended availability in time and space	Separation of contexts; extended availability in time and space
Range of symbolic cues	Multiplicity of symbolic cues	Narrowing of range of symbolic cues	Narrowing of range of symbolic cues
Action orientation	Oriented towards specific others	Oriented towards specific others	Oriented towards an infinite range of potential recipients
Dialogical/ monological	Dialogical	Dialogical	Monological
Example	Face-to-face conversation	Letters, telephone	Books, newspapers, (broadcast) radio and TV

Thompson's insights about 'interaction' provide some restraint to the fortunes of 'interactivity' in literature on the Internet. Just as Thompson points out that broadcast media are capable of interaction, we are also compelled to accept that the Internet is not just about interactivity – its various submedia are also capable of broadcast communication, such as bulk e-mails and bulletin board postings. In turn, it needs to be asked why technologically extended 'interactivity' is so closely associated with the Internet and not with, say, the entire history of telephony. In fact, the Internet is not an easy host to such a blanket characterization, as it provides a platform for an array of communication functions: information retrieval, advertising, browsing, commerce and many forms of anonymous communication. The only submedia of the Internet that provides a communication form which cannot be found in other media is Usenet or WWW-hosted discussion groups as they are capable of scales of participation not possible in embodied fora. Even with these, interactivity cannot be so easily heralded as a kind of special property.

Sheizaf Rafaeli is a key theorist who can assist in understanding interaction within computer-mediated communication (CMC). Rafaeli (1988) distinguishes between connectivity, reactivity and interactivity. Connectivity refers to the technical way **network** architecture makes interactivity possible, but also important is the way communication histories within CMC determine the nature of the interactivity that happens within it. Two-way communication does not, in itself, guarantee interactivity. If an exchange does not develop into a relationship where one utterance becomes a context for another, the discourse may become closed and self-referential. Conversely, reactive communication is not just typical of broadcast communication, but is possible within **networks**.

Rafaeli and Fay Sudweeks (1997) have argued that online interactivity should be thought of as existing across an entire network, not simply between two given interlocutors. Two-way communication must be part of a chain of interrelated messages for genuine interactivity to occur. Every message 'must take into account not just messages that preceded them, but also the manner in which previous messages were reactive' (Rafaeli and Sudweeks, 1997). If this view of interactivity is adopted, it suggests that much of the way in which the Internet is used is seldom interactive, especially if the question of anonymity in CMC discussion groups is addressed (see **identity**).

The views of Thompson – that traditional media can enable interactivity – and Rafaeli – that new media do not, in themselves, guarantee interactivity – arrest much of the popular usage of this concept. The limitations of the concept of interactivity become apparent the more it is empiricized or made exclusively reducible to one or other technical medium. This, in turn, underpins the historicism of second media age thinkers, for whom interactivity becomes synonymous with the 'interactive society'.

Another alternative account distinguishes between interaction and *integration*. In this distinction, interaction is still important, but needs also to be viewed in terms of the fact that all concrete interactions occur in the context of four dominant frames of communicative integration (see Table 13). Following C.H. Cooley, Craig Calhoun explores forms of *indirect social relationships* enabled by complex communication systems and through which individuals are nevertheless able to form integrating bonds of intimacy and many-sided recognition.

Where such recognition occurs in large volumes, interaction is no longer a condition of social connection, as individuals become integrated indirectly by the agency of technologically extended media forms. Thus, the integration thesis rejects the idea that the study of communication is reducible to the documentation of empirically observable kinds of *interaction*, be they interpersonal or extended (Calhoun, 1986, 1992).

Table 13 Calhoun's four types of social relationship (developed from Calhoun, 1992, in Jones, 2003)

Type of relationship	Primary (from Cooley)	Secondary (from Cooley)	Tertiary	Quaternary
Characteristics	Affective ties	Impersonal groups	No embodied co-presence; 'mediated' but parties aware of relationship	One party unaware of relationship
Direct/indirect	Direct	Direct	Indirect	Indirect
Example	Family/ friendship groups	Committees	The corporation; correspondence; information technology	Surveillance via information technology

FURTHER READING

John Thompson's extensive discussion of 'The rise of mediated interaction', the third chapter of *The Media and Modernity* (1995), provides a sobering discussion of the theoretical and historical background of 'interaction'. Without mentioning the Internet or cyberculture, Thompson's discussion is invaluable for its unravelling of the spatial and temporal conditions of interactivity in human communication. A text that draws on Thompson, Anthony Giddens and Bourdieu to explain the communicative forms of the Internet is Roy Slevin's *The Internet and Society* (2003).

Mass

> *Related concepts*: audience, broadcasting, culture, culture industry, modern, popular/populist, public sphere, tabloidization.

Two primary conditions often cited for the emergence of mass society – or, more commonly, 'the masses' – are the rapid urbanization processes driven by industrialization, together with the emergence of mass communications systems used to integrate large-scale massing of populations.

Epitomized by Charlie Chaplin's 1936 film *Modern Times*, a key moment in which the forces of industrial modernity and mass media converged was that following the Great Crash of 1929. The mass armies of the unemployed, concentrated in the crowded conditions of the metropolis, were introduced to the mass mediums of radio and cinema which, together with cheaper newsprint, magazines and books, offered, in different ways, a means of social integration.

Although they had nineteenth-century precursors, it was also from this time that a range of theories dealing with mass society, mass culture and mass media emerged. These included the mass/elite framework, the culture industry approach and, later, theories of 'mass society'.

MASS/ELITE

The mass/elite framework and **culture industry** analysis were both responses to the emergence of the **popular**, which was seen to threaten both the traditions of high art and the long-standing values of traditional communities that had been broken up and made vulnerable to the manipulations of mass culture. Stable communities and traditions were conceived as being replaced by isolated vulnerable individuals. As with the uses of **populist**, this critical perspective could be from 'right' or 'left'.

The intellectual anxiety could thus be about 'too much' democratization or the risk of proto-fascist **populism**.

For Raymond Williams (1990: 297), the risk in *both* these tendencies was that 'masses was a new word for mob'. Accordingly, he felt that they further risked continuing a nineteenth-century practice of attributing the characteristics of 'gullibility, fickleness, herd-prejudice, lowness of taste and habit' to all popular gatherings and popular taste (1990: 298). There were, Williams (1990: 300) polemicized, in fact *no* masses, 'only ways of seeing people as masses'. This discussion comes in the conclusion to Williams' *Culture and Society*, a work that traced the tensions in nineteenth- and twentieth-century British political and cultural debate about the consequences of the struggles to expand the right to vote in what was the first of the industrial capitalist societies.

European mass/elite frameworks can be traced to aspects of the work of Friedrich Nietzsche, José Ortega y Gasset and Mathew Arnold. To varying degrees, and often with much qualification, these frameworks articulated the anxiety that the rise of liberalism, democracy, the popular press and popular education and literacy were forces by which the rule of the elite might give way to the reign of the mob.

Variants of twentieth-century 'mass culture' arguments often share elements of this mass/elite framework, usually in a contradictory manner. Without an educated elite being able to define 'the good', 'culture' and civilization itself, social and cultural anarchy might ensue. As Bennett (1982) notes in his still useful overview, the British debate over these issues was dominated by literary figures and the US one (below) by sociologists (including some members of the Frankfurt School).

In the UK, some elements of the mass/elite motif were visible in the early work of the *Scrutiny* group formed around F.R. and Q.D. Leavis. Bennett cites Q.D. Leavis' advocacy of a 'select, cultured element of the community that set the standards of behaviour and judgement, in direct opposition to the common people' in her 1932 *Fiction and the Reading Public* (1968: 202; see also Bennett, 1982: 38). The *Scrutiny* perspective was more complex than this suggests, however. Even in the 1930s, they recognized the threat market forces posed to public education, literature and art as a cause of declining 'standards', rather than an inherent failing in 'the masses' – a view that at least overlaps with the critique of the '**culture industry**' developed in the 1940s by Frankfurt School members Max Horkheimer and Theodor Adorno. F.R. Leavis even advocated the abolition of advertising and lamented the **tabloidization** of journalism. While Adorno and Horkheimer saw the reduction of aesthetics to saleability as a somewhat inevitable rationalizing process, the Leavisites launched a programme of cultural re-education.

Crucially, however, neither the Frankfurt School nor *Scrutiny* wished to impose one class's taste as a 'way of life' on another – as they are still both commonly portrayed. For Leavis and Thompson (1937: 82), consistent with Matthew Arnold, for example, the educated 'are not to be identified with any social class'. Such an account of the 'purely' class–elitist cultural argument is found in T.S. Eliot's *Notes Towards the Definition of Culture* (1948). It was this Eliot tract that drove Williams (1990) to write one of the claimed foundational texts of cultural studies, *Culture and Society*, cited above (see also **culture**).

131

US TRADITIONS OF 'MASS COMMUNICATIONS'

In the United States, the development of communications studies was also heavily influenced by a form of mass society theory, which, in turn, stemmed from functionalist traditions in sociology. These traditions saw social systems as innately equilibrating, yet in need of management in order to create harmony. Mass communication had a key role in such management and 'administrative research' was primarily aimed at measuring the effects that messages had on societal and 'mass' behaviour (see **media effects**). In his foundational text of 1948, 'The structure and function of communication in society', Harold Lasswell argued that mass communications served three major functions for social reproduction:

- the monitoring of a society's value consensus to provide feedback in cases when consensus deteriorates
- better integration of the various subsystems and institutions of society to maintain that consensus
- cultural transmission of history and tradition, which also helps with the achievement of social solidarity.

By the 1960s, Daniel Bell (1962) argued that the mass society paradigm was the most influential in the Western world at that time.

Sociological mass *society* theories in the United States thus differed from the European traditions, in that they often saw the media as a key institution though which large-scale social (re)integration could occur. US critiques of mass *culture* analogous to the Leavises' – such as Dwight Macdonald's (1953) – certainly did exist, however (see also Bennett, 1982; Bramson, 1967). Likewise, more nuanced analyses of popular culture, such as David Riesman's study of popular music, emerged very early in the US sociological tradition. Riesman (1990) had recognized in 1950 that even the products of the emergent consumer culture might be creatively consumed in subcultural *milieux* and not necessarily be indicators of consumerist 'conformism'. Such early revisions of the mass culture model anticipated a later enthusiastic intellectual fascination with the **popular**, most notably in the UK within later cultural studies and in France by its postmodern celebration. In its **populist** variants, cultural studies was capable of privileging the soap opera over the novel, *The Simpsons* over Dickens. Others remained more circumspect (see **culture**; **popular**; **tabloidization**).

More recently, two participants in key moments in the US mass communication research tradition, Kurt Lang and Gladys Engel Lang (2009), have mounted a spirited defence of that tradition against its critics (notably Bell). In part, they argue that 'masses' were conceived not necessarily as models of society but, rather, as more discrete formations that only qualified as 'masses' if they met particular requirements. From this view, mass formations are somewhat analagous to the UK understanding of **moral panics.**

FINDING THE MASS IN NEW MEDIA

One challenge to the populist cultural studies approach to **popular** culture is the development of new media and cyberculture, which do not so easily fit into a 'mass' model.

The question of whether or not the Internet is a mass medium, for example, is problematic (Morris and Ogan, 1996.) As the most common usage of Internet submedia is asynchronous, non-linear and point-to-point, its suitability for the mass broadcast of messages is limited. The Internet is a medium capable of broadcast, but it does not command audiences in the sense that print, radio and television do. As a diffused domestic communications media, the Internet has had a limited impact on television's role as a 'gathering place' (Adams, 1992), in which audiences can step into a current of simultaneous event reception. The electronically extended massing of viewers via television has created a peculiar kind of '**public**' (Dayan, 2001) that Internet submedia are unable to match in scale or solidarity.

As David Holmes (2005) argues, attempts to understand the Internet highlight a basic misunderstanding of mass media **audiences**. The orthodox view of audiences is that they are a pre-given demographic that needs to be reached by broadcasters, whereas a media sociology view sees audiences as *constituted* by the **broadcast** event. Central to this perspective is the impor-tance of simultaneous event reception afforded by broadcast media. This is often confused with the idea of liveness, where, for example, an event might be televized in real time. What is more important for broadcast audiences, however, is that when a given text is 'live for the audience' there are simulta-neous viewers.

Online counterparts to liveness, such as 'live blogging' or Twitter, do not feed into simultaneous event reception. They may be live at the point of production, but not live for a mass that they have helped create. The fact that broadcast media are capable of synchronous reception and of constituting a mass audience internal to the broadcast event challenges popular definitions of a mass medium. It also menaces the idea that the Internet can have an audience or be a mass medium in that it is used asynchronously and its content is entirely open-ended and horizon-tally networked.

Morris and Ogan (1996) argue, however, that the Internet *is* a mass medium, in the sense that it commands the attention of millions and, therefore, provides a 'popular' alternative to other forms of media literacy. As the Internet does not afford the kind of para-socal interaction and identification with an image that a broadcast does, its popular attraction lies in the illusion of anonymous control over a simulated reality.

The invention of the graphic user interface (GUI) has been a key feature of this attraction. Indeed, Anna Everett (2003: iii) argues that GUI has created a new kind of consumer pleasure, defined by the simplicity and ubiquity of clicking a mouse, video game joystick or Web-TV remote control. At least, it is the power and pleasure of the 'click' that produces a consumer-driven on-demand environment of media services and gives the consumer an illusion of autonomy over new media. From the human/media interface, 'click theory' points towards the need for new accounts of the relationship between users/audiences and media texts that mass media paradigms are unable to accommodate.

133

FURTHER READING

A still useful survey of mass society theories in relation to media studies can be found in Tony Bennett's 'Theories of the media, theories of society' (1982). It can be fruitfully contrasted with Lang and Lang (2009). For an application of a similar conception of mass society theory to new media, see Neuman (2000). The Modleski collection, *Studies in Entertainment: Critical approaches to mass culture* (1986), marks an important transition point between the 1950s/1960s debates and later forms of cultural analysis as well as the gendering of these debates. For an argument that the popularity of the Internet is a key condition for it being characterized as a mass medium, see Merrill Morris and Christine Ogan (1996). A contrary view, that the Internet is not a mass medium, can be found in Holmes (2005). See also the Further reading sections for **culture**, **popular** and **tabloidization**.

Media effects

> *Related concepts*: audience, criticism/critique, identity, influence, media/medium, modern.

Few concepts have consumed more time, and a greater percentage of research budgets, in communications research than the study of media effects. Although today the term is sometimes retrospectively applied to models of media influence and manipulation guided by variants of the concept of **ideology**, effects studies were, and remain, principally empirical research projects.

The empirical study of media effects in communication studies is an outgrowth of the process model of communication established in the 1940s in the USA. A foundation text of this tradition is Harold Lasswell's 'The structure and function of communication in society' (1948). In it, the process model of *communication* becomes an 'effects' model when applied to the study of mass media or *communications*.

To understand this important transition, and what is meant here by media 'effects', the main features of the process model must be reviewed. The process model is properly directed towards the study of communication, regardless of whether such communication is between humans, machines or animals. Beginning with Claude E. Shannon and Warren Weaver's *The Mathematical Theory of Communication* (1949), a result of research conducted for the AT&T telecommunications company, communication is examined as a linear event between only two entities. The effect of sending a message to a receiver is the analogue for this model and communication is measured according to how a unit of information produced by a sender at one end of a communication channel is faithfully reproduced at the other end by a receiver. The model is not concerned with meanings produced at either end but, rather, the technical success of getting a message across.

The purpose of measuring such success is to make communication more efficient and accurate. The process model borrows from *information theory* the idea that the content of information can be separated from the means of its carriage, while, from cybernetics, the need for accuracy and corrective feedback.

The source may be speech on the telephone, writing in a book, beeps on a telegraph wire, which is conducted on a channel (a wire, magazine or book) and received by another person with or without the aid of a 'decoding' device. Cybernetics, also known as 'communication engineering', is directed towards the construction of communication 'systems' in which the success of communication can be totally controlled. The ability to control the success of communication events amounts to one primary aim: to eradicate interference or 'noise' between the sender and receiver (see Figure 6). The possible sources of interference are many and varied and characterized as unwelcome 'variables' in the communication process.

The idea that a noise source can interfere with the message presupposes that the message is already a unit of self-identity. The informational sign faithfully stands in for the thing to which it refers and the language in which it is conveyed is assumed to be transparent. Language is assumed to embody or stand in for the real. The meanings attributed to objects and events can be faithfully reproduced between senders and receivers. Communication is regarded mostly as a question of selecting the right signifier to convey the correct message. Thus, in everyday language, many reflexive statements made in interpersonal communication provide *de facto* support for this process model, so we have, for example, 'I am searching for the word I mean' (language is nomenclature in which meanings are fixed and misunderstanding simply results from a poor choice of words), 'Do you follow what I am saying?' (is the message being faithfully reproduced?) or 'Am I getting through to you?' (is there interference in the signal?).

In interpersonal communication, communication can be thought of as a process, yet it makes no sense to attribute 'effects' to speech because dialogue is not, by definition, unilinear. What the process model describes as 'feedback' is exchanged in every moment of a conversation by dense verbal and non-verbal cues.

MEDIA EFFECTS IN MASS COMMUNICATIONS

Such assumptions, however, do not apply to mass communication, where nearly all communication events constitute a 'speech without a response' or at least a

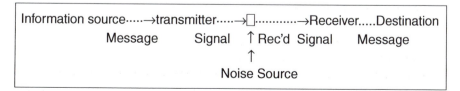

Figure 6   Shannon's conduit metaphor (from Day, 2000: 806)

response that is instantaneous and mutual. In mass communication, the addressee is widened to include the audience.

Mass communication needed a different methodological approach from personal communication because it has many more 'open' variables. The variables involved in mass communication received their first and very famous elaboration in Lasswell's (1948: 178) question 'Who, Says What, In Which Channel, To Whom And With What Effect?'. Lasswell's framing of communication theory in this way proliferated into an array of sub-branches looking at content, control, audience and impact.

Lasswell argues that, to understand the effect of any particular communication event, it is necessary to understand these variables. He describes the study of the motivations and intentions that guide the communicator as 'control analysis' (note the resonance with cybernetics). The 'says what' component is understood by a quantitative 'content analysis', while the content itself is influenced by the kind of channel, which, for Lasswell, was mainly radio, press or film. Then there is the question of who the message 'reaches' or who is attracted to the message in the channel via which it is conveyed. When these motivations and contexts are understood, the analysis can then look at the impact of the communication on its audience.

For the early Lasswell (1949) at least, the template was provided by wartime propaganda and the appropriate methodological instrument was quantitative content analysis. From such data, an inferred 'effect' was derived using a behaviourist stimulus–response model. It was also a model much beloved by researchers of media violence, the most enduring of the effects researchers.

It is important to consider the historical contexts in which this model of communication was developed. As a response to the Second World War and the need to make information secure and efficient, Ron Day (2000) argues, the process model appealed to an acutely scientist self-image to stamp its authority on communication theory. The process model merges with a general concern with functionalism in sociology and psychology. Sociological functionalism insists that all social systems are innately equilibrating and tend towards harmonic function. Behaviourist psychology aimed to better classify types of individuality and this information was thought to feed back into the better running of society. In communication studies, communication was seen as a vital agent in such harmony. Thus, from this period, 'communication' branched into 'organizational communication', of firms and bureaucracies and the manufacture of industry, many of which adopted a linear and instrumental approach to the organization and management of social relations. Thus, the linear process model of communications in many respects mirrors the Fordist mode of production that characterized the assembly-line approach in factories and workplaces. Both were concerned with managing communication, society and work practices during a time of rapid industrial change.

'ADMINISTRATIVE' RESEARCH AND MEDIA EFFECTS

The specific development of 'media effects' research within the US context became associated with the notion of 'administrative research', which, following Lazarsfeld (1941) is contrasted with 'critical' research (see **criticism/critique**). Its name derives primarily from its commissioned status and arose during a famous dispute in the USA in the 1940s between European *émigrés* who had fled Nazism, namely the social researcher Paul Lazarsfeld and key Frankfurt School member Theodor Adorno.

For Adorno – and the philosophy of social science generally – the more appropriate term for 'administrative' would be 'positivist' and, indeed, Lazarsfeld had been close to the Vienna positivist circle. In this context, positivism refers to the attempt to emulate the predictability and validity of 'hard' physical scientific methods within the social sciences (see **modern**). Adorno, a modernist composer of 'fine music' and major philosophical aesthetician, chafed at the constraints within the research environment of Lazarsfeld's Columbia Bureau, which required him to work on popular music.

Lazarsfeld's 'administrative research' was certainly a term compatible with Adorno's critique of the role of the **culture industry** within an 'administered capitalism'. Where the Frankfurt Institute for Social Research had been free, in its early days, to research what and how it liked due to a generous endowment, Lazarsfeld's situation required him to become an early research entrepreneur. Initially a project of the Rockefeller Foundation, his early US work (Lazarsfeld and Gaudet, 1944, for example) was dominated by voting studies that understood 'effects' as media influence on voting choice.

Significantly, these studies were credited with establishing much of the apparatus of modern opinion polling, which is highly administrative research, *and* modern political communication research, today often quite critical. Techniques developed here included the use of panel groups – that is, repeated surveys of the same group of people, in-depth interviews and open-ended questionnaires. This research project was a significant check on stimulus–response models, but later became subject to the charge that it contributed to the underestimation of (news) media **influence**. It is fair, in hindsight, to regard Lazarsfeld (together with colleague Robert Merton) as having shifted the ground of such effects research from a purely positivist quantitative domain to a more qualitative one, if at times it took the form of difficult methodological compromises.

Nonetheless, as a measure of the ambiguities here, Lazarsfeld also made one of the more bizarre contributions to effects research. He designed the 'programme analyser' or 'profile machine' with Frank Stanton, a psychologist and director of research at CBS. Viewers pressed buttons to record their positive or negative responses. The research was to be fed back into the production of messages, in a continuous process that could refine the effectiveness of almost any genre, advertising, entertainment, factual broadcasting and so on. The programme analyser's contemporary legacy can be seen in Hollywood test screenings and some of the more simplistic forms of tabloid 'vox pop' pseudo-surveys. Even this, however, has been claimed as an advance in qualitative analysis (Levy, 1982).

Lazarsfeld's 1941 essay conceded a key point of Adorno's culture industry thesis: that 'promotional culture' already prevailed. His frustration with Adorno's critical theory, expressed more forcefully in a much later essay (Lazarsfeld, 1972), was that it was so difficult to 'operationalize' – that is, translate into a set of empirical research tasks that could be undertaken by a research assistant.

Such questions remain pertinent today in a period when evidence-based empirical research has undergone a revival. Some defenders of the effects tradition sought to redefine Lazarsfeld's terminology and translate administrative as simply 'empirical' (Rogers, 1981). This is misleading as even Lazarsfeld could see the potential of 'operationalizing' the critical perspective into an empirical project. It is important to distinguish Lazarsfeld's administrative resort to a *positivist* focus on predictive research from critically informed contemporary evidence-based research that employs methods developed by both Lasswell and Lazarsfeld, among others, on issues close to their original concerns (see **influence**). (Likewise, Lazarsfeld's collaborator, Elihu Katz, went on to play a major role in later work on media **ritual**.)

The general point here would be that empirical methods should not be seen as permanently 'contaminated' by their positivist conditions of development. Indeed, C. Wright Mills (1959) had famously dismissed Lazarsfeld's work as 'abstract empiricism' – that is, a set of methods in search of a rationale.

Despite the continuance of instrumental research noted above, the formerly sharp divide between administrative and critical research has become far less relevant, if not obsolete, today (Lievrouw and Livingstone, 2006). This is partly because not all externally funded research comes under the same pressures and some commissioned research pursues quite critical goals. A good indication here is the shifting views of Adorno's student in critical theory, Jürgen Habermas. He initially emulated Adorno's pessimism and suspicion about administrative research and its consequences for the critical value of its results. More recently, however, he has seen the need for a fruitful collaboration between the critical research imperative of his **public sphere** thesis and contemporary evidence-based political communication research (Habermas, 2006a, for example). Even so, the ethical dilemmas Lazarsfeld and Adorno struggled with still speak loudly to a present in which attracting research funds from the commercial world is very often a career imperative for many communications researchers.

FURTHER READING

Claude Shannon and Warren Weaver's *The Mathematical Theory of Communication* (1949) is a key text, representing the influence of information theory on the effects model. Likewise, Harold Lasswell's 'The structure and function of communication in society' (1948) illustrates how the effect model migrated from dyadic communication exchange to mass communication and its distinctive understanding of the audience. Lazarsfeld's 'Remarks on administrative and critical communications research' (1941) is the foundational text for the distinction between instrumental, administratively orientated research and 'critical communication(s) research'. The 'Ferment in the field' special issue of *Journal of Communication* (1983: 33 (3)) is still regularly cited as well. David Gauntlett's 'Ten things wrong with the media "effects model"' (1998) critiques many of the assumptions of effects research, while marvelling at the historical persistence of the model in research on the effects of the mediated portrayal of violence. For a fuller history, see Hanno Hardt (1992), D.G. McDonald (2004) and the special issue of the *Annals of the American Academy of Political and Social Science* (Simonson, 2006) devoted to the work of Elihu Katz, which covers much of this territory. There is a companion volume on political communication in this SAGE series (Lilleker, 2006). See also the Further reading for **influence**.

Media/medium

> **Related concepts**: *communication(s), cultural form, digital, identity, image, interactivity, mobile privatization, network (society), technoculture, time–space compression.*

The challenge of explaining the concept of media or medium relates to the fact that it has different meanings for audiences, media consumers, media producers and media theorists.

THREE METAPHORS FOR MEDIA

In commonsense usage, 'media' is regarded as the plural of 'medium'. Nevertheless, there are several orthodox ways in which both media and medium are conceptualized, the dominant one being conduit. In this definition, a medium is likened to a container or vessel, a 'means of connection' or means of carriage between interactants. For such a metaphor to work, a strong distinction is drawn between the container and its content, which are radically separated, with a privileging of content.

Typically, when we try to interpret the meaning of a message, the medium is overlooked as the conduit metaphor demands that we uncover the intentionality of the message, rather than the way it might be shaped by the medium. The fact that the medium is overlooked in accounting for the production of meaning suggests the persistence of the 'transport' or 'process' model of communication (see **media effects**), in which a medium is regarded as transparent. In this case, the meaning of a message is regarded as a self-identical unit that remains stable no matter how it is conveyed – whether be it on the telephone, in writing or by other means.

The transport definition of medium goes some way towards explaining how diverse communication mediums, from print, to radio and television, can be clustered together as 'the media'. When it is held that a 'story' is 'all over the media', the assumed singularity of the story is reinforced by the assumption that all media provide a transparent means of connection to it. At the same time, the influence attributed to the mass apparatus of broadcasting as 'the media' suggests an homogenous

139

sphere in which messages circulate and signs can jump from one channel to another as self-identical units of meaning (see **sign**).

To the conduit metaphor can be added two other metaphors of medium: medium as language and medium as environment (Meyrowitz, 1999).

Medium as language is of most significance to media producers, whether it be on canvas, in print or electronic. As Holmes (2005: 116) explains, Meyrowitz (1999) proposes that, 'Medium as language treats a medium *like a language* with its own grammar'. This grammar of production exhibits a range of variables, such as font type, camera angle, sound reverberation or, we could add with new media, the sublanguage of computers or, on the Web, hypertext markup language (HTML).

The production of meaning in any medium requires a set of conventions and rules of expression peculiar to that medium. It is impossible to 'cut to a close-up' in a novel. The production values of radio do not fit with the codes of television. The craft of producing content for these media relies on technical knowledge and canonized modes of working with them.

The fact that each medium has its own language necessitates an 'adaptation industry', to convert novels into film or films into television series and Web designers who can translate publicity into a hypertext medium. It is not simply that a screenplay or HTML template is needed but also the entire translation of possibilities of expression. The fact that an adaptation industry exists challenges both the widespread experience of medium as transparent conduit and the assumption the same content can be reproduced in any medium.

The third metaphor is that of medium as environment, which is of most interest to 'medium theorists' and scholars of media in general. Tracing the origins of this metaphor takes us straight to the engine room of medium theory, in the work of Marshall McLuhan and Harold Innis.

As Holmes explains (2005: 41), for McLuhan 'anything that can extend the body's senses and biological capabilities (psychic or physical) earns the status of media'. Typically, such extensions are equated with information and communication systems and, indeed, the passage from communication to 'communications', the development of an entire superstructure of technologically extended systems of mediation, particularly with the broadcasting industries, coinciding with the emergence of 'media' as a social category.

For McLuhan, media can be non-technological. A situation may become a medium if it adds a new form of *mediation* between individual and environment. In the broad horizon of McLuhan's definition, the lecture theatre can be a medium, clothes can be a medium, as can a code or technique of communication, such as those found in the fine arts. Moreover, not only do media mediate our relationship with the world but they also substitute for that world and can become a new environment, in relation to which the 'outer' environment is diminished. These new environments remain largely unperceived as environments, as the senses become enveloped. It is the medium and the fact of interaction with it that is more important than the content of the medium, yielding McLuhan's (McLuhan and Fiore, 1967) most famous maxim – 'The medium is the message'.

In creating a new, substitute environment, media tend to work on, and extend, one of the human senses (McLuhan and Fiore, 1967: 68):

> Environments are not passive wrappings, but are, rather, active processes which work us over completely, massaging the ratio of the senses and imposing their silent assumptions.

The personal music device privileges the ear while changing the physical sense of place of the user. Electric light is a medium that annuls the dependence on daylight and extends vision around the clock. Clothing allows us to extend our bodies into the public domain and environments too harsh for our skin, while becoming a shield from such environments.

THE BIASES OF MEDIA

Most of McLuhan's work deals with the mass consumption of media, such as print, film, radio and television, which he claimed worked to massage the senses with particular sensory biases.

McLuhan's concern with sensory bias was influenced by Harold Innis' (1950, 1951) historical study of media. Innis' account of modernity focuses on the bias of printed media and its relationship to social power. In contrast to oral, time-bound cultures that build extremely strong worlds of tradition, the concentration of knowledge in the printed word leads to the political control of space. As James Carey (1968: 280) explains in comparing McLuhan to Innis, 'Printing fostered the growth of nationalism and empire; it favoured the extension of society in space. It encouraged the growth of bureaucracy and militarism, science and secular authority'.

In McLuhan's work, the culture of print – what he calls the Gutenberg Galaxy, in reference to the European inventor of the printing press – is a culture of uniformity, repetition and centralism. He contrasts it with electronic media, which is decentralized, instantaneous and simultaneous. The simultaneity created by communication at 'light speed' (McLuhan, 2003) generates extreme interdependence and involvement of individuals in electronic assemblies at the expense of physical assemblies.

Whereas print exaggerated the eye, electronic media, or 'cybernation', exaggerates the ear. Television and the Internet are both technologies of aural culture, of information enveloping the senses in an all-at-once movement. With all electric media, McLuhan (2003: 125) argues that 'the visual' is only one component of a complex interplay: 'Since, in the age of information, most transactions are managed electrically, the electric technology has meant … a considerable drop in the visual component, … and a corresponding increase in the activity of other senses'.

MEDIA ECOLOGY

Since McLuhan, the study of media environments has been extended in the USA with the media ecology perspective, also influenced by Neil Postman. The media ecology perspective focuses upon how particular cultures emerge out of different media environments. Adherents argue that 'just as bacterial cultures grow within a biological medium, human cultures grow within a technological medium'.

The media ecology perspective can be summarized by three theoretical propositions:

- That communication media 'are not neutral, transparent, or value-free conduits for carrying data or information from one place to another'. Rather, the physical and symbolic nature of media shape 'what and how information is to be encoded', transmitted and decoded (Lum, 2006: 32). In other words, particular media shape and constitute the message, and the message cannot be considered in isolation from the former.
- Each medium exhibits a 'unique set of physical as well as symbolic character-istics [and] carry with them a set of biases', which can be intellectual, emo-tional, temporal, spatial, political, social, metaphysical and content biases (Lum, 2006: 32–3). The peculiarity of a medium's symbolic forms might induce particular intellectual or emotional dispositions, while its technical architecture might delimit temporal and spatial experiences. For example, online communication normalizes the importance of the electronic assembly over physical proxemics, whereas, with the medium of the lecture, the reverse is true. Political biases derive from different kinds of access to media that are inherent to those media, while content bias suggests that some symbolic forms are only suitable to some media, such as when it is suggested that a novel is not suitable as a screenplay for cinema. As Joshua Meyrowitz neatly summarizes, the combination of physical characteristics unique to a particular media mark that medium as distinctive. To paraphrase Meyrowitz (1999), they relate to:

  o the type of sensory information the medium can transmit
  o the speed and immediacy that is allowed for a communicative event
  o whether it is unidirectional, bidirectional or multidirectional
  o whether the interaction is sequential or simultaneous
  o what the physical requirements for using the medium are
  o how easy it is to learn to use the medium.

- The intrinsic biases of media have effects or consequences that impact culture in profound ways.
- McLuhan argues that these 'media effects' are systemic. In *The Medium is the Massage: An inventory of effects* (McLuhan and Fiore, 1967: 16), he proclaims that 'Electric circuitry has overthrown the regime of "time" and "space" and pours upon us, instantly and continuously the concerns of all other men. It has reconstituted dialogue on a global scale. Its message is Total Change, ending psychic, social, economic and political parochialism'. McLuhan's account of globalization, suggested by his notion of the global village, is one of electronic interdependence, where individuals and states become extremely involved in each other's affairs.

TECHNOLOGICAL DETERMINISM IN MEDIUM THEORY

McLuhan's interest in the technological mediation of experience has been extremely influential in the sociology of technology and social theory as it provides a powerful account of the role of media in identity construction and the relationship between media and social power. The role Innis and McLuhan give to media in social change, however, has been the subject of much criticism. As McLuhan (McLuhan and Fiore, 1967: 8) comments, 'It is impossible to understand social and cultural changes without a knowledge of the workings of media'. To claim that media are the decisive factors in historical evolution and revolution has been labelled historicist and **technologically determinist**.

Tom Nairn argues that McLuhan has ignored the influence of European imperialism in the formation of a 'global village'. It is not television, but the culture of capitalism and its need to gain control over property and labour, by means of the gun if necessary, that has been central to the current world picture. These forces are overwhelmingly pre-electronic and he (1968: 150) argues that television has served to reinforce, rather than overturn, our acceptance of capitalist culture and its class contradictions: 'The *potential* of electric media is, in fact, in *contradiction* with a great deal of the actual social world'.

Raymond Williams has also pointed out that McLuhan's characterization of the emancipatory potential of new media is contextless. It does not take into account the decisive influence of media regulation in the concentration and diffusion of media technologies and their content (see **technological determinism** and Jones, 2000a). As Williams (1974a: 128) suggests: 'The physical fact of instant transmission, as a technical possibility, has been uncritically raised to a social fact, without any pause to notice that virtually all such transmission is at once selected and controlled by existing social authorities.' Williams challenges the assumption that media have the freedom to drive historical change because the argument is too singularly focused on the media and relegates all other historical forces to mere 'effects'.

Yet, Williams conceded that his critique of technological determinism 'should not, however, be understood to mean that a given medium does not have specific properties crucial to understanding how it works' (Heath and Skirrow, 1986: 11). At worst, McLuhan's was a 'sophisticated technological determinism' that did not simply argue the latest was the best. Williams recognized that McLuhan's sense–ratio model required a fuller alternative he later labelled 'Means of Communication as Means of Production' (1980a; see also Jones, 2004). Moreover, it is not often noticed that Williams' much-quoted critique does not stop at the charge of technological determinism. Williams also draws attention to a variant of the linguistic metaphor of medium (or, for Williams, not so much a metaphor as part of medium's historical semantic range of usage), an aesthetic sense, as in the artist's choice of 'the medium of oils'. This sense permeates throughout McLuhan's work and occludes the role of distribution and regulatory systems. It strongly informs the famous 'medium is the message' declaration that Williams identified with *formalist* techniques of cultural analysis. The charge of (excessive) formalism stands equally

143

with that of technological determinism in Williams' critiques. While it enables McLuhan to provide insights unavailable to contemporary effects studies, McLuhan nonetheless tends to treat media technologies as well as media content *only* to the extent a formalist analysis can encompass. In Williams' view, McLuhan confuses several dimensions of the means of communication and occludes social contexts of communication practice (see **modern**; **cultural form**).

FURTHER READING

Two of McLuhan's most readerly texts are *Understanding Media* (1964) and *The Medium is the Massage* (McLuhan and Fiore, 1967). The first contains his most consolidated elaboration of medium as message as well as an accessible introduction to 'hot' and 'cool' media. The second is a picture book, replete with 1960s counterculture images and subversive layout designed to challenge the linear consumption of text. For later developments in medium theory, Lance Strate's (2004) article contains a full introduction to media ecology figures, such as McLuhan, Jacques Ellul, Lewis Mumford, Innis, Walter Ong and Postman. An alternative introduction that attempts to apply McLuhan to digital and online media is provided by Paul Levinson (1999). For a reconstruction of Williams' own account of medium's semantic formation, see Jones (2004). For a defence of McLuhan against Williams' critique, see Martin Lister et al. (2009).

Mobile privatization

> *Related concepts*: broadcasting, capitalism, mass, modern, technological determinism.

144

Raymond Williams developed the concept of mobile privatization as part of his criticism of the failings of **technological determinism** and its role in accounts of media history. It plays a central role in his alternative *social shaping* account of the development of radio and television **broadcasting**. It was also developed as an explicit alternative to accounts of the power of the media that relied on the concept of 'mass communication' or '**mass media**'. As the components of its name suggest, however, it obviously has great potential relevance to 'post-broadcasting' media, particularly the mobile phone and other ICTs that facilitate **mobility**.

Williams' own shorthand definition in *Television* (1974a) develops from his assessment of a kind of technology that first became commonplace in the early twentieth century and is exemplified by the car and motorcycle, the first portable cameras, home electrical appliances and, most relevantly here, radio. For Williams (1974a: 26), 'this complex is characterized by the two paradoxical yet deeply connected tendencies of modern urban industrial living: on the one-hand mobility, on the other hand the more apparently self-sufficient family home' and these technologies 'served an at once mobile yet home-centred way of living: a form of *mobile privatization*'.

MOBILE PRIVATIZATION'S EMERGENCE

The idea of mobile privatization arose from Williams' reflections on modern car traffic in the 1960s. Our personal use of privately owned cars and the enormous social organization involved in sustaining this form of transportation pointed to major transformations not only in industrial **capitalism** but also in how we understand the everyday social world around us:

> Looked at from right outside, the traffic flows and their regulation are clearly a social order of a determined kind, yet what is experienced inside them – in the conditioned atmosphere and internal music of this windowed shell – is movement, choice of direction, the pursuit of self-determined private purposes. All the other shells are moving, in comparable ways but for their own different private ends. And if all this is seen from the outside as in deep ways determined, or in some sweeping glance as dehumanized, that is not at all how it feels like inside the shell, with people you want to be with, going where you want to go. (Williams, 1983a: 188)

Modern transport networks are, of course, as much part of the communications system as **information** networks, as Williams (1973: 296) reminds us. Such traffic became necessary not only because of the increasing distance between workplaces and homes but also because of the increasing *social* distance between production and consumption. Food is the most obvious example. Whereas in traditional and other agricultural societies most food sources were 'close to home', agricultural food production becomes increasingly 'socially invisible' in urban industrial societies. This is the sting in the 'apparently' in Williams' phrase 'apparently self-sufficient family home' in the above definition of mobile privatization. Such homes 'might appear private and self-sufficient but could be maintained only by regular funding and supply from external sources' (1974a: 27).

Mobile privatization thus draws our attention to social relations rendered 'socially invisible' in everyday life, especially those in which *physical* distance provides the precondition for *social* distance.

This is the key to Williams' understanding of its role in the formation of broadcast media. The domestic radio receiver was, of course, one of those new consumer 'gadgets' that arrived in the family home in the early twentieth century. It is well known that it could have been designed as 'interactive' from the beginning – as the inventor Guglielmo Marconi intended it for the use of navies – but was, instead, domestically configured on broadcasting's model of a centralized transmitter broadcasting to multiple receivers. Williams (1974a: 27) emphasizes that broadcasting's classic technical configuration established 'a new kind of "communication": news from "outside", from otherwise inaccessible sources'. Thus, mobile privatization 'socially shaped' traditional broadcasting as we know it. Yet, its paradoxical dynamic was also pivotal to the long historical trend since the 1920s towards ever-increasing portability of both broadcast and post-broadcast media – from transistor radios to MP3 players.

MOBILE PRIVATIZATION IN DOMINANCE

The *social shaping of the technical configuration of broadcasting* thus provided a means of redressing the communicative consequences of the social and physical isolation of 'the apparently self-sufficient family home':

> The new consumer technology which reached its first decisive stage in the 1920s served this needs complex well within just these limits and pressures. There were immediate improvements of the condition and efficiency of the privatised home; there were new facilities in private transport, for expeditions from the home; and then, in radio, there was a facility for a new type for social input – news and entertainment brought into the home. (Williams, 1974a: 27)

This 'needs complex' is now usually characterized by Antonio Gramsci's term 'Fordism'. Analysts of Fordism (such as Harvey, 1989) have emphasized the relative stabilization of capitalist production relations in the leading economies of the first half of the twentieth century around disciplined factory labour, higher wages, production lines, consumer credit *and* a stabilized domestic sphere. All of these rested on markedly gendered divisions of labour, most famously that between a male breadwinner and a female domestic labourer. Williams' specific contribution to such a perspective is his focus on Fordism's required increase in 'internal mobility' of the workforce – what would now be called commuting – and the role of the 'apparently self-sufficient family home' as a private retreat.

As Roger Silverstone (1994: 52–77) elaborates – in one of the fullest engagements with the concept to date – the full sociocultural realization of mobile privatized broadcasting occurred in mid-twentieth-century suburbia. This way of life developed unevenly across different nation states. Australia, for instance, was claimed to have become 'the first suburban nation' by the early 1960s (Horne, 1964). The private home also became the basis of radio and television **cultural forms** – most notably the soap – that take mobile privatized suburban existence as a given. As David Morley argues of more recent developments, however, suburbia for later generations – and for much of its US history – was also a 'geography of exclusion', culminating in phenomena such as 'gated communities'. Similarly, many of the related television narratives treat any form of disruption to the rhythms of the suburban way of life as a threat (Medhurst, 1997; Morley, 2000: 128ff.).

The legacy of mobile privatization's contribution to the shaping of broadcasting certainly risked, in Williams' own assessment, such a form of *social insularity*. Consistent with his work on **hegemony,** Williams regarded mobile privatization as having shifted since the 1920s from an *emergent* to *dominant* position within late **modern** societies. Referring again to the 'shells' of mobile privatization, he commented (1983a: 189):

> Thus at a now dominant level of social relations, systems quite other than settlement, or in any of its older senses community, are both active and continually reproduced. The only disturbance is when movements from quite outside them – movements which are the real workings of the effective but taken-for-granted public system – slow the flow ... forcing a truly public world back into chosen and intensely valued privacy.

As Morley reminds us, however, Williams did not see such insularity as a necessary consequence of mobile privatization. It remained 'an ambivalent process' precisely because of its 'paradoxical' dynamic and the contestable status of all forms of social **hegemony**.

EXTENDING WILLIAMS' ANALYSIS

Williams thought that mobile privatization described the modern configuration of broadcast media outside totalitarian societies such as Nazi Germany more accurately than 'mass media'. Unlike those subjected to such regimes, members of democracies were not compelled to physically assemble as 'masses' to attend broadcasts. (An analogy with such societies was often implicit in uses of the term 'mass'.) Rather, the typical site of broadcast media use in modern liberal democracies was the family home and, later, the 'shells' established by portable media that enabled such privatization to become mobile.

Driving Williams' development of the concept was an attempt to delineate the specific everyday forms of media technology and their social use. So how can we apply it today?

Most subsequent applications of mobile privatization focus on radio and, especially, television broadcasting. These of course remain highly relevant, but one effect of this emphasis has been to neglect Williams' own emphasis on the *portability* of technical devices – and so the mobility of the privatization – in his original analysis. While it's true, as Silverstone argues, that this analysis seems best suited to the car, if we look again at the opening citation above, it is the 'conditioned atmosphere and internal music of this windowed shell' that is the key to its role in mobile privatization – that is, it is a portable *mediated* privacy.

So here is one way to begin looking at the current array of portable devices as mobile privatized ones. We can also say that these devices increase the trend noted by Williams towards individuated rather than 'collective' family use. Much research on the mobile phone, for example, emphasizes its capacity to 'emancipate' teenagers from parental constraint (Ling and Yttri, 2006). Yet, true to mobile privatization's contradictory character, the mobile phone also sustains communication – and potentially surveillance – *within* the contemporary family (Wajcman et al., 2007). A more crucial difference is that Williams tended to assume that the portable means of communication were dedicated receivers and so, to this extent, primarily part of a broadcast network. Mobile telephony – and, indeed, all telephony – of course, does not operate like this and today the content of other devices can be user-driven to greater degrees.

We also need to attend to Williams' ambivalence about the consequences of mobile privatization:

> And why I think it's ambivalent is this; because it has given people genuine kinds of freedom of choice and mobility which their ancestors would have given very much for. At the same time the price of that space has never been accounted. The price of that space has been paid in the deterioration of the very conditions which allow it. I mean that it all depends on conditions which people, when this consciousness was formed, thought were permanent. Full employment, easy cheap credit, easy cheap petrol. All the conditions of this kind of life were assumed to be abundant and permanent. (Williams, 1989a: 171–172)

Some 25 years after these lines were first written, the broader social assumptions of Fordist suburban mobile privatization seem even further away. Likewise, Williams (1983a) anticipated increasing pressure on mobile privatization's 'private retreat' from a globalized economy. So, for each case situation, we need to consider a checklist such as the following:

- the changed rhythms of work towards more 'flexible', casual labour and the degree of change away from a Fordist gendered division of labour
- the recomposition of habitation within and beyond cities by migration, the expansion of suburbanization and/or the increased density of apartment living
- the consequences for each nation-, city- or locale-based transport system, public and private.

Many of our mobile, **time–space compressing** media have been designed to fit this new, post-Fordist 'complex of needs', with mixed success (McGuigan, 2007; Schiller, 2007). Today, for example, many treasure the mobile phone as a means of maintaining 'work–life balance' – often while commuting – yet it is also resented for its capacity to intrude on our private life (Wajcman et al., 2007). The consequences of all this need not be greater social insularity, however. Equally, in many modern cities, for example, we can note greater cosmopolitanism. Mobile privatization's capacity to increase private withdrawal, however, does have consequences for how we think of the **public sphere** today.

FURTHER READING

See Williams (1974a, 1983a, 1989a) for his own accounts. Jim McGuigan (2007) has written a very useful overview of technological determinism and mobile privatization applied to the case of the mobile phone. Dan Schiller's 'Privatized' chapter (2007) is an important updating of Williams' argument in the context of both mobile phones and flexible labour markets. Lyn Spigel's (1992) considerable body of feminist work on gender, television, suburbanization and the domestic sphere (mainly in the USA) developed a critical dialogue with this concept. Morley (2000), like Silverstone (1994), has also linked his interest in domestication (see **articulation**) with this concept.

Modern

> **Related concepts**: *capitalism, criticism/critique, culture industry, deconstruction, discourse, ideology, media/medium, postmodernism, time–space compression.*

'Modern' is an unusually distinctive signifier. It was one of Raymond Williams' central keywords – arguably the most central to his later work. Some keywords for Williams' historical semantics signify key points around which other keywords cluster. Modern is plainly one of those. So, unlike a key *concept*, the possibilities of ambiguity and contestation of meaning are extremely high. There can be little prospect of pointing to an intellectual consensus concerning a core definition of it. Nor is 'modern' a mere precursor concept of **postmodern(ism)**, even when limited to its aesthetic sense. Moreover, we have taken 'modern' as our defining term for this entry so that we can point to its central ambiguity, namely that, as an adjective, it can appear to denote any of three nominal sources:

- *aesthetic* modernism
- the (dominantly sociological) conception of modernity
- the now much-derided notion of modernization.

These three informing denotations are the concern of this entry. All have considerable ramifications for understandings of media and communications.

SETTING ASIDE MODERNIZATION

The concept of 'modernization' is consistent with what is probably the most well-known commonsense meaning of 'modern' – a process of steady advance or revolutionary 'progress' primarily or entirely enabled by technological innovation. Thus, to modernize is usually thought to mean bringing some aspect of social and cultural life 'up to date'. It implies a lag. So, for example, regulatory laws relating to any aspect of technological innovation are often said to be 'lagging behind' the latest scientific advance. In short, modernization, in most of its usage, is a variant of **technological determinism**.

149

In sociology, modernization theory is usually taken to refer to a largely US-centric understanding of how nation states might 'develop' in the mid-twentieth century. It is closely related to the view that 'technological diffusion' would encourage such development. Communications technology was often thought to be a key component of this technological diffusion. At its worst, this perspective would enable the export of armaments into civil conflicts; at its best, it might encourage a less simplistic conception of progress, such as facilitating literacy programmes. As with critiques of **technological determinism**, then, the alternative is not a denial of technologies' potential benefits but, rather, the avoidance of the view that a technology or device, *by itself*, will bring about major advances in social and cultural life. For example, the recent campaigns worldwide 'to put a laptop on every student's desk' point to a real need, but fail as panaceas without adequate broadband connectivity, provision of teaching staff, solutions to student truancy and so on.

Modernization theory also figures prominently as a major bête noire in the debates about *cultural imperialism* (see **capitalism**). The question as to *why* such a reduced conception of human progress proliferated was met first among those working with the richer concept of *modernity*.

MODERNITY AS CORE

Much of the rhetoric relating to the 'postmodern' and 'cultural' turns centred on the idea of a canon, an apparently arbitrary set of revered texts around which a 'grand narrative' of the discipline had been constructed. Aesthetically based disciplines of great significance to media and communications, such as English/literary studies and visual arts, were the most vulnerable to challenges regarding their canonical formulations. For example, their canons of 'great works' were frequently criticized as being embodiments of white patriarchal selection.

Sociology was unusually resistant to this understanding, for its core concept, on many definitions, was *modernity* and, indeed, German sociology had been founded on its own 'cultural turn' (see below). Many sociologists could remember very recent 'sociological turns' in the aesthetic disciplines. Many of sociology's canonical texts, most notably the works of Max Weber, demonstrated highly nuanced approaches to modernity and culture. In other words, these canonical texts already practised the kind of reflexivity frequently advocated for other disciplines in the postmodern and cultural turns. This sociological resistance culminated in Jürgen Habermas' (1996b) definitive critique of the idea of postmodernity, which, in turn, strongly echoes the premises of his **public sphere** thesis. Anthony Giddens (1990), for example, defends 'classical' sociology similarly, but advocates that sociologists should pay more heed to the consequences of phenomena like **time–space compression** and the changing role of face-to-face interaction.

To some extent, the tension can be explained by the unusually accelerated German intellectual trajectory on these issues. German sociology confronted, much earlier than the French and US traditions, the failure of *positivist* models of knowledge. First promulgated by Auguste Comte for French sociology, positivism asserts that the model of the experiment in nineteenth-century natural science should be the template for all other 'modern' disciplines. The most notable continuity of this model in the twentieth century was the 'rats and stats' model of human psychology known as behaviourism. Much early communications research – such as the notorious 'stimulus–response' model of **media effects** – was premised on this limited model of experimentally based scientific knowledge.

Within German sociology, Max Weber pointed to the limits of such models and their implications for the Enlightenment ideals that had informed Marx's work. Crucial to the earliest versions of positivism was the Enlightenment confidence that the pursuit of human reason *necessarily* entailed the pursuit of progressive social goals. For example, key figures in the early days of the US Republic, such as Benjamin Franklin and Thomas Jefferson, had been scientific 'tinkerers' as well as publishers and advocates of freedom of the press (see **freedom of communication**).

By the late nineteenth and certainly early twentieth century, however, advocates of positivism tended to detach that experimental template from emancipatory Enlightenment ideals. One key figure in early communication studies, Harold Lasswell (1949; see also Splichal, 2008), was unusually explicit in this regard in his advocacy of quantitative content analysis. This separation became known in critical sociology as the 'reason/values split'.

What has all this to do with 'modern'? For Weber and much sociology, the developing reason/values split was *a constitutive feature of modernity*, where modernity was understood to entail a period from the eighteenth century (if not earlier) to the present. It was *this* conception of Enlightenment that Theodor Adorno and Max Horkheimer (1979) adopted, and criticized, within their larger project, which included their work on the **culture industry**. This, in turn, formed the basis of Adorno's hostility to Paul F. Lazarsfeld's 'administrative research' (see **media effects**; **criticism**).

In short, the reason/values split meant that scientific methods and related technological innovation could be used to *any* purpose in order to fulfil any 'values'. For Adorno, this provided a powerful explanatory motif for understanding how Germany could also have become a society in which the Nazis' reorganization of all aspects of social life – including the Holocaust – could be conducted with 'scientific' precision. Anything, even the most horrific, now seemed possible and the development of the **culture industry** was, for him, part of this contemporary reality. Within the German tradition, Habermas' **public sphere** thesis was initially designed as a corrective to the pessimistic consequences of Adorno's development of Weber's conception of modernity. For all these thinkers, however, positivism was an unacceptable intellectual option – some form of *critical* research was necessary.

151

(AESTHETIC) MODERNISM AND MODERNITY/*MODERNITÉ*

While 'modernity' can be found in English usage from the late seventeenth century, its French formulation, 'modernité', dates from only the mid-nineteenth century and is predominantly aesthetic in its initial reference (Calinescu, 1987: 42). Moreover, as this initial usage is dominated by the writings of symbolist poet

Charles Baudelaire, French formulations of modernité are also strongly linked to the legacy of aesthetic reactions to the relatively new bourgeois forms of 'everyday life'. In the French case, these were developing within a period also characterized by relatively frequent revolutionary upsurges (1830, 1848, 1870). In short, the French tradition of reflection on modernité – which contributed most directly to the twentieth-century formulations of **postmodernism** – is, from the beginning, ambivalent about the Enlightenment promises of the bourgeoisie (see **capitalism**) and focuses, instead, on the bourgeoisie's contemporary failings and the offerings of the avant-gardes (see below).

In French and French-derived usage, then, it is difficult to separate modernism as an aesthetic/cultural movement from the broader conception of modernity. French usage tends to conflate the two as 'modernité' while 'Germanic/English' usage tends to distinguish modern aesthetic developments as *cultural modernity*, one phase within the centuries of existence of modernity. Likewise, usages of 'postmodernism' tend to confuse the aesthetic movements and works labelled postmodernist ('after' twentieth-century aesthetic modernism) with the broader question of whether there has been an epochal interruption/alteration to the Enlightenment project of modernity, a putative postmodernity.

To put this more plainly, it is possible to acknowledge the existence of a series of postmodern aesthetic developments (now arguably ended), while also rejecting the view that we have entered an era of 'postmodernity' rendering obsolete the project of Enlightenment modernity. Table 14 moves from this premise.

Table 14   Major aesthetic movements within 'cultural modernity'

Period of emergence/ dominance (all dates contested)	Dominant/significant *aesthetic* movement(s)	Some distinguishing features
1700s	Neoclassical	Allusions to Ancient Greece and Rome, the preferred 'cloak' of eighteenth-and nineteenth-century revolutions (Marx)
Early–mid 1800s	Romantic	Critical of Enlightenment focus on 'reason' at expense of emotions; much interest in 'folkloric' culture
Mid-nineteenth– mid-twentieth century	Modernist	Avant-gardes a key feature; break with deference to tradition; much enthusiasm for modernizing technoscientific features enabling 'new media' for artistic experimentation
Mid-/late twentieth century	Postmodernist	Abandonment of any sense of linear 'progress' within arts; all styles permanently available and mixable: pastiche

AVANT-GARDES, 'MEDIA' AND CULTURAL THEORY

The very French formulation, avant-garde, captures this ambivalence perfectly. Based on *vanguard*, the military term for an advance component of an army in battle, the aesthetic modernist and other avant-gardes (from the mid-nineteenth to mid-twentieth century) sought to revolutionize everyday life. Although they issued party-like manifestoes, they did not usually seek change by violent means, unlike the political revolutionaries within the communist parties, who saw themselves as members of a 'vanguard party' (Lenin's term). Instead, avant-gardes usually saw themselves leading *by example*. The Italian futurists' proto-fascist formulations would be a notable exception, while the Russian avant-gardes tended to act in support of the Bolshevik Revolution until the suppression of artistic autonomy in the Soviet Union.

A key feature of avant-gardes was thus a tendency to reject ossified aesthetic traditions and embrace 'the new'. Accordingly, most avant-gardes were especially sympathetic to new technologies, primarily understood as *new means of artistic expression* (Poggioli, 1968). The most visible legacy of these is perhaps the architectural avant-gardes' enthusiasm for steel, concrete and sheet glass over brickwork; this is something we continue to see reproduced in every major city of the world. It was the avant-gardes who traced important aesthetico-cultural consequences of phenomena such as speed, so contributing to our understanding of **time–space compression**.

In communications, too, however, new techniques were embraced, particularly (for the high period of aesthetic modernism, 1880–1920s), photography and cinema. New means of communication were expected to produce a 'shock effect' that would aid a process of 'defamiliarizing' publics from their 'bourgeois' routines and so contribute to the revolutionizing of everyday life. It was very much in this cultural context that Walter Benjamin (2008) wrote his pivotal surrealist-influenced 1936 essay on photography and cinema: 'The work of art in the age of its technological reproducibility' (see **culture industry**).

Benjamin's translation of avant-gardist aesthetic innovation echoed the earlier practice of the Russian Formalists, who undertook a more elaborate theoretical construction based on the practice of the Russian Futurist avant-garde (see **cultural form**). Russian Formalists laid the groundwork for much of the structuralist project (see **sign**).

The most decisive catalyst for the development of what is now usually called 'cultural theory' was the work of Marshall McLuhan. McLuhan was heavily inspired by both the French symbolist avant-garde and the literary formalism of Northrop Frye (1957). He brought formalist techniques of analysis to bear on media content, neatly summarized in his 'the medium is the message' slogan, which echoed the usual summary explanation of formalism as the prioritization of 'form over content' (see **media/medium**). Moreover, McLuhan's intellectual practice was closely modelled on that of modernist avant-gardes – he claimed his work was not accountable to the usual scholarly norms as it was a series of 'probes', plainly designed to produce a 'shock effect'. His lectures and media appearances operated in a similar mode, most notable for their very early academic use of the quote as a 'soundbite'. For this reason, many regard his work as highly prefigurative of **postmodernism** (Ferguson, 1991). It points to an irony concerning both post-modernist and poststructuralist media and cultural theory – that their innovations were often not postmodern at all, but based firmly in (aesthetic) modernism.

FURTHER READING

Matei Calinescu (1987) provides one of the clearest accounts of the semantic minefield here, but, for a broader sociological frame, see also Alan Swingewood (1998), especially Chapter 8 on 'modernity 1' and 'modernity 2'. Habermas' (1996b) famous essay, 'Modernity: an unfinished project', originally a public lecture, is very readable, especially in the fuller version. Eugene Lunn (1985) maps the Marxian tradition in relation to aesthetic modernism; see especially Chapter 6, 'Avant-garde and culture industry' for a very good detailed exposition of the Adorno/Benjamin 'debate'. Andrew Murphie and John Potts (2003) also cover the aesthetic modernist ground well in relation to media technologies. Glenn Willmott (1996) provides a sympathetic account of McLuhan's relationship with aesthetic modernism. John Thompson (1995) builds on Giddens' understanding of time–space 'distanciation' in traditional and modern societies (Giddens, 1995) and features an innovative account of mediated 're-mooring of tradition' within modernity. On related themes, see also the important contributions of Craig Calhoun (1992), Graham Murdock (1993) and Nicholas Garnham (2000).

Moral panic

Related concepts: discourse, freedom of communication, ideology, influence, news values, populism, public sphere, regulation, tabloidization.

Moral panic has undergone considerable transformations in usage since Stan Cohen's definitive book, *Folk Devils and Moral Panics*, was first published in 1972. His much-quoted initial definition stands up well:

> Societies appear to be subject, every now and then, to periods of moral panic. A condition, episode, person or group of persons emerges to become defined as a threat to societal values and interests; its nature is presented in a stylized and stereotypical fashion by the mass media; the moral barricades are manned by editors, bishops, politicians and other right-thinking people; socially accredited experts pronounce their diagnoses and solutions;

ways of coping are evolved or (more often) resorted to; the condition then disappears, submerges or deteriorates and becomes more visible. ... Sometimes the panic passes over and is forgotten, except in folklore and collective memory; at other times it has more serious and long-lasting repercussions and might produce such changes as those in legal and social policy or even in the way the society conceives itself. (Cohen, 1980: 9)

Several key points emerge from this initial definition:

- Moral panics are *societal overreactions* to 'labelled deviance' that leads to an increase in the 'tightening' of rule-like societal norms. In plainer language, they resemble 'law and order' campaigns.
- Overreaction refers to the *disproportionate response* to a 'real' or imagined threat to 'social order' – typically by overreporting, increased policing, new legislation.
- The deviant 'folk devil' can range from actual 'criminals' to innocent bystanders who happen to be 'different'. It may have been clearer if Cohen had called these figures 'folk witches' – as in 'witch hunt'.
- Cohen's own analysis is not 'mediacentric' (Schlesinger, 1990). Rather, he holds that the social roots of moral panics develop *prior* to their mediated representation. This last point is well demonstrated in his own initial case study, now known as 'the classic moral panic'.

Figure 7 usefully maps Cohen's circuit or 'amplification spiral'. It is a good visual representation of Cohen's central ideas of a moral panic as a kind of feedback loop, *once underway*. Like much subsequent use of Cohen in media studies, however, it

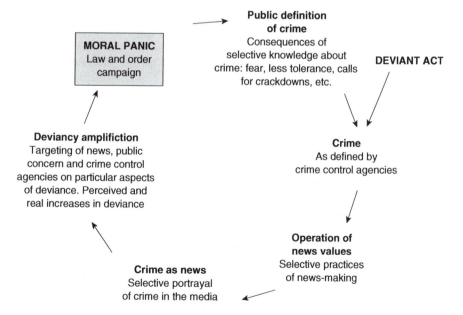

Figure 7   Circuit of a moral panic, emphasizing crime (reproduced from Taylor et al., 1995)

155

renders the commencement of the process in a somewhat more 'mediacentric' manner than he does. In fact, what Taylor et al. (1995) simply shift 'offscreen' as the 'deviant act' is the key to the whole process.

'THE CLASSIC MORAL PANIC': THE CONSTRUCTION OF THE MODS AND ROCKERS

The mid-1960s British panic about the mods and rockers was not the *first* moral panic. Rather, it was the instance Cohen chose as his case study and Thompson (1998) christened the *classic* moral panic. Nor were the mods and rockers the first youth subcultures in Britain or other advanced capitalist societies. By the 1960s, however, a powerful conjunction of circumstances that fulfilled Cohen's definition above had developed in Britain, or at least in London and the south coast seaside holiday/retirement towns that were the main scenes of clashes between the mods and rockers.

It is important to note the disjunction in Cohen's analysis between 'real events' and the process of social overreaction, in which the media feature heavily but not exclusively. The predominantly male mods and rockers really did develop as distinct working-class youth subcultures. Like their predecessors, such as the teddy boys, they chose not to dress in the traditional working-class male 'cloth cap' workers' style of their parents' and grandparents' generations. The mods did develop their own style. There were clashes between the two groups.

Crucially, for Cohen, however, the subcultural participants were *constructed* as 'folk devils' – a threat to society completely out of proportion to the actual social disruption they caused. So, the key labels applied to the youths that signified their folk devil status were terms such as 'hooligan' and 'sawdust Caesars'. These terms were picked up and/or elaborated by national news media and cited by magistrates in their judgements, which were often harsher than usual. These judgements, in turn, provided further elaborations on the perceived societal threat posed by the youths. At the extreme end of this process, special parliamentary legislation was passed and the army placed on alert.

Cohen's research featured fieldwork interviews with key participants in the societal reaction. Central to these was 'Geoffrey Blake', Cohen's renamed hotelier in one of the coastal towns, who has much in common with Basil Fawlty, the now legendary British television character later created by John Cleese.

Blake agitated locally against the mods and rockers. He tried to have their actions curtailed by increased policing and related regulation. He also sought media publicity for his cause. He was thus a key link between what Cohen calls the 'initial misperception' phase of a moral panic and the escalating amplification of the stereotypical portrayal of the folk devil. While Cohen stresses a Blake cannot be found in every moral panic, his self-righteous advocacy is very typical of what Howard Becker (1963), one of Cohen's major influences, calls a *moral entrepreneur*.

Cohen assessed the role of the media primarily via a qualitative and quantitative content analysis of newspaper coverage. Part of his case for the societal overreaction turned on a statistical demonstration of the overreporting of the clashes and related events. His qualitative analysis of thematics within the news coverage also drew on long-standing terms of criticism – such as stereotyping – of a tendency we would now characterize as **tabloidization**. These elements constituted Cohen's 'media inventory'.

Finally, Cohen warned his readers that moral panics are exceptional and not all such reportage induces a societal overreaction.

STUART HALL AND THE CCCS: MORAL PANIC AS CRISES OF HEGEMONY

The concept of moral panic played a key role in the emergent British sociology of news and early cultural studies work at the Birmingham Centre for Contemporary Cultural Studies (CCCS) in the 1970s under the direction of Stuart Hall.

The CCCS rapidly established research programmes on both youth subcultures and the media that drew on Cohen's work as well as Cohen's US antecedents within 'Chicago School' sociology (see **culture**). These were combined with the CCCS's interests in semiotics, Louis Althusser's conception of **ideology** and Antonio Gramsci's conception of **hegemony**. Detailed case studies of the British youth subcultures were undertaken.

Most importantly, the increasingly significant theme that emerged from these studies was the phenomenon of racism as a recurrent source of 'folk devilling'. Perhaps more importantly, where Cohen's book was a retrospective assessment of events almost a decade old, the CCCS work – rapidly produced initially as 'stencilled papers' – had a sense of contemporary urgency. These efforts culminated in the second most influential text in studies of moral panics, *Policing the Crisis: Mugging, the State and law 'n' order* (Hall et al., 1978; unsourced references below are also from this source).

Hall pinpointed 'mugger' as the folk-devilling label. It had been introduced shortly beforehand into British usage, and in news reports it was increasingly associated with youths of Afro-Caribbean descent. It became a coded means of signifying 'black crime against whites'. It is important to remember here that the folk devil may even have committed a violent crime, but forms of societal reaction, such as harsh sentencing, can still be disproportionate and, thus, evidence of a moral panic. This was the case with the Birmingham mugging that Hall took as the triggering 'deviant action' in the mugging panic.

Hall also made key changes to moral panic analysis and incorporated the concept into his analysis of **hegemony,** broadly using it to replace the role of 'societal control culture' in Cohen's analysis and, similarly, replacing Cohen's qualitative content analysis with a semiotic analysis. Table 15 summarizes the conceptual transformations Hall and his colleagues made to the moral panic model. Hall shifted the focus from Cohen's emphasis on the discrete character of moral panics to their *systemic* place within a nonetheless contingent crisis of British hegemony in the 1970s and 1980s. Race was 'the signifier of the crisis' and the development of an authoritarian consensus was the societal response.

Perhaps the key transformation was Hall's usage of Gramsci's understanding of the role of *common sense* within hegemony (see **articulation**). Common sense, for both Gramsci and Hall, coincides with the term's everyday use: an obvious taken-for-granted set of assumptions understood as practical knowledge one needs to operate effectively in everyday life. For Hall, its English variant has close links with the role of empiricism in English ruling class ideology. Common sense is, however, most closely identified with working-class belief systems, such as the 'traditionalist worldview' subscribed to by much of the 'respectable' working class and documented by Richard Hoggart in his 1957 *The Uses of Literacy* (1976) (and partly based on his reminiscences of earlier decades).

Historically, from the late nineteenth century, this 'sedimented' common sense took a settled form as the British working class established its own corporate class culture and consciousness following its successful securing of male suffrage and a more secure place within British industrial capitalism. Crucially, then, common sense is not merely traditionalist but also a site of critical resources.

Consistent with the CCCS's extensive work on subcultures and race, Hall followed Cohen in tracking the *social anxiety* within this challenged common sense

Table 15 Conceptual transformations of Cohen's moral panic model by Stuart Hall et al. (1978, as developed in Jones, 1997)

Folk Devils and Moral Panics	Policing the Crisis, Parts 2–4
Labelling	Signification
Amplification	Signification spiral
Disproportionality of societal reaction (understood largely statistically)	Disproportionality of societal reaction (understood as ideological misrepresentation)
Societal control culture	State (formed from dominant bloc) exercising hegemony
Discrete 'moral panics'	Convergence of multiple panics into 'general panic', crisis of authority/ hegemony
'Moral consensus'	(Gramscian) consent (contingently, an authoritarian consensus)
Public opinion	Ideological articulation of common sense (later understood as Hoggart's 'traditionalist worldview')

that was the fertile ground for moral entrepreneurship or, as Hall would later put it, **populist** ideological interpellation. Hall sourced these anxieties – and, indeed, 'the subcultural solution' – to post Second World War developments, such as 'affluence', and subsequent restructuring of the economy that impacted heavily on this corporate working-class culture, its neighbourhood forms *and* its common sense (Hall et al., 1978: 150–65).

RECENT WORK AND FURTHER READING

Hall and Gramsci's mutual interest in common sense points to its structural role in other societies. The broader claim Hall made was that Gramsci's terrain of the national popular – and so of common sense and moral panics – was a key site of **populist** contestation in struggles between 'the people' and 'the power bloc' in all comparable nations. This intellectual perspective waned as neoliberalism consolidated in the 1980s, but has risen again in the wake of challenges to working-class communities' survival by economic globalization and related moral panics folk-devilling migrants, diasporic communities and asylum seekers. The Australian tradition here is quite strong, culminating in the collection *Outrageous!* (Poynting and Morgan, 2007). In his introductions to the second and third editions of *Folk Devils and Moral Panics*, Cohen tracks later panics and also provides his own commentary on others' use of the concept. In the third edition (Cohen, 2002), he identified asylum seekers as the latest folk devils. Perhaps because so much of the earlier empirical research focused on Anglo-working-class cultures and racism, research interest in moral panics remained focused on the UK and Australia.

Almost simultaneously with the initial publication of *Folk Devils*, the favourite band of the 1960s mods, The Who, produced a rock opera, *Quadrophenia*, based on the mods and rockers clashes. They also financed a well-regarded film of the same name in which many of the original participants in the beachside events happily re-enacted their battles (see www.quadrophenia.net). The key (republished) CCCS texts from the 1970s on subcultures are Stuart Hall and Tony Jefferson (1976) and Dick Hebdige (1979). Hall and Jefferson includes the short but very useful 'Some notes on the relationship between the societal control culture and the news media'. Hall (1974b) also produced a rare Open University TV programme based on analysis of media coverage of the Birmingham Handsworth mugging; it stands up surprisingly well today. There is a parallel, but more 'mediacentric' US project, laid down in Barry Glassner (2000). Its thesis about overreporting of crime strongly informed the Michael Moore film, *Bowling for Columbine* (2002). The first large-scale emulation of *Policing the Crisis* in the USA, by Steve Macek (2006), interestingly extends the case to TV drama and cinema. Chas Critcher, one of the *Policing the Crisis* team, has produced an excellent textbook introduction and related set of readings (2003, 2006). Thompson's earlier textbook (1998) remains very useful.

Network (society)

> **Related concepts**: *broadcasting, capitalism, communication(s), cyberculture, digital, information society, technoculture, time–space compression.*

Unlike its immediate forebear, the **'information society'**, the concept of the 'network society' refers less to a principle of organization than to a condition of self-organization. Whereas information can be controlled by elites for the purposes of defining bounded entities, such as states, corporations or society itself, networks are non-linear complexes of structures and flows.

Information typically plays a central role in the reproduction and regulation of complex systems, 'the knowledge economy', 'the post-industrial society', but such systems are usually confined to the boundaries of the nation state or the closed systems of supranational actors, such as transnational corporations. Networks, however, do not have any boundaries and their structure is made ambiguous by the multiplicity of points to which, and from which, information circulates.

A network, be it technical or social, has a different architecture from hierarchical forms of assembly. The networked assembly is decentred and distributed. Networks can be interpersonal, as in the practice of 'networking' to accumulate social contacts, or technologically extended when they are mediated by an apparatus of communication, such as the Internet, which makes 'online social networking' possible.

TECHNOLOGICALLY EXTENDED NETWORKS

The Internet itself is a distributed form of communication of connected routers and servers that, in turn, serve individual users. The function of the routers is completely separate from the content sent and received from each interconnected point. The routers form the architecture of distribution and do not in any way alter such content and are not 'gatekeepers' of the message.

Distributed networks (see Figure 8) are different from decentralized networks in that, in the former, the packets of information sent along them are 'held' across the network itself and never reside at one point. This principle of information distribution was created by Paul Baran (1964) on behalf of the Rand Corporation as a way of guarding the USA against nuclear attack. If data is always 'on the move' and never centralized, it makes it very difficult for an adversary to destroy command, control and communication systems. In other words, the entire network would need to be attacked for the system to break down, as one of the jobs of routers is to reroute information to wherever it is assured of integrity, as malfunctioning routers are ignored.

Alexander Galloway has argued, however, that, while distributed, decentralized apparatuses of communication tend to view information as 'anarchic', in fact, it is 'highly controlled' (Galloway, 2004: 8). Such control is to be found in the

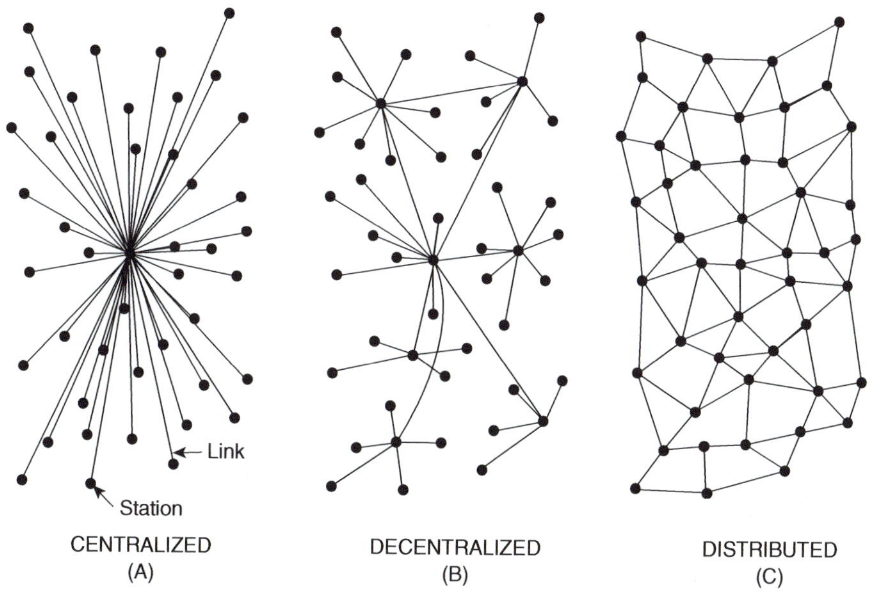

Figure 8   Centralized, decentralized and distributed networks (reproduced from Baran, 1964)

'protocological' nature of neworks, which develop their own self-reproducing systems of regulation, that do not allow for a 'single central point' of control (Galloway, 2004: 11). According to Galloway (2004: 42): 'The ultimate goal of the Internet protocols is totality. The virtues of the Internet are robustness, contingency, interoperability, flexibility, heterogeneity, pantheism.' These characteristics make it difficult to undermine protocological systems, even in the face of partial systems failure.

Thus, while the Internet is distributed rather than simply decentralized, it is nevertheless governed by 'inbuilt' protocols that give it a collective robustness and it does not rely on a central point of production and transmission, as centralized, or even decentralized, networks do.

A decentralized network is typically comprised of a collection of remote hubs, which are themselves points of centralized 'transmission'. For example, a 'network' of syndicated television broadcasters (a 'television network') could be said to be 'decentralized', in that there are several hubs of transmission (albeit of the same content) that pertain to defined audiences, typically separated in time and space. Moreover, a decentralized network does not give each user autonomy over the transmission and reception of messages; that is determined by the television broadcaster.

The Internet, however, is a network of networks that allows users (particularly with the aid of Web 2.0) to be their own gatekeepers in a variety of ways.

THE NETWORK SOCIETY

A social condition anticipated by the 'information society' thesis, the 'network society' is not simply a communications architecture but has also been elevated to the reorganization of political, social and economic life on a planetary scale (Castells, 2000a; Van Dijk, 1999b). It shares the historicism of the information society thesis, but information is no longer limited to the content of social exchange. Rather, the network society arises when information technologies become embedded at all levels of social reproduction, as environments rather than tools. Such an environment, characterized by 'spaces of flow' rather than spaces of place, is seen to challenge age-old hierarchies of states and capitalist organization by enabling alternatives to corporate and political power.

According to Castells, networks have actually existed for thousands of years of human history, determined largely by transportation technologies, wind-powered vessels, message runners, horseback, steam-powered ships and trains. The capacity of technological infrastructures to facilitate the rise of a network society has been historically subordinated 'to the logic of vertical organizations, whose power was inscribed in the institutions of society and distributed in one-directional flows of information and resources' (Castells, 2004a: 4).

Castells (2004a: 5) argues that a 'network society' was not possible until certain 'material limits' to networked social organization could be overcome. These limits are linked to available technology, but also the scale of social organization that they make possible. That is, 'beyond a certain threshold of size, complexity, and volume of exchange, (networks) become less efficient than vertically organized command and control structures, *under the conditions of pre-electronic communication technology*' (Castells, 2004a: 5).

With pre-electronic networks, 'the time lag for the feedback loop in the communication process' privileges a one-way flow of information and command, co-opting the power of a given network to centralized vertical forms of organization (Castells, 2009: 22, 24):

> It was because of available electronic information and communication technologies [made possible by the micro-electronics revolution] that the network society could deploy itself fully, transcending the historical limits of networks as forms of social organization and interaction.

The infrastructure provided by microelectronics allows the inherent social benefits endemic to all networks to be historically realized. These features are 'flexibility, scalability and survivability' (Castells, 2004a: 5). In their electronic form, such as the Internet, it is easy to see how networks can flexibly circle around communications blockages. They can also grow and contract in a self-regulatory fashion, without political command, and are immune from attack because they have no centre.

INFORMATIONALISM

The content of the network society is information rather than 'energy', which is what characterized industrial society. What is new about the 'network society' is the way information has become embedded in microelectronics-based technologies, which Castells (2004a: 8) calls 'informationalism' or the 'information mode of development': 'Informationalism is the technological paradigm that constitutes the material basis of early twenty-first-century societies.'

Castells claims, however, that his approach differs from the conceptual framework defining our societies as 'information or knowledge societies'. That is because, he (2004a: 6) argues, 'all known societies are based on information and knowledge as their source of power, wealth and meaning'. Here he wants to clear up any confusion arising from the fact that he 'gave in to the fashion of the times in my labels by characterizing our historical period as the "information age"' (see **information society**).

Informationalism refers to the augmentation of human capability for information processing and communication; it is a paradigm shift from what is afforded by printing, the telegraph and the analogue telephone. The **digital** nature of the microelectronics revolution creates a communicative sphere of self-proliferating networks of unprecedented volume, complexity and speed. Moreover, such technologies hold emergent qualities related to endless possibilities for reconfiguration, convergence and recombination – what Van Dijk (1999a: 9) has called the 'integration of transmission in communications'. This entails the **convergence** of telecommunications, data communications and mass communications into one medium, to the point where the separate identity of such media will one day disappear.

GLOBAL SPACES OF FLOW

The networking of previously separate electronic media invariably led to the establishment of an information-driven, post-industrial global economy. Competition within such an economy is not driven, by labour control as it is by using networked information to gain an advantage, be this in financial markets, research and development, commodity trading, the mobility of multinational corporations or the latter's internal communications.

The culture of such a form of globalization is defined not by place but by flows – of people, ideas, commodities and information. It is not unlike Paul Baran's (1964) notion of information never residing in one place in a network; the space of flow subordinates place to that of nodes. Even large cities become nodes that service the needs of the informational economy.

In the networked society, then, information does not exist to service cities but, rather, cities are relay points for information networks. In turn, spaces of flow 'disembod[y] social relationships, introducing the culture of real virtuality' (Castells, 2010: 386).

CRITIQUE

An opening criticism that can be levelled at Castells' account of the network society is its inability to distinguish itself from the 'information society' thesis. Castells' account of the term 'network' is not all that different from Daniel Bell's portrayal of 'information'. Both are tied to a post-industrial condition and both place central importance on the role of information in the new economy. The only real departure is Castells' emphasis on digital technology and the homeostatic nature of networks.

A related problem that Castells shares with Bell is **technological determinism**. While Castells claims to have a dialectical view of the interaction between technology and society, Van Dijk points out that he does have an *instrumental* view of technology producing an autonomous development which can be used and supported, or not. Van Dijk (1999b: 136) cites Castell's use of Melvin Kranzberg's first law on the relationship between technology and society: 'Technology is neither good, nor bad, nor is it neutral. It is a force.'

This force is the 'information mode of development' discussed earlier, one that Castells sees as having a transhistorical role in all modes of development. The 'information mode of development' is distinguished from the 'capitalist mode of production'. According to Frank Webster (1995: 195), the mode of development, which determines the 'level of production', replaces what Marx described as the 'forces of production' (see **capitalism**). Whereas for Marx, the forces of production stand in a dialectical relation to the social relations of production, for Castells (1989: 11) 'modes of development evolve according to their own logic'. Webster (1995: 195) comments: 'This may seem to be rather strange talk for a Marxist ... since what is being suggested is that social change may in fact be determined – to an unspecified degree – by technical advances in production'.

Castells' assertion that the informational mode of development is autonomous from capitalism leads to a monocausal account of social reproduction. Moreover, the decentred nature of the network that drives informationalization makes it easy to characterize the network as an 'out-of-control' category of social determination. As Van Dijk (1999b: 136) reports, in an interview with a Dutch newspaper, Castells expressed the view that with networks 'we have created a machine which is dynamic, full of opportunities but is controlled by no one'. This echoes a trope often found in the genre of science fiction, of a systemic networked machine that acquires not simply a logic but also a life of its own, where human beings finally lose control over their own self-organization – a theme that also appears in the young Marx – that of alienation.

FURTHER READING

Castells' oft-cited trilogy (first published 1996 (2000a), 1997 (2004b), 1998 (2000b)) on the network society, *The Information Age: Economy, society and culture*, is based on 15 years of research conducted in the USA, Asia, Latin America and Europe. These volumes cover the impact of information technology on the global economy, the flexible nature of work, social movements, identity politics and the increasingly globally constituted processes of social change. A summary of Castells' main argument can be found in his 2004 essay. A critique of Castells' trilogy can be found in Van Dijk (1999b) and Nicholas Garnham (2004). Castells has extended this work (Castells et al., 2007) to encompass mobile communication (which some had argued was underrepresented in his trilogy) and his *Communication Power* (2009) has a fuller engagement with media and communications studies literatures.

News values

> **Related concepts**: *capitalism, freedom of communication, ideology, modern, public sphere, regulation, tabloidization.*

The relationship between 'news' and 'values' is perhaps one of the most confusing relationships of all for the media and communications studies initiates. As with comparable terms, the ambiguities are largely a result of social contestation over meanings – much is at stake, within and beyond the academy, in claiming that yours is the 'definitive' account of the responsibilities and practices of news producers.

We have chosen 'news values' as our point of entry to this cluster of issues because it operates very much like one of Raymond Williams' keywords – that is, its meaning is 'shared' between an academic sense, developed among researchers of news, and an ordinary language sense, developed among news producers themselves. This topic also opens up wider issues in the field, which this entry maps. The 'values' in 'news values' can refer to two quite distinct issues: newsworthiness and 'editorial values'.

NEWS VALUES AS NEWSWORTHINESS

The core definition of news values according to 'newsworthiness' is thus: the criteria by which news stories are selected *as* being newsworthy and prioritized within a news publication. 'Value' in this dominant sense refers to the degree of newsworthiness or, more bluntly, what the story is 'worth' *as news* compared to its potential rivals. For a 'jobbing' journalist perhaps more than a communications degree-bearing professional, this inevitable process of selection and prioritization was traditionally referred to as an 'instinct' or 'sixth sense'.

From the academic researchers' perspective, it was precisely such unreflective presumptions as 'sixth sense' – even 'common sense' – that were the most interesting sociologically. So, lists of explicit 'de facto' criteria began to be developed.

The most cited of these is by Johan Galtung and Mari Holmboe Ruge (1970). These were 'hypotheses' derived mainly from cybernetic theory and 'common sense perception psychology' and tested in a quantitative content analysis of inter-national news agency stories. Most are self-descriptive:

i **frequency** – compatibility with the news medium's publication time frame
ii **threshold** – the scale of a story's scope, such as the numbers of people directly and indirectly affected by a disaster
iii **unambiguity**
iv **meaningfulness** – cultural proximity (including a 'necessary' ethnocentrism) and relevance
v **consonance** – compatibility with journalists' expectations of certain types of event
vi **unexpectedness**
vii **continuity**
viii **composition**
ix **reference to élite nations**
x **reference to élite people**
xi **personalization** – the tendency to attribute 'causes' of *all* events to single individuals rather than social circumstance, which is *not* reducible to 'celeb-rity news' or 'human interest stories'
xii **negativity** – 'bad news' is more newsworthy than 'good news'.

This list, and amended variants, have been reproduced endlessly (Allan, 1999; Hartley, 1982), but often not in Galtung and Ruge's original order, as above.

They all usefully point to the socially constructed character of who and what is newsworthy. Galtung and Ruge's concern was not merely to tease out into a kind of transparency such unstated prioritizations so that they might be consciously 'taught', for example (although they later were). Only two ('continuity' and 'com-position') relate directly to the 'craft' of story composition, what might now be called 'news narrative' devices (Schudson, 2004). For the others, a pattern of unequal power relations is implicit.

Galtung and Ruge's article was originally published in *The Journal of International Peace Research*. Its main **critical** purpose was to highlight the means by which news stories from outside the advanced capitalist societies of 'the Northwest' were *depri-oritized*. They considered their first 8 news value as *not* culture-bound and, thus, likely to occur within news produced in most cultures. Their last 4 news values, however, were thought to be highly culture-bound to 'the Northwestern' perspective and accounted for much of the deprioritization of stories outside that 'first world'.

All news values were nonetheless often regarded academically as **ideological**. Such recognition intermeshed strongly with emerging debates about cultural imperialism (see **capitalism**) and rising concerns about sexist/gendered and racist news values. The sense of ideology at stake here is fairly straightforwardly a legiti-mating/masking one (see **ideology**), but it proved problematic. News values were now thought (by academic researchers) to be socially constructed rather than 'natural', contra to what their 'instinctive' journalistic recognition had suggested. To take one famous formulation, the 'masking' derived from news media's being seen to be *agenda-setting* (McCombs and Shaw, 1972). This term implied that their influence was not direct in requiring 'what citizens think' but, rather, set an agenda for 'what citizens think about'. It functions in a kind of parallel with the two-step flow thesis about patterns of **influence** on and within audiences. As some issues were selected as newsworthy, others were, in effect, concealed, in that they dropped off the metaphorical public agenda.

Accounting for the role of journalistic practitioners in this process, however, was more vexing. First, as salaried journalists, these practitioners of this set of ideological assumptions were *not* members of any conventional 'ruling' social group (as a vulgar Marxist account would have required). Second, their professional wing at least insisted that their entire raison d'être – often drawn from **freedom of communication** principles – was, instead, to hold powerful social groups to account.

The role of journalists in this apparently contradictory process thus raised questions that sent researchers further into questions of social and cultural theory for conceptual solutions, as well as to more careful empirical engagement with journalistic practices (Allan, 1999: 48–82). It would be fair to say that this process remains ongoing. One outcome, however, is that Galtung and Ruge's basic thesis of core news values – developed from a content analysis – has tended to be broadly confirmed by surveys of and interviews with journalists.

Discussions of news values came to be addressed within a larger set of 'organizational constraints' – that is, day-to-day realities of the journalistic labour process as required by employing organizations and the news 'market' (McNair, 1998: 61–81). In principle, this would separate unreflective practices such as newsworthiness evaluation from *declared professional journalistic ethics* (see below), but this ideal-type distinction is not quite so straightforward, especially in recent times.

EDITORIAL VALUES: THE PROBLEM OF 'BIAS' AND OBJECTIVITY

Significantly, sociological accounts of news production's implication in networks of power tended not to use the term most non-specialists first resort to in complaints about journalism: *bias*. Journalists certainly bridle at such a suggestion for both the ordinary language and professional use of 'bias' suggests conscious manipulation and distortion. Indeed, Gans' (1979) classic study of news selection at the major US TV networks found 'conscious bias' was those journalists' very definition of ideology. Even early social research on journalism suggested something more complex, such as, at the very least, an unconscious or 'structured' bias (Epstein, 1981).

Similarly, while the core *editorial value* of 'objectivity' is posited by journalists as the opposite of bias, non-journalists might regard it as an impossible claim that only invites cynical dismissal. The rise of critical scepticism towards any kind of emulation of natural scientific claims to 'truth' within the social sciences and humanities (in the wake of **postmodernism** and other recent intellectual movements) only added to suspicion of this journalistic ideal, not least among higher education students.

If we think of objectivity, however, as a professional 'strategic ritual' (Tuchman, 1972) or as a set of practices and texts composed according to the conventions of specified **cultural forms**, much of this scepticism can be situated as a form of misrecognition. This misrecogniton arises in part from conflicting meanings attached by journalists and non-journalists to powerful signifiers such as 'truth'. Journalists'

167

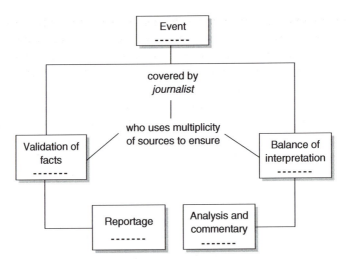

Figure 9 'Objective journalism' (reproduced from McNair, 1998: 68)

professional claim to 'truthful' objectivity and avoidance of bias is actually quite modest. As McNair's (1998: 68) diagram in Figure 9 suggests, it primarily relates to conventions for sourcing stories.

While both newsworthiness values and 'editorial values' are 'ritualized' within professional journalistic practice, *only* editorial values are routinely published. These can take the form of codes of ethics of professional associations, usually for purposes of professional self-regulation. In turn, however, they can become the basis of newspaper publisher-organized complaints systems, often called press councils, and, more rarely, formal content-based media **regulations** (especially in the case of broadcasting). Most public service broadcasters (PSBs) routinely publish their editorial guidelines.

If we follow the left side of McNair's diagram, we can see that the 'objective truth' being claimed in such professional ethics is little more than a system of reliable – but by no means infallible – verification/validation. It has much in common with the academic practice of authoritative sourcing via citation and referencing systems required in most student essay-writing and academic publication. Hence, plagiarism is an ethical concern in both fields. Where academic authoritative sources are usually located in texts, however, journalistic ones are usually people 'in the field' of reporting and are obtained via interviews, press/media conferences and 'soundbites'.

Both sets of conventions rest on a distinction that resembles the one Jürgen Habermas (1991) makes between 'mere opinion' and 'informed opinion' in his public sphere thesis. Mere opinion is relatively unreflective and might include, for example, accusations about someone based on no more than simple prejudice or rumour. By contrast, informed opinion is a product of some actual or, in the case of journalism, textually juxtaposed, interaction between differing opinions, including the accused's entitlement to provide a 'balancing' response to such accusations.

Facts, in this sense, are assertions/opinions that have survived this process of verification/validation/balance. Journalistic texts – news stories – that adhere to these editorial values are organized according to textual conventions that display these sources. Accordingly, informed opinions adopted by readerships are those based on facts and informed commentary. This process does not make these 'facts' irrefutable – they are, in turn, subject to processes of correction. For this reason, another core editorial value is the textual separation of verified facts from opinion and commentary (as per the right side of McNair's diagram). Newspapers routinely use section headings to delineate these distinctions. Post-print news media demonstrate this distinction less plainly, however. Most notably, online newspapers in HTML format tend to obscure these distinctions. Table 16 lays out some of the classic distinctions used in print and broadcast news and current affairs.

This is, of course, an account of the ideal. It is important for analysts of journalism to be clear about this ideal typology, however, in order to acknowledge the rationale behind journalists' impatient rejection of charges of 'bias'. Similarly, while we could add 'citizen journalism' and blogging to a prospective third 'new media' column, the issue of their professional self-regulation would immediately arise (see **freedom of communication**).

That said, the vulnerability of this validation process to overt and covert abuse – understood by journalists as unethical conduct – is considerable. Over the last decade, there has been a spate of cases in major US news organizations, such as *The New Republic* and *The New York Times*, where journalists abused the mutual trust – with both their colleagues and publics – that ensures each journalist validates facts and does not 'make up' sources. As a result, these news organizations have introduced increasingly formalized audit-like 'fact-checking' procedures in which stories' sources are randomly double-checked and so 'revalidated'.

Table 16   Transformation of cultural formal conventions in editorial values (Jones, 2000b)

	Editorial value	Print – cultural forms	Broadcast – cultural forms
News	'Objective' news reporting	News pages	News bulletins
	In-depth reporting	Investigative features	Investigative current affairs
Opinion	Diversity of opinion	Op-ed pages consisting of: • editorial (AKA leader) • letters to editor • 'expert' opinion pieces and 'opinionated' columnists	Broadcast current affairs: • 'balanced' debates • interviews and discussion (NB: In most regulated broadcast systems and PSBs, overt 'editorializing' in broadcast media is restricted; this has changed dramatically since multichannelling and deregulation)

Journalistic professional routines are similarly vulnerable to increasing pressure from public relations practitioners available 'for hire' or employed within organizations, most notably today in governmental agencies. Often themselves ex-journalists, public relations practitioners' tasks can include providing press releases of ready-made 'stories' stylistically suited to publication (or 'cutting and pasting'). Unchecked use of these stories' contestable claims by journalists also constitutes a violation of the professional validation process. An Australian study of leading political journalists (Ester, 2007) found that they regarded this rising 'PR state' as the most serious threat to their professional autonomy.

'PRIMARY DEFINERS' AND THE JOURNALISTIC 'CONSENSUS'

In a highly influential critique of the validation process itself, Stuart Hall (1974b) argued that journalists' reliance on authoritative sources – combined with the temporal pressures of news routines – created a 'pyramid of access' to (print and broadcast) newsmedia.

Hall's central point – based largely on semiotically informed content analyses of newspapers – was that not all those consulted in the process of report validation were regarded as holding equal validatory authority. Most notably in crime reporting, and especially in times of crisis, figures such as police chiefs were permitted initial access to the definition of a 'crime wave'.

Hall's argument was not limited to the resulting agenda-setting implications of such inequality but, rather, proposed that the public **signification** of an issue was ideologically situated. Accordingly, he called such overaccessed authoritative sources *primary definers*, to underscore their centrality to the professional **encoding** of news. Significantly, Hall (1974b) explicitly positioned this critique of news production against conspiratorial charges of 'bias' and simpler accounts of the ideological role of news. It was precisely the most professional of editorial values, he argued (Hall et al., 1978: 58–9), that meant news media tended to reproduce the definitions of the powerful and keep dissenting sources to the margins. Hall (1974b) also had in mind the fact that such procedures were required to be practised in all UK broadcasting as a key component of its **regulation**.

Hall's argument was subjected to numerous critiques (most notably Schlesinger, 1990), which rightly pointed to the relative contingency of the source–journalist relation – that is, some 'non-primary' sources might well become more powerful over time or in differing areas of reporting, such as the 'primary defining' role of Greenpeace in many environmental news stories today. Indeed, as Hall's thesis was a subordinate component of a larger argument about racism, crime, **moral panics**, **ideology**, **hegemony** and authoritarian **populism**, his evidence for an enduring role for his primary definers was necessarily slim. To be fair, however, his conception of hegemony required that such relations should be 'unstable equilibria' and subject to the rise of contesting social movement organizations, such as Greenpeace today. Likewise, his broader Vološinovian/Gramscian theoretical claim that the signification of reported news is part of a contested field of social hegemony has survived in critical **discourse** theory.

Thus, despite its empirical limits, Hall's thesis could also be read to suggest that Galtung and Ruge's final four 'culture-bound' news values might 'contaminate' editorial values not only in 'foreign news' but also in 'domestic' news. The result, Hall argued, was a set of 'consensus values' with which journalists 'mapped' social issues. Around the same time, Herbert Gans (1979) concluded that US journalists shared a similar set of 'Progressive era' (a period in US politics) values, such as ethnocentrism, responsible capitalism, small-town pastoralism, individualism and moderation.

UNIVERSAL OR WESTERN NEWS/EDITORIAL VALUES?

In a major comparative study of European nations and the USA, Daniel C. Hallin and Paolo Mancini (2004) remind us that the modern professional *editorial* values of journalism are, in Jean K. Chalaby's (1996) phrase, 'an Anglo-American invention'. Their struggle with notions of facts and truth are part of the Enlightenment dimension of **modernity**. For all the claims to objectivity, much journalism maintains a *normative* orientation towards democratization, usually articulated in terms of **freedom of communication** 'values'. This coupling of an ostensibly objective method and social progress is another characteristic Enlightenment mixture (see **modern**).

Hallin and Mancini's key point, however, is that, like democratic institutions, the newsmedia–democracy relationship is configured differently within different nation states. An equally prominent tradition of *partisan* journalism was historically more common and survives in parts of Europe in the form of newsmedia based in political parties. This partisan tradition, however, is yielding to the Anglo-American model of professional journalism in a globalizing process.

Yet the expansion of the Anglo-American model also entails an increasing tendency towards commercial pressures on both news values and editorial values. Together they are referred to as **tabloidization**. Often in tandem with these pressures has been the development of online platforms for news. They have placed enormous pressures on editorial values in particular. Most of these new platforms rely heavily on (recycled) traditional journalism. Moreover, it is to those same editorial values that we turn in order to assess the reliability of online reporting and amateur/citizen-initiated journalism.

As we saw above, the development of news values 'lists' was a means of highlighting how culturally bounded those traditional selection criteria were. Especially given the Western dominance of international news agencies (such as Reuters), which provided many news organizations' 'foreign' news, many thought that 'a New World Information (and Communication) Order' (NWICO), sponsored by UNESCO, was required to redress that Western focus. That initiative failed because a challenge to Western *news(worthiness)* values was misunderstood (or misrepresented) by its opponents as a challenge to professional *editorial* values. The rise of the Arabic satellite television news service Al Jazeera in the 1990s can be partly explained by the lack of such an alternative to those Western news agencies. At least initially, Al Jazeera claimed to be, precisely, a news organization that practised professional editorial values but upheld very different news(worthiness) values, evident, for example, in the 'infamous' prioritization of graphic footage of war casualties.

FURTHER READING

The literature here is vast and includes a companion volume in the *Sage Key Concepts* series, *Journalism Studies* (Franklin et al., 2005), which provides many vocational perspectives on these issues that are not addressed here. Michael Schudson's (2004, 2008) work provides succinct overviews, aimed mainly at the US reader. He (2008: Chapter 6) has provided an update, for example, of Gans' consensus values of journalists. Although his own views have shifted radically since, John Hartley's *Understanding News* (1982) remains one of the best exegeses of the informing assumptions of the critique of news(worthiness) values and, especially, of Hall's work. See also Rodney Tiffen (1989) for a distinctive analysis of news values. James Curran (1991, 2000, 2005) provides the best linkage between editorial values and the public sphere literature. In a global context, on NWICO and news agencies as well as overviews of world journalism, see Arnold S. de Beer and John C. Merrill (2009), as well as Angela R. Romano and Michael S. Bromley (2005) and, on Al Jazeera, see Mohamed Zayani (2005). Barbie Zelizer (2004) is a highly insightful series of discussions of the relationship between journalism and different academic disciplines. On online and 'citizen journalism', see Stuart Allan (2006) and Stuart Allan and Einar Thorsen (2009).

USEFUL WEBSITES

The Pew Research Center for the People & the Press: http://people-press.org

The Pew Research Center's Project for Excellence in Journalism: www.journalism.org

BBC editorial guideliness: www.bbc.co.uk/guidelines/editorialguidelines

Ofcom's programme codes: www.ofcom.org.uk/static/archive/itc/itc_publications/codes_guidance/programme_code/index.asp.html

Popular/populist

> *Related concepts*: audience, cultural form, culture industry, deconstruction, encoding/decoding, hegemony, ideology, moral panic, popular.

Variants of 'popular', such as 'popular media' and 'popular culture', remain key categories within media and communications, but they have functioned less as concepts than as terms guiding ordinary language. So, the usage of 'popular' is closer to the original sense of what Raymond Williams called keywords than the contemporary notion of key concepts. Its shifting and contested meanings indicate a field of discussion rather than conceptual precision.

In contrast, populist has developed a more systematic – if also contested – sense within the work of Ernesto Laclau, Stuart Hall and Jim McGuigan. Indeed, to a large extent, the emergence of 'populist' as a concept is closely tied to attempts to overcome ambiguities and tensions in the concept of 'popular'. It can be preliminarily defined as an intellectual or political appeal 'directly' to – or from – 'the people', often in explicit avoidance or rejection of formal democratic institutions or mediated cultural forms, such as journalism. Accordingly, this entry begins with a discussion of the semantic tensions of 'popular'.

POPULAR – BELONGING TO THE PEOPLE?

As a keyword, 'popular' has a long history of association with 'political', going back to its Latin root meaning of 'belonging to the people', which carried over into English usage (Williams, 1983b: 236–7). This, however, was shadowed by a derogatory sense of 'low' and 'base' and, later, 'of inferior quality'. Yet, by the late eighteenth century, the dominant meaning had shifted to 'widely favoured' and 'well-liked'. Thus, there is a primary tension of perspective – 'top-down' versus 'bottom-up' – that, by the nineteenth century, was increasingly crisscrossed by the protodemocratic associations of 'belonging to the people'.

The pivotal derogatory sense of popular – which leads us towards populist – is 'deliberately setting out to win favour' (Williams, 1983b: 239), implying that something is done at the expense of nobler or more ethically driven purposes. Significantly, it can be applied to the two main fields relevant to media: popular politics and popular culture. It can also be applied from varying political perspectives.

A key historical example here is the emergence of tabloid journalism – today consolidated as a general trend known as **tabloidization** – as it is within this cultural form that the political and aesthetico-cultural aspects of 'popular' come most obviously into conflict. Moreover, to a considerable extent, this cultural form triggers many of the twentieth-century intellectual concerns about 'popular culture'. In the British case, tabloid journalism was a concern even in the Leavisite prehistory of cultural studies (Thompson, 1939, for example). The early Raymond Williams and Richard Hoggart, similarly, tended to agree that tabloid journalism was 'deliberately setting out to win favour' – that is, its linguistic mode of address was a kind of bad faith parody of the everyday argot of the popular classes. Williams later characterized this 'demotic style' as an 'idiomatic facsimile' (Heath and Skirrow, 1986: 7–8; see **tabloidization**).

Williams and Hoggart disagreed violently, however, on the more generally posed issue of the relationship between commodified popular culture and the social classes to whom it was addressed. Williams accused Hoggart of equating such popular culture with a putative 'working-class culture' in Hoggart's *The Uses of Literacy* (1976).

For Williams, this equation destroyed the normative potential of 'belonging to the people'. Commercially produced popular culture failed to meet this criterion, Williams (1957) insisted, as it was produced and distributed by the bourgeoisie. He struggled to identify a viable contemporary example of 'class belonging'. Famously, he declared trade unions and the British Labour Party key institutions of working-class culture, but later acknowledged that they had become **hegemonically** incorporated. He certainly did find justification for his criteria in the history of the British popular press (see **tabloidization**).

Williams' position on the related forms of folk culture and folklore shifted in the opposite direction. While he felt that these met his 'belonging' criterion, his initial estimate was that folk cultural forms were residual and offered no prospect of a counterhegemonic alternative culture. Here, his and Hoggart's position shared much with F.R. Leavis' view that an 'authentic' popular culture had once existed, but had been destroyed by industrial capitalism.

Later, Williams acknowledged the more resilient continuity into modernity of everyday folk-cultural forms, such as jokes (Heath and Skirrow, 1986: 5). Significantly, as he did so, he complained about the trend in cultural studies – which took its name from the CCCS Hoggart had founded at Birmingham – 'where there is an unwillingness either to isolate the pre-industrial or pre-literate folk or to make categorical distinctions between different phases of internal and autonomous, sometimes communal, cultural production' (1983b: 137).

Williams' increasing dissatisfaction with Birmingham cultural studies' intellectual absorption with popular cultural consumption fits well into McGuigan's (1992: 75) typology of 'productionist' and 'consumptionist' trajectories taken to reconcile the tensions in popular culture and populism. Williams certainly saw the reorganization of the *means of cultural production* as the primary solution to what he had interpreted to be an historical dislocation in the social relations of cultural production. Accordingly, he regarded the central tasks for redressing this inequity to be the use of **regulation** and policy for democratic institutional design of the means of **communication** and popular education as appropriate means of widening the social base of cultural producers. His typology of forms of artistic/cultural autonomy within what became the **culture industries** – to which he alludes in his complaint above – also points in this direction. Unquestionably, cultural studies moved along a 'consumptionist' trajectory, but this path has remained uneven.

STUART HALL: FROM POPULAR ART TO AUTHORITARIAN POPULISM

Indeed, earlier in his career, Hall had used just those categorical distinctions Williams claimed were lacking in later cultural studies. So, in his 1964 book, co-authored with Paddy Whannel, significantly entitled *The Popular Arts*, Hall argued that twentieth-century means of **communication** enabled the recomposition of the quasi-communal dimensions of folk art as popular art. In a line of argument later used by popular music analysts in relation to major figures such as Bob Dylan and David Bowie, Hall discusses Charlie Chaplin. His filmic performances provide an expert rendering of popular/folk cultural genres, devices and conventions developed in nineteenth-century music hall (vaudeville) and early cinema. Crucially, however, the exploitative dimension of populist address is eschewed in favour of a respect for the audience, as follows (Hall and Whannel, 1964: 65):

> The quality of style suggests not only the way in which the popular artist makes *art* of the welter of experiences but the respect which he (Chaplin) always holds for his art and his audience. It is expressive of popular taste, but does not exploit it. Though this kind of art never reckons its audiences in terms of numbers ... it is an art which thrives only when varied audiences find something common and commonly valued in their appreciation of it; one of the preconditions for this being that the institutions which carry this art should be open institutions widely available – as the music hall was, in comparison with the legitimate theatre today ...

Some 20 years later, Hall's assessment had altered dramatically. The key to this change is his shift from assessing popular culture as a field of aesthetic practices to one primarily constituted in relation to politics and the state.

Following Gramsci's inclusion of the 'national popular' as a domain of contestation for **hegemony**, Hall's analyses of popular culture increasingly focused on its instrumentalization in contestations of power. Famously, he once stated, 'I don't gave a damn' about popular culture, except in its role as a space of contestation between 'the power bloc' and 'the people' (1981: 239). Of the several definitions of popular culture he weighs up in the same article, Hall (1981: 234ff.) opts for one that recognizes the continuing tension between the popular and a dominant ideology/culture, albeit one understood as a process of **articulation**.

This position was some distance from Williams' foregrounding of 'belonging to the people' in his *Keywords* book and other discussions. For Hall, following Valentin Vološinov's conception of ideologies as sites of semiotic contestation, he was at pains to avoid all Marxian formulations that took as given a 'necessary class belonging'. He developed the concept of **articulation** in order to demonstrate that ideological and cultural forms needed to be *articulated with* social blocs. As these relations were never 'given', the process of articulation was a labour of construction.

In a sense, this was Williams' position, too: he did not take 'class belonging' as a given but, rather, a normative goal. Where Williams saw the constructive task as primarily the responsibility of institutions and policy, Hall most often had in mind the *discursive* **articulation** of ideologies in popular beliefs and defined 'common sense' as a means of winning the consent of alternative social blocs.

Thus, *authoritarian populism* was Hall's further elaboration of his Gramscian conception of an authoritarian *consensus*, previously developed within his work on **moral panics**. Hall developed this concept from Nicos Poultanzas' 1978 (2000) work on 'authoritarian statism'.

Both Hall and Poulantzas argued that authoritarian state practices were expanding, notably for Hall in the late 1970s (and earlier), into areas of policing and related criminalizing legislation. In Althusserian terms, Hall filled out the cultural and political 'levels' of Poulantzas' thesis. Where Poulantzas had concentrated on the State, Hall developed Laclau's work on populism to account for consent to that expanded authoritarianism. This work became the template for Hall's (1988) quasi-journalistic writings on 'Thatcherism', particularly his analysis of Thatcherism's apparently popular support.

CULTURAL POPULISM

McGuigan's (1992: 4) definition of cultural populism is quite succinct:

> the intellectual assumption, made by some students of popular culture, that the symbolic experiences and practices of ordinary people are more important analytically and politically than Culture with a captial C.

The key addition here is the highlighting of the role of intellectuals in this 'bottom-up' emphasis.

McGuigan's scepticism about the version of cultural populism that developed in the 1980s owes much to its abandonment of the critical dimensions of the framework of **hegemony** that dominated the CCCS and related work in the 1970s and 1980s for what James Curran (1996a) characterized as 'a new revisionism'. In effect, the intellectual shift was one from concerns with the organization of culture and media production – the traditional foci of political economy and related policy studies – to a relatively uncritical focus on cultural consumption. Moreover, Curran regards such studies of consumption as neglecting the role of the political economy of media and related policy in shaping cultural consumption options.

These matters are quite complex, especially in relation to the role of the rising wave of feminist research on popular culture, primarily within the 'active **audience**' literature. The shift towards studies of gendered popular cultural consumption – especially television 'soaps' – was consistent with more general feminist critiques of Marxian emphases on the priorities set by a Fordist framework of production: a highly masculinized conception of social class and related elements of popular culture that confined women to an 'unproductive' domestic sphere. Women's popular cultural consumption within Fordist relations had thus been doubly excluded from intellectual attention. The 'revaluing' of the relatively neglected dimensions of gendered consumption within Fordism and, later, the forms of gendered popular culture in post-Fordist social relations (from the 1970s onwards) was thus long overdue.

McGuigan argues that revisionism and cultural populism are more persuasive when addressed to those who make *general* claims about the increased significance of popular cultural consumption than those who make specific claims based on cases of marginalization of specific constituencies. The key figure here for McGuigan's 1992 analysis was John Fiske.

Fiske starts out with Hall's primary opposition between 'the power bloc' and 'the people', but then removes most of the protocols that Hall established regarding the contingency of any counterhegemonic success of a popular practice. For

Fiske, evaluative perspectives like Hall's are too pessimistic and they underestimate the folkloric dimensions of popular culture. Where Laclau had initially retheorized hegemonic incorporation as contingent articulation, Fiske (1989: 187–94) believes the lessons of empowerment derived from some feminist readings of popular romances (such as Radway, 1984, and his own of Madonna) suggest an overlooked micropolitics with counterhegemonic potential.

This may be so, but, as a general claim, it remains vulnerable to McGuigan's critique. Nancy Fraser's (1993) model of counterhegemonic practice within **public sphere** theory, for example, sets more discerning criteria for what constitutes counterhegemonic discourses and practices.

FURTHER READING

Frankfurt School member Leo Löwenthal (1961) provided one of the most remarkable early overviews of these issues during the 'mass culture' debates of the 1950s and 1960s. See also Peter Goodall (1995) and John Storey (2003). James Curran (1996b) and David Morley (1996a, 1996b) conducted a fruitful and still pertinent debate about the fallout from Curran's 'revisionism' thesis about active audience studies and populism. An influential critique of Fiske et al. within cultural studies was Meaghan Morris' (1990). See Christine Gledhill (1996) for a contemporaneous overview of the feminist literature, as well as Joke Hermes (2005). Analysts of popular music often have the deepest insight into these issues and Simon Frith's (1991) much republished critique of cultural populism is one of the best pieces written on this topic.

Postmodernism

> **Related concepts**: culture industry, deconstruction, identity, modern, simulacra, technoculture.

177

Few concepts that have entered daily usage since the Second World War have been as imprecise and broadranging as 'postmodernism'. Disagreements about when 'postmodernism' begins and ends, whether it is solely an aesthetic movement or a total cultural revolution in Western modernities, have never been resolved.

In range, 'postmodernism' doubles as a term for an aesthetic movement in architecture, art, literature and film *as well as* an intellectual movement in the human sciences, sometimes used interchangeably with poststructuralism. Its most popular usage, however, is for denoting a social form – postmodernity.

POSTMODERNITY

Postmodernity is thought of as a distinct break from the period of Western modernity, as well as the decline of the grand narratives and aspirations towards totality attributed to the modern period. A decisive text in which this distinction is made is Jean-François Lyotard's *The Postmodern Condition* (1984: xxiii):

> I will use the term *modern* to designate any science that legitimates itself with reference to a metadiscourse ... making an explicit appeal to some grand narrative, such as the dialectics of Spirit, the hermeneutics of meaning, the emancipation of the rational or working subject, or the creation of wealth.

The 'grand narratives' referred to here conceive of history as an inexorable spirit of progress, the 'scientific' interpretation of deep causal laws, liberation of the individual or classes from social structure and expansion of capitalist accumulation. According to Lyotard, all of these narratives begin to lose their credibility when 'information', translated into complex, computerized systems of data, becomes the new productive force in society.

Increasingly, Lyotard argues, knowledge only becomes operational if it is translated into quantities of information that can be rendered and translated into computer language. Data banks are 'the Encyclopedias of tomorrow. They transcend the capacity of each of their users. They are "nature" for postmodern man' (Lyotard, 1984: 194).

The rise of 'information' as a ubiquitous force leads to a genuine 'recognition of the heteromorphous nature of language-games' (Lyotard, 1984: 51), which is at the heart of the postmodern condition. Lyotard (1984: xxiv) says:

> I define postmodern as incredulity toward metanarratives, thus articulating a pervasive scepticism about the existence of any general "truths" about social organisation on which to base a project of the just society and the good life.

This attitude to modernity is both a theoretical and an aesthetic one. Theoretical individualism (poststructuralism) takes the place of collective theoretical movements, while the anti-aesthetic rejection of aura and essence in the arts replaces the historical separation of high culture and mass culture.

AESTHETIC POSTMODERNISM

According to Andreas Huyssen in 'Mapping the postmodern' (1986b), postmodernism first appeared in literary studies in the 1950s (Irving Howe and Harry Levin) and, in the 1960s, in the divergent work of Leslie Fiedler and Ihab Hassan. By the 1970s, 'the term gained much wider currency encompassing first architecture, then dance, theater, painting, film and music' (Huyssen, 1986: 184). By the early 1980s, 'the modernism/postmodernism constellation in the arts and the modernity/postmodernity constellation in social theory had become one of the most contested terrains in the intellectual life of Western societies' (Huyssen, 1986: 184).

An essay often cited in discussions of the role of media in the rise of postmodernism is Walter Benjamin's 'The work of art in the age of mechanical reproduction' (1969). In it, Benjamin examines what he calls 'the tremendous shattering of tradition' that results from the mass reproducibility and circulation of artworks and images. Benjamin (1969: 224) argues that, 'To an ever greater degree, the work of art reproduced, becomes the work of art designed for reproducibility'. The mechanical or, today, electronic reproduction of media images and texts saturates aesthetic culture to a degree not envisaged by Benjamin. His foundational premise that, with every increase in the technical means of representation, art begins to be produced *only* according to how well it is received in the sphere of consumption, gives us a useful lead into what postmodernism is, or was.

The main characteristics of postmodern media culture are the collapse of the distinction between 'high culture' and mass culture, and the celebration of media culture as the agent of such a demise. In postmodern culture, the distinction between surface and depth, copy and original is menaced by the 'coloniziation of the unconscious' with 'the image', which, Frederic Jameson (1991: 18), citing Guy Debord, calls the 'final form of commodity reification'. Jameson accounts for this by distinguishing between 'pastiche' and 'parody'.

For Jameson (1991: 17), the practice of pastiche, which characterizes all postmodern art, first arises out of the immense fragmentation of 'the explosion of modern literature into a host of distinct private styles and mannerisms'. Such fragmentation results in a breakdown in aesthetic norms by which 'new art' obtains its meaning. This represents a loss of a sense of stylistic norms, in relation to which there can be ironic, comic or even tragic deviations.

When this norm disappears (Jameson, 1991: 17):

> parody finds itself without a vocation ... and ... pastiche slowly comes to take its place ... Pastiche is, like parody, the imitation of a peculiar or unique, idiosyncratic style, the wearing of a linguistic mask, speech in a dead language. But it is a neutral practice of such mimicry, without any of parody's ulterior motives, amputated of the satirical impulse, devoid of laughter and of any conviction that alongside the abnormal tongue you have momentarily borrowed, some healthy linguistic normality still exists.

It can be generalized, then, that, in the communication of style, postmodernism employs pastiche, as described above, but also makes frequent references to the 'death of the subject'. Not only are the great modernist writers and artists forgotten by postmodernism, their importance has always been exaggerated and the idea of gifted individuals who possesses a 'unique personal identity' is challenged.

Moreover, Jameson (1983: 115–16) argues that the inventory of the great modern styles has been exhausted:

> Hence, once again, pastiche: in a world in which stylistic innovation is no longer possible, all that is left is to imitate dead styles, speak through the masks and voices stored up in the imaginary museum of a now global culture. But this means that contemporary or postmodernist art is going to be about art itself in a new kind of way; even more, it means that one of its essential messages will involve the necessary failure of art and the aesthetic, the failure of the new, the imprisonment in the past.

Thus, postmodern art and artefacts attract the curious label of 'anti-aesthetic' (Foster, 1983). The image circulates more than it ever has, but there is a waning of affect and a disappearance of depth in which the historical meaning and tradition of art becomes totally decontextualized.

POSTMODERNISM AND POPULAR CULTURE

In film and television texts, the disappearance of depth is represented by the recycling of genres in which 'art becomes submerged and mixed in with mass culture, in the composition of postmodern popular culture, as well as providing another convenient store of images for advertisers' (Strinati, 2000: 240). Strinati provides numerous examples from popular cinema of genre pastiche and recycling, including films that combine the 'B' film crime genre with French new wave art film (such as *Reservoir Dogs*, 1991, and *Pulp Fiction*, 1994), combining the love story with the disaster movie (such as *Titanic*, 1997), science fiction, monster and disaster genres (such as *Godzilla*, 1998). The TV series, *The X Files* 'brings together the detective story with the science fiction and horror genres', while *Twin Peaks* 'combine[s] a wide range of genres including the soap opera, the detective story, the murder mystery, horror, science fiction, comedy and *film noir*' (Strinati, 2000: 241–2).

Then there are genres in film that are about 'the media' as their content, such as *The Player* (1992), *Speaking Parts* (1989), *Family Viewing* (1987) and *American Beauty* (1999). These films narrativize the extent to which everyday life has become organized around media and the image.

In popular music, the 1980s saw the anti-humanist rejection of morality in punk rock and grunge music, while pop had a moment where it turned on itself in a genre of anti-love songs, emblematized by John Lydon's 'This is not a Love Song'.

By the late 1980s and 1990s, postmodernism became synonymous with the consumption of popular culture, but popular texts and the 'conspicuous consumption' of commodity culture were also seen to provide the means of expressing alternative and subaltern voices (McRobbie, 1994). Thus, popular culture began to be viewed as a discourse poised against grand theory and the grand narratives of modernity.

THE WANING OF POSTMODERNISM

By the turn of the new millennium, postmodernism had begun to slip from the lexicon of sociology and communication studies, as 'globalisation became the new master signifier' (Huyssen, 2006) and one of its foremost theoreticians, Ihab Hassan (2003: 3), proclaimed: 'I know less about postmodernism today than I did thirty years ago'.

Five years into the new millennium saw proclamations about the end of posmodernism and attempts to understand what it *was*. Some commentators argued that it had been overtaken by the rise of new media networks and globalism, while we can also point to the ideological climate of the 'clash of civilizations' as a contest between alternative modernities in which postmodernism does not make any sense. A genre of books and journal special issues began to appear in which postmodernism was prefixed with *'After'* (Huyssen, 2006; López and Potter, 2001; Shaw, 2001; Simons and Billig, 1994).

A damaging attack on postmodern theory was made in 1996 by scientist Alan Sokal in his article in *Social Text*, 'Transgressing the boundaries: towards a transformative hermeneutics of quantum gravity' (1996a). This article was a spectacular hoax and parodied the solipsistic tendencies of postmodern theory. Fabricated evidence and ludic arguments were passed off as postmodern discourse finding its way into science studies. *Social Text*, a leading journal in postmodern studies, published it without amendment. Then came the revelation, by Sokal (1996b: 62), in *Lingua Franca*, that the entire article was a prank, a 'mélange of truths, half-truths, quarter-truths, falsehoods, non-sequiturs, and syntactically correct sentences that have no meaning whatsoever'.

Sokal followed up his stunt with a book (co-authored with Joan Bricmont), *Intellectual Impostures* (1999), that, while recognizing postmodern art, savaged the idea that postmodernism could ever provide an epistemology that would be useful to the social and natural sciences. In addition to a familiar dismissal of the extreme relativism of postmodernism, that there are no universal truths, Sokal and Bricmont (1999: 174) included charges of 'an excessive interest in subjective beliefs independently of their truth or falsity; an emphasis on discourse and language as opposed to the facts to which those discourses refer'.

However postmodernism is regarded – as an antimodernist or anti-aesthetic movement – the term captures a new and paradoxical attitude towards 'theory'. While some have accused postmodern thinking of being wilfully theoretical, others see it as an exhaustion of theory.

The anti-essentialism and antifoundationalism of postmodern thought rejects the possibility of universal truths or transcendental forms of knowledge. Rather, its extreme individualism and relativism is of a kind that differs from itself, leading to the paradox that it must denounce theoretical unity and its own speaking position if it is not to become the kind of grand narrative that it claims to have dismantled.

FURTHER READING

The literature on postmodernism is extensive. As an intellectual movement, it survives as a 'perspective' in the human sciences, but attempts to characterize it as a contemporary period were accomplished by the mid-1990s. In 1984, Jameson's famous essay: 'Postmodernism, or the cultural logic of late capitalism', was published in *New Left Review* (Jameson, 1984) and, in addition, the English translation of Lyotard's *The Postmodern Condition* was published. These texts were distinctive in characterizing postmodernism as, at once, an intellectual, aesthetic and historical movement. They were followed by disputes between neo-Marxists and postmodern cultural studies that academics celebrated or condemned 'the postmodern' as either a moment of late capitalism (Callinicos, 1989) or pronounced the irrelevance of Marxist analysis to the same. More recently, Steve Matthewman and Douglas Hoey (2006) have argued that 'postmodernism' has only ever been a term of convenience for fin-de-siècle critics, who, paradoxically, gave it the character of a coherent intellectual movement. For a useful collection, see Hal Foster (1983). For an insightful indication of postmodernist confusions about 'popular culture', see Andrew Goodwin's (1992) superb critique of postmodernist readings of the cultural form of music videos.

Public sphere

> **Related concepts**: audience, capitalism, communication, criticism/critique, culture, culture industry, ideology, influence, mass, media effects, media/medium, modernity, news values, popular, regulation.

This increasingly influential term is most closely associated with the work of Jürgen Habermas (1974: 49), who defined it in 1964, summarily, as 'a realm of our social life where something approaching public opinion might be formed' and which 'mediates between society and the state' (1974: 50). For Habermas, this realm definitely includes the media.

The tentative shape of that short formulation also indicates the deeper complexities of the concept. Perhaps most significantly, 'might be formed' points to both Habermas' *normative* (that is, related to a critical ideal criterion) hopes for its use and his concern that that hope remained unfulfilled. For, like other critical thinkers such as Pierre Bourdieu (1993), Habermas does not equate public opinion with the latest opinion poll results. Rather, for Habermas, public opinion *should* be a product of *informed deliberation among citizens in a democracy*, rather than the measurement of what he calls 'mere prejudice'.

It is in this context that the media become central to the public sphere thesis. They provide the means by which citizens obtain information and contribute to the sphere of public debate. Moreover, consistent with the liberal norms relating to **freedom of communication**, they hold public authority to account. The abiding theme within Habermas' writings on this question is that the media should remain sufficiently independent to perform these roles. To this extent, his argument echoes older arguments many readers would have met in citizenship or civics classes about the relationship between citizens, independent journalism and democracy that are often invoked by (confusing) phrases such as the 'fourth estate'. Habermas, however, regards such rights and freedoms as minimal preconditions of a public sphere.

THE RISE OF THE MODERN PUBLIC SPHERE

What makes Habermas' somewhat idealized account more plausible – and original – is his historical account of the emergence of the public sphere within European **modernity**. This was first detailed in his 1962 book, *The Structural Transformation of the Public Sphere* (STPS; 1991), but has been revised and improved many times since.

Habermas' conception of the modern public sphere is *not* the same as earlier historical examples, such as the Ancient Greek agora. Rather, it is specifically tied to the rise of a new social class across Europe – the 'rising middle class' or bourgeoisie (see **capitalism**). It is this social class that pioneers many features of our modern conceptions of privacy and intimacy as well as publicness.

Britain is Habermas' paradigmatic case. The kind of deliberative debate Habermas values initially emerges *in practice* within literary critical discussion in eighteenth-century London coffee houses. These coffee houses fostered a new form of 'society', independent of the court society that clustered around the monarch. Coffee house debate was closely tied to new cultural forms, such as the overlapping of early modern journalism and the novel. These discussions shifted from debates about literature to those about politics. Thus, a *literary* public sphere grows into the broader public sphere that exists 'between state and society', facilitating the emergence of the modern 'public use of reason'. This sphere was able, via 'the vehicle of public opinion', to 'put the state in touch with the needs of society' (Habermas, 1991: 31). Comparable developments, such as the French literary salons, took place elsewhere in Europe.

The transition to democracy can thus be seen as the development of a 'political public sphere' focused on matters of relevance to the state, now centred on a parliament rather than a monarch. Habermas distinguishes the political public sphere from the literary one 'when public discussion deals with objects connected to the activity of the state' (1974: 49). This tight 'feedback' relationship between the public sphere and the state remains a consistent feature of Habermas' model.

As Habermas readily admitted, his account in STPS was overly pessimistic about later developments of the public sphere. He applies a variant of Theodor Adorno's **culture industry** thesis, which leaves little room for an 'active **audience**'. While the new print-based cultural forms of the novel and political journalism contributed to the emergence of the modern public sphere in the eighteenth century, twentieth-century cultural forms and newer media were seen to merely replace the cultural debaters of the eighteenth-century literary public sphere with passive cultural consumers. Relying heavily on Paul Lazarsfeld's early **audience** research, based on electoral studies, STPS paints a very pessimistic picture of the modern election campaign process as a 'pseudo-public sphere'.

Debates have raged around these issues ever since STPS was published and then, again, when it was finally translated into English in 1989. Before reviewing these, it is important to note that, as with Adorno's **culture industry** thesis itself, such pessimistic scenarios certainly speak to strong *tendencies* within contemporary media and society. Many of us might be able to cite elections we have voted in – or chosen not to – that had at best 'pseudo-public spheres', for example.

PUBLIC SPHERE AND MEDIA

The public sphere thesis became well known in English language media studies initially in the 1980s because it was drawn on as a defence of public service broadcasting (PSB). PSBs, it was argued, embody most of the Habermasian ideals.

Habermas had not initially argued this, but others soon did for the German case (Negt and Kluge, 1993: 191). In Europe, PSBs had enjoyed monopoly or dominant positions since the advent of radio broadcasting. It was easy, then, to regard the provision of quality programming by PSBs and, especially, the high journalistic standards of their news programming, as *the* public sphere of those nation states. The simultaneity of audience reception of such programming could be characterized as 'society communing with itself'. The threat to these broadcasters by rival, increasingly commercial service providers based in satellite and cable broadcasting provided PSB defenders with an opportunity to rerun Habermas' pessimistic account of the fate of the twentieth-century public sphere. In short, the era of media addressing their audiences as citizens seemed to be threatened by a new consumerist one.

Of course, for those nations that did not have such PSB-dominance, this framework did not fit so readily. Transnational satellite broadcasting might actually enable rather than compromise the prospect of viable public spheres; cable networks might offer quality alternatives to the dominant. Most obviously, the advent of the Internet led to the quite different argument that a completely new media technology might facilitate a mediated public sphere, also enabling a level of **interactivity** – perhaps on a global scale – unimaginable within broadcasting. This shift in turn redressed a tendency to focus on face-to-face and print-based communication in Habermas' original argument (Thompson, 1995).

A key point of contestation within the literature on media and public sphere thus tends to be the conceptualization of the normative role of journalism and news and related media organizations. Such specificities of **regulation** have rarely been addressed by Habermas in his major writings. Instead, he broadly defends 'the independence of a self-regulated media system'. Such a 'media system' (see Figure 10) is his blanket term derived from Thompson's (1990: 260–4) characterization of the UK broadcast (FTA) regulatory system as 'regulated pluralism' and from the broader field of normative political communication studies (such as Gurevitch and Blumler, 1990; see also Habermas, 1996a: 378).

PSB defenders often highlight the defence of quality journalism and Habermas (2009) has also written explicitly on this theme himself. Yet, the philosophical reworking of the public sphere thesis in his later work is arguably just as compatible with a view of public deliberation found in 'horizontal' online discussion and activism. Habermasians remain concerned about the quality of that deliberation and wary of any tendencies towards **tabloidization** and populism, however.

CRITICISMS AND REMODELLINGS

The different applications of the public sphere thesis to different media in different contexts echo detailed sociological and philosophical critiques of the concept. At their heart was the view that Habermas had inadvertently idealized the particular form of public sphere, and its related media, established by the propertied white bourgeoisie. It so overlooked struggles by other social groups, and their own (mediated) public spheres, for recognition in the history of democracy. As James Curran (1991) made plain, even in Habermas' 'paradigmatic' case of Britain, radical plebeian presses played a crucial role in the expansion of the suffrage and the history of journalism in the nineteenth century. Especially in the context of the rise of **identity** politics in the late-twentieth century, this oversight seemed especially serious.

Significantly, many of these critics acknowledged the significance of the concept and sought to improve rather than replace it. Easily the most influential of these has been Nancy Fraser's (1993) feminist critique. It has become a focal point in assessments of Habermas' ongoing dialogue with his feminist critics.

Fraser drew together much of the existing critical literature on *The Structural Transformation*, especially that related to its inattention to subaltern histories and the *constitutive* role gender exclusion played in the 'classical' bourgeois public sphere. She advocates a multiple publics model (see Figure 10), in which subaltern counterpublics (more or less associated with social movements and identity politics) have a 'Janus-faced' relationship with their own constituencies and the

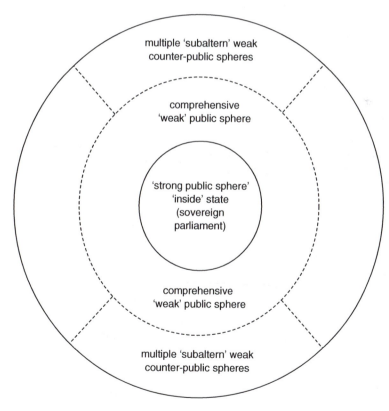

Figure 10 Fraser's multiple publics model (based on Fraser, 1993, as developed in Jones, 2000b)

public posited by the 'comprehensive' public sphere. That is, counterpublics provide both 'internal' means of collective affirmation and make 'external' claims, ultimately on the state.

Perhaps more than any other text, Fraser's points to the plausibility of Habermas' hope that his reconstitution of Frankfurt critical theory might provide an opening for discussions that inform social movements. Fraser's use of the Gramscian term 'subaltern' for her counterpublics also suggests a means of thinking about public sphere and hegemony together. The sociocultural terrain of public sphere and hegemony, in principle, overlap in civil society, but while one is primarily directed optimistically towards the success of the participatory goals of democratic political communication, the other assesses the consequences of its failure.

THE 'LIVE WHITE MALE' KEEPS GOING PUBLIC

One of the curiosities of the public sphere literature is Habermas' own continuing involvement. He was quite young when he published STPS in 1962 and, consistent with his own view of the reconstructive role of immanent critique, he has maintained a productive dialogue with his critics. In 1989, he responded to a major series of critical engagements with STPS – including Fraser's – that marked its translation into English (Calhoun, 1992). In 1996, he published a reworking of the entire public sphere argument in the context of his major work on law (1996a). In 2006, he examined the argument again in light of more recent empirical research on political communication (Habermas, 2006a).

Unusually, then, for such a major concept in media and communication studies, we can match the critics' views with the responses of the concept's leading advocate. For media studies particularly, the most telling 'unfulfilled promise' in all these responses by the later Habermas is his recognition of the gap between the original formulation of the public sphere model and subsequent developments in audience research, such as Hall's encoding/decoding model and active audience theory (Habermas, 1993a: 439, 1996a: 377). Despite these acknowledgements, at certain points in his recent rethinking, Habermas considers 'resistant' publics not as actively decoding media audiences but, instead, in something like Fraser's terms, as members of social movements. With rare exceptions, however, social movements are minority movements and possibly quite fragmentary.

A number of public sphere theorists have thus been drawn to Todd Gitlin's (1998) suggestive image of relatively isolated 'sphericules'. Yet Fraser's more elaborate model reminds us that one can be a member of a social movement and/or hold a subaltern minority identity within a counterpublic/sphericule *as well as* being a member of the comprehensive public that democratic leaders address as 'the people' or 'the nation'.

Although new media play an ever-increasing role in the democratic process, as long as television remains the chief source of political information for that comprehensive public, the question of the relationship between the public sphere and the consumption of such political communication will remain a key research issue in media and communications. Figure 10 aims to capture the dynamics of Fraser's model and Figure 11 is one of several slides Habermas used in his 2006 paper (2006b), which

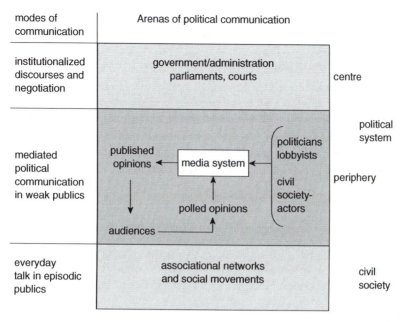

modes of communication	Arenas of political communication	
institutionalized discourses and negotiation	government/administration parliaments, courts	centre
mediated political communication in weak publics	published opinions ← media system ← politicians lobbyists / civil society-actors / polled opinions / audiences	political system / periphery
everyday talk in episodic publics	associational networks and social movements	civil society

Figure 11   Public sphere and contemporary political communication (reproduced from Habermas, 2006b)

displays not only his revised understanding of the public sphere within modern **political communication** but also his debt to Fraser's 'weak publics' and, despite its decidedly non-spherical shape, a similar centre/periphery formulation.

FURTHER READING

Nicholas Garnham initially introduced the public sphere thesis to Anglophone media studies in his 1986 paper, an argument he later revised and updated several times (1986, 1992, 1993, 2000). Garnham and democratic theorist John Keane conducted an insightful and still relevant debate about the relationship between public spheres and PSBs in 1995 (Keane, 1995a, 1995b; see also Garnham, 1995); plus, see Keane (1991) and his related conception of 'monitory democracy' (2009). Curran's (2000, 2005, for example; see also Jones, 2000b) policy-orientated development of his critique of Habermas – which has gone through several variants – is much recommended. The best of the more recent overviews of Habermas and the public sphere for media-orientated readers is that by Luke Goode (2005), but see also Richard Butsch's (2007) collection. The collection edited by Craig Calhoun (1993), based on the conference marking the English translation of STPS, remains the definitive one on the broader contours of this topic, but see also Johanna Meehan's (1995) collection of feminist readings. For a similarly pitched broader account of the public sphere thesis and other normative models of (journalistic) media, see Clifford G. Christians et al.

(2009). John B. Thompson (1995) is similarly systematic. A useful US media sociology perspective can be found in David Croteau and William Hoynes (2006). The literature on the Internet and the public sphere is also vast (for example, Buchstein, 1997; Curran and Witschge, 2009; Dahlberg, 2001; Dahlgren, 2001; Dean, 2003; Hand and Sandywell, 2002; Sparks, 2001b). An important more recent collection is Sonia Livingstone's (2005), especially her own papers on audiences and publics and the role of new media in differing conceptions of the relationship between private and public. Jeffrey C. Alexander's *The Civil Sphere* (2006) offers a major alternative model that builds on the concept of a civil society rather than the public sphere. On the increasing significance of the literary/cultural/aesthetic public sphere model in contemporary use, see Jim McGuigan (2005), Maria Pia Lara (1998) and Paul Jones (2007). For sanguine assessments of the relationship between public sphere theorists and 'cultural populists', see Jonathan Simons (2003) and John Michael Roberts and Nick Crossley (2004). The highly relevant journal *Javnost: The Public* (available free online) has an impressive archive of themed issues. See also the US Social Science Research Council's growing online resources (at: http://publicsphere. ssrc.org/guide/differentiation-of-the-public-sphere/production-structures/ interaction-of-institutional-fields/politics-media-economy).

Regulation

> **Related concepts**: *capitalism, criticism/critique, communication(s), freedom of communication, modern, news values, public sphere, tabloidization.*

The relationship between post-print media/communications and regulation varies dramatically among nation states to this day, despite media globalization and attempts at forms of global governance. That is because the question of whether or not the media should be regulated is still largely answered at the level of the nation state. Supranational bodies such as the European Union and international 'free trade' agreements have certainly challenged the supremacy of nation states, but national governments remain the most common initiators of regulatory regimes. That is so even if, in democratic societies, they are usually administered by more or less independent agencies collectively known as 'regulators'. While this is very much an 'in practice' administrative domain, it is strongly informed by the kinds of conceptual distinctions that are the concern of this book.

Indeed, two major distinctions are of significance here in ordering our understanding of the role of regulation. The first, following from debates within free speech literatures, makes the fairly self-descriptive separation between content regulation and structural regulation (see **freedom of communication** for further elaboration). The second distinction is more complex than the first and turns on conceptual distinctions outlined elsewhere in this book. It refers to the difference between moral and cultural regulation, on the one hand, and the regulation of journalism and information on the other. Similarly, all these modes of regulation by the state, and its related regulators, generate fields of policy practice and governance.

It is perhaps most useful, then, to start with the distinction between journalistic and moral/cultural regulation. The rise of moral/cultural regulation as a form of structural regulation is closely tied to the 'cultural turn' and the increasing recognition of the **culture industries** as an economic force and policy field. So, we might include here policies and regulations that seek to protect and encourage cultural producers within a nation state for reasons of national cultural identity and the perceived threat of cultural imperialism (see **capitalism**). Film and television drama subsidies, tax incentives and quota systems have thus been common. They became difficult to sustain with the rise of neoliberal 'free trade' agreements in the 1990s. Likewise, the rise of minority cultural identities within many nation states have been met by ('positive') regulatory cultural policies (such as subsidies, dedicated broadcast frequency allocations and so on). These are often allied to multi-culturalism policies that aid the circulation (and perhaps production) of appropriate cultural forms, usually administratively recognized as such by the presence of minority languages. Both these areas of subsidization also significantly overlap with the field of cultural policy practice that has grown out of former and continuing national arts policies.

There is, however, a longer history of content regulation for 'moral' purposes and this sense of 'moral' is closely allied to that encompassed within '**moral panic**' – that is, where the actions of the state and regulators resemble (or, indeed, are) forms of censorship based on 'moral standards'. Regulation of matters relating to 'taste and decency' (and often violence, especially in the USA), chiefly developed in relation to cinema and television, but, historically, also related to printed fiction and images, form a major part of the history of regulation. So, early forms of censorship of literary pornography and erotica through to the development of photography, cinema and later media is a common strand. Proposals for this form of censorship remain very active in debates today about 'Internet filtering'.

A key feature of this tradition is a (patriarchal) notion of moral guardianship, initially understood to protect the interests of women and children, but today conceived mainly in relation to children and/or 'family values'. (For the feminist tradition here, see **freedom of communication**.) It is also the case that a similarly morally conservative estimation of 'the mainstream market' may lead powerful forces within the culture industries to practise their own form of pre-emptive moral self-censorship.

In the 1980s and 1990s, such moral regulation resurfaced significantly in the wake of neoliberalism (see **capitalism**), especially in the UK and USA. Part of the academic response to this trend, especially in the UK, was a tendency to (re)conceptualize all regulation per se as necessarily 'moral' in a related Foucaultian/disciplinary sense (see especially Thompson, 1997). The term 'cultural policy' was often used similarly in a blanket manner to include all media regulation.

These views tended to exclude an equally well-established role for media regulation and policy: of being primarily focused on matters relating to freedom of speech and informed citizenship, often glossed in regulatory and legal literatures as 'the public interest' (Feintuck, 1999, 2004). Thus, there is a kind of division of labour between these two senses of regulation: moral and cultural regulation tend to be concerned with 'aesthetic–cultural' materials, while regulation for informed citizenship tends to be concerned primarily with journalism and other 'information' materials.

Accordingly, we could make the broad distinctions represented in Table 17.

That said, it must be acknowledged immediately that such distinctions in modes of regulation are by no means hard and fast in practice and vary significantly from nation state to nation state. Most notably, in structural/institutional terms, public service broadcasters (PSBs), such as the BBC, were established to operate across at least two, if not all three, of the domains in Table 17. In content regulation, requirements for quotas of 'quality' children's television programming arguably fulfil the requirements of all three modes, which perhaps explains their relative success. Conceptually, these porous boundaries echo similar tensions relating to **tabloidization** and the relationship between **culture** and **public sphere**, as well as changing understandings of **influence** – a term often invoked in much policy debate. Nonetheless, we would stress the usefulness of the table for orienting the initiate.

Table 17 Examples of structural and content regulatory practices across three modes of regulation

Mode of regulation	Journalism/ information ('media policy')	Cultural (aesthetic and multi)	Moral
Structural	Ownership and diversity rules, establishment of PSBs, newspaper subsidies	Subsidies, provision of dedicated (multicultural) channels – establishment of PSBs	Restriction of 'immoral' imported materials
Content	Content regulation tied to commercial broadcast licences, compulsory impartiality codes administered by regulator, self-regulatory industry codes, editorial accountability guidelines published by PSBs	Content regulation tied to commercial broadcast licences, quota systems for broadcast and cinema content – usually based on promotion of 'national identity'	Content regulation tied to commercial broadcast licences, overt banning/ censorship or classification system administered by state or 'taste and decency' regulator, compulsory Internet filtering, self-regulatory industry codes

DEREGULATION, MARKETS, DIGITALIZATION/CONVERGENCE

Much of the regulatory regimes sketched above turned on a simple 'technical' premise that held from the 1920s to the 1980s in most nations. It was that, unlike paper, the resource requirements of post-print media were scarce. In particular, the electromagnetic spectrum that enabled broadcasting was finite and required state intervention to regulate frequency allocations.

'Spectrum scarcity' is the conventional shorthand for this assumption. It provided the technical necessity for licensing and so enabled conditions to be placed on those licences, especially for commercial licensees. Today, such assumptions have been almost completely reversed. Newsprint is regarded as an increasingly finite resource and 'digital abundance' is an almost truthful catchphrase, *if* one understands it to mean an abundance of infrastructure 'channels' rather than a diversity of content. In the terms used above, structural diversity is real, but content diversity is more problematic (see **tabloidization**).

The prospect of digital **convergence** between telephony, broadcasting and computing – anticipated from the 1970s – only increased the recognition that a major reorganization of regulatory regimes was inevitable. Telephony had been regulated separately in many nation states by 'communications' (as opposed to 'broadcast' or 'media') regulators, but the US practice of a single regulator – the Federal Communications Commission (FCC) was soon emulated, most notably in the UK.

On what basis should a 'converged' regulator manage a digitally converged system? Could it? Before rushing to declare such systems obsolete in the wake of media globalization and the Internet, it is important to pause and consider separately the different effects of digitization on different media.

Most notably, 'free-to-air broadcasting' remains a remarkable de facto institution with considerable social inertia, due to its apparent 'freedom' from cost. The 'to air' component contains an important key to its continuing social success.

Printed forms of ongoing distribution, notably newspapers and magazines, relied on subscriptions or the cover price. Advertising became a significant revenue source with the later developments of the newspaper.

With rare exceptions, broadcasting was always 'subsidized' by either advertising revenue or the PSB licence fee (or its general tax equivalent). Such arrangements enabled the removal of a point-of-sale consumption charge or even the impression that there was such a charge 'to air'.

In contrast, telephony became another 'utility' with monthly or similar periodical billing. Although often called a 'subscription', to a large degree it is telephony's revenue model that has been applied to 'converged' digital media. Payment by 'consumers' is a much more transparent process and makes it appear to be an 'optional' service that might be reduced in hard times.

Free-to-air broadcasting – especially in its PSB form – appealed to those advocating public interest-based media regulation precisely because it did assemble an audience – albeit with relatively little channel choice – and so a potential public (Scannell, 1989). Accordingly, some of the most significant policy debates in recent years have been about expansions to the free-to-air configuration – notably digital multichannelling of television and radio (and high-definition (HD) television).

191

A parallel case emerges with free wi-fi. In such instances, the maintenance of such 'free' public availability has required the initiative of a state authority committed to such provision – such as the Singapore government's commitment to publicly available wi-fi – or, in the case of digital multichannelling, the creative reinterpretation of the remit of a PSB – as in the BBC's 'freeview' initiative (Born, 2004).

Professional/industry 'self-regulation' was the preferred position for many in commercial media industries, deriving in part from newspapers' historical exemption from most broadcast-era regulation on freedom of speech grounds. The dominant assumption in the neoliberal period, however, was that markets would provide the most appropriate means of reorganizing regulatory regimes and so *deregulation* became an important catchcry (Freedman, 2008). That these developments coincided with the fall of European communism – and subsequent transitions from authoritarian media systems – only increased the pressure to abandon 'statist' models of media regulation in the 'old' democracies. Undoubtedly, much of this deregulatory pressure arose from corporate opportunism – in particular, the hostility of many media corporations to regulations that sought to limit concentrations of ownership. The scale of deregulation actually achieved appears to have been inversely related to the strength of the public service culture in the particular nation state. A further factor has been the extent of the ability of critical intellectuals and policy activists to rethink the rationale for PSBs and regulation of commercial systems with such innovative discursive tactics as the **public sphere** thesis and a revived understanding of positive **freedom of communication** norms (Garnham, 1986; McChesney, 2007).

Indeed, perhaps the greatest surprise in recent years has been the institutional survival of PSBs in the neoliberal and digital environments, not least because of their reputation as trusted providers of online news services. In the main, they have demonstrated themselves to be anything *but* State-controlled monoliths. Despite their neoliberal 'disciplining' towards more marketized practices (Freedman, 2008), the loss of PSB hegemony in many national media systems and their continuing vulnerability to funding pressures, they remain some of the most autonomous and accountable media institutions in existence.

FURTHER READING

David Ward (2008) provides a good global survey of television/media regulation practices. Justin Lewis and Toby Miller (2002) and Jim McGuigan (2004) provide good guides to the 'cultural policy' moment (see also Jones, 1994). Georgina Born (2004) provides one of the most detailed accounts available of the neoliberal disciplining of a PSB. David Croteau and William Hoynes (2006) provide an exceptionally clear account of 'market v. public sphere' understandings of regulation of media in the US case. Their other book (Croteau and Hoynes, 2003: Chapter 3) is equally strong on the distinctions between these modes and 'moral regulation' in the USA. Edwin Baker (2007) gives a powerful restatement of the case for ownership regulation in the digital environment. (See also the Further reading sections for **public sphere** and **freedom of communication**.)

Related concepts: audience, communication(s), culture, genre, identity, influence, media/medium.

Ritual communication and the redefinition of 'ritual' in relation to '**media**' have opened up as a new branch of study in recent years. At least some of the impetus for the turn to **ritual** is frustration with the repetitive orthodoxy of 'effects analysis' and the transmission model of **communication**. Apart from anthropology (Ginsburg, 2005; Rothenbuhler and Coman, 2005), however, the analysis of media ritual struggles to find a paradigmatic home. Part of this quandary is that media rituals are seen to be qualitatively different from communal rituals, the focus of anthropological study, or those that characterize modern festivals.

An interesting forerunner to the discussion of media rituals can be found in Walter Benjamin's essay 'The work of art in the age of mechanical reproduction' (1969). Benjamin contrasts the status of ritualized 'cult' art with the fate of art after the inception of its **mass** circulation in **modern**ity. In ancient societies, he claims, art was always indissociable from ritual, first as magic then through religious ritual. It is only since the 'first truly revolutionary means of reproduction, photography [that] … for the first time in world history, mechanical reproduction emancipates the work of art from its parasitical dependence on ritual' (Benjamin, 1969: 224).

Instead, Benjamin argues, what counts for art today is more determined by politics than ritual, but there is another interesting difference between mediatized art and ritual or 'cult' art. Modern art can only demonstrate an 'aura' if it is on view, circulated in galleries or by other means, whereas, for social reasons, cult art was rarely ever on view. For example, cave art might have been shared, but it was intended for the spirits, as are many of the figures found in organized religions. For example, in the Orthodox Church, its Madonnas stay covered nearly all year round and much of the artistic detail of many religious buildings are well above ground level, inaccessible to worshippers. What ritual might be attributed to the modernist aesthetic is entirely anchored to its circulation and reproducibility.

THE SPECIFICITY OF MEDIA RITUALS

The reproducibility of images in the mass media generates an entirely different order of ritual. Nick Couldry (2003, 2005) who is one of the foremost theorists of ritual media, argues that media rituals should not be seen as extensions or representations of other kinds of ceremonies. Oft-cited examples, such as a coronation, do not capture what is involved in ritual media.

Couldry (2003: 3) distinguishes between three types of ritual:

- ritual as habitual action
- ritual as formalized action
- ritual as action associated with transcendental values.

It is this transcendental form of ritual that has the most bearing on the role of media in social integration. For Couldry (2003: 22–3), media represent a 'wider space of ritualization', which has a range of transcendental functions beyond individual habits of media consumption. Rather, the rituals of media are distinguished by the way they reify a powerful boundary between a concentrated centre of media power and an excluded reality of everyday life.

The important feature of this division, however, is that the 'mediated centre' (2003: 2, 47) is mythical, both imaginary and real. Media appear to occupy the centre of social life, an appearance that is convincing and therefore real. This 'imaginary' relationship between social life and media somehow makes media seem to sit legitimately at the centre of social life and encourages ritual relationships to them. Couldry (2003: 52) describes a condition in which every member of modern society believes that the media are our 'access point to society's centre'. Consequently, the media itself enjoys a virtual monopoly over the power of naming, and 'defining-the-situation' (Couldry, 2003: 43).

Everyday practices of ritual socially sanction the concentration of power in the media. According to Couldry, media rituals differ from other forms of ritual in that they are not geared solely to 'preserving' the past (such as the transmission of culture) but also generate connections to society 'right now', from minute to minute, hour to hour. Nevertheless, media rituals are not subservient to some underlying impulse to preserve the social order. Media is related to power, but not functionally. Media rituals do not simply maintain social integration ('community'); they enable the 'management of conflict and the masking of inequality' (Holmes, 2005: 166). The power of central media provides for 'spaces of ritualization', which rest on one 'central inequality: the historic concentration of symbolic power in media institutions' (Couldry, 2003: 134). This inequality is naturalized by means of habitual daily practices: 'liveness', media events, media pilgrimages, reality TV and talk shows.

These rituals perpetuate the 'myth of the mediated centre' rather than society itself. The practices of genres and mediums that give us access to this mediated centre attain very high status, while practices that do not connect with them are rendered mundane, ordinary and profane. Liveness is a particularly important aspect of this division.

For example, consider the newspaper, the 'morning prayer of modern man', as Georg Wilhelm Hegel called it. Its power derives from its currency, its immediate relevance to the here and now, where its capacity to concentrate the specular consciousness of its readers is most intense. Few people would read yesterday's newspaper if they had today's edition and, if they did, it would be in order to review information in some kind of 'academic' way.

Likewise, it is a very different experience listening to prerecorded music, unless it is the very latest 'release', than it is when we 'tune in' to hear **broadcast** music, which we might relate to via a radio host or simply by stepping into the 'simultaneous current of event reception', as this redetermines such music as a mediated event.

Then there is also the study of spectacular events, which may be celebratory (for example, the Olympics or a political event) or of a kind that shocks and interrupts (Cottle, 2006; Dayan and Katz, 1992). The difference between these two kinds of events is that the celebratory ones are planned and have a build-up of weeks or months, while the conflicted media events are generally unplanned and unexpected. (Except perhaps by those planned to highjack airtime by creating the spectacle in question.) These kinds of media events may involve **moral panics**, disaster marathons, a so-called 'media scandal' or a mediatized public crisis (Cottle, 2006).

According to Couldry, the ritual event still does not provide an appreciation of the mythical relationship audiences have to *central* media and their **genres**. To this end, Couldry also gives examples of media-*related* practices, which are not simply about directly consuming media, but indirect practices where the reification of the 'media–ordinary' boundary is recreated. Such is the case with 'media pilgrimages', where fans visit a place made famous by a celebrity, group or individuals who once made a miraculous pilgrimage from being 'nobodys' to being 'a name'. Another example is the 'pervasiveness' of 'celebrity **culture**' (discourse about celebrity inside and outside media). Such culture is not confined to everyday practices of viewing. Rather, their appearance in magazines and high up in **news values** communicates the idea that 'celebrity actions demand special attention' (Couldry, 2006: 128). Regardless of our individual likes and dislikes regarding celebrities, every member of society is forced into practices (which can range from idle chat to pretending not to notice a celebrity who has walked into a room) to maintain 'a constant point of reference with them' (Couldry, 2006: 46).

With celebrity culture providing the most accessible examples, Couldry (2003: 12) explains that 'Ritualisation … encourages us to look at the links between ritual actions and wider social space, and in particular at the practices and beliefs, found right across social life that make specific actions possible'.

THE CRITIQUE OF FUNCTIONALISM AND INSTRUMENTALISM

Couldry's work is an advance on the early work of James Carey, who can be credited with critiquing the pervasive 'instrumentalism' of communication studies in his exploration of ritual ontologies of communications. This involved undoing the entrenched dualism of thinking about communication in subject–object terms, in which communication is a realm that does not have its own culture. The title of his book, *Communication as Culture* (1989), makes the point that communication does not exist as a service or 'apparatus' *for* culture, but constitutes its own system of culture.

For Carey, social reality is partly *produced* in communication, not simply reflected by it. To support his argument, Carey cites John Dewey (in Carey, 1989: 14)

195

as follows: 'Society exists not only by transmission, by communication, but it may fairly be said to exist in transmission, in communication.' Thus, the role of communication in social reproduction is accented in Carey, but in a non-functionalist way. For example, the functionalism of the dominant ideology thesis or the culture industry argument that media and communications are shaped by the logic of capital or 'the needs of fractions of capital' is qualitatively different from the ritual perspective. Communications are considered to be diffused in the very possibilities of sociability rather than being a kind of 'moral improvement' of the same. Such communications are not the object of consumer choice, but are indispensable to social reproduction.

Carey (1989: 18) argues that, 'A ritual view of communication is directed not toward the extension of messages in space but toward the maintenance of society in time; not the act of imparting information but the representation of shared beliefs'. Thus, communications are not simply functional subsystems that enhance the connections between different areas of culture but are themselves a cultural form.

In developing a non-functionalist approach to ritual, Carey makes a strong distinction between ritual and transmission conceptions of **communication**. In the transmission model, symbols are taken to be representations 'of' and rituals are representations 'for'. Whereas the transmission approach is concerned with 'content', dyadic models of interaction and 'mediation', ritual is concerned with integration via mediums and their *genres*.

A key difference setting ritual apart from **medium** theory is that the latter deals with the extension of the senses and sensorial bias, whereas ritual theory looks at how content or messages gain their power from a medium to create 'genres'.

For example, a ritual approach is useful for analysing the sources from which the news derives its authority. News is not information, but a form of drama. News is a premier genre for invoking audience anxieties and providing a daily fix of highly stylized and codified narratives that do less to convey information and more to rehearse a predictable format. A transmission point of view, however, assumes that individual viewers simply 'use' media to overcome their anxieties (a variant being the 'uses and gratifications approach') and not that the media produce the behaviour that is supposed to be overcome. Carey (1989: 20) writes:

> If one examines a newspaper under a transmission view of communication, one sees the medium as an instrument for disseminating news and knowledge, sometimes *divertissement*, in larger and larger packages over greater distances. Questions arise as to the effects of this on audiences, news as enlightening or obscuring reality, as changing or hardening attitudes, as breeding credibility or doubt. … [A ritual view of communication on the other hand] will focus on a different range of problems in examining a newspaper. It will, for example, view reading a newspaper less as sending or gaining information and more as attending a mass, a situation in which nothing new is learned but in which a particular view of the world is portrayed and confirmed.

News is probably the best example of the totemic function of media genres, the greatest of which is to provide a sense of continuity and constancy. News producers know the importance of such constancy all too well. Unlike any other genre, the timing of news is upheld with immovable reverence. A television station will rarely delay the evening news programme for other forms of programming and radio is even more rigid – even an interview with a head of state will be cut short and sacrificed to the hallowed calling of the hourly news bulletin.

FURTHER READING

A foundational text on ritual is Carey's *Communication as Culture* (1989), which develops the significance of ritual by contrast with the dominant 'transmission' paradigm of communication. Eric W. Rothenbuhler and Mihai Coman provide a useful compendium of anthropological approaches to media ritual in *Media Anthropology* (2005). More recently, Nick Couldry has attempted to take the non-functionalist direction, which Carey inaugurated, much further – looking at media itself as a kind of research optic for understanding social relations in general. Couldry has also carried this perspective into empirical research with Sonia Livingstone and Tim Markham in an important study of news consumption and political communication (Couldry et al., 2007).

Sign

Related concepts: cultural form, deconstruction, discourse, encoding/decoding, ideology, popular.

Sign is the most central concept in the field of semiotics or semiology. Semiotics (the more commonly used term) in turn provided a powerful resource in challenging all *quantitative* approaches to media 'content' or 'messages'. For this reason, it has become somewhat inseparable from the related semiotic concept of code. Together, these concepts made perhaps their greatest impact on media studies via Stuart Hall's (1980a) 'Encoding/decoding' paper.

Non-quantitative or *qualitative* approaches to media content certainly already existed when semiotics was introduced into media studies in the 1970s, but the contrast with quantitative methods makes the appeal of semiotics clearer. That is because the problem facing all communications researchers is primarily one of scale. How does one delimit the sheer amount of material under analysis and still make claims to understand the meaning of, say, television crime dramas? The vast amounts of such media content produced could hardly *all* be analysed.

Quantitative methods rely in part on sampling, taking a block of time of programming or a certain number of months of newspapers from distinct parts of a nation state, for example. The appeal of early semiotic approaches was the implicit, at times explicit, claim to have discovered something like 'eternal laws' of what would later be called signification, the formation of meaning(s). A similar appeal developed for the overlapping forms of analysis of mediated **cultural forms** via **genre** and narrative methods.

THE LINGUISTIC TURN

The 'prequel' of such developments was the expansion of the influence of a particular branch of linguistics, the study of language. Ferdinand de Saussure's breakthrough in structural linguistics in the early years of the twentieth century provides us with the central definition of the sign. It is the accompanying model of language as a *system*, however, that becomes the template for a 'linguistic turn' – initially understood outside linguistics as *structuralism* – that swept the humanities and social sciences. The phrase 'structured like a language' was soon applied in philosophy and to anthropological myths, ideologies and mediated cultural forms.

There are two basic premises for Saussure, both of which proved controversial: his Principle 1 and Principle 2.

Saussure's Principle 1 is the arbitrary character of the sign. Saussure's most basic premise is to reject the 'naming' conception of the relationship between words and their meanings that most of us are initially taught and assumes a 'natural' relation between 'words' and 'things'. In order to facilitate his break with this commonsensical presumption, Saussure uses the concepts of the (linguistic) sign and its (analytic) components, signifier and signified. The signifier is the auditory means ('sound image') of the sign, while the signified is the meaning ('concept') it carries.

In asserting the sign's 'arbitrary' character, Saussure (1966: 65–70) implies that the signifier–signified bond is not 'natural' and, in principle, any meaning can be conveyed by any auditory means. In his *Cours*, Saussure uses the example of the French word for tree, 'arbre', for which, in principle, any other signifier could be substituted ('named'), as any bilingual or multilingual person can attest (see Figures 12 and 13). While Saussure understood signs to be primarily composed from language, the possibility of thinking of non-linguistic signs in similar terms was already possible.

For Saussure, there is, nonetheless, a tree beyond the signified, which he terms the 'referent'. He sets it aside – or 'brackets' it – however, for the purposes of his analysis. One implication of this distinction is to suggest that different languages 'carve up reality' differently, as in the apocryphal stories of Inuit/Eskimo peoples and their signification of 'snow'. In more radical formulations of semiotics, it is claimed that we *only* access 'reality' via language.

While we might claim that our senses, most obviously our sight, provide us with non-linguistic 'input', only via language can we communicate what we see to others and, some would argue, even to ourselves. In itself, this distinction

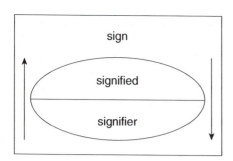
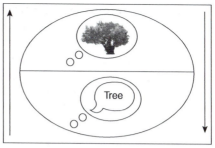

Figures 12 and 13   Saussure's conception of sign (reproduced from Chandler, 2007, as adapted from Saussure, 1966)

might seem pedantic, but as this last more radical implication of the linguistic turn was adopted directly in Louis Althusser's theory of **ideology**, for example, its influence is considerable.

Saussure's Principle 2 is the langue/parole distinction. This is one of several (more) binary dichotomies Saussure usually represents visually by axes. Put simply, this position simply asserts that linguistic users do not understand the deep structure of a language – the rules by which it shapes meaning – in the same way that a driver need not understand the workings of a car. Indeed, the immersive 'unconsciousness' that a learner driver has to achieve to employ reflexes when driving a car is a little like this. Similarly, successful learners of a second language must attain such familiarity via immersion rather than repeated 'conscious' translations into their first language.

'Langue' is thus the 'system' constituted by the conventions of linguistic practice that are unreflectively 'known' by each speaker and 'confronted as a state' (Saussure, 1966: 9). 'Parole' is the manifest speech that results from the operations of those conventions. Diachrony, in this context, is the horizontal axis of incremental changes; synchrony the vertical axis of overarching paradigmatic rules within which change may occur. The 'state' of achieved conventions is extremely conservative, however, despite the 'facts' Saussure acknowledges, namely the frequent changes in signifier–signified relations (Saussure, 1966: 74).

THE VOLOŠINOVIAN CRITIQUE OF SAUSSURE

Sausure's influence outside linguistics relied on a now well-mapped set of influences and migrations via 'the Prague Circle'. The most famous member of this group was Roman Jakobson. From him, the French anthropologist Claude Lévi-Strauss learnt the principles of structural linguistics and applied them to anthropology. From thereon, structuralism was usually considered part of 'the new French thought'. There was an earlier phase of Saussurean influence among the post-revolutionary Russian artistic **modern**ist avant-gardes of the 1920s, however, especially the Futurists (a group in which Jakobson had participated) and the related Russian formalist literary critics and theorists.

From that phase came a Russian critique of Saussure's work published under the name of Valentin Vološinov, which was not translated into English until 1973. Vološinov sought in *Marxism and the Philosophy of Language* (1973) to criticize both Saussure and orthodox Marxism. Thus, his priorities were not unlike those of Gramsci, whose major work was being translated into English simultaneously.

Vološinov features prominently in Stuart Hall's work of this period, as a means of tempering the effects of structuralism on Althusser's conception of ideology. Hall was especially drawn to Vološinov's thesis of the relationship between signs, ideologies and social class.

Vološinov's conception of the domain of signification/**ideology** is remarkably similar to Gramsci's non-reductive conception of **hegemony**. As the field of signification is socially shared across social classes, social struggles can also manifest as *contests in signification*. For Vološinov, signs are thus *multiaccentual*; that is, the same sign – democracy or freedom, for example, could be inflected with different social accents by different social groups or blocs of social forces. These dimensions fed directly into Hall's conceptualization of **articulation** (Hall, 1982). More recently, Vološinov's work has been taken up within critical **discourse** analysis (CDA).

Vološinov's critique of Saussure received a more elaborate reconstruction and extension in the work of Raymond Williams (1977a: 21–44). Both Williams and Vološinov consider the Saussurean project *formalist* – a term developed in Russian literary theory to refer to the prioritization of the formal properties of signifying practices that 'produce' meaning at the expense of considering the broader social relations and conventions within which those signifying practices are developed (see **cultural form**). In the case of poetry, for example, the formalist emphasis shifts to poetic *devices* such as metaphor.

In the case of the arbitrary nature of the sign, Williams accepts the premise that no 'natural' bond between signifier and signified exists, but he insists that the use of the term 'arbitrary' to characterize this non-correspondence conceals the *social conventions* by which the signifier–signified relation is 'fused' (Williams, 1977a: 27).

Williams and Vološinov each criticize the conservatism of both Saussure's conception of change within his synchrony/diachrony model and subsequent structuralist theories that either privilege synchrony over diachrony or work with an impoverished conception of the diachronic. They also reject the signifier–signified binary.

FROM SIGN TO CODE

The critical tension implicit in the Vološinov/Williams charge of formalism is to some extent reproduced within the work of Roland Barthes, the French figure most associated with semiology and semiotics.

Barthes applied the Saussurean conception of the sign to non-linguistic phenomena such as photographs. So the issue of the relationship between signification and social conventions and related practices was even more important. In the case of news photographs, for example, there was no question for Barthes in 1961 (1977b: 15) that *semiological* analysis was limited to 'the message', while *sociological* analysis was required to examine the message's production and reception. Revealingly, a few years earlier in *Mythologies* (Barthes, 1972: 112), in direct response to the charge of (ahistorical) formalism, he quipped, 'the more a system is specifically defined in its forms, the more amenable it is to historical criticism. To parody a well-known saying, I shall say that a little formalism turns one away from History, but that a lot brings one back to it'.

Indeed, for the early Barthes at least, such a self-description is borne out in his analyses, especially in relation to mediated forms. What he tends to bring his detailed formal analyses 'back to', however, is not quite 'History', but **ideology** (understood in its masking sense). In *Mythologies*, Barthes (1972) argued for a second-order system of signification where both language and extra-linguistic signs, such as photographs, signified – primarily by connotation – 'myths' (see Figure 14). As linguistic signifiers denote signifieds, so too do such signs signify myths. Myths dehistoricize and some myths – especially those associated with nationalist rhetoric – seek to naturalize political ideologies. The systems of 'cultural' familiarity on which such connotations relied Barthes called *codes*.

In a famous 1964 analysis of a French pasta advertisement, Barthes examined the different layers of signification present within the text of the advertisement's message. His primary distinction in this instance is between denotation and connotation. Photography fascinated Barthes as it short-circuited the Saussurean portrayal of the signifier–signified relationship in Figures 12 and 13. Such a photographic message is not 'arbitrary', as linguistic signs are. The signifier resembles the signified; it is *iconic*. A photographed tomato signifies a tomato. That is only a primary, *denotative* level of signification, however. The message of the entire advertisement also relies on the anchoring of such images to connotative codes by the linguistic message – here, rather subtly; more typically, quite explicitly in advertising.

The mythical dimension of the Panzani advertisement (Figure 15) is the 'Italianicity' connoted by the advertisement within the second order of signification. 'Italianicity' relies for its decoding on a paradigmatic chain of cultural stereotypes. Precisely because the denotative and connotative messages are simultaneously 'received' by the reader, however, the overall implication is to 'naturalize' the cultural work of the advertisement and such stereotypes. Hence, for Barthes, it also works ideologically.

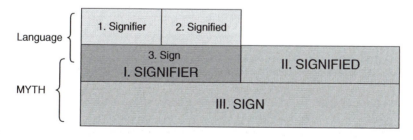

Figure 14   Myth and its relation to signs and signifiers (reproduced from Barthes, 1972: 115)

Figure 15 Panzani advertisement (reproduced from Barthes, 1977a)

The anchoring of signification also indicated the phenomenon of _polysemy_ – literally definable as 'multiplicity of meanings' – but, especially for the later Barthes and related approaches, the semiotic form that generates polysemy is a floating chain of signifiers, the meaning of which otherwise remains 'unfixed'. Such a conception also supported the increasing 'textualization' of social phenomena – that is, to read non-linguistic phenomena not only as if they were structured like a language but also _as if_ they were no more than texts. Two problems for 'textualizing' approaches arise:

- how to distinguish between the textual and extra-textual
- how to account for the relationship between the textual and the extra-textual.

The second problem is addressed broadly within media studies as one of **articulation**. On the first issue, Williams (1995: 208–9) proposed a model of (liquid) solution as a way of clarifying this potential impasse – that the extent to which a textual analysis of a non-linguistic 'object' could be legitimate depended on the 'degree of solution of a signifying practice within otherwise organised social relations'. That is, another form of analysis – such as one modelled on social action as used in discussions of **interactivity** – was often also required.

Nonetheless, the fixing and unfixing of meaning also suggested a more fluid form of critico-political practice that emerged most notably in media studies around conceptions of **popular**.

EXCURSUS

At stake in such nuances of application of the linguistic/textualist models is the question of non-object-like *values* that also need to be rendered linguistically and, so, semiotically. While we can debate the 'reality' of a tree as signified and referent and its relevance or not to the signifier 'tree', something quite different happens if we replace 'tree' with 'justice'. If we argue that such normative concepts are mere constructions of language, it is plain that something has gone amiss in the formalist construction of the issue as one of 'arbitrariness'. For, even by the linguistic definition, concepts such as justice and democracy are *not* arbitrary. They can be 'benchmarked' by parameters such as the independence of a judiciary, **freedom of communication** and so on. Yet, we do not need to debate their tree-like material 'reality' to establish this. While a tree plausibly can be considered an object, normative concepts refer to (at least) *intersubjective* relations between fellow 'subjects', humans or citizens. The 'materiality' of such concepts is hardly as relevant until we discuss their **embodiment**. Equally, however, an unfixed signifying chain might also be thought compatible with the unfulfilled – and so unfixed – utopian promise of an idea such as democracy that is at the heart of immanent **critique**.

FURTHER READING

Semiotics 'primers' are ubiquitous. Daniel Chandler's *Semiotics: The basics* (2007) is one of the best (see also www.aber.ac.uk/media/Documents/S4B/the_book. html). For the work of Roland Barthes, see Michael Moriarty (1991). On messages in media studies, see the 'Codes and cultural analysis' chapter in Corner (1998). Typical cultural studies accounts of this literature can be found in Hall (1997) and Chris Barker (2000).

Simulacra

> **Related concepts**: *broadcasting, culture, embodiment, image, mobile privatization, popular/populist, sign, technoculture.*

203

'Simulacra' is a concept popularized in the work of sociologist and media theorist Jean Baudrillard. The plural of simulation, simulacra refers to the vast field of signs and sign objects that have become separated from their referents. Thus, simulation is not the same as a copy. Rather, it is the copy of a copy, the circulated meaning of which does not rest on an original signified object.

The signs that constitute simulacra do not conform to a logic of representation, nor do they measure up to the real – they are their own reality or 'hyperreality'.

AN ANTHROPOLOGY OF THE SIGN

Baudrillard's concept, which erases the distinction between surface and depth, is frequently cited as central to postmodernism. Baudrillard, however, rejects the characterization of his work as postmodern – the source of it can be traced back, instead, to French anthropology.

In an important work, William Merrin (2005) has salvaged Baurdillard's work from his postmodern contemporaries by tracing the influences of Émile Durkheim, Marcel Mauss and the College of Sociology influential in Paris in the 1930s. Merrin argues that the key to understanding the popularized concept of 'simulacra' is to understand the significance of 'symbolic exchange' in his work.

Rather than being a supporter of what many see as the decadent fatalism of postmodern thought, Baudrillard sees the development of modern media in terms of a great fall in the history of human communication. The passage from symbolic gift exchange societies to modern mass societies has resulted in a steady decline of human communication. He (1981b: 169) makes the apparently absurd claim that 'mass media fabricate non-communication'. For Baudrillard, there is no communication without an act of exchange. Modern mass media, on the other hand, constitute a form of 'speech without a response' (Baudrillard, 1981b: 169).

Tribal society is based on symbolic gift exchange: 'The symbolic is neither a concept, an agency, a category, nor a "structure", but an act of exchange and *a social relation which puts an end to the real*, which resolves the real, and, at the same time, puts an end to the opposition between the real and the imaginary' (Baudrillard, 1981a: 133). Bound up in this exchange is the opportunity for the giver to attain a kind of honour and prestige that is seldom seen in media societies, in which the mass audience has no opportunity to 'give'.

Thus, mass media do not provide an environment in which there can be a *group recognition* of reciprocity that gives people access to the sacred and the divine. In several texts, Durkhem and Mauss describe how, in premodern societies, the organized offering of gifts and sacrificial goods at festivals and religious rituals results in an intense convulsive and euphoric release of energy, which lifts individuals out of the mundane and everyday.

In media societies, communication of the gift is replaced by the consumption of communications, the only message of which is the communication of consumption: 'the media induce a social relation [that] involves … the abstraction, separation and abolition of exchange itself' (Baudrillard, 1981b: 169).

Television is an example of people 'no longer speaking to each other', isolated in the face of a 'speech without response' (Baudrillard, 1981b: 169). In echoes of Guy Debord's *Society of the Spectacle* (1977), audiences' only recourse to reclaim exchange is via an abstract circuit of consumption. Through consumption, individuals can realize the meaning of the image that is attached to the commodity, but, when this becomes systemic, it leads to the 'total organization of everyday life' (Baudrillard, 1998: 29). This is what Baudrillard calls the realm of the semiotic or simulacra.

FROM THE SYMBOLIC TO THE SEMIOTIC

When the symbolic is translated into the semiotic, 'the lived, unique, eventual character of the world is transformed into images of itself' (Baudrillard, 1998: 122–3). 'We live, sheltered by signs in the denial of the real' (Baudrillard, 1998: 34), consuming reality as a sign. The real is replaced by a 'neo-reality', which assumes the force of a reality. The hyperreal stage of simulacra corresponds to mass media.

Baudrillard charts the historical cultural significance of simulacra in 'The precession of simulacra' (Baudrillard, 1994). They proceed in four phases or 'orders', conforming to phases of the image that progress within a framework of representation as follows (Baudrillard, 1994: 6):

- It is the reflection of a profound reality
  - it masks and denatures a profound reality
  - it masks the *absence* of a profound reality
  - it has no relation to any reality whatsoever: it is its own pure simulacrum.

In the first phase, 'representation is of the sacramental order' (Baudrillard, 1994: 6), which is when the image must be faithful to reality, as in European landscape and oil painting. While it can easily be recognized in hundreds of years of European expressive realism, it survives in the code of journalists today, who, with their narrow conventions and frameworks of objectivity, bias and neutrality, embrace the prospect of a correspondence between reality and representation.

The second phase is recognized in various understandings of ideology, namely the assumption that representation is an order of malfeasance, false consciousness and a distortion of real conditions.

The third phase is probably the most difficult to understand. Here, Baudrillard argues that an objective representation of the real is impossible because the referent is already a simulational reality. Therefore, representation hides not 'the truth' but the fact that there is no 'truth'. Famously, he claimed that the function of theme parks, such as Disneyland, is to encourage us to think that the rest of society is somehow 'real', whereas, for Baudrillard (1981b: 180), the semiotic world is a 'cybernetic illusion'.

The fourth phase marks a limit to representation itself. A line is crossed and representation leaves the orders where signs either simulate or dissimulate the real to enter an order where signs dissimulate that there is nothing to simulate. It is a simulacrum that 'never exchanged for the real, but exchanges for itself, in an uninterrupted circuit without reference or circumference' (Baudrillard, 1994: 6). It is the ubiquity of electronic media that produces this decisive transition. Television, in particular, constitutes a vast simulation machine in which the displacement of communication by a 'speech without response' becomes total.

THE TOTALITARIAN NATURE OF MASS MEDIA

In the chapter 'Requiem for the media' in *For a Critique of the Political Economy*, Baudrillard (1981b: 181) remarks:

> In its present form, equipment like television or film does not serve communication but prevents it. It allows no reciprocal action between transmitter and receiver: technically speaking, it reduces feedback to the lowest point compatible with the system.

For Baudrillard, what the process model would call 'feedback' is part of the 'cybernetic illusion'. Genres of media that formally appear to set up a 'reversibility' of circuits (such as letters to the editor, phone-in programmes, polls and so on) integrate the contingency of all possible responses in advance. These genres rely on the illusion of responsibility in exchange but, in fact, they co-opt a fraction of the audience for the benefit of cybernetic illusion.

In symbolic exchange, power is accumulated by those who can give without needing to be repaid. Reciprocity is achieved, however, over time via the potlatch (system of gift exchange). In media societies, all of the power belongs to mass media as the system of simulacra cannot be democratized.

That is why, for example, Baudrillard argues that the 'abstraction' of media constitutes a total system of power and control that cannot be subverted. He says: 'All vague impulses to democratise content … control the information process, contrive a reversibility of circuits, or take power over media are hopeless – unless the monopoly of speech is broken' (1981b: 170). The common misconception that 'feedback' (the process model) is reversible is a potent apologia for non-response, but it is another device for the abolition of exchange, merely the simulation of a response.

Baudrillard discusses the futility of 'using' media as a form of protest in relation to the failed French revolution of May 1968. For Baudrillard, there was a brief moment of reversibility, where protestors appeared to use the media against the power structure, but for him this just provided content destined to be co-opted into the media's system of power. When the **discourse** of the protest is 'transformed into models, neutralized into signs', their meaning is eviscerated. The momentum of the protest is short-circuited by being made over in the abstract bureaucratic model of 'habitual social control'. Once transformed into the familiar models of meaning habituated by mass media, the 'revolutionary' events begin to be read according to the models and codes of particular mediums. Television, in particular, can never accommodate a model of subversion, but, on the contrary, finds a situation where 'the media have never discharged their responsibilities with more efficiency' (Baudrillard, 1981b: 173). In other words, what television does best is mould the ephemerality and spontaneity of events into a coded narrative that audiences are forced to make sense of according to other narratives peculiar to TV (especially if they are spectacles). Thus, the operation of symbolic communication, only successful offscreen, always finds its way on to the screen or the screen becomes the totem via which people make sense of it. As Baudrillard (1981b: 176–7) writes:

> The real revolutionary media during May were the walls and their speech, the silk-screen posters and the hand-painted notices, the street where speech began and was exchanged – everything that was an *immediate* inscription, given and returned, spoken and answered, mobile in the same space and time, reciprocal and antagonistic. The street is, in this sense, the alternative and subversive form of the mass media, since it isn't, like the latter, an objectified support for answerless messages, a transmission system at a distance. It is the frayed space of the symbolic exchange of speech – ephemeral, mortal: a speech that is not reflected on the Platonic screen of the media. Institutionalized by reproduction, reduced to a spectacle, this speech is expiring.

As with his romantic yearning for the tribal foundations of communication, the street seems to represent the last remnant of symbolic exchange, at once glorified and abolished. What Baudrillard does not explain, however, is how street forms of communication might nevertheless be made sense of by way of the code of television, and why the street is exempted from the power of simulacra.

Baudrillard's bleak view of **media** as totalitarian displays a number of problems that had become apparent by the 1990s. One was the challenge of computer-mediated communication (CMC) to the unilinear model of media of which Baudrillard complains. Clearly, online forms of contact and community allow for degrees of reciprocity that are not extinguished by the semiotic code. Thus, Baudrillard's account of simulacra becomes specific to mass media rather than mediation in general. The status of the image in broadcast environments is completely different from its status in online media.

Even within mass media, Baudrillard's account of simulacra is implicitly challenged by the turn to 'active audience' analysis. His construction of the masses as passive is vulnerable to the kind of critique that Williams made of McLuhan in 1974 – that medium theory, which renders the audience as inert, is technologically determinist.

FURTHER READING

The most accessible entry point into Baudrillard's account of the semiotic and his theory of simulacra is his chapter 'Requiem for the media' (1981b: Chapter 9). In it, Baudrillard's pessimism regarding the fate of human communication under the conditions of electronic media is expressed succinctly. It also reveals his anthropological approach to human communication deriving from sociologists Durkheim and Mauss and the College of Sociology, who rallied around Alexandre Kojeve in 1930s Paris. The argument that Baudrillard has been long mischaracterized as a postmodernist and he is, in fact, more of a romantic modernist is persuasively put by William Merrin in *Baudrillard and the Media* (2005).

Tabloidization

The term 'tabloid' derives from 'tablet' and referred to the practice of printing certain kinds of popular newspapers in the tabloid format as opposed to the 'broadsheet' format used by the 'quality press'; a tabloid was initially half a broadsheet. Today, the distinction has outlived the term's origin as many broadsheets have adopted the tabloid format and the tabloid v. quality distinction has been applied across all post-print media.

Some source the 'tablet' metaphor to compound medicines of the late nineteenth century (Ray, 2006), others to the shape of inscribed stone tablets. The mere format distinction today resembles the 'portrait v. landscape' opposition in page-formatting options in software programs and the increasing usage of the term 'tablet computer' for miniaturized multifunction digital devices.

Initially, the term 'tabloid' also invoked a significant contemporary cultural distinction of more significance. In the USA, use of 'tabloid' also refers to very unusual newspaper publications – the 'supermarket tabloids' – composed mostly of fictional stories of the 'Martian stole my baby' genre, rather than the mainstream understanding deriving from British practice. A similar distinction in US usage applies to the extension to 'tabloid TV', which includes non-news or borderline news programmes, such as news on celebrity TV channels that is referred to as 'infotainment' (Gripsrud, 2000).

Perhaps for this reason, US media analysts tend to refer to 'infotainment' and a 'media malaise thesis' as much as the British-derived 'tabloidization' (Norris, 2000). All these terms denote an alleged decline in editorial standards, as well as an alteration in dominant **news values** towards 'tabloid' ones across (usually all) news media. 'Infotainment' specifically concerns the tendency of programme producers to address even free-to-air television news as just another audience-maximizing product, without regard to its public interest role.

In short, the chief concern among critics of tabloidization is that professional standards of journalism are being compromised and, as a result, journalism's 'information function' in modern democracies – as specified in many notions of freedom of the press – is also being compromised. Many advocates of the tabloidization/malaise thesis are former or practising journalists (for example, Fallows, 1996). Defenders of tabloids, if not tabloidization *per se*, point to the more socially inclusive style of the tabloids and their capacity to reach a broader audience that more readily includes women, those on lower incomes and the less well educated.

The lines of debate thus resemble those relating to the terms **popular** and **populist** and the **culture industries**. Where the normative reference point in debates around popular culture is usually art and/or popular aesthetic tastes, however, tabloidization's counterpoint is more often the normative ideals of democracy, most recently those gathered around the **public sphere** and, specifically, informed citizenship. As James Curran (1991: 33) has noted, however, even for traditional liberal conceptions of democracy, 'entertainment is problematic' – as prefigured by early Romantic conceptions of the irreconcilability of art and the market (see **culture**). Moreover, the role of 'the market' (and, indeed, **capitalism**) in this process provides a somewhat starker case for economic analysis.

HOTELLING'S EFFECT

Critics of tabloidization regard it chiefly as a business strategy rather than evidence of a popular 'will' articulated via the market (Fallows, 1996: 145). Although it has been a long-standing feature of the self-justifications of market systems, neoliberal claims that markets were more reliable indicators of public/popular demand became strident in the period of media de**regulation** from the 1980s. For example, the neoliberal reorientation of the USA's regulator, the Federal Communications Commission (FCC), during Ronald Reagan's presidency is an overt instance. As Mark Fowler (cited in Calabrese, 2000), its then director and his aide, advocated in 1982:

> Instead of defining public demand and specifying categories to serve this demand, the FCC should rely on the broadcasters' ability to determine the wants of their audience through the normal mechanisms of the marketplace. The public's interest, then, defines the public interest.

There are no 'normal mechanisms of the marketplace', however, nor, indeed, a singular spatially fixed 'marketplace' – unless one imagines entire national populations still living in small eighteenth-century European and US market towns.

Of most concern to critics of tabloidization is the tendency for media markets to homogenize under the influence of 'Hotellings effect'. As it happens, US network TV was just such an instance. As Collins and Murroni (1996: 62–3) have usefully put it:

> many doubt that competitive media markets, even those with more than one firm supplying relevant products and services, do deliver diverse, quality media products. They characteristically point to broadcast television in the USA where there is significant convergence of programming content. … Economic theory names this phenomenon 'Hotelling's effect'.

> Hotelling's effect applies under special circumstances, namely where there is non-price competition (e.g. between advertising-funded television channels). Economically rational competitors will then crowd in the middle of the spectrum of consumer tastes rather than provide a diverse range of products. Assuming consumer tastes can be arranged in a continuum, it can be argued that two firms that did not compete on price would do best by positioning their products 'where the demand is', in the middle of the continuum. New entrants would face the same incentives, resulting in an undue tendency for competitors to imitate each other. Advertising funded, profit maximizing television is a case in point. (Collins and Murroni, 1996: 62–3)

Many media markets are configured according to such 'non-price competition' to follow 'common denominator' marketing logics. These are premised on an *estimate* of majority tastes, strongly informed by imitation of competitors' programmes and scheduling. Historically, the result was that free-to-air channels tended to schedule very similar programmes against each other (Beebe, 1977). Indeed, free-to-air analogue broadcasting is the classic instance, but often so are, for example, the channels competing *within* a digital subscription television service (Waterman, 1992).

In effect, as Hotelling (1929) argued for such markets generally, many media markets follow this tendency *unless* there is direct intervention by a regulator via content **regulation** (as in programme codes) or a media policy that structurally facilitates qualitative competition via PSB-like market participants, committed to certain 'less common denominator' programme standards. The more orthodox economic view is that increasing the number of 'players' should lead to the 'natural' market development of more 'quality' consumer choices. Despite increasing fragmentation and restructuring of traditional media markets, however, such 'quality' market provision is rare. Examples are HBO's production of *The Sopranos*, *The Wire* and so on in recent US television production.

Thus, deregulation of structured media markets and 'tabloidization' typically go hand in hand. The need for PSB provision of 'quality products' tends to be an example of 'market failure', namely that the supposedly 'natural' configuration of the market has failed to provide such choice. In the case of journalism specifically, cost also becomes a problematic *production* (rather than market competition) issue, because tabloid journalism is usually cheaper to produce than investigative journalism, for example (Curran et al., 1980).

THE DANGERS OF TABLOIDIZATION: FOX NEWS AND NINETEENTH-CENTURY RADICAL PRESSES AS LIMIT CASES

Even given the 'market bias' towards tabloidization, the issue remains of just what is problematic about the content of such cultural forms. From the perspective of professional editorial values, it does not follow that traditional tabloid newspapers are necessarily inferior. Many tabloids routinely follow the same professional norms of validation and sourcing as 'the qualities'.

More typically, it was in **news**(worthiness) **values** that the traditional distinction between tabloid and quality journalism was drawn. Tabloids have historically prioritized 'human interest' stories and generally placed less routine emphasis on the domain of electoral politics, especially policy debates, than the broadsheets (Curran et al., 1980). More recently, tabloid news values have shifted heavily towards celebrities and what McNair has called 'striptease culture' and, predictably, Hotelling's effect is playing its role in television programming too (McNair, 2002: especially 95–6). Tabloids tend not to routinely address their readers and audiences as citizens seeking to become informed on a range of policy issues. They have fewer features and less background analysis and their commentary may be based less on expertise than in the qualities. They are also more prone than 'quality' journalistic outlets to go into 'campaign mode' during elections and practise forms of populist jingoism in times of war.

Most notoriously, it is the rise of News Corp's US Fox News that demonstrates, for many, the ultimate tabloidization of editorial values, in a similar fashion to *The Sun* newspaper in the UK. Here, expanded popularity is combined with overt political influence and the overt abandonment of the traditional editorial values of fact validation and the separation of fact from 'opinion'.

Nevertheless, Fox News is a somewhat exceptional case in that its proprietor, Rupert Murdoch, is also continuing the role of a nineteenth-century 'politically minded press owner' (Chalaby, 1997), rather than merely practising Hotelling's market logic. That is, he really does have a long track record of orienting his news outlets to follow a political 'line', most often in terms of party affiliation and support for military interventions. Moreover, even by the internal standards of his own global corporation, Fox News is an extreme case (perhaps due to national differences in regulation). It has more in common with its deregulated US cousin, the aggressive talk(back) radio format that developed in the USA in the 1990s, than mainstream tabloid culture.

Back in Australia, Murdoch's nation of origin (where he has not held FTA broadcast licences for many years), the deregulation of commercial television news and especially current affairs in the 1990s followed an almost classic pattern of prioritization of ratings over professional ethics and 'hard' news values (Turner, 2001).

Yet, those who doubt the recent critiques of tabloidization rightly argue that these instances are hardly justifications for an argument that there has been an overall decline. Tabloids exist and proliferate, of course, but an overall claim of ongoing tab-loid*ization* requires a longer view. Indeed, even more overt partisanship – and, often, a capacity to entertain – was once the norm in nearly all journalism. If we follow Schudson's (2008) account of the US case, for example, the 'social responsibility' tradition that promoted professional editorial values was a relatively recent historical development and replaced a much more partisan model of journalism.

Here, the debates about **populism** are of relevance. Partisan presses can be argued to have had a direct linkage to readerships via popular association with large popular political parties and similar social movements. As the commercial press – both quality and tabloid – in Britain was, to a considerable degree, built on the destruction of the older nineteenth-century 'unstamped' or 'radical' partisan presses (Boyce, 1978; Curran and Seaton, 2009: Chapter 2; Williams, 1961), the loss of this more diverse partisanship is often an implicit historical reference point in not only this debate but also core liberal understandings of diversity of opinion and so freedom of speech (Curran, 1991).

While no **postmodernist**, Raymond Williams argued on a number of occasions that the radical presses were actually *replaced* by a commercial '*simulacrum* of popular journalism' in the nineteenth century that continued to dominate at the time he wrote (1970: 16 [emphasis added]; 1989b: 261). What he means by this is that while open political repression had failed to eliminate the popular radical presses, commercial replacement had succeeded.

Radical political writing was *the* dominant form of daily popular newspaper in early-nineteenth-century Britain. Papers such as *The Black Dwarf* routinely outsold nascent qualities such as *The Times*. The future tabloid news priorities of crime and scandal entered via the later development of the Sunday press, but were still usually mixed with radical political writing at this point.

From the 1840s, the commercial 'simulacra' of this popular radicalism took the newer prototabloid content and manufactured it on an industrial scale, but excluded the original radical political content. Williams' simulacra of popular radical journalism were the core 'content' of a restructuring of mid-nineteenth-century commercial popular newspapers that rested on the development of steam-powered presses and their use in increased capitalization of production and distribution. These developments finally rendered 'obsolete' the old hand presses, from which the word 'press' had been derived (Williams, 1970). For Williams (1978: 49), however, these developments also meant, crucially, a reorientation of 'social relations between journalists and their readers and between both and their proprietors'. More detailed and sophisticated historical accounts of these developments have followed (see especially Chalaby, 1998; Curran, 1977, 1978, 2002).

Williams' (1978) deliberate linkage of this press history with his work on popular culture – notably theatrical melodrama – has ensured that his account remains a frequent reference point in the tabloidization debates. In a powerful critique of Williams, for example, Martin Conboy (2002) argued that the moment of the radical presses should be regarded as an historical exception. Indeed, the period was one characterized by the struggle for expanded suffrage as well as freedom of the press, so neatly fitting Habermas' distinction between public sphere in crisis/formation and public sphere 'at rest' (Habermas, 1996a: 379ff).

Conboy (2002: 178) suggests that, in analysing what has now become normalcy, we must accept that 'popular' can now only be defined numerically by circulation or its equivalent: 'authenticity is now economically marked'. Further, for Conboy, we must examine tabloid culture for its contemporary rhetorical modes of presenting itself *as* authentic in the old sense – that is, 'of the people'. Conboy's recommendations lead us directly (back) into the discursive analysis of **populism** and the Gramscian 'national popular' and echo strongly Justin Lewis' (2001) contemporary cultural analysis of opinion polls (see **hegemony**). Indeed, Conboy has gone on to provide an excellent case study of 'Tabloid Britain' as a discursively constructed national community (Conboy, 2006).

Yet, both Conboy and Williams regard popular culture as a mixture of (potentially radical) 'popular engagement' (Conboy, 2002: 178) *and* 'ways of adapting, from disadvantage, to a dominant social order, finding relief and satisfaction or diversion inside it' (Williams, 1970: 22). The 'realistic' mapping Conboy advocates resembles what Williams characterized as a 'social structure' of such media where that structure includes a nuanced account of not only the business model of the publisher but also the embedded cultural relations between cultural producers and readerships/viewerships.

It is temping, then, to bracket Hotelling's effect as 'economic tabloidization' and separate it from the tabloidization of content. Indeed, Conboy is drawn to those who would define tabloidization entirely by its rhetorical devices. Yet if we were speaking of other aspects of popular culture, most notably popular music, we would not make such a separation. A Hotelling-like pursuit of 'the middle of the market' via the simulacra of 'authenticity' is the music business's stock in trade. We can equally note what is still called in everyday language the 'authentically innovative and creative', even 'autonomous', that is always celebrated by each new wave of musical innovators and pitched against a corporate orthodoxy of homogenization. Given the increasing prominence of user-generated reportage, some similar 'popular' critique of tabloidization – perhaps about whether or not tabloid content belongs on the latest tablet computers – may also emerge.

FURTHER READING

Martin Conboy's (2002) study of the British popular press is perhaps the most sustained and historically informed analysis of the issues at stake, within and beyond print media. His *Tabloid Britain* (2006) is a contemporory analysis informed by critical discourse analysis (CDA). Frank Esser (1999) locates the issue more broadly within Europe than its usual Anglo-American frame and G.N. Ray (2006) provides an Indian perspective. On the rise of 'infotainment' globally, see Daya Kishan Thussu (2007). Some of the strongest critics of tabloidization come from a legal justice perspective; Fox et al. (2007) is indicative. John Hartley's (1996) sympathetic reading of tabloid culture is one of the most influential and shares some aspects of John Fiske's (1989) broader defence of popular culture. On the role of gender in the tabloidization debates, see Carter et al. (1998), Macdonald (2000) and Conboy (2006: Chapter 6). For a US critique of Hotelling-like homogenization, see David Croteau and William Hoynes (2006). Within media economics literatures, Rudolf Steiner (1952) is usually considered the classic initial employment of Hotelling's Effect to analyse media markets – for more recent examples, see David Waterman (1992) and A. Brown (1996). The US collection edited by Barbie Zelizer (2009) focusses on stylistic tabloidization, while the UK/European-based collections on tabloidization and related issues edited by Peter Dahlgren and Colin Sparks (1992), Michael Bromley and Hugh Stephenson (1998) and Colin Sparks and John Tulloch (2000) remain very valuable.

Technoculture

Related concepts: cyberculture, embodiment, mobile privatization, modern, technological determinism, time–space compression.

The historical emergence of the concept of 'technoculture' in the last half of the twentieth century marks a distinct shift in the relationship between technology and society, culture and nature. The development, during this period, of technologies of a qualitatively different character from those associated with modernity, has deeply problematized the widespread instrumental view that technology is a central index of moral improvement (Carey, 1989).

The advance of nuclear, cybernetic, DNA, gene-splicing, information and nano-technologies into the daily lives of individuals in technological societies becomes central to the definition of those societies. Thus, technological historicism – the idea that there are one or two technologies that characterize a social period, such as 'the steam age', nuclear age, computer age, video age and so on – is replaced by the general conditions of technological society.

Technoculture distinguishes itself from 'Enlightenment' technology and science in that it is not concerned with discovering 'laws of nature' but the reinvention of nature itself. Technoculture reconstitutes the world by ignoring the constraints of the natural world. The manipulation of nature at the atomic, molecular, cellular and DNA levels affords the opportunity to substitute nature and natural processes.

POSTMODERN TECHNOCULTURE V. MODERN TECHNOLOGY

Such a relationship to nature is very different from the technologies and tech-niques of modernity, which accept the limits of nature and work within its con-straints, or at least towards 'harnessing' the power of nature with some intrinsic regard for its sustainability. The fact that 'sustainability' has recently become a scientific and technological buzzword indicates this changing relationship to nature; science and science policy now set their own limits.

Both postmodern technoculture and modern technology can be seen as out-comes of the scientistic Enlightenment narrative of emancipation, in which tech-nology is applied to liberate human beings from the 'realm of necessity' (see **modern**). Whether a technological development works within the constraints of nature to reduce dependence on it or nature is replaced by simulation, the aim in each case is emancipation. Thus, all technologies are placed on a modernization continuum of emancipatory potential and descriptions, such as the 'best available technology', cutting-edge or 'state-of-the-art' technology proliferate.

Jean-François Lyotard (1984) sees postmodern technoscience as a kind of end game (final stage in a protracted negotiation) of such grand narratives, which involves, first, the accumulation of knowledge about nature and society and then the application of such knowledge to moral and physical improvement. Such an instrumental culture of technology represents a kind of Copernican revolution – in science, the secular idea that human knowledge can be released from theological foundations, such as realizing that the movement of celestial bodies can be discov-ered by direct observation rather than as a worldview controlled by a world religion.

FROM NATURE TO 'NEW NATURE'

Thus, Enlightenment science has sought material emancipation from nature at the same time as a release from theology. There are, however, some problems with such a view of science and technology.

First, nature is assumed to be benign and inert; technology is seen to improve the human condition; and nature is assumed to remain constant and unchanging, rather than placed 'in crisis' by human activity itself.

Second, in pursuit of the 'realm of freedom' from nature, human beings have created their own 'new nature' (Garnham, 2000; Lyotard, 1984). Here, new nature refers to the creation of human-made environments that plunge human beings into a new kind of enslavement. This is the argument that, in technological societies, technology itself creates its own kind of deprivation. While technological society has effected a huge leap in productivity, it has created more alienating division of labour and bureaucratic administration, which has 'put in place a new systems world that dominated humans and restricted their freedom as effectively as nature had previously done' (Garnham, 2000: 65–6).

The high-modern notion of being 'slaves to the machine' is an expression of this particular reversal of dominance and subordination of nature and culture (Postman, 1993). The machine can be a bureaucracy, a factory system or, in post-industrial societies, the demands of communications media (layers of communication mediums that require attention). Modern communications mediums differ from the machine-like environments of the workplace or institution, in that they involve electronic rather than physical assemblies. The way that they become embedded in social life, however, and come to mediate the very possibility of sociability is extensive. Checking messages on telephones, texts, e-mails, online chat, online social networking, as well as the calling of popular culture, in film, music, print and television, occupy so much of our daily routine as to make sociability a new form of labour, although the ideology of such communications mediums is that they are labour-saving and convenient.

THE DISCOURSE OF TECHNOLOGICAL PROGRESS

It is true that modern technology 'speeds up' processes of work, entertainment and communications, but it is not true that this translates into more efficiency and convenience. Rather, countless studies of the use of domestic technologies show that their main impact is to raise social expectations of the time in which activities can be achieved, such as the mechanization of housework, with machines to clean dishes and clothes, or e-mailing documents as attachments rather than relying on postal services. Notions of efficiency and speed are therefore not related to the technologies themselves but social norms that are established in relation to the embeddedness of these technologies in social life.

While Enlightenment views of science have been criticized by romantics, critical theorists and postmodernists, the technological discourse of progress remains deeply embedded in popular culture and scientific norms. The frontiers of such progress have been extended to the most macro levels, such as astrophysics and deep-space exploration, and the most micro, such as nuclear, DNA and nanotechnology. The discourses of discovery and moral improvement that can be found at such frontiers are, however, scarcely different from those that legitimated scientific research conducted over the past 200 years in technological societies.

There are two discourses at play in the technological conquest of nature – instrumentalism and **technological determinism**. These discourses, which are also perspectives on the application of science, arise from maintaining a strong distinction between 'technology' and 'society' and yet there is a recursive relationship between the two.

An instrumental perspective 'treats technology as subservient to values established in other social spheres (e.g. politics and culture)' (Feenberg, 1991: 5). This 'use or abuse' approach mainly views technology as a tool for the moral improvement of society. Therefore, it tends to side with utopian views of science and technology. The flipside to this is dystopian, even apocalyptic, attitudes to technology played out in science fiction, from Mary Shelley's *Frankenstein* to *Terminator 2*. Where technology fails – a nuclear accident or a collapsed bridge, for example – science is blamed.

Technological determinism also maintains a sharp causal distinction between science and society, but posits technology as a relatively autonomous power that, historically, develops independently of social influences, yet has profound impacts on society (Bimber, 1994; Misa, 1988). Consequently, entire periods of social history are tied to technology, such as the 'steam age', 'atomic age', 'digital age' and so on.

A third approach to technology is the 'substantivist' view, associated with Martin Heidegger's philosophy of technology (Feenberg, 1991; Heidegger, 1997). In this approach, 'technology constitutes a new type of cultural system that restructures the entire social world as an object of control' (Feenberg, 1991: 5). This is very different from the instrumental or determinist approaches, in that the opposition between science and society is broken down. Rather, it considers technology as already a part of the social sphere and, in fact, a unique aspect of social relations that often reveals our values, even what it means to be human. The substantivist view is sometimes taken to be technologically determinist, because of the importance it places on technology.

Its view is historical in another way, however: technology has not always been a key element of social life. It has only become so in recent times. The more technology mediates the kinds of engagement and interaction individuals have with the world, the more it assumes the character of an environment rather than a tool. This is what Heidegger (1997) calls enframing.

Enframing is the way technology reveals the threshold between human and machine, culture and nature. That is to say, questions, such as what it means to be human, are actually revealed when human beings begin to instrumentally intervene in and substitute natural functions, including the workings of the brain and human reproduction, or replace limbs with prosthetics, for example. Age-old questions, such as where does the mind end and the body begin, are thrown up in the process of substituting organs with machines. Equally, our ability to function in everyday life, as part of an assembly of machine and human, is revealed when a technology breaks down. In particular, when electronic technologies fail, we are typically propelled towards reconnecting with physical realities that have been replaced by the technologically extended substitutes for face-to-face communication or reliance on print. We also come to realize the extent to which we depend on electronic environments in everyday life and the social expectations according to which we conduct our life within these environments.

FURTHER READING

Heidegger's essay 'The question concerning technology' (1997) is a difficult read but foundational for understanding technoculture. Other forerunners include Jacques Ellul (1964) and, particularly relevant to media studies, Neil Postman (1993). A neo-Marxist analysis of the relationship between technology and the reproduction of capitalist culture can be found in Kevin Robins and Frank Webster (1999). The classic postmodern position on technology as 'new nature' is represented by Lyotard (1984). In an important essay, Andrew Feenberg (2003) has sought to link the Heideggerian literature with the social shaping critique of technological determinism.

Technological determinism

> **Related concepts**: articulation, broadcasting, communication(s), information society, interactivity, media/medium, mobile privatization, modern.

Few have ever labelled themselves technological determinists but, once recognized, we can see that technological determinism (TD) is a pervasive commonsensical assumption. It is the view that technologies achieve dramatic effects on society *of their own accord*. 'Technology' and 'society' are so thought of as more or less separate entities. It is important to remember that TD is a *pejorative* critical term, usually employed as a criticism of others.

Raymond Williams has provided what is certainly the most influential definition of TD employed within media studies. The following much-cited passage sets the scene for this discussion as well as the related concept of **cultural form** (Williams, 1974a: 13):

> It is an immensely powerful and now largely orthodox view of the nature of social change. New technologies are discovered, by an essentially internal process of research and development, which then sets the conditions for social change and progress. Progress, in particular, is the history of these inventions, which 'created the modern world'. The effects of these technologies, whether direct or indirect, foreseen or unforeseen, are as it were the rest of history. The steam engine, the automobile, television, the atomic bomb, have *made* modern man [sic] and the modern condition.

So TD is a commonsense assumption rather than an elaborated 'theory'. Accordingly, it is most readily found in 'gee whizz' journalism and press releases, colour

217

supplements and coffee-table books (such as Bunch and Hellemens, 1994; Harpur, 1982) and other popular forms, such as science fiction.

A powerful audiovisual illustration of the technologically determinist view of progress can be found within the opening titles of a version of the *Star Trek* television series, *Enterprise*. The *Enterprise* series is a 'prequel', set in the next century, and so sets out to link 'our present' in the twenty-first century with the period portrayed in the very first series (the twenty-third century). The opening of *Enterprise* establishes this transition via a visual montage of *past, present and future* images of technical inventions associated with exploration and discovery: cartography, sextants, sailing ships, early aeroplanes and, most notably, famous NASA missions, including the Apollo Moon landings of the 1960s, the shuttle programme, Mars Rover probes and the International Space Station. With this momentum established, animations of *Star Trek* shuttlecraft and star ships are seamlessly interwoven as the logical *linear extension* of this powerful body of past and present technical achievement. Thus, TD is not only a potent means of summing up the past but often a first resort in many imaginings of the future.

What TD most obviously overlooks is that 'technology' is part of 'society', not separate from it. The major alternative perspectives are thus called *social shaping* and/or *social constructivist* approaches. Against what Williams describes above as TD's assumption of an 'essentially internal process of research and development', the social shaping perspective locates technical inventions and the shape of their social configuration as technologies within a much broader social context. Famous early case studies by social shapers included the typewriter, military technology and the refrigerator (MacKenzie and Wajcman, 1999; Wajcman, 1994). Feminist research has been especially influential here (Wajcman, 1991, 2004).

TECHNOLOGICAL DETERMINISM AND COMMUNICATIONS TECHNOLOGIES

There are four different ways of discussing communications technologies in which the struggle between TD and social shaping alternatives are significant. In practice, these dimensions can be difficult to separate, but it is important to be aware of the distinctions between them.

- *Industrial–institutional* As most social shaping literature is focused on the 'industrial' and utilitarian roles of technology, this is the chief terrain of direct relevance of the critique of TD to media studies. Williams' account of the development of the **broadcasting** configuration of radio and television is the classic example of this practice within media studies. He argues that the reason radio was not configured more interactively than broadcasting's single sender–multiple receiver configuration was that that configuration was more amenable to the emerging reorganization of modern social life around consumerism and a relatively isolated pseudo-independent domestic sphere of suburbanized family life (see **mobile privatization**). For Williams (1989c), such configurations more properly bear the name 'technology' than the technical inventions (valves, cathode ray tubes and so on) from which they are composed. The broadcasting configuration was compatible with both the commercial advertising and public service models of broadcasting organizations.

- *Qualitative transformations of social relations* achieved by 'the **medium**'. These effects are peculiar – and arguably 'inherent' – to communications technologies as media – for example, **mediated interaction, time–space compression** and the shift away from the 'visual linearity' of print literacy that Marshall McLuhan and others believed new media were facilitating. These tend to be the concern of 'medium theorists', such as Joshua Meyrowitz (see **media/medium**). Arguments for such effects are, by themselves, not guilty of TD. It is extremely contentious, however, to argue, as McLuhan often implied, that these qualitative transformations are communications technologies' *only* social effect or **influence**. Such an assertion risks endorsing whatever might be the prevailing media **regulation** regime – no matter how concentrated the **ownership** of media organizations or how little **freedom of communication** is permitted. Ironically, in this scenario, communications technologies become just as removed from 'society' as in any TD account. It was because of this conservative consequence of his work that Williams (1974a: 127) accused McLuhan of 'sophisticated technological determinism'.

- *Future projections* In a process not unlike Roland Barthes' **sign**-based understanding of the role of denotation and connotation in social myths, we can speak of first and second orders of TD. The first refers to specific technical inventions, while the second level consists of what Williams (1974a) calls 'projections'. These are speculative visions of an imminent new social and/or cultural order that a new technology, purportedly, will bring about: McLuhan's global village, Daniel Bell's post-industrial society, the **information society**, for example.

- *Emancipatory–democratic norms* TD can be explained as a result of the diminution of the Enlightenment conception of **modernity**. Advocates of the Enlightenment assumed that the pursuit of scientific enquiry and technological innovation would *necessarily* entail comparable work in attaining social equity and so a greater social good. This was exemplified by 'universal men' such as the USA's Benjamin Franklin (scientist, 'tinkerer', constitutionalist, diplomat, printer/publisher). Second-order TD still promises a greater good, but ignores non-technological forms of 'social progress' – that is, *emancipatory norms* such as democracy and the expansion of human rights. Unlike the case of most other technologies today, communications technologies are still often thought to *combine* these two discourses of 'progress'. The social struggles by political and social movements for the expansion of the right to vote went hand in hand with the struggle to establish **freedom of communiation**. TD can also inflect or diminish even *this* combination today, however, by reducing 'freedoms' themselves to the causal effects of a technology, as in the title of de Sola Pool's classic text, *Technologies of Freedom* (1983). The risk here is even greater than in 'industrial' versions of TD – that whole social movements can be written out of history and replaced by a printing press or a more democratic future might seem to rest solely on the latest technical developments within communications (as in early speculation about the Internet). So the restoration of a social context here is crucial. One related feature of this normative dimension is also worthy of note: 'press' and 'printing' are not synonyms. 'Press' has always carried a strong normative connotation of the democratic process of an independent institution holding governments and other powerful bodies to account. 'Media' and even 'information technology' do not carry this connotation as strongly. As 'media' has tended to replace both 'press' *and* 'printing', the strong normative dimensions in phrases like 'press (media) conference' has faded.

DIFFICULTIES AND COMPLEXITIES

Difficulties can arise with this concept if one misunderstands the motivation of critics of TD. *No participant in these debates is arguing that technical innovation has neither social nor cultural implications.* Rather, debate usually centres on what scale or quality of 'effects' can reasonably be attributed to the technology itself. This is particularly important for considering the particular 'effects' associated with communications technologies.

Even if we confine ourselves to the 'industrial' role of communications technologies, it is plain that the pace of technical innovation is faster than ever before. We have clearly left far behind a time when innovation in these technologies might be the province of a single inventor or set of discrete inventions. Moreover, the **convergence** enabled by digital technologies of the formerly discrete technologies of telephony, computing and **broadcasting** has constituted a whole new terminology – information and communication technologies (ICTs) – that have a *systemic* form, which also needs to be recognized.

Can such innovations still be thought of as being 'socially shaped'? Paschal Preston (2001) has made the useful suggestion that communications technologies are 'reshaped' and we should distinguish different kinds of reshaping innovation in terms of their wider industrial effects:

- *incremental innovations* (usually 'market-driven'), such as the self-defrosting fridge, also seems applicable to isolated 'artefacts'
- *radical innovations* – distinctly novel devices – the result of deliberate R&D – usually 'sectoral' in their (industrial) influence, such as television
- *major new technology systems (MNTS)* – similar to radical innovations, except pervasive across industrial sectors in their influence, such as electricity and ICTs (digital convergence).

Preston's rethinking is consistent with a broader intellectual trend that problematizes another of our routine assumptions about technology, namely that we are necessarily always referring to discrete, machine-like artefacts. Especially when we want to consider technologies that serve powerful social interests, it is useful to broaden our conception of the semantic reach of 'technology'. What does it mean to suggest, for example, that society itself increasingly functions like a machine? A wide range of thinkers have argued that the expansion of machine-like routine or instrumentalized practice across *all* fields of social life can be characterized as, variously, rationalization (Max Weber), technologies of power (Michel Foucault) or instrumental reason/rationality (Theodor Adorno, Max Horkheimer, Jürgen Habermas).

The increasingly popular work of Bruno Latour configures this dilemma differently. Characteristic of much French post-structuralist theory, he decentres humans and focuses on the specificity of the technology itself, granting it a kind of social agency. Latour christens this acting technology an 'actant', a term derived from Formalist literary theory (Jones, 2010; Latour, 1992, 1994, 1995, 1997, 1999; see **cultural form**).

In much the same way that literary formalists refocused analytic attention from authors to literary 'devices', Latour suggests doorstoppers, for example, demonstrate a kind of 'delegated agency'. Accordingly, he proposes that we consider actants and humans to be co-implicated in **networks**. His approach is thus usually referred to as actor–network theory or ANT. As Latour has himself suggested, his work might thus be fruitfully compared with McLuhan's. The gains and losses are similar: a capacity to follow the micro dimensions of the actual uses of (media) technologies that can be difficult to (re)connect with 'macro' dimensions of economy and policy (Jones, 2010).

Latour's work is part of a general trend in the broader field of science and technology studies (STS) to increasingly read technologies as 'texts'. This was thought to be one way to reduce the likelihood of technologically determinist accounts. For example, corporately developed new technological artefacts in particular are now routinely subjected to 'user trials' in which the 'interpretation' of the product by the user is evaluated. Famously, even these did not adequately anticipate the degree to which the mobile phone would be 'interpreted' as a device for sending messages instead of making calls. This 'textual turn' peaked in the 1990s and, thus, postdates similar developments in **audience** studies, especially debates around **encoding/decoding** (but it also moves in parallel with the domestication school's understanding of **articulation**). Yet the problems were similar. If technologies were texts, was their range of possible interpretations unlimited? Was user interpretation at the point of consumption the only form of social shaping? What about the kind of 'macro' social shaping Williams had argued for in the configuration of broadcasting?

In a very strong echo of Stuart Hall's 'preferred reading' model (see **encoding/decoding**), Ian Hutchby (2001) suggested that the psychological term 'affordance' may provide a 'third way', that avoided all determinisms. By 'affordance', Hutchby means the delimited degree to which a technological artefact exists beyond any possible ambiguity of its interpretation or, to put it more bluntly, its non-textual dimension. Affordances thus have a limited causality, so mobile phones' multiple uses can only be 'interpreted' in a particular way if a technical capacity for each possible use – its affordance – actually exists. No one 'interpreted' the first generation of mobile phones as cameras, but a camera function 'affords' its interpretation/usage as a camera. Affordances thus set constraints on user interpretation and, it should follow, are themselves socially shaped by 'macro' social processes.

All these more recent figures and debates have questioned the Enlightenment assumption that social good is necessarily embedded within scientific enquiry and technological innovation – and, indeed, 'a free press'. What remains an open question today is whether or not and how we might try to ensure that future technical innovation *does* serve a social good.

Andrew Feenberg (1991) has suggested that this requires a democratization of the process of designing and developing new technologies. If he is right, then the long historical association between communications technologies and democracy will be all the more important. Moreover, the social design of communication technologies that facilitate a **public sphere** of debate – including debates about the social configuration of new technologies – emerges as perhaps one of the most important priorities of our time.

FURTHER READING

As noted above, Williams' groundbreaking discussion in his *Television: Technology and cultural form* (1974a) remains exemplary for media studies. Des Freedman (2002) provides a very useful unpacking and updating of this text. Donald A. MacKenzie and Judy Wajcman (1999) provide the definitive collection on social shaping. It includes a very useful introductory essay, but has relatively little on communication technologies. Perhaps the perfect complement is the extremely impressive collection *Handbook of New Media: Social shaping and the consequences of ICTs* (Lievrouw and Livingstone, 2006). The work of Latour is usefully reviewed in the same 'ICT' context by Eric Monteiro (2004). A more recent application of 'affordance' to the case of blogging is Lucas Graves (2007).

Time–space compression

> **Related concepts**: capitalism, cyberculture, globalization, mobile privatization, technoculture.

'Time–space compression' is a concept largely developed by economic geographers (Harvey, 1989; Massey, 1999), but it has become a keyword in the study of communications. The origin of the concept is Karl Marx's analysis of the need for **capitalism** to speed up the circulation time of capital. The faster that money can be turned into the production of goods and services, which then turn back into money in the form of profit (M-C-M), the greater the power of capital to expand or valorize itself. The most abstract manifestation of this is

globalization. More specifically, in relation to competition between capitalists, capital that circulates too slowly, in relation to other capital, will not survive. With capitalism, time literally *is* money.

This concept is relevant to communications in that the turnover time of capital is enormously assisted by innovations in transportation and communications, to an extent unforeseen by Marx. Improvements in the means of communication, the transport of messages, commodities and bodies have two principle effects: reduction of the cost of capital circulation, and a shrinking of the globe in terms of circulation time (what Marx called the 'annihilation of space with time'). Marx's thesis in the *Grundrisse* (1973a: 539) is:

> while capital must on one side strive to tear down every spatial barrier to intercourse, i.e. to exchange, and conquer the whole earth for its market, it strives on the other side to annihilate this space with time, i.e., to reduce to a minimum the time spent in motion from one place to another. The more developed the capital, therefore, the more extensive the market over which it circulates, which forms the spatial orbit of its circulation, the more does it strive simultaneously for an even greater extension of the market and for greater annihilation of space by time.

In other words, while capitalism requires a universal 'free market' and uninhibited possibilities of market exchange, it transforms and compresses the spaces in which it does this, threatening nation states, nationally-based capitals and the national **identity** of individuals. For example, the city is privileged over country, the motorway over the main street and the shopping mall over the high street. In communications, the screen is of greater importance than the face-to-face; mobile communications replace fixed telecommunications systems; and perpetual contact is more important than sense of place.

THE HISTORY OF TIME–SPACE COMPRESSION

The influence of communications on time–space compression begins with improvements in means of transportation. Prior to the telegraph, physical transport was the only means by which messages could be circulated on a global scale. Geographers narrate these developments according to the speed of transportation systems. For example, Harvey (1989: 241) sketches a figure of the shrinking globe that begins with the timeworld of the horse-drawn coach and sailing ship (10 mph) from 1500–1840, to steam ships (36 mph) and steam trains (66 mph) from 1850–1930, propeller aircraft (300–400 mph) from the 1950s and jet aircraft (700mph) today. When electronic communications were brought in after the invention of the telegraph in the 1830s, however, this kind of continuum really became pointless.

As Carey (1989: 213) argues, more than any other technology, it was the telegraph that first marked a 'decisive separation of "transportation" and "communication"'. The transport of bodies and messages by the wheel, sail and steam was, for the first time, challenged by the transport of messages at speeds dramatically different from what had previously existed. The telegraph dramatically increased the speed of communication to a velocity where the time taken for a message to be sent became a minute fraction of that afforded by physical transport.

Since the telegraph, the development of radio and cinema in the 1910s, telephony in the 1920s, and television in the 1940s and 1950s, made available new means of instantaneous communications. Also, during the first half of the twentieth century, access to electronic communications increased in exponential ways. Between 1940 and 1970, the cost of an international telephone call fell by more than 80 per cent and, between 1970 and 1990, by 90 per cent. Since the 1980s, telecommunications traffic has been expanding by an average 20 per cent a year. The Internet is now used by upwards of 1 billion people and the numbers are doubling every two years.

In 1995, the number of messages sent by e-mail in the USA exceeded those sent by post for the first time. In 2000, the global trade in TV programming was growing by 15 per cent a year and the number of mobile phone users stood at over 1 billion, exceeding that of landlines.

THE EXPERIENCE OF TIME–SPACE COMPRESSION

One of the consequences of this acceleration in communication time is how it changes the individual's experience of space. Before the telegraph, the speed of transport and the mechanical timepiece dominated the experience of space and time. The annihilation of space by the speeding up of transportation, then communication, saw the end of cultures of the *longue durée*, where time was regulated by the slow pace of maritime activity or crop cultivation, where relatively few unexpected events would intrude into everyday life.

The availability of faster transport and its potential for bringing close what is far changes the individual's sense of place. Even if such transport is never used by an individual, it is the *potential* availability of places that are otherwise too distant to be considered part of one's world that provides people with a sense of living in a smaller world. Conversely, the experience of travelling is, typically, one in which speed transforms the local and the landscape into a more abstract geographic space.

Wolfgang Schivelbusch (1987), in his writings on the railway journey, documents how the railway was a decisive transportational medium that severed the traveller's connection to landscape. The application of speed to the body abolishes the foreground and substitutes a closed space that is constructed between departure and destination. The train's velocity 'dissolve[s] the foreground', and thus the traveller is 'removed from that "total space" which combined proximity and distance' and 'he became separated from the landscape he saw' (Schivelbusch 1987: 63).

The relationship between speed and space that can be observed on a train is true also for modern motorway and aircraft travel, but the scales of compression those forms of transport afford cannot be compared to the instantaneousness of electronic communications, which make possible universal forms of electronic assembly and new senses of abstract space, such as 'electronic **audience**' and 'cyberspace'.

The circulation of images on coins in antiquity made possible the first abstract audiences, but the telegraph can be regarded as the first kind of cyberspace (Stratton, 1997). The telegraph facilitated the introduction of coordinated time-zones, first to regulate train timetables (Kern, 1983: 2) and, later, all kinds of flows of commodities, money and people in a global and homogenous spatial zone. As Holmes (2001: 11) observes:

> Whereas the invention of the mechanical clock in the fourteenth century enabled the recognition of a *uniform* public time within national frameworks, the telegraph beckoned the development of a *global* standard time – realising Newton's projection of a mathematic objective linear time.

TIME–SPACE COMPRESSION TODAY

The production of global space by the telegraph has been consolidated by optic fibres and satellite communication systems, but these are simply extensions of features that were embryonic in the telegraph. The difference between the telegraph and the Internet is often exaggerated. Of course, they each represent degrees of time–space compression that are internal to telecommunications, but the telegraph remains the first medium to break away from transport as a means of communication.

Nevertheless, today, the Internet is viewed by some theorists, such as Arthur Kroker and Weinstein (1994) and Paul Virilio (1997), as spawning a new empire of space: 'the Internet does not simply lay down a mesh of connections between real-life nodes/computers, annihilating space; it creates and maintains its own simulated world to replace the physical world of spatial distances' (Nunes, 1997: 166).

For some, it is the site of 'hyper-deterritorialisation' (Stratton, 1997: 257) and 'technofear' (Jordan, 1999), inhabited by nowherians who have, in some measure, forfeited identities they might have had in the physical world of space, which has been left behind (Iyer, 2000).

Of course, the Internet and other digital technologies differ from the telegraph in bandwidth and their ability to convey complexity, but Brian Winston (1998) argues that they have done little to accelerate global time–space compression. Moreover, the work of scholars examining 'when old technologies were new' (James Carey's analysis of the telegraph (1989), Gitelman and Pingree, (2004), Stephen Kern (1983) and Mattelart (2000), for example) suggests that, in the nineteenth century, relative to the world population at the time, time–space compression was much more intense than today.

Arguably, today, the democratization and diffusion of communications technologies point to a greater percentage of the world's population being influenced by this process than ever before. For example, the fact that 2007 was the year in which, for the first time, more than half the world's population could be said to live in cities, is a very important indicator of time–space compression. Cities become the nodal points in which the culture of global capitalism usurps local or ethnically defined forms of culture and creates the idea of an omnipolis, a generalized urbanism on which all cities are modelled. As more people live in cities, they also become exposed to accelerated flows of bodies, commodities, images, information and ideas. This, in turn, leads to what Hartmut Rosa (2003) has called 'social acceleration', as we become subject to the 24-hour society.

FURTHER READING

A first primer for exploring this concept is David Harvey's *The Condition of Postmodernity* (1989), which also makes important links to aesthetic modernism and postmodernism. A point of origin for time–space compression is Marx's chapter on method in the Grundrisse (1973a), which deals with the speeding up of circulation time in modern capitalism. In relation to communications and transportation, Stephen Kern's (1983) examination of the acceleration of social exchange from 1880 to 1918 looks at how technologies like railways and the wireless telegraph alter perceptions of time and space as expressed in art, politics and even war. There is also a genre of 'when old technologies were new' that resets the study of 'new media' back to the nineteenth century and beyond. It provides a *de facto* critique of hubristic notions of new media today. See also Lisa Gitelman and Geoffrey B. Pingree (2004) and Armand Mattelart (2000).

Abercrombie, N. and Longhurst, B. (1998) *Audiences: A sociological theory of performance and imagination*. London: Sage.

Abu-Lughod, L. (1997) 'The interpretation of cultures after television', *Reflections*, 59: 109–34.

Adams, P. (1992) 'Television as gathering place', *Annals of the Association of American Geographers*, 82 (1): 117–35.

Adorno, T.W. (1945) 'A social critique of radio music', *Kenyon Review*, 8 (2): 208–17.

Adorno, T.W. (1969) 'Scientific experiences of a European scholar in America', in D. Fleming and B. Bailyn (eds.), *The Intellectual Migration: Europe and America*. Cambridge, MA: Harvard University Press. pp. 338–70.

Adorno, T.W. (1977) 'Adorno to Benjamin, 18 March 1936', in R. Taylor (ed. and tr.), *Aesthetics and Politics*. London: NLB. pp. 120–6.

Adorno, T.W. (1984) 'Cultural criticism and society', in T.W. Adorno, *Prisms*. Cambridge, MA: MIT Press. pp. 17–34. (1st edition, 1955; 1st English translation, 1967.)

Adorno, T.W. (1991a) 'Culture industry reconsidered' (A.G. Rabinbach, tr. 1975), in T.W. Adorno, J. Bernstein (ed.), *The Culture Industry: Selected essays on mass culture*. London: Routledge. pp. 85–92. (1st edition, 1967.)

Adorno, T.W. (1991b) 'Transparencies on film' (Y.T. Levin, tr.), in T.W. Adorno, J. Bernstein (ed.), *The Culture Industry: Selected essays on mass culture*. London: Routledge. pp. 154–61. (1st edition, 1967.)

Adorno, T.W. and Horkheimer, M. (J. Cumming, tr.) (1979) *Dialectic of Enlightenment*. London: Verso. (1st edition, 1947; 1st English translation, 1972.)

Alasuutari, P. (ed.) (1999) *Rethinking the Media Audience*. London: Sage.

Alexander, J.C. (1981) 'The mass news media in systemic, historical and comparative perspective', in E. Katz and T. Szecskö (eds.), *Mass Media and Social Change*. London: Sage. pp. 17–52.

Alexander, J.C. (2006) *The Civil Sphere*. Oxford: Oxford University Press.

Allan, S. (1998) 'News from nowhere: television news discourse and the construction of hegemony', in A. Bell and P. Garrett (eds.), *Approaches to Media Discourse*. Oxford: Blackwell. pp. 105–41.

Allan, S. (1999) *News Culture*. Buckingham: Open University Press.

Allan, S. (2006) *Online News: Journalism and the Internet*. Buckingham: Open University Press.

Allan, S. and Thorsen, E. (eds.) (2009) *Citizen Journalism: Global perspectives*. New York: Peter Lang.

Allen, R.C. (ed.) (1987) *Channels of Discourse: Television and contemporary criticism*. London: Methuen.

Althusser, L. (B. Brewster, tr.) (1971) *Lenin and Philosophy and Other Essays*. New York: Monthly Review Press.

Althusser, L. (G. Lock, tr.) (1976) *Essays in Self-criticism*. London: NLB.

Althusser, L. (B. Brewster, tr.) (1982) *For Marx*. London: Verso. (1st English translation, 1969.)

Ang, I. (1985) *Watching Dallas: Soap opera and the melodramatic imagination*. London: Methuen.

Arnold, M. (1960) *Culture and Anarchy*. Ed. J. Dover Wilson. Cambridge: Cambridge University Press. (1st pub. 1869.)

Arthurs, J. (2004) *Television and Sexuality: Regulation and the politics of taste*. Buckingham and New York: Open University Press.

Artz, L. and Kamalipour, Y.R. (eds.) (2003) *The Globalization of Corporate Media Hegemony*. Albany, NY: State University of New York Press.

Askew, K. and Wilk, R. (eds.) (2002) *The Anthropology of Media: A reader*. Oxford: Blackwell.

Auge, M. (J. Howe, tr.) (1995) *Non-places: Introduction to an anthropology of supermodernity*. London: Verso.

Baker, C.E. (2002) *Media, Markets and Democracy*. Cambridge: Cambridge University Press.

Baker, C.E. (2007) *Media Concentration and Democracy*. Cambridge: Cambridge University Press.

Baran, P. (1964) *On Distributed Communications*. Santa Monica, CA: Rand Corporation Publications. Introduction. (Available online at: www.rand.org/pubs/research_memoranda/2006/RM3420.pdf)

Barendt, E. (1991) 'Press and broadcasting freedom: does anyone have any rights to free speech?', *Current Legal Problems*, 44: 63–82.

Barendt, E. (1993) *Broadcasting Law: A comparative perspective*. Oxford: Clarendon Press.

Barendt, E. (2005) *Freedom of Speech*. Oxford: Oxford University Press.

Barker, C. (2000) *Cultural Studies: Theory and practice*. London: Sage.

Barrett, M. (1988) *Women's Oppression Today: The Marxist/feminist encounter*. London: Verso. (1st edition, 1980.)

Barrett, M. (1991) *The Politics of Truth: From Marx to Foucault*. Cambridge: Polity Press.

Barthes, R. (A. Lavers and C. Smith, tr.) (1967) *Elements of Semiology*. New York: Hill & Wang. (1st edition, 1964.)

Barthes, R. (A. Lavers, tr.) (1972) *Mythologies*. St Albans: Paladin. (1st edition, 1957.)

Barthes, R. (S. Heath, tr.) (1977a) 'Rhetoric of the image', in R. Barthes, *Image, Music, Text*. London: Fontana. pp. 32–51. (1st edition, 1964.)

Barthes, R. (S. Heath, tr.) (1977b) 'The photographic message', in R. Barthes, *Image, Music, Text*. London: Fontana. pp. 15–31. (1st edition, 1961.)

Barthes, R. (S Heath, tr.) (1977c) 'Introduction to the structural analysis of narratives', in R. Barthes, *Image, Music, Text*. London: Fontana. pp. 79–124. (1st edition, 1966.)

Baudrillard, J. (I.H. Grant, tr.) (1981a) *Symbolic Exchange and Death*. London: Sage.

Baudrillard, J. (C. Levin, tr.) (1981b) *For a Critique of the Political Economy of the Sign*. St Louis, MO: Telos Press.

Baudrillard, J. (S. Faria Glasser, tr.) (1994) 'The precession of simulacra', in J. Baudrillard, *Simulacra and Simulation*. Ann Arbor, MI: University of Michigan Press. pp. 1–42.

Baudrillard, J. (J. Benedict, tr.) (1996) *The System of Objects*. New York: Verso.

Baudrillard, J. (C. Turner, tr.) (1998) *Consumer Society: Myths and structures*. London: Sage.

Bauman, Z. (1998) *Globalization: The human consequences*. New York: Columbia University Press.

Bauman, Z. (2000) *Liquid Modernity*. Cambridge: Polity Press.

Baym, N. (2000) *Tune in, Log on: Soaps, fandom, and online community*. London: Sage.

Bazin, A. (H. Gray, tr.) (1974). 'The myth of total cinema', in A. Bazin, *What is Cinema?* Berkeley, CA: University of California Press. pp. 17–22.

Becker, H. (1963) *Outsiders: Studies in the sociology of deviance*. New York: Free Press.

Beebe, J. (1977) 'Institutional structure and program choices in television markets', *The Quarterly Journal of Economics*, 91 (1): 15–37.

de Beer, A. and Merrill, J. (2009) *Global Journalism: Topical issues and media systems*. Boston, MA: Pearson. (1st editon, 1983.)

Bell, A. and Garrett, P. (1998) *Approaches to Media Discourse*. Oxford: Wiley-Blackwell.

Bell, D. (1962) *The End of Ideology: On the exhaustion of political ideas in the fifties*. Glencoe, IL: Free Press.

Bell, D. (1973) *The Coming of Post-industrial Society: A venture in social forecasting*. New York: Basic Books.

Bell, D. (1979) 'The social framework of the information society', in M.L. Dertouzos and J. Moses (eds), *The Computer Age: A twenty-year view*. Cambridge, MA: MIT Press. pp. 163–211.

Bell, D. (1989) 'Communication technology: for better or for worse?', in J. Salvaggio (ed.), *The Information Society*. Hillsdale, NJ: LEA. pp. 89–103.

Bell, D. (1996) *The Cultural Contradictions of Capitalism*. New York: Basic Books. (1st edition, 1976.)

Bell, D. (1999) 'The axial age of technology: Foreword: 1999', in D. Bell, *The Coming of Post-industrial Society*. New York: Basic Books. pp. ix–lxxxvi.

Benedikt, M. (ed.) (1992) *Cyberspace: First steps*. Cambridge, MA: MIT Press.

Benjamin, W. (1969) 'The work of art in the age of mechanical reproduction' [1936], in W. Benjamin, H. Arendt (ed.), *Illuminations*. New York: Shocken Books. pp. 217–50.

Benjamin, W. (2008) 'The work of art in the age of its technological reproducibility: second version', in M.W. Jennings, B. Doherty and T.Y. Levin (eds.) (E. Jephcott and H. Zohn, tr.), *The Work of Art in the Age of its Technological Reproducibility, and other Writings on Media*. Cambridge, MA: Belknap Press. pp. 19–55.

Bennett, T. (1982) 'Theories of the media, theories of society', in M. Gurevitch, T. Bennett, J. Curran and J. Woollacott (eds.), *Culture, Society and the Media*. London: Routledge. pp. 30–55.

Bennett, T. and Martin, G. (1977) 'Popular culture and high culture: a rejoinder', in Open University Mass Communication and Society Course Team, *The Study of Culture*. Buckingham: Open University Press. pp. 53–71.

Bennett, T., Grossberg, L. and Morris, M. (eds.) (2005) *New Keywords: A revised vocabulary of culture and society*. Oxford: Blackwell.

Bennett, W.L. (2008) *News: The politics of illusion*. New York: Longman. (1st edition, 1983.)

Berker, T., Hartmann, M., Punie, Y. and Ward, K. (2006) *Domestication of Media and Technology*. Buckingham: Open University Press.

Bimber, B. (1994) 'Three faces of technological determinism', in M.R. Smith and L. Marx (eds.), *Does Technology Drive History? The dilemma of technological determinism*. Cambridge, MA: MIT Press. pp. 79–100.

Bird, S.E. (2010) *The Anthropology of News and Journalism: Global perspectives*. Bloomington, IN: Indiana University Press.

Blumler, J. and Gurevitch, M. (1982) 'The political effects of mass communication', in M. Gurevitch, T. Bennett, J. Curran and J. Woollacott (eds.), *Culture, Society and the Media*. London: Routledge. pp. 236–67.

Blythe, M. (2002) 'The work of art in the age of digital reproduction: the significance of the creative industries', *Journal of Art and Design Education*, 20 (2): 144–50.

Bolter, J.D. and Grusin, R. (1999) *Remediation: Understanding new media*. Cambridge, MA: MIT Press.

Boorstin, D. (1961) *The Image*. Harmondsworth: Pelican.

Born, G. (2004) *Uncertain Vision: Birt, Dyke and the reinvention of the BBC*. London: Secker & Warburg.

Bourdieu, P. (1991) 'On symbolic power', in P. Bourdieu, J. Thompson (ed.) (G. Raymond and M. Adamson, tr.), *Language and Symbolic Power*. Cambridge, MA: Harvard University Press. pp. 163–70. (1st English translation, 1977.)

Bourdieu, P. (1993) 'Public opinion does not exist', in P. Bourdieu (R. Nice, tr.), *Sociology in Question*. London: Sage. pp. 149–57. (1st edition, 1968.)

Bourdieu, P. (2005) 'The political field, the social science field and the journalistic field', in R. Benson and E. Neveu (eds.) (R. Nice, tr.), *Bourdieu and the Journalistic Field*. Cambridge: Polity Press. pp. 29–47. (1st edition, 1995.)

Bowden, M. (2008) 'The angriest man in television', *The Atlantic Monthly*, January/February: 50–6.

Boyce, G. (1978) 'The fourth estate: the reappraisal of a concept', in G. Boyce, J. Curran and P. Wingate (eds.), *Newspaper History: From the seventeenth century to the present day*. London: Constable. pp. 19–40.

boyd, d. (2007) 'Why youth © social network sites: The role of networked publics in teenage social life', in *Youth, Identity and Digital Media*. Ed. D. Buckingham. Cambridge, MA: MIT Press. pp. 119–42.

Boyd-Barrett, O. and Rantanen, T. (eds.) (1998) *The Globalization of News*. London: Sage.

Boyer, M.C. (1996) *Cybercities: Visual perception in the age of electronic communication*. New York: Princeton Architectural.

Bramson, L. (1967) *The Political Context of Sociology*. Princeton, NJ: Princeton University Press.

Brantlinger, P. (1990) *Crusoe's Footprints: Cultural studies in Britain and America*. New York: Routledge.

Briggs, A. and Burke, P. (2009) *A Social History of the Media: From Gutenberg to the Internet*. Cambridge: Polity Press.

Bromley, M. and Stephenson, H. (eds.) (1998) *Sex, Lies, and Democracy: The press and the public*. London: Longman.

Brooker, W. and Jermyn, D. (2003) *The Audience Studies Reader*. Abingdon: Routledge.

Brown, A. (1996) 'Economics, public service broadcasting and social values', *Journal of Media Economics*, 9 (1): 3–15.

Brunsdon, C. and Spigel, L. (eds.) (2008) *Feminist Television Criticism*. Buckingham: Open University. (1st edition, 1997.)

Bryman, A. (1999) 'The Disneyisation of society', *The Sociological Review*, 47 (1): 25–47.

Buchstein, H. (1997) 'Bytes that bite: the Internet and deliberative democracy', *Constellations*, 4 (2): 248–63.

Buck-Morss, S. (2003) *Thinking Beyond Terror: Islam and critical theory on the left*. London: Verso.

Bunch, B. and Hellemans, A. (1994) *The Timetables of Technology: A chronology of the most important people and events in the history of technology*. New York: Simon & Schuster.

Butler, J., Laclau, E. and Zizek, S. (2000) *Contingency, Hegemony, Universality: Contemporary dialogues on the Left*. London: Verso (Phronesis).

Butsch, R. (ed.) (2007) *Media and Public Spheres*. Houndmills, Basingstoke: Palgrave Macmillan.

Calabrese, A. (2000) 'Political space and the trade in television news', in C. Sparks and J. Tulloch (eds.), *Tabloid Tales: Global debates over media standards*. Lanham, MA: Rowman & Littlefield. pp. 43–62.

Calabrese, A. and Sparks, C. (eds.) (2004) *Toward a Political Economy of Culture: Capitalism and communication in the twenty-first century*. Lanham, MD: Rowman & Littlefield.

Calhoun, C. (1986) 'Computer technology, large-scale social integration and the local community', *Urban Affairs Quarterly*, 22 (2): 329–49.

Calhoun, C. (1992) 'The infrastructure of modernity: indirect social relationships, information technology, and social integration', in H. Haferkamp and N. Smelser (eds.), *Social Change and Modernity*. Berkeley, CA: UCLA Press. pp. 205–36.

Calhoun, C. (ed.) (1993) *Habermas and the Public Sphere: Critical debates*. Cambridge, MA: MIT Press. (1st edition, 1992.)

Calhoun, C. (1998) 'Community without propinquity revisited: communications technology and the transformation of the urban public sphere', *Sociological Inquiry*, 68 (3): 373–97.

Calinescu, M. (1987) *Five Faces of Modernity: Modernism, avant-garde, decadence, kitsch, postmodernism*. Durham, NC: Duke University Press.

Callanan, R. (2004) 'The changing role of broadcasters within digital communications networks', *Convergence*, 10 (3): 28–38.

Callinicos, A. (1989) *Against Postmodernism*. Cambridge: Polity Press.

Carey, J. (1968) 'Harold Adams Innis and Marshall McLuhan', in R. Rosenthal (ed.), *McLuhan: Pro and con*. Baltimore, MD: Pelican. pp. 270–308.

Carey, J. (1989) *Communication as Culture*. London: Routledge.

Carey, J. (2008) *Communication as Culture: Essays on media and society* (online edn). Hoboken, NJ: Taylor & Francis. (1st edition, 1989.)

Carter, C., Branston, G. and Allan, S. (eds.) (1998) *News, Gender and Power*. Abingdon: Routledge.

Carvalho, A. (2008) 'Media(ted) discourse and society', *Journalism Studies*, 9 (2): 161–77.

Casey, N., Casey, B., Lewis, J., Calvert, B. and French, L. (2002) 'Genre', in N. Casey, B. Casey, J. Lewis, B. Calvert and L. French. *Television Studies: The key concepts*. Abingdon: Routledge. pp. 108–11.

Castells, M. (1989) *The Informational City: Information technology, economic restructuring, and the urban regional process*. Oxford, UK, and Cambridge, MA: Blackwell.

Castells, M. (2000a) *The Rise of the Network Society*, Vol. 1, *The Information Age: Economy, society and culture*. Cambridge, MA, and Oxford, UK: Blackwell. (1st edition, 1996.)

Castells, M. (2000b) *End of Millennium*, Vol. 3, *The Information Age: Economy, society and culture*. Cambridge, MA, and Oxford, UK: Blackwell. (1st edition, 1998.)

Castells, M. (2001) *The Internet Galaxy*. Oxford: Oxford University Press.

Castells, M. (2004a) 'Informationalism, networks, and the network society: a theoretical blueprint', in M. Castells (ed.), *The Network Society*. Cheltenham: Edward Elgar. pp. 3–48.

Castells, M. (2004b) *The Power of Identity*, Vol. 2, *The Information Age: Economy, society and culture*. Cambridge, MA, and Oxford, UK: Blackwell. (1st edition, 1997.)

Castells, M. (2009) *Communication Power*. Oxford: Oxford University Press.

Castells, M. (2010) *End of Millenium: The information age: Economy, society, and culture*. Oxford: Blackwell.

Castells, M., Fernandez-Ardevol, M., Qiu, J.L. and Sey, A. (2007) *Mobile Communication and Society: A global perspective*. Cambridge, MA: MIT Press.

Chalaby, J. (1996) Journalism as an Anglo-American invention', *European Journal of Communication*, 11 (3): 303–26.

Chalaby, J. (1997) 'No ordinary press owners: press barons as a Weberian ideal type', *Media, Culture and Society*, 19: 621–41.

Chalaby, J. (1998) *The Invention of Journalism*. Houndmills, Basingstoke: Macmillan.

Chandler, D. (2007) *Semiotics: The basics*. London: Routledge.

Chouliaraki, L. (2008) 'Discourse analysis', in T. Bennett and J. Frow (eds.), *Sage Handbook of Cultural Theory*. London: Sage. pp. 674–98.

Chouliaraki, L. and Fairclough, N. (1999) *Discourse in Late Modernity: Rethinking critical discourse analysis*. Edinburgh: Edinburgh University Press.

Christians, C., Glasser, T., McQuail, D., Nordenstreng, K. and White, R. (2009) *Normative Theories of the Media: Journalism in democratic societies*. Chicago, IL: University of Illinois Press.

Clarke, J., Hall, S. Jefferson, T. and Roberts B. (1977) 'Subcultures, cultures and class', in S. Hall and T. Jefferson (eds.), *Resistance through Rituals: Youth subcultures in post-war Britain*. London: Hutchinson. pp. 9–74. (1st edition, 1974.)

Cohen, J. and Arato, A. (1992) *Civil Society and Political Theory*. Cambridge, MA: MIT Press.

Cohen, S. (1980) *Folk Devils and Moral Panics*. Oxford: Martin Robinson. (1st edition, 1972.)

Cohen, S. (2002) *Folk Devils and Moral Panics*. Abingdon: Routledge. (3rd edition.)

Collins, R. and Murroni, C. (1996) *New Media, New Policies: Media and communications strategies for the future*. Cambridge: Polity Press.

Compaine, B. (ed.) (2001) *The Digital Divide: Facing a crisis or creating a myth?* Cambridge, MA: MIT Press.

Conboy, M. (2002) *The Press and Popular Culture*. London: Sage.

Conboy, M. (2004) *Journalism: A critical history*. London: Sage.

Conboy, M. (2006) *Tabloid Britain: Constructing a community through language*. Abingdon: Routledge.

Corner, J. (1998) *Studying Media: Problems of theory and method*. Edinburgh: Edinburgh University Press.

Corner, J. (1999) *Critical Ideas in Television Studies*. Oxford: Oxford University Press.

Corner, J. (2000) '"Influence": the contested core of media research', in J. Curran and M. Gurevitch (eds.), *Mass Media and Society*. London: Arnold. pp. 376–97. (1st edition, 1991.)

Corner, J. (2001) 'Ideology: a note on conceptual salvage', *Media, Culture and Society*, 23 (4): 525–33.

Cottle, S. (2006) 'Mediatized rituals: beyond manufacturing consent', *Media, Culture and Society*, 28 (3): 411–32.

Couldry, N. (2003) *Media Rituals: A critical approach*. London: Sage.

231

Couldry, N. (2005) 'Media rituals: beyond functionalism', in E. Rothenbuhler and M. Coman (eds.), *Media Anthropology*. Thousand Oaks, CA: Sage. pp. 59–70.

Couldry, N. (2006) *Listening Beyond the Echoes: Media, ethics, and agency in an uncertain world*. Boulder: Paradigm.

Couldry, N., Livingstone, S. and Markham, T. (2007) *Media Consumption and Public Engagement: Beyond the presumption of attention*. Houndmills, Basingstoke: Palgrave Macmillan.

Crang, M., Crang, P. and May, J. (eds.) (1998) *Virtual Geographies: Bodies, space and relations*. Abingdon: Routledge.

Crary, J. (1990) *Techniques of the Observer: On vision and modernity in the nineteenth century*. Cambridge, MA: MIT Press.

Critcher, C. (2003) *Moral Panics and the Media*. Buckingham: Open University Press.

Critcher, C. (ed.) (2006) *Critical Readings: Moral panics and the media*. Buckingham: Open University Press.

Crossley, N. (2005) 'Discourse ethics', in N. Crossley, *Key Concepts in Critical Social Theory*. London: Sage. pp. 64–7.

Croteau, D. and Hoynes, W. (2003) *Media/Society: Industries, images, and audiences*. Thousand Oaks, CA: Pine Forge. (1st edition, 1997.)

Croteau, D. and Hoynes, W. (2006) *The Business of Media: Corporate media and the public interest*. Thousand Oaks, CA: Pine Forge.

Cruz, J. and Lewis, J. (1994) 'Reflections upon the encoding/decoding model: an interview with Stuart Hall', in J. Cruz and J. Lewis (eds.), *Viewing, Reading, Listening: Audiences and cultural reception*. Boulder, CO: Westview Press. pp. 253–74.

Cubitt, S. (2006) 'Analogue and digital', *Theory, Culture and Society*, 23 (2–3): 250–1.

Cunningham, S. (2005) 'Creative enterprises', in J. Hartley (ed.), *Creative Industries*. Oxford: Blackwell. pp. 282–98.

Curran, J. (1977) 'Capitalism and control of the press, 1800–1975', in J. Curran, M. Gurevitch and J. Woollacott (eds.), *Mass Communication and Society*. London and Buckingham: Edward Arnold/Open University Press. pp. 195–230.

Curran, J. (1978) 'The press as an agency of social control: an historical perspective', in G. Boyce, J. Curran and P. Wingate (eds.), *Newspaper History: From the seventeenth century to the present day*. London: Constable. pp. 51–75.

Curran, J. (1979) 'Press freedom as a property right: the crisis of press legitimacy', *Media, Culture and Society*, 1: 59–82.

Curran, J. (1991) 'Rethinking the media as a public sphere', in P. Dahlgren and C. Sparks (eds.), *Communication and Citizenship: Journalism and the public sphere*. Abingdon: Routledge. pp. 27–56.

Curran, J. (1996a) 'The new revisionism in mass communication research: a reappraisal', in J. Curran, D. Morley and V. Walkerdine (eds.), *Cultural Studies and Communications*. London: Arnold. pp. 256–78.

Curran, J. (1996b) 'Media dialogue: a reply', in J. Curran, D. Morely and V. Walkerdine (eds.), *Cultural Studies and Communications*. London: Arnold. pp. 294–9.

Curran, J. (2000) 'Rethinking media and democracy', in J. Curran and M. Gurevitch (eds.), *Mass Media and Society*. London: Edward Arnold. pp. 82–117. (1st edition, 1991.)

Curran, J. (2002) 'Media and the making of British society, c. 1700–2000', *Media History*, 8 (2): 135–54.

Curran, J. (2005) 'Mediations of democracy', in J. Curran and M. Gurevitch (eds.), *Mass Media and Society*. London: Hodder Arnold. pp. 122–52. (1st edition, 1991.)

Curran, J. and Seaton, J. (2009) *Power without Responsibility: Press, broadcasting and the Internet in Britain*. Abingdon: Routledge. (1st edition, 1981.)

Curran, J. and Witschge, T. (2009) 'Liberal dreams and the Internet', in N. Fenton (ed.), *New Media, Old News: Journalism and democracy in the digital age*. London: Sage. pp. 102–18.

Curran, J., Douglas, A. and Whannel, G. (1980) 'The political economy of the human interest story', in A. Smith (ed.), *Newspapers and Democracy*. Cambridge, MA: MIT Press. pp. 288–348.

D'Acci, J. (2004a) 'Television, representation and gender', in R.C. Allen and A. Hill (eds.), *The Television Reader*. Abingdon: Routledge. pp. 373–88.

D'Acci, J. (2004b) 'Cultural studies, television studies and the crisis in the humanities', in L. Spigel and J. Olsson (eds.), *Television After TV: Essays on a medium in transition*. Durham, NC: Duke University Press. pp. 418–45.

Dahlberg, L. (2001) 'Democracy via cyberspace', *New Media and Society*, 3 (2): 157–77.

Dahlgren, P. (2001) 'The public sphere and the Net: structure space and communication', in W. Bennett and R. Entman (eds.), *Mediated Politics: Communication in the future of democracy*. Cambridge: Cambridge University Press. pp. 33–55.

Dahlgren, P. and Sparks, C. (1992) *Journalism and Popular Culture*. London: Sage.

Day, R. (2000) 'The "conduit metaphor" and the nature and politics of information studies', *Journal of the American Society for Information Science*, 51 (9): 805–11.

Dayan, D. (2001) 'The peculiar public of television', *Media, Culture and Society*, 23 (6): 743–65.

Dayan, D. and Katz, E. (1992) 'Defining media events: high holidays of mass communications', in *Media Events: The live broadcasting of history*. Cambridge, MA: Harvard University Press. pp. 1–24.

Dean, J. (2003) 'Why the Net is not a public sphere', *Constellations*, 10 (1): 95–112.

Debord, G. (F. Perlman and J. Supak, tr.) (1977) *Society of the Spectacle*. Detroit, MI: Black & Red.

De Certeau, M. (Steven Rendall, tr.) (1988) *The Practice of Everyday Life*. Berkeley, CA: University of California Press.

Derrida, J. (G.C. Spivak, tr.) (1976) *Of Grammatology*. Baltimore, MD: Johns Hopkins University Press.

Derrida, J. (A. Bass, tr.) (1978) *Writing and Difference*. London: Routledge & Kegan Paul.

Derrida, J. (A. Bass, tr.) (1979) *Positions*. London: The Athlone Press.

Derrida, J. (1980) 'The law of genre', *Critical Inquiry*, 7 (1): pp. 55–81.

Derrida, J. (B. Johnson, tr.) (1981) *Dissemination*. Chicago, IL: University of Chicago Press.

Derrida, J. (A. Bass, tr.) (1982a) 'Signature, event, context', in J. Derrida, *Margins of Philosophy*. Sussex: Harvester. pp. 307–30.

Derrida, J. (A. Bass, tr.) (1982b) 'White mythology: metaphor in the text of philosophy', in *Margins of Philosophy*. Sussex: Harvester. pp. 207–72.

Derrida, J. (K. McLaughlin, tr.) (1983) 'The time of a thesis: punctuations', in A. Montefiore (ed.), *Philosophy in France Today*. Cambridge: Cambridge University Press. pp. 34–50.

Derrida, J. (C.V. McDonald, ed; P. Kamuff, tr.) (1985) *The Ear of the Other: Otobiography, transference, translation: texts and discussions with Jacques Derrida*. New York: Schocken.

Derrida, J. (S. Weber, tr.) (1988) *Limited Inc*. Evanston, IL: Northwestern University Press.

Devereux, E. (2003) *Understanding the Media*. London: Sage.

Dornsife, R. (2006) 'Coming to (digital) terms: the work of art in the age of non-mechanical reproduction', *Radical Pedagogy*. (Online journal, available at: http://radicalpedagogy.icaap. org/content/issue8_1/dornsife.html)

Downey, J. (2008) 'Recognition and the renewal of ideology critique', in D. Hesmondhalgh and J. Toynbee (eds.), *The Media and Social Theory*. Abingdon: Routledge. pp. 59–74.

Dworkin, A. (1985) 'Against the male flood: censorship, pornography, and equality', *Harvard Women's Law Journal*, 8: 1–29.

Eade, J. (ed.) (1997) *Living the Global City: Globalisation as a local process*. London: Routledge.

Eagleton, T. (2000) *The Idea of Culture*. Oxford: Blackwell.

Eagleton, T. (2003) *Sweet Violence: The idea of the tragic*. Oxford: Blackwell.

Eliot, T.S. (1948) *Notes Towards the Definition of Culture*. London: Faber.

Ellul, J. (J. Wilkinson, tr.) (1964) *The Technological Society*. New York: Knopf.

Epstein, E.J. (1981) 'The selection of reality', in E. Abel (ed.), *What's News: The media in American Society*. San Francisco, CA: Institute for Contemporary Studies. pp. 119–32.

233

Escobar, A. (1994) 'Welcome to Cyberia: notes on the anthropology of cyberculture', *Current Anthropology*, 43 (5): 775–86.

Esser, F. (1999) '"Tabloidization" of news: a comparative analysis of Anglo-American and German press journalism', *European Journal of Communication*, 14 (3): 291–324.

Ester, H. (2007) 'The media', in C. Hamilton and S. Maddison (eds.), *Silencing Dissent: How the Australian government is controlling public opinion and stifling debate*. Crows Nest, NSW: Allen & Unwin. pp. 101–23.

Everett, A. (2003) 'Digitextuality and click theory: theses on convergence media in the digital age', in A. Everett and J. Caldwell (eds.), *New Media: Theories and practices of digitextuality*. Abingdon and New York: Routledge. pp. 1–28.

Fainstein, S. and Judd, D. (1999) 'Global forces, local strategies, and urban tourism', in D. Judd and S. Fainstein (eds.), *The Tourist City*. New Haven, CT and London: Yale University Press. pp. 1–17.

Fairclough, N. (1995) *Media Discourse*. London: Arnold.

Fallows, J. (1996) *Breaking the News: How the media undermine American democracy*. New York: Pantheon.

Featherstone, M. (1995) *Undoing Culture: Globalization, postmodernism and identity*. London: Sage.

Featherstone, M. (1998) 'The *flaneur*, the city and virtual public life', *Urban Studies*, 35 (5–6): 909–25.

Featherstone, M. and Burrows, R. (eds.) (1995) *Cyberspace, Cyberbodies, Cyberpunk*. London: Sage.

Feenberg, A. (1991) *Critical Theory of Technology*. Oxford: Oxford University Press.

Feenberg, A. (1992) 'Subversive rationalisation: technology, power and democracy', *Inquiry*, 35 (3/4): 301–22.

Feenberg, A. (2003) 'Modernity theory and technology studies: reflections on bridging the gap', in T.J. Misa, P. Brey and A. Feenberg (eds.), *Modernity and Technology*. Cambridge, MA: MIT Press. pp. 74–104.

Feintuck, M. (1999) *Media Regulation, Public Interest and the Law*. Edinburgh: Edinburgh University Press.

Feintuck, M. (2004) *'The Public Interest' in Regulation*. Oxford and New York: Oxford University Press.

Ferguson, M. (1991) 'Marshall McLuhan revisited: 1960s zeitgeist victim or pioneer postmodernist?', *Media, Culture and Society*, 13: 71–90.

Fiske, J. (1987) *Television Culture*. London: Routledge.

Fiske, J. (1989) *Understanding Popular Culture*. London: Unwin Hyman.

Fiske, J. (1991) *Introduction to Communication Studies*. London: Routledge. (1st edition, 1982.)

Fiske, J. (1996a) *Media Matters: Race and gender in US politics*. Minneapolis, MN: University of Minnesota Press.

Fiske, J. (1996b) 'Opening the hallway: some remarks on the fertility of Stuart Hall's contribution to critical theory', in D. Morley and K. Chen (eds.), *Stuart Hall: Critical dialogues in cultural studies*. London: Routledge. pp. 212–22.

Flew, T. (2005) 'Creative economy', in J. Hartley (ed.), *Creative Industries*. Oxford: Blackwell. pp. 344–60.

Fortunati, L. (2005) 'Mediatization of the Net and Internetization of the mass media', *Gazette: The International Journal for Communication Studies*, 67 (1): 27–44.

Foster, H. (ed.) (1983) *The Anti-Aesthetic: Essays on postmodern culture*. Washington, DC: Bay Press.

Foucault, M. (R. Swyer, tr.) (1971) 'Orders of discourse', *Social Science Information*, 10 (2): 7–30.

Foucault, M. (A. Sheridan, tr.) (1979) *Discipline and Punish: The birth of the prison*. Harmondsworth: Penguin.

Foucault, M. (R. Goldstein and J. Zinovich, tr.) (1991) *Remarks on Marx*. New York: Semiotext(e). (1st edition, 1981.)

Fox, R.L., Van Sickel, R.W. and Steiger, T. (2007) *Tabloid Justice: Criminal justice in an age of media frenzy*. Boulder, CO: Lynne Rienner. (1st edition, 2000.)

Frankfurt Institute for Social Research (1973) *Aspects of Sociology*. London: Heinemann. (1st edition, 1956.)

Franklin, B., Hamer, M., Hanna, M. and Kinsey, M. (2005) *Key Concepts in Journalism Studies*. London: Sage.

Fraser, N. (1993) 'Rethinking the public sphere: towards a critique of actually existing democracy', in C. Calhoun (ed.), *Habermas and the Public Sphere: Critical debates*. Cambridge, MA: MIT Press. pp. 109–42.

Freedman, D. (2002) 'A technological idiot? Raymond Williams and communications technology', *Information, Communication and Society*, 5 (3): 425–42.

Freedman, D. (2008) *The Politics of Media Policy*. Cambridge: Polity Press.

Friedberg, A. (1993) *Window Shopping: Cinema and the postmodern*. Berkeley, CA: University of California Press.

Frith, S. (1991) 'The good, the bad, and the indifferent: saving popular culture from the populists', *diacritics*, 21 (4): 101–15.

Frye, N. (1957) *Anatomy of Criticism: Four essays*. Princeton, NJ: Princeton University Press.

Fuchs, C. (2010a) 'Grounding critical communication studies: an inquiry into the communication theory of Karl Marx', *Journal of Communication Inquiry*, 34 (1): 15–41.

Fuchs, C. (2010b) 'New imperialism: information and media imperialism?', *Global Media and Communication*, 6 (1): 33–60.

Fukuyama, F. (1992) *The End of History and the Last Man*. New York: Random House.

Fuller, S. (2002) *Knowledge Management Foundations*. London: Butterworth-Heinemann.

Galloway, A.R. (2004) *Protocol: How control exists after decentralization*. Cambridge, MA: MIT Press.

Galtung, J. and Ruge, M.H. (1970) 'The structure of foreign news', in J. Tunstall (ed.), *Media Sociology: A reader*. London: Constable. pp. 259–98. (1st edition, 1965.)

Gans, H. (1979) *Deciding What's News: A study of CBS evening news, NBC nightly news, Newsweek, and Time*. New York: Pantheon Books.

Garnham, N. (1986) 'The media and the public sphere', in P. Golding, G. Murdock and P. Schlesinger (eds.), *Communicating Politics: Mass communications and the political process*. Leicester: University of Leicester Press. pp. 37–53.

Garnham, N. (1990) *Capitalism and Communication: Global culture and the economics of information*. London: Sage.

Garnham, N. (1992) 'The media and the public sphere', in C. Calhoun (ed.), *Habermas and the Public Sphere*. Cambridge, MA: MIT Press. pp. 359–76.

Garnham, N. (1993) 'The mass media, cultural identity, and the public sphere in the modern world', *Public Culture*, 5 (2): 251–65.

Garnham, N. (1995) 'Comments on John Keane's "Structural transformations of the public sphere"', *The Communication Review*, 1 (1): 23–5.

Garnham, N. (2000) *Emancipation, the Media and Modernity: Arguments about the media and social theory*. Oxford: Oxford University Press.

Garnham, N. (2004) 'Information society theory as ideology', in F. Webster (ed.), *The Information Society Reader*. New York: Routledge. pp. 165–84. (1st edition, 1998.)

Garnham, N. (2005a) 'The information society debate revisited', in J. Curran and M. Gurevitch (eds.), *Mass Media and Society*. London: Hodder Arnold. pp. 287–302. (1st edition, 1991.)

Garnham, N. (2005b) 'From cultural to creative industries: an analysis of the implications of the "creative industries" approach to arts and media policy making in the United Kingdom', *International Journal of Cultural Policy*, 11 (1): 15–28.

Gauntlett, D. (1998) 'Ten things wrong with the media "effects model"', in R. Dickinson, R. Harindranath and O. Linné (eds.), *Approaches to Audiences: A Reader*. London: Arnold. (Available online at: www.theory.org.uk/effects.htm)

du Gay, P., Hall, S., Janes, L. and Mackay, H. (1997) *Doing Cultural Studies: The story of the Sony Walkman*, Vol. 1: *Culture, Media and Identities*. London: Sage.

Geertz, C. (1973) *The Interpretation of Cultures*. New York: Basic Books.

Geraghty, C. (1991) *Women and Soap Opera: A study of prime-time soaps*. Cambridge: Polity Press.

Gergen, K.J. (1991) *The Saturated Self: Dilemmas of identity in contemporary life*. New York: Basic Books.

Gibbons, T. (1992) 'Freedom of the press: ownership and editorial values', *Public Law*: 279–99.

Giddens, A. (1990) *The Consequences of Modernity*. Stanford, CA: Stanford University Press.

Giddens, A. (1995) *A Contemporary Critique of Historical Materialism*. Houndmills, Basingstoke: Macmillan. (1st edition, 1981.)

Gilder, G. (1994) *Life After Television*. New York: Norton.

Ginsburg, F. (2005) 'Media anthropology: an introduction', in E. Rothenbuhler and M. Coman (eds.), *Media Anthropology*. Thousand Oaks, CA: Sage. pp. 17–25.

Ginsburg, F., Abu-Lughod, L. and Larkin, B. (eds.) (2002) *Media Worlds: Anthropology on new terrain*. Berkeley, CA: University of California Press.

Gitelman, L. and Pingree, G.B. (eds.) (2004) *New Media 1740–1915*. Cambridge, MA: MIT Press.

Gitlin, T. (1978) 'Media sociology: the dominant paradigm', *Theory and Society*, 6: 205–53.

Gitlin, T. (1980) *The Whole World is Watching: Mass media in the making and unmaking of the new left*. Berkeley, CA: UCLA Press.

Gitlin, T. (1994) 'Prime time ideology: the hegemonic process in television entertainment' (first published 1979), in H. Newcomb (ed.), *Television: The critical view*. pp. 516–36. (1st edition, 1976.)

Gitlin, T. (1998) 'Public sphere or public sphericules?', in T. Liebes and J. Curran (eds.), *Media, Ritual, Identity*. Abingdon: Routledge. pp. 168–75.

Gitlin, T. (2000) *Inside Prime Time*. Abingdon: Routledge. (1st edition, 1983.)

Gitlin, T. (2002) *Media Unlimited: How the torrent of images and sounds overwhelms our lives*. New York: Henry Holt.

Glassner, B. (2000) *The Culture of Fear: Why Americans are afraid of the wrong things*. New York: Basic Books.

Gledhill, C. (1996) 'Feminism and media consumption', in J. Curran, D. Morley and V. Walkerdine (eds.), *Cultural Studies and Communications*. London: Arnold. pp. 306–22.

Golding, P. and Murdock, G. (1991) 'Culture, communications and political economy', in J. Curran and M. Gurevitch (eds.), *Mass Media and Society*. London: Edward Arnold. pp. 11–30. (1st edition, 1977.)

Goodall, P. (1995) *High Culture, Popular Culture: The long debate*. Sydney: Allen & Unwin.

Goode, L. (2005) *Jürgen Habermas: Democracy and the public sphere*. London: Pluto.

Goodwin, A. (1988) 'Sample and hold: pop music in the digital age of reproduction', *Critical Quarterly*, 30 (3): 34–49.

Goodwin, A. (1992) *Dancing in the Distraction Factory: Music, television and popular culture*. Minneapolis, MN: University of Minnesota Press.

Goodwin, A. (2004) 'Rationalization and democratization in the new technologies of popular music', in S. Frith (ed.), *Popular Music: Critical concepts in media and cultural studies*, Vol 2. Abingdon: Routledge. pp. 147–68. (1st edition, 1992.)

Gramsci, A. (Q. Hoare and G. Nowell-Smith, tr.) (1976) *Selections from the Prison Notebooks*. London: Lawrence & Wishart. (1st edition, 1971.)

Gramsci, A. (1978) 'Some aspects of the Southern question' (first published, 1930), in A. Gramsci (Q. Hoare, tr.), *Selections from Political Writings 1921–1926*. London: Lawrence & Wishart. pp. 441–62.

Graves, L. (2007) 'The affordances of blogging: a case study in culture and technological effects', *Journal of Communication Inquiry*, 31 (4): 331–46.

Greider, W. (1997) *One World, Ready or Not: The manic logic of global capitalism.* New York: Simon & Schuster.

Gripsrud, J. (2000) 'Tabloidization, popular journalism and democracy', in C. Sparks and J. Tulloch (eds.), *Tabloid Tales: Local debates about media standards.* Lanham, MD: Roman & Littlefield. pp. 285–300.

Gripsrud, J. (2004) 'Broadcast television: the chances of its survival in a digital age', in L. Spiegel and J. Olsson (eds.), *Television After TV: Essays on a medium in transition.* Durham, NC: Duke University Press. pp. 210–23.

Grossberg, L. (1993) 'Can cultural studies find true happiness in communication?', *The Journal of Communication,* 43 (4): 89–97.

Grossberg, L. and Carey, J. (2006) 'James Carey in conversation with Lawrence Grossberg, Parts 1 and 2', in J. Packer and C. Robertson (eds.), *Thinking with James Carey.* New York: Peter Lang.

Grosz, L. (1986) 'Derrida and the limits of philosophy', *Thesis Eleven,* 14: 26–44.

Gurevitch, M. and Blumler, J. (1990) 'Political communication systems and democratic values', in J. Lichtenberg (ed.), *Democracy and the Mass Media.* Cambridge: Cambridge University Press. pp. 269–89.

Habermas, J. (1974) 'The public sphere: An encyclopedia article (1964)', *New German Critique,* 1 (3): 49–55. (First published 1964.)

Habermas, J. (T. Berger with F. Lawrence, tr.) (1991) *The Structural Transformation of the Public Sphere.* Cambridge, MA: MIT Press. (1st edition, 1962; 1st English translation, 1989.)

Habermas, J. (T. Burger, tr.) (1993a) 'Further reflections on the public sphere', in C. Calhoun (ed.), *Habermas and the Public Sphere.* Cambridge, MA: MIT Press. pp. 421–61.

Habermas, J. (1993b) 'Concluding remarks', in C. Calhoun (ed.), *Habermas and the Public Sphere.* Cambridge, MA: MIT Press. pp. 418–79.

Habermas, J. (W. Rehg, tr.) (1996a) *Between Facts and Norms: Contributions to a discourse theory of law and democracy.* Cambridge: Polity Press. (1st edition, 1992; 1st English translation, 1996.)

Habermas, J. (1996b) 'Modernity: an unfinished project', in S. Benhabib and M. Passerin d'Entreves (eds.), *Habermas and the Unfinished Project of Modernity.* Cambridge: Polity Press. pp. 38–55. (Lecture delivered in 1980.)

Habermas, J. (2006a) 'Political communication in media society: does democracy still enjoy an epistemic dimension? The impact of normative theory on empirical research', *Communication Theory,* 16 (4): 411–26.

Habermas, J. (2006b) 'Political communication in media society: does democracy still enjoy an epistemic dimension? The impact of normative theory on empirical research', paper presented at the 56th Annual International Communication Association Conference, Dresden, Germany, 20 June.

Habermas, J. (2009) (C. Cronin, tr.) 'Media, markets and consumers: the quality press as the backbone of the public sphere', in *Europe: The faltering project.* Cambridge: Polity Press. pp. 131–8.

Hall, S. (1972) 'The determinations of news photographs', *Working Papers in Cultural Studies,* 3: 53–87.

Hall, S. (1973a) 'Encoding and decoding in the television discourse', Centre for Contemporary Social Studies Stencilled Occasional Paper No 7. Birmingham: Centre for Contemporary Cultural Studies (CCCS).

Hall, S. (1973b) 'The "structured communication" of events', Centre for Contemporary Social Studies Stencilled Paper No 5. Birmingham: Centre for Contemporary Cultural Studies (CCCS).

Hall, S. (1974a) 'Marx's notes on method: a "reading" of the "1857 introduction"', *Working Papers in Cultural Studies,* 6: 132–71.

Hall, S. (1974b) *Mugging: A case study in communication* (video recording). Buckingham: Open University.

Hall, S. (1977a) 'Culture, the media and the "ideological effect"', in J. Curran, M. Gurevitch and J. Woollacott (eds.), *Mass Communication and Society*. London and Buckingham: Edward Arnold/Open University Press. pp. 315–418.

Hall, S. (1977b) 'The "political" and "economic" in Marx's theory of classes', in A. Hunt (ed.), *Class and Class Structure*. London: Lawrence & Wishart. pp. 15–60.

Hall, S. (1977c) 'Rethinking the "base-and-superstructure" metaphor', in J. Bloomfeld (ed.), *Class, Hegemony and Party*. London: Lawrence & Wishart. pp. 43–72.

Hall, S. (1978) 'The hinterland of science: ideology and the "sociology of knowledge"', in Centre for Contemporary Social Studies (CCCS), *On Ideology*. London: Hutchinson. (1st edition, 1977.)

Hall, S. (1980a) 'Encoding/decoding', in S. Hall, D. Hobson, A. Love and P. Willis (eds.), *Culture, Media, Language: Working papers in cultural studies, 1972–79*. London: Hutchinson. pp. 128–38.

Hall, S. (1980b) 'Popular–democratic *vs* authoritarian populism: two ways of "taking democracy seriously"', in A. Hunt (ed.), *Marxism and Democracy*. London: Lawrence & Wishart. pp. 157–85.

Hall, S. (1981) 'Notes on deconstructing "the popular"', in R. Samuel (ed.), *People's History and Socialist Theory*. London: Routledge. pp. 227–40.

Hall, S. (1982) 'The rediscovery of ideology: the return of the repressed in media studies', in M. Gurevitch, T. Bennett, J. Curran and J. Woollacott (eds.), *Culture, Society and the Media*. London: Methuen. pp. 56–90.

Hall, S. (1985a) 'Signification, representation, ideology: Althusser and the post-structuralist debates', *Critical Studies in Mass Communication*, 2 (2): 91–114.

Hall, S. (1985b) 'Authoritarian populism: a reply to Jessup et al.', *New Left Review*, I/151: 115–24.

Hall, S. (1988) *The Hard Road to Renewal: Thatcherism and the crisis of the Left*. London: Verso.

Hall, S. (1994) 'Reflections on the encoding/decoding model: an interview with Stuart Hall', in J. Cruz and J. Lewis (eds.), *Viewing, Reading, Listening: Audiences and cultural reception*. Boulder, CO: Westview Press. pp. 253–74.

Hall, S. (1996a) 'The problem of ideology: Marxism without guarantees' (first published in 1983), in D. Morley and K. Chen (eds.), *Stuart Hall: Critical dialogues in cultural studies*. London: Routledge. pp. 25–46.

Hall, S. (1996b) 'Gramsci's relevance for the study of race and ethnicity' (first published 1986), in D. Morley and K. Chen (eds.), *Stuart Hall: Critical dialogues in cultural studies*. London: Routledge. pp. 411–40.

Hall, S. (1996c) 'On postmodernism and articulation' (first published 1986), in D. Morley and K. Chen (eds.), *Stuart Hall: Critical dialogues in cultural studies*. London: Routledge. pp. 131–50.

Hall, S. (1997) 'The work of representation', in S. Hall (ed.), *Representation: Cultural representations and signifying practices*. London and Buckingham: Sage/Open University Press. pp. 13–74.

Hall, S., Connell, I. and Carti, L. (1976) 'The "unity" of current affairs television', *Working Papers in Cultural Studies*, 9: 51–94.

Hall, S., Crichter, C., Jefferson, T., Clarke, J. and Roberts, B. (1978) *Policing the Crisis: Mugging, the State and law 'n' order*. London: Macmillan.

Hall, S., Hobson, D., Lowe, A. and Willis, P. (eds.) (1980) *Culture, Media, Language*. London: Hutchinson.

Hall, S. and Jefferson, T. (eds.) (1976) *Resistence Through Rituals: Youth subcultures in post-war Britain*. London: HarperCollins Academic. (1st pub. 1974.)

Hall, S. and Whannel, P. (1964) *The Popular Arts*. London: Hutchinson.

Hallin, D.C. (1994) *We Keep America on Top of the World: Television journalism and the public sphere*. New York: Routledge.

Hallin, D.C. and Mancini, P. (2004) *Comparing Media Systems: Three models of the media and politics*. Cambridge: Cambridge University Press.

Hand, M. and Sandywell, B. (2002) 'Etopia as cosmopolis or citadel: on the democratizing and de-democratizing logics of the Internet, or toward a critique of the new technological fetishism', *Theory, Culture and Society*, 19 (1): 197–225.

Hardt, H. (1992) *Critical Communication Studies: Communication, history and theory in America.* Abingdon: Routledge.

Harpur, P. (ed.) (1982) *The Timetable of Technology: A record of our century's achievements.* London: Joseph.

Hartley, J. (1982) *Understanding News.* London: Methuen.

Hartley, J. (1996) *Popular Reality: Journalism, modernity, popular culture.* London: Arnold.

Hartley, J. and Hawkes, T. (1977) 'Popular culture & high culture: history and theory', in *Mass Communications and Society.* Buckingham: Open University Press. pp. 53–71.

Hartmann, M. (2006) 'The triple articulation of ICTs: media as technological objects, symbolic environments and individual texts', in T. Berker, M. Hartmann, Y. Punie and K.J. Ward (eds.), *The Domestication of Media and Technology.* Buckingham: Open University Press. pp. 80–102.

Harvey, D. (1989) *The Condition of Postmodernity.* Oxford: Blackwell.

Harvey, D. (2005) *A Brief History of Neoliberalism.* Oxford: Oxford University Press.

Hassan, I. (2003) 'Beyond postmodernism: toward an aesthetic of trust', *Angelaki: Journal of the Theoretical Humanities*, 8 (1): 3–11.

Heath, S. and Skirrow, G. (1986) 'An interview with Raymond Williams', in T. Modleski (ed.), *Studies in Entertainment: Critical approaches to mass culture.* Bloomington, IN: Indiana University Press. pp. 3–17.

Hebdige, D. (1979) *Subculture: The meaning of style.* London: Methuen.

Heidegger, M. (1997) 'The question concerning technology', in M. Heidegger (William Lovitt, tr.), *The Question Concerning Technology and Other Essays.* New York: Torchbooks. pp. 3–35.

Herman, E. and McChesney, R. (1997) *Global Media: New missionaries of corporate capitalism.* London: Continuum.

Hermes, J. (2004) 'A concise history of media and cultural studies in three scripts: advocacy, auto-biography and the chronicle', in J. Downing, D. McQuail, P. Schlesinger and E. Wartella (eds.), *The Sage Handbook of Media Studies.* London: Sage. pp. 251–70.

Hermes, J. (2005) *Re-reading Popular Culture.* Oxford: Blackwell.

Herring, S. (2004) 'Slouching towards the ordinary: current trends in computer-mediated communication', *New Media and Society*, 6 (1): 26–36.

Hesmondhalgh, D. (2007) *The Cultural Industries.* London: Sage. (1st edition, 2002.)

Hesmondhalgh, D. (2008) 'Cultural and creative industries', in T. Bennett and J. Frow (eds.), *Sage Handbook of Cultural Theory.* London: Sage. pp. 467–87.

Hesmondhalgh, D. and Toynbee, J. (2008) 'Why media studies needs better social theory', in D. Hesmondhalgh and J. Toynbee (eds.), *The Media and Social Theory.* Abingdon: Routledge. pp. 1–24.

Hills, M. (2001) 'Virtually out there: strategies, tactics and affective spaces in on-line fandom', in S. Munt (ed.), *Technospaces: Inside the new media.* London: Continuum. pp. 147–60.

Hirst, P. and Thompson, G. (1996) *Globalisation in Question: The international economy and the possibilities of governance.* Cambridge: Polity Press.

Hitchens, L. (2006) *Broadcasting Pluralism and Diversity: A comparative study of policy and regulation.* Oxford: Hart.

Hoggart, R. (1976) *The Uses of Literacy: Aspects of working-class life with special reference to publications and entertainments.* Harmondsworth: Penguin. (1st edition, 1957.)

Holmes, D. (1989) 'Deconstruction: a politics without a subject', *Arena*, 88: 73–116.

Holmes, D. (ed.) (1997) *Virtual Politics: Identity and community in cyberspace.* London: Sage.

Holmes, D. (ed.) (2001) *Virtual Globalisation: Virtual spaces, tourist spaces.* Abingdon: Routledge.

Holmes, D. (2005) *Communication Theory: Media, technology and society.* London: Sage.

Horne, D. (1964) *The Lucky Country: Australia in the sixties.* Ringwood, Victoria: Penguin.

Hotelling, H. (1929) 'Stability in competition', *The Economic Journal*, 39 (153): 41–57.

Howarth, D. (2000a) *Discourse*. Buckingham: Open University Press.

Howarth, D. (2000b) 'Applying Discourse Theory: the method of articulation', in D. Howarth, A.J. Norval and Y. Stavrakakis (eds.), *Discourse Theory and Political Analysis*. Manchester: Manchester University Press. pp. 316–49

Hutchby, I. (2001) 'Technologies, texts and affordances', *Sociology*, 35 (2): 441–56.

Hutchison, D. (1999) *Media Policy: An introduction*. Oxford: Blackwell.

Huyssen, A. (1986) *After the Great Divide: Modernism, mass culture, postmodernism*. Bloomington, IN: Indiana University Press. (1st edition, 1984.)

Huyssen, A. (2006) 'Introduction: modernism after postmodernity', *New German Critique*, 99: 1–5.

Innis, H. (1950) *Empire and Communications*. Oxford: Oxford University Press.

Innis, H. (1951) *The Bias of Communication*. Toronto: University of Toronto Press.

Ives, P. (2004) *Language and Hegemony in Gramsci*. London: Pluto.

Iyer, P. (2000) *The Global Soul: Jet lag, shopping malls and the search for home*. London: Bloomsbury.

Jacobs, R. (2006) 'American television as a global public sphere', paper presented to World Congress of International Sociological Association, Durban, July.

Jameson, F. (1984) 'Postmodernism, or the cultural logic of late capitalism', *New Left Review*, 146: 53–92.

Jameson, F. (1991) *Postmodernism, or the cultural logic of late capitalism*. London: Verso.

Jansen, S. (2002) *Critical Communication Theory: Power, media, gender, and technology*. Lanham, MD: Rowman & Littlefield.

Jappe, A. (1993) *Debord*. Berkeley, CA: University of California Press.

Jay, M. (1984) *Adorno*. London: Fontana.

Jay, M. (1996) *The Dialectical Imagination*. Berkeley, CA: University of California Press. (1st edition, 1973.)

Jenkins, H. (2006a) 'Democratizing television? The politics of participation', in *Convergence Culture: Where old and new media collide*. New York: New York University Press. pp. 240–60.

Jenkins, H. (2006b) '"Worship at the altar of convergence": a new paradigm for understanding media change', in H. Jenkins (ed.), *Convergence Culture: Where old and new media collide*. New York: New York University Press. pp. 1–24.

Jensen, K.B. (1995) *The Social Semiotics of Mass Communication*. London: Sage.

Jensen, K.B. (2010) *Media Convergence: The three degrees of network, mass and interpersonal communication*. Abingdon: Routledge.

Johnson, R. (1986) 'What is cultural studies anyway?', *Social Text*, 16: 38–80.

Johnston, J. (ed.) (1997) *Frederich Kittler Essays: Literature, media, information systems*. Amsterdam: G & B Arts International.

Jones, P. (1994) 'The myth of "Raymond Hoggart": on "founding fathers" and cultural policy', *Cultural Studies*, 8 (3): 394–416.

Jones, P. (1997) 'Moral panic: the legacy of Stan Cohen and Stuart Hall', *Media International Australia*, 85: 6–16.

Jones, P. (2000a) 'McLuhanist societal projections and social theory: some reflections', *Media International Australia*, 94: 39–56.

Jones, P. (2000b) 'Democratic norms and means of communication: public sphere, fourth estate, freedom of communication', *Critical Horizons*, 1 (2): 307–39.

Jones, P. (2001) 'The best of both worlds? Freedom of communication and "positive" broadcasting regulation', *Media Culture and Society*, 23 (3): 407–17.

Jones, P. (2003) 'Beyond "ages" and "eras": avoiding societal "projections" by typologising ICTs', in B. Miège and G. Tremblay (eds.), *2001 Bogues: Globalisme et pluralisme, Tome 1: TIC et société*. Les Sainte-Foy, Quebec: Les Presses de l'Université de Laval. pp. 111–28. (Available online at: www.er.uqam.ca/nobel/gricis/actes/bogues/Jones.pdf)

Jones, P. (2004) *Raymond Williams's Sociology of Culture*. Houndmills, Basingstoke: Palgrave Macmillan.

Jones, P. (2006) 'Thirty years of *Keywords*', *Sociology*, 40 (6): 1209–15.

Jones, P. (2007) 'Beyond the semantic "big bang": cultural sociology and an aesthetic public sphere', *Cultural Sociology*, 1 (1): 73–95.

Jones, P. (2010) 'Raymond Williams and Bruno Latour: "formalism" and the sociology of culture and technology', *Sociologie de l'Art*, OpuS 15/16: 59–84.

Jones, S. (ed.) (1995) *CyberSociety, Computer-mediated Communication and Community*. London: Sage.

Jordan, T. (1999) *Cyberpower: The culture and politics of cyberspace and the internet*. London: Routledge.

Jowett, G.S. (1981) 'Extended images', in R. Williams (ed.), *Contact: Human communication and its history*. London: Thames & Hudson. pp. 183–98.

Joyrich, L. (1996) *Re-viewing Reception: Television, gender, and postmodern culture*. Bloomington, IN: Indiana University Press.

Katz, E. and Lazarsfeld, P. (1955) *Personal Influence: The part played by people in the flow of mass communication*. Glencoe, IL: Free Press.

Keane, J. (1991) *The Media and Democracy*. Cambridge: Polity Press.

Keane, J. (1995a) 'Structural transformations of the public sphere', *The Communication Review*, 1 (1): 1–22.

Keane, J. (1995b) 'A reply to Nicholas Garnham', *The Communication Review*, 1 (1): 27–31.

Keane, J. (2009) 'Monitory democracy and media-saturated societies', *Griffith Review*, 24. (Available online at: www.griffithreview.com/edition-24-participation-society/222-essay/657.html)

Kellner, D. (1990) *Television and the Crisis of Democracy*. Boulder, CO: Westview Press.

Kern, S. (1983) *The Culture of Time and Space: 1880–1918*. Cambridge, MA: Harvard University Press.

Kittler, F. (1997) 'Gramophone, film, typewriter', in J. Johnston (ed.), *Friedrich Kittler Essays: Literature, media, information systems*. Amsterdam: G & B Arts International. pp. 28–49.

Klein, N. (2000) *No Logo*. Hammersmith: Flamingo.

Kompare, D. (2006) 'Publishing flow: DVD box sets and the reconception of television', *Television and New Media*, 7 (4): 335–60.

Kroker, A. and Kroker, M. (1996) *Hacking the Future: Stories for the flesh-eating 90s*. Montreal: CTheory.

Kroker, A. and Weinstein, M. (1994) *Data Trash: The theory of the virtual class*. New York: St Martin's Press.

Kumar, K. (1995) *From Post-industrial to Post-modern Society: New theories of the contemporary world*. Oxford: Blackwell.

Lacey, N. (2000) *Narrative and Genre*. Houndmills, Basingstoke: Palgrave Macmillan.

Laclau, E. (1977) *Politics and Ideology in Marxist Theory: Capitalism, fascism, populism*. London: Verso.

Laclau, E. (2005) *On Populist Reason*. London: Verso.

Laclau, E. and Mouffe, C. (W. Moore and P. Cammack, tr.) (1985) *Hegemony and Socialist Strategy*. London: Verso.

Laclau, E. and Mouffe, C. (1987) 'Post-Marxism without apologies', *New Left Review*, 1 (161): 79–106.

Lacroix, J.-G. and Tremblay, G. (1997) 'Trend report: "the information society" and cultural industries theory', *Current Sociology*, 45 (4): whole issue.

Lang, K. and Lang, G. (2009) 'Mass society, mass culture, and mass communication: the meaning of mass', *International Journal of Communication*, 3: 998–1024.

Lara, M. (1998) *Moral Textures: Feminist narratives in the public sphere*. Cambridge: Polity Press.

Larrain, J. (1979) *The Concept of Ideology*. London: Hutchinson.

Larrain, J. (1984) 'Three different concepts of ideology in Marx? A rejoinder to Márkus', *Canadian Journal of Political and Social Theory*, 8 (3): 151–61.

Lash, S. and Lury, C. (2007) *Global Culture Industry: The mediation of things*. Cambridge: Polity Press.

Lasswell, H. (1948) 'The structure and function of communication in society', in B. Berelson and M. Janowitz (eds) *Reader in Public Opinion and Communication* (2nd edition). New York: The Free Press. pp. 178–90.

Lasswell, H. (1949) 'Why be quantitative?', in H.D. Lasswell, N. Leites, R. Fadner, J. Goldsen, A. Grey, I. Janis, A. Kaplan, A. Mintz, I. De Sola Pool, S. Yakobsen and D. Kaplan, *Language of Politics: Studies in quantitative semantics*. New York: George W. Stewart. pp. 40–54.

Latour, B. (1992) 'Where are the missing masses? The sociology of a few mundane artifacts', in W. Bijker and J. Law (eds.), *Shaping Technology/Building Society: Studies in sociotechnical change*. Cambridge, MA: MIT Press. pp. 225–58.

Latour, B. (1994) 'On technical mediation: philosophy, sociology, genealogy', *Common Knowledge*, 3 (Fall): 29–64.

Latour, B. (1995) 'A door must either be open or shut', in A. Feenberg and A. Hannay (eds.), *Technology and the Politics of Knowledge*. Bloomington, IN: Indiana University Press. pp. 271–91.

Latour, B. (1997) 'On actor network theory: a few clarifications', Working Paper, CSTT, University of Keele, Staffordshire. (Available online at: www.nettime.org/Lists-Archives/nettime-l-9801/msg00019.html)

Latour, B. (1999) 'On recalling ANT', in J. Low and J. Hassard (eds.), *Actor Network Theory and After*. Oxford: Blackwell. pp. 15–25.

Lazarsfeld, P.F. (1941) 'Remarks on administrative and critical communications research', *Studies in Philosophy and Social Science*, IX (1): 2–16.

Lazarsfeld, P.F. (1972) 'Critical theory and dialectics', in P.F. Lazarsfeld, *Qualitiative Analysis: Historical and Critical Essays*. Boston, MA: Allyn & Bacon.

Lazarsfeld, P.F. and Gaudet, H. (1944) *The People's Choice*. New York: Duell, Sloan & Pearce.

Leavis, F.R. (1965) 'Literature and society', in F. Leavis (ed.), *The Common Pursuit*. London: Chatto & Windus. pp. 182–94. (1st edition, 1952.)

Leavis, F.R. and Thompson, D. (1937) *Culture and Environment*. London: Chatto and Windus. (1st pub. 1933.)

Leavis, Q.D. (1968) *Fiction and the Reading Public*. London: Chatto & Windus. (1st edition, 1932.)

Lent, J. (ed.) (1995) *A Different Road Taken: Profiles in critical communication*. Boulder, CO: Westview Press.

Lerner, D. (1958) *The Passing of Traditional Society*. Glencoe, IL: Free Press.

Levinson, P. (1999) *Digital McLuhan: A guide to the information millennium*. Abingdon: Routledge.

Lévi-Strauss, C. (1973) *Totemism*. Harmondsworth: Penguin. (1st edition, 1962.)

Levy, M. (1982) 'The Lazarsfeld-Stanton program analyzer: an historical note', *Journal of Communication*, 32 (4): 30–8.

Lewis, J. (1983) 'The encoding/decoding model: criticisms and redevelopments for research on decoding', *Media, Culture and Society*, 15: 179–98.

Lewis, J. (1991) *The Ideological Octopus: An exploration of television and its audience*. New York: Routledge.

Lewis, J. (1996) 'Decoding television news' (revised and reprinted) in J. Corner and S. Harvey (eds.), *Television Times: A reader*. London: Arnold. (1st edition, 1985.)

Lewis, J. (1999) 'Reproducing political hegemony in the United States', *Critical Studies in Mass Communication*, 16 (3): 251–67.

Lewis, J. (2001) *Constructing Public Opinion*. New York: Columbia University Press.

Lewis, J. and Miller, T. (eds.) (2002) *Critical Cultural Policy Studies: A reader*. Malden, MA: Blackwell.

Lichtenberg, J. (1990) 'Foundations and limits of freedom of the press', in J. Lichtenberg (ed.), *Democracy and the Mass Media*. Cambridge: Cambridge University Press. pp. 102–35.

Lievrouw, L. and Livingstone, S. (eds.) (2006) *Handbook of New Media: Social shaping and the consequences of ICTs*. London: Sage.

Lilleker, D. (2006) *Key Concepts in Political Communication*. London: Sage.

Ling, R. and Yttri, B. (2006) 'Control, emancipation and status: the mobile telephone in the teen's parental and peer group control relationships', in R. Kraut, M. Brynin and S. Kiesler (eds.), *Computers, Phones, and the Internet: Domesticating information technology*. Oxford: Oxford University Press. pp. 219–34.

Lister, M., Dovey, J., Giddings, S., Grant, I. and Kelly, K. (2009) *New Media: A critical introduction*. Abingdon: Routledge. (1st edition, 2003.)

Littlemore, S. (1996) *The Media and Me*. Sydney: ABC Books.

Livingstone, S. (1996) 'On the continuing problem of media effects', in J. Curran and M. Gurevitch (eds.), *Mass Media and Society*. London: Edward Arnold. pp. 305–24.

Livingstone, S. (1998a) 'Audience research at the crossroads: the "implied audience" in media and cultural theory', *European Journal of Cultural Studies*, 1 (2): 193–217.

Livingstone, S. (1998b) *Making Sense of Television: The psychology of audience interpretation*. Abingdon: Routledge. (1st edition, 1990.)

Livingstone, S. (1998c) 'Relationships between media and audiences: prospects for audience reception studies', in T. Liebes and J. Curran (eds.), *Media, Ritual and Identity: Essays in honour of Elihu Katz*. Abingdon: Routledge. pp. 237–55.

Livingstone, S. (2004) 'The challenge of changing audiences: or, what is the audience researcher to do in the age of the Internet?', *European Journal of Communication*, 19 (1): 75–86.

Livingstone, S. (ed.) (2005) *Audiences and Publics: When cultural engagement matters for the public sphere*. Bristol: Intellect.

Livingstone, S. (2006) 'The influence of Personal Influence on the study of audiences', in P. Simonson (ed.), 'Politics, social networks, and the history of mass communications research: re-reading personal influence', *The Annals of the American Academy of Political and Social Science*, 608: 233–50.

Livingstone, S. (2007a) 'On the material and the symbolic: Silverstone's double articulation of research traditions in new media studies', *New Media and Society*, 9 (1): 16–24.

Livingstone, S. (2007b) 'The challenge of engaging youth online', *European Journal of Communication*, 22 (2): 165–84.

López, J. and Potter, G. (2001) *After Postmodernism: An introduction to critical realism*. London: Athlone.

Löwenthal, L. (1961) *Literature, Popular Culture, and Society*. Upper Saddle River, NJ: Prentice Hall.

Lukács, G. (1971) *History and Class Consciousness*. London: Merlin.

Lum, C.M.K. (2006) *Perspectives on Culture, Technology and Communication: The media ecology tradition*. Cresskill, NJ: Hampton Press.

Lunn, E. (1985) *Marxism and Modernism*. London: Verso.

Lury, C. (2008) 'Cultural technologies', in T. Bennett and J. Frow (eds.), *Handbook of Cultural Theory*. London: Sage. pp. 570–86.

Lyotard, J.-F. (G. Bennington and B. Massumi, tr.) (1984) *The Postmodern Condition: A report on knowledge*. Manchester: Manchester University Press.

Lyotard, J.-F. (1992) *The Postmodern Explained to Children: Correspondence 1982–1985*. Sydney: Power Publications.

MacCannell, D. (1999) *The Tourist: A new theory of the leisure class*. Berkeley, CA: University of California Press.

MacCabe, C. (2008) 'An interview with Stuart Hall, December 2007', *Critical Quarterly*, 50 (1–2): 12–42.

McChesney, R. (2007) *Communication Revolution*. New York: The New Press.

McChesney, R. (2008) *The Political Economy of Media: Enduring issues, emerging dilemmas.* New York: Monthly Review Press.

McCombs, M. and Shaw, D. (1972) 'The agenda-setting function of the mass media', *Public Opinion Quarterly*, 15 (2): 65–70.

Macdonald, D. (1953) 'A theory of mass culture', *Diogenes*, 1 (3): 1–17.

McDonald, D.G. (2004) 'Twentieth-century media effects research', in J. Downing, D. McQuail, P. Schlesinger and E. Wartella (eds.), *The Sage Handbook of Media Studies*. London: Sage. pp. 183–200.

Macdonald, M. (2000) 'Rethinking personalization in current affairs journalism', in C. Sparks and J. Tulloch (eds.), *Tabloid Tales: Global debates over media standards*. Lanham, MD: Rowman & Littlefield. pp. 251–66.

McGuigan, J. (1992) *Cultural Populism*. Abingdon: Routledge.

McGuigan, J. (2004) *Rethinking Cultural Policy*. Buckingham and Maidenhead: Open University Press and McGraw-Hill.

McGuigan, J. (2005) 'The cultural public sphere', *European Journal of Cultural Studies*, 8 (4): 427–43.

McGuigan, J. (2007) 'Technological determinism and mobile privatization', in V. Nightingale and T. Dwyer (eds.), *New Media Worlds: Challenges for convergence*. Oxford and Melbourne: Oxford University Press. pp. 5–18.

McGuigan, J. (2009) *Cool Capitalism*. London: Pluto Press.

MacKenzie, D.A. and Wajcman, J. (eds.) (1999) *The Social Shaping of Technology: How the refrigerator got its hum*. Buckingham: Open University Press. (1st edition, 1985.)

McLuhan, M. (1964) *Understanding Media: The extensions of man*. London: Abacus.

McLuhan, M. (1971) 'Marshall McLuhan Convocation Address, The University of Alberta', McLuhan Studies, Issue 5. (Available online at McLuhan: http://projects.chass.utoronto.ca/mcluhan-studies/v1_iss5/1_5art3.htm)

McLuhan, M. (2003) *Understanding Me: Lectures and interviews*. Eds. S. McLuhan and D. Staines. Toronto: McClelland and Stewart.

McLuhan, M. (2008) *McLuhanisms*, Los Angeles, Marshall McLuhan Center on Global Communications. (Available online at: www.mcluhanmedia.com/m_mcl_quotes_003.html)

McLuhan, M. and Fiore, Q. (1967) *The Medium is the Massage: An inventory of effects*. London: Penguin.

McNair, B. (1998) *The Sociology of Journalism*. London: Arnold.

McNair, B. (2002) *Striptease Culture: Sex, media and the democratization of desire*. Abingdon: Routledge.

Macnamara, J. (2010) *The 21st Century Media Revolution: Emergent communication practices*. New York: Peter Lang.

McRobbie, A. (1994) *Postmodernism and Popular Culture*. Abingdon: Routledge.

Macek, S. (2006) *Urban Nightmares: The media, the right and the moral panic over the city*. Minneapolis, MN: Minnesota University Press.

Mansell, R. and Silverstone, R. (eds.) (1996) *Communication by Design: The politics of information and communication technologies*. Oxford: Oxford University Press.

Marc, D. (2000) 'What was broadcasting?', in H. Newcomb (ed.), *Television: A critical view*. Oxford: Oxford University Press. pp. 629–49. (1st edition, 1976.)

Márkus, G. (1983) 'Concepts of ideology in Marx', *Canadian Journal of Political and Social Theory*, 7 (1–2): 84–103.

Márkus, G. (1987) 'Ideology, critique and contradiction in Marx: an answer to J. Larrain', *Canadian Journal of Political and Social Theory*, 11 (3): 74–88.

Márkus, G. (1995) 'On ideology critique: critically', *Thesis Eleven*, 43: 66–99.

Martin, H.P. (1997) *The Global Trap: Globalization and the assault on prosperity and democracy*. London: Zed Books.

Marvin, C. (1988) *When Old Technologies were New: Thinking about communication in the late nineteenth century*. New York: Oxford University Press.

Marwick, A. and boyd, d. (2010) 'I tweet honestly, i tweet passionately: Twitter users, context collapse, and the imagined audience', *New Media and Society*, 13: 114–33.

Marx, K. (1950a) 'Preface to a contribution to the critique of political economy', in K. Marx and F. Engels, *Selected Works*, Vol. 1. London: Lawrence & Wishart.

Marx, K. (1950b) *The Eighteenth Brumaire of Louis Bonaparte*, in K. Marx and F. Engels, *Selected Works*, Vol. 1. London: Lawrence & Wishart.

Marx, K. (1973a) *Grundrisse*. London: Penguin. (1st edition, 1939.)

Marx, K. (1973b) 'The 1857 Introduction', in *Grundrisse*. London: Penguin. (1st edition, 1939.)

Marx, K. (B. Fowkes, tr.) (1976) *Capital* (Vol 1). London: Penguin/New Left Books.

Marx, K. and Engels, F. (1967) *The Communist Manifesto*. Harmondsworth: Penguin.

Marx, K. and Engels, F. (1976) *The German Ideology*, in K. Marx and F. Engels, *Collected Works*, Vol. 5, *1845–1847*. London: Lawrence & Wishart.

Massey, D.B. (1999) 'Space-time, "science" and the relationship between physical geography and human geography', *Transactions of the Institute of British Geographers*, 24 (3): 261–76.

Mattelart, A. (2000) *Networking the World, 1794–2000*. Minneapolis, MN: University of Minnesota Press.

Matthewman, S. and Hoey, D. (2006) 'What happened to postmodernism?', *Sociology*, 40 (3): 529–47.

Mazzoleni, G., Stewart, J. and Horsfield, B. (eds.) (2003) *The Media and Neo-Populism*. Westport, CT: Praegar.

Medhurst, A. (1997) 'Negotiating the gnome zone: versions of suburbia in British popular culture', in R. Silverstone (ed.), *Visions of Suburbia*. London: Routledge. pp. 240–68.

Meehan, J. (ed.) (1995) *Feminists Read Habermas*. New York: Routledge.

Mellencamp, P. (1998) 'The news as performance: the image as event', in M. Morse (ed.), *Virtualities: Television, media art, and cyberculture*. Bloomington, IN: Indiana University Press. pp. 36–71.

Merrill, J. (1974) *The Imperative of Freedom: A philosophy of journalistic autonomy*. New York: Freedom House.

Merrin, W. (2005) *Baudrillard and the Media: A critical introduction*. Cambridge: Polity Press.

Meyrowitz, J. (1985) *No Sense of Place: The impact of electronic media on social behaviour*. New York: Oxford University Press.

Meyrowitz, J. (1990) 'Television: the shared arena', *The World and I*, 5 (7): 464–81.

Meyrowitz, J. (1999) 'Understandings of media', *ETC: A Review of General Semantics*, 56 (1): 44–53.

Michaels, E. (1986) *The Aboriginal Invention of Television in Central Australia 1982–1986*. Canberra: Australian Institute of Aboriginal Studies.

Michaels, E. (1987) *For a Cultural Future: Francis Jupurrurla makes TV at Yuendumu*. Malvern, Victoria: Artspace.

Miège, B. (1989) *The Capitalization of Cultural Production*. New York: International General.

Mill, J. (1991) *On Liberty and Other Writings*. Cambridge: Cambridge University Press.

Mills, C.W. (1959) *The Sociological Imagination*. New York: Oxford University Press.

Misa, T. (1988) 'How machines make history and how historians (and others) help them to do so', *Science, Technology and Human Values*, 13 (3–4): 308–31.

Mitchell, W.J.T. (2003) 'The work of art in the age of biocybernetic reproduction', *Modernism/Modernity*, 10 (3): 481–500.

Modleski, T. (ed.) (1986) *Studies in Entertainment: Critical approaches to mass culture*. Bloomington, IN: Indiana University Press.

Monteiro, E. (2004) 'Actor network theory and cultural aspects of interpretive studies', in C. Avgerou, C. Ciborra and F. Land (eds.), *The Social Study of Information and Communication Technology: Innovation, actors, and contexts*. Oxford: Oxford University Press. pp. 129–39.

Moores, S. (2000) *Media and Everyday Life in Modern Society*. Edinburgh: Edinburgh University Press.

Moriarty, M. (1991) *Roland Barthes*. Cambridge: Polity Press.

Morley, D. (1980) *The Nationwide Audience: Structure and decoding*. London: British Film Institute (BFI).

Morley, D. (1996a) 'Populism, revisionism and the "new" audience research', in J. Curran, D. Morley and V. Walkerdine (eds.), *Cultural Studies and Communications*. London: Arnold. pp. 279–93.

Morley, D. (1996b) 'Media dialogue: reading the readings of the readings', in J. Curran, D. Morley and V. Walkerdine (eds.), *Cultural Studies and Communications*. London: Arnold. pp. 300–5.

Morley, D. (2000) *Home Territories*. Abingdon: Routledge.

Morley, D. and Brunsdon, C. (1997) *The Nationwide Television Studies*. London: Routledge.

Morley, D. and Silverstone, R. (1990) 'Domestic communication: technologies and meanings', *Media, Culture and Society*, 12 (1): 31–55.

Morris, M. (1990) 'Banality in cultural studies', in P. Mellencamp (ed.), *Logics of Television: Essays in cultural criticism*. London: BFI Publishing. pp. 14–43.

Morris, M. and Ogan, C. (1996) 'The Internet as mass medium', *Journal of Communication*, 46 (1): 39–50.

Mosco, V. (2003) 'Brand new world? Globalization, cyberspace and the politics of convergence', in B. Miège and G. Tremblay (eds.), *2001 Bogues: Globalisme et pluralisme, Tome 1: TIC et Société*. Les Sainte-Foy, Quebec: Les Presses de l'Université de Laval. pp. 31–52.

Mosco, V. (2004) *The Digital Sublime: Myth, power and cyberspace*. Boston, MA: MIT Press.

Mosco, V. (2009) *The Political Economy of Communication*. Thousand Oaks, CA: Sage. (1st edition, 1996.)

Mulhern, F. (2000) *Culture/Metaculture*. London: Methuen.

Murdock, G. (1993) 'Communications and the constitution of modernity', *Media, Culture and Society*, 15 (4): 521–39.

Murphie, A. and Potts, J. (2003) *Culture and Technology*. Houndsmills: Palgrave Macmillan.

Nairn, T. (1968) 'McLuhanism: the myth of our time', in R. Rosenthal (ed.), *McLuhan: Pro and Con*. Baltimore, MD: Pelican. pp. 140–64.

Nealon, J. and Irr, C. (eds.) (2002) *Rethinking the Frankfurt School: Alternative legacies of cultural critique*. Albany, NY: SUNY Press.

Negroponte, N. (1995) *Being Digital*. Sydney: Hodder & Stoughton.

Negt, O. and Kluge, A. (P. Labanyi, J.O. Daniel and A. Oksiloff, tr.) (1993) *Public Sphere and Experience: Toward an analysis of the bourgeois and proletarian public sphere*. Minneapolis, MN: University of Minnesota Press. (1st edition, 1972.)

Negus, K. (1997) 'The production of culture', in P. du Gay (ed.), *Production of Culture/Cultures of Production*. London: Sage. pp. 67–118.

Neuman, W.R. (2000) 'The impact of the new media', in W. Lance Bennett and Robert M. Entman (eds.), *Mediated Politics: Communication in the future of democracy*. New York: Cambridge University Press. pp. 299–320.

Newcomb, H. (2004) 'Narrative and genre', in J. Downing (ed.), *The Sage Handbook of Media Studies*. Thousand Oaks, CA and London: Sage. pp. 413–28.

Nightingale, V. (1996) *Studying Audiences: The shock of the real*. London: Routledge.

Nightingale, V. and Ross, K. (eds.) (2003) *Critical Readings: Media and audiences*. Buckingham: Open University Press.

Norris, C. (1987) *Derrida*. London: Fontana.

Norris, P. (2000) *A Virtuous Circle: Political communications in postindustrial societies*. Cambridge: Cambridge University Press.

Nunes, M. (1997) 'What space is cyberspace?', in D. Holmes (ed.), *Virtual Politics: Identity and community in cyberspace*. London: Sage. pp. 163–78.

Ohmae, K. (1995) *The End of the Nation State: The rise of regional economies*. London: HarperCollins.

O'Shaughnessy, M. and Stadler, J. (2005) *Media and Society: An introduction.* Oxford: Oxford University Press. (1st edition, 1999.)

Ouellette, L. and Hay, J. (2008) *Better Living Through Reality TV: Television and post-welfare citizenship.* London: Wiley-Blackwell.

Park, D. and Pooley, J. (2008) *The History of Media and Communication Research: Contested memories.* New York: Peter Lang.

Peters, J.D. (1999) *Speaking into the Air: A history of the idea of communication.* Chicago, IL: Chicago University Press.

Plant, S. (1992) *The Most Radical Gesture: The situationist international in a postmodern age.* London: Routledge.

Plant, R. (2009) *The Neo-Liberal State.* Oxford: Oxford University Press.

Poggioli, R. (1968) *The Theory of the Avant-Garde.* Cambridge, MA: Belknap. (1st edition, 1962.)

Poster, M. (1995) *The Second Media Age.* Cambridge: Polity Press.

Postman, N. (1993) *Technopoly: The surrender of culture to technology.* New York: Vintage.

Poulantzas, N. (1976) *Political Power and Social Classes.* London: NLB. (1st edition, 1968.)

Poulantzas, N. (2000) *State, Power, Socialism.* London: Verso. (1st edition, 1978.)

Poynting, S. and Morgan, G. (eds.) (2007) *Outrageous!: Moral Panics in Australia.* Hobart: ACYS Publishing.

Preston, P. (2001) *Reshaping Communications: Technology, information and social change.* London: Sage.

Propp, V. (L. Scott, tr.) (1968) *Morphology of the Folktale.* Austin, TX: University of Texas Press. (1st edition, 1927.)

Radway, J. (1984) *Reading the Romance: Women, patriarchy, and popular literature.* Chapel Hill, NC: University of North Carolina Press.

Rafaeli, S. (1988) 'Interactivity: from new media to communication', in R.P. Hawkins, J.M. Wiemann and S. Pingree (eds.), *Advancing Communication Science*, Vol. 16, *Sage Annual Reviews of Communication Research*. Beverley Hills, CA: Sage. pp. 110–34.

Rafaeli, S. and Sudweeks, F. (1997) 'Networked interactivity', *Journal of Computer Mediated Communication*, 2 (4).

Rantanen, T. (2005) *The Media and Globalization.* London: Sage.

Ray, G. (2006) 'Tabloidization of the media: the page three syndrome', address by Mr Justice G.N. Ray, Chairman, Press Council of India at Seminar organized by the Public Relations Society of India and Mass Media Centre, Government of West Bengal on 25 August 2006. (Available online at: http://presscouncil.nic.in/Decisions/Oct-Rew-1-239.pdf)

Real, M. (1984) *Supermedia.* Thousand Oaks, CA: Sage.

Rheingold, H. (1994) *The Virtual Community.* London: Secker & Warburg.

Riesman, D. (1990) 'Listening to popular music', in S. Frith and A. Goodwin (eds.), *On Record.* Abingdon: Routledge. (1st edition, 1950.)

Ritzer, G. (1993) *The Maconaldization of Society: An investigation into the changing character of contemporary social life.* Newbury Park, CA: Pine Forge Press.

Riva, G. and Galimberti, C. (1998) 'Computer-mediated communication: identity and social interaction in an electronic environment', *Genetic, Social and General Psychology Monographs*, 124: 434–64.

Rizzo, T. (2007) 'Programming your own channel: an archaeology of the playlist', in A.T. Kenyon (ed.), *TV Futures: Digital television policy in Australia.* Carlton, Victoria: Melbourne University Press. pp. 108–29.

Roberts, J.M. and Crossley, N. (eds.) (2004) Special issue on the public sphere, *The Sociological Review*, 52 (Supplement 1).

Robertson, R. (1992) *Globalization: Social theory and global culture.* London: Sage.

Robins, K. and Webster, F. (1999) *Times of the Technoculture: From the information society to the virtual life.* Abingdon: Routledge.

Robinson, W. (2006) 'Catching the waves: considering cyberculture, technoculture, and elecronic consumption', in D. Silver and A. Massanari (eds.), *Critical Cyberculture Studies*. New York: New York University Press. pp. 55–67.

Rogers, E. (1981) 'The empirical and critical schools of communication research', *Communication Yearbook* 5. Brunswick, NJ: Transaction. pp. 125–44.

Rojek, C. (2007) *Cultural Studies*. Cambridge: Polity Press.

Rojek, C. and Urry, J. (1997) *Touring Cultures: Transformations of travel and theory*. London: Sage.

Romano, A. and Bromley, M. (eds.) (2005) *Journalism and Democracy in Asia*. Abingdon: Routledge.

Rosa, H. (2003) 'Social acceleration: ethical and political consequences of a desynchronized high-speed society', *Constellations*, 10 (1): 3–33.

Rose, N. (1999) *Powers of Freedom: Reframing political thought*. Cambridge: Cambridge University Press.

Rosen, J. (2003) 'PressThink: An introduction', PressThink: The Ghost of Democracy in the Media Machine blog (at: http://journalism.nyu.edu/pubzone/weblogs/pressthink/2003/09/01/intro-duction_ghost.html)

Ross, K. and Nightingale, V. (2003) *Media and Audiences: New perspectives*. Buckingham: Open University Press.

Rothenbuhler, E.W. and Coman, M. (eds.) (2005) *Media Anthropology*. Thousand Oaks, CA: Sage.

Sassoon, D. (2002) 'On cultural markets', *New Left Review*, 17: 113–26.

de Saussure, F. (1966) *Course in General Linguistics*. New York: McGraw-Hill. (1st edition, 1916.)

Scannell, P. (1989) 'Public service broadcasting and modern public life', *Media, Culture and Society*, 11 (2): 135–66.

Schauer, F. (1982) *Free Speech: A philosophical enquiry*. Cambridge: Cambridge University Press.

Schiller, D. (1996) *Theorizing Communication*. Oxford: Oxford University Press.

Schiller, D. (1999) *Digital Capitalism*. Cambridge, MA: MIT Press.

Schiller, D. (2007) *How to Think About Information*. Urbana, IL: University of Illinois Press.

Schiller, H. (1971) *Mass Communication and American Empire*. New York: Beacon. (1st edition, 1969.)

Schivelbusch, W. (1987) *The Railway Journey*. New York: Urzen Books.

Schlesinger, P. (1990) 'Rethinking the sociology of journalism: some strategies and the limits of media-centrism', in M. Ferguson (ed.), *Public Communication: The new imperatives*. London: Sage. pp. 61–83.

Schudson, M. (2004) *The Sociology of News*. New York: Norton.

Schudson, M. (2008) *Why Democracies Need an Unlovable Press*. Cambridge: Polity Press.

Schultz, T. (2000) 'Mass media and the concept of interactivity: an exploratory study of online forums and reader email', *Media, Culture and Society*, 22 (2): 205–21.

Selden, R. and Widdowson, P. (1993) *A Reader's Guide to Contemporary Literary Theory*. Lexington, KY: University Press of Kentucky.

Shannon, C.E. and Weaver, W. (1949) *The Mathematical Theory of Communication*. Urbana, IL: University of Illinois Press.

Sharp, C. (1966) 'Introduction to the first edition, 1917', in O.D. Campbell and C. Sharp, *English Folk Songs from the Southern Appalachian Mountains*. Oxford: Oxford University Press.

Shaw, G.D. (ed.) (2001) 'Happy in our chains? Agency and language in the postmodern age', *History and Theory*, 40 (4): 1–9.

Shields, R. (ed.) (1996) *Cultures of the Internet: Virtual spaces, real histories, living bodies*. London: Sage.

Shklovsky, V. (1965) 'Art as technique' (first published 1917), in L. Lemon and M. Reis (eds and tr.), *Russian Formalist Criticism: Four essays*. Lincoln, NE: University of Nebraska Press. pp. 3–24.

Shuttleworth, A., de Camargo, M. and Hall, S. (1975) *Television Violence, Crime-Drama and the Analysis of Content*. Birmingham: Centre for Contemporary Cultural Studies (CCCS).

Silver, D. (2000) 'Looking backwards, looking forward: cyberculture studies 1990–2000', in D. Gauntlett (ed.), *Web.studies: Rewriting media studies for the digital age*. London: Arnold. pp. 19–30.

Silver, D. (2006) 'Where is Internet studies? Introduction', in D. Silver and A. Massanari (eds.), *Critical Cyber-Culture Studies*. New York: New York University Press. pp. 1–14.

Silverstone, R. (1994) *Television and Everyday Life*. London: Routledge.

Silverstone, R. (1999) *Why Study the Media?* London: Sage.

Simmel, G. (K. Wolf, ed.) (1950) *The Sociology of Georg Simmel*. New York: Free Press.

Simmel, G. (1971) 'The metropolis and mental life', in G. Simmel, *On Individuality and Social Forms*. Chicago, IL: University of Chicago Press. pp. 324–39.

Simons, H.W. and Billig, M. (1994) *After Postmodernism: Reconstructing ideology critique*. London: Sage.

Simons, J. (2003) 'Popular culture and mediated politics: intellectuals, elites and democracy', in J. Corner and D. Pels (eds.), *Media and the Restyling of Politics*. London: Sage. pp. 171–89.

Simonson, P. (ed.) (2006) *Politics, Social Networks, and the History of Mass Communications Research: Re-reading Personal Influence. The Annals of the American Academy of Political and Social Science*, 608 (whole issue).

Slevin, R. (2003) *The Internet and Society*. Cambridge: Polity Press.

Sokal, A. (1996a) 'Transgressing the boundaries: towards a transformative hermeneutics of quantum gravity', *Social Text*, 46/47: 217–52.

Sokal, A. (1996b) 'A physicist experiments with cultural studies', *Lingua Franca*, May/June: 62–4.

Sokal, A. and Bricmont, J. (1999) *Intellectual Impostures*. London: Profile.

de Sola Pool, I. (1983) *Technologies of Freedom*. Cambridge, MA: Belknap Press.

Sparks, C. (2001a) 'Development, imperialism and globalization: the implications of the paradigm shifts in international communication', in R. Srinivas and S. Rao (eds.), *Critical Issues in Communication: Looking inward for answers*. London and New Delhi: Sage. pp. 357–85.

Sparks, C. (2001b) 'The Internet and the global public sphere', in W. Bennett and R. Entman (eds.), *Mediated Politics: Communication in the future of democracy*. Cambridge: Cambridge University Press. pp. 75–98.

Sparks, C. (2007) *Globalization, Development and the Mass Media*. London: Sage.

Sparks, C. and Tulloch, J. (eds.) (2000) *Tabloid Tales: Global debates over media standards*. Lanham, MD: Rowman & Littlefield.

Special Issue: Ferment in the field (1983) *Journal of Communication* 33 (3): 4–362.

Spigel, L. (1992) *Make Room for TV: Television and the family ideal in postwar America*. Chicago, IL: University of Chicago Press.

Splichal, S. (2008) 'Why be critical?', *Communication, Culture & Critique*, 1: 20–30.

Steemers, J. (1999) 'Broadcasting is dead. Long live digital choice', in H. Mackay and T. O'Sullivan (eds.), *The Media Reader: Continuity and transformation*. London: Sage. pp. 231–49.

Steger, M. (2009) *Globalisms: The great ideological struggle of the twenty-first century*. Lanham, MD and Oxford: Rowman & Littlefield.

Steiner, R. (1952) 'Program patterns and preferences, and the workability of competition in radio broadcasting', *Quarterly Journal of Economics*, 66 (2): 194–223.

Steinert, H. (2003) *Culture Industry*. Cambridge: Polity Press.

Stevenson, N. (2002) *Understanding Media Cultures: Social theory and mass communication*. London: Sage. (1st edition, 1995.)

Storey, J. (2003) *Inventing Popular Culture: From folklore to globalization*. Oxford: Blackwell.

Strate, L. (2004) 'Introduction: a media ecology review', *Communication Research Trends*, 23 (2): 3–48.

Stratton, J. (1997) 'Cyberspace and the globalization of culture', in D. Porter (ed.), *Internet Culture*. London: Routledge. pp. 253–71.

249

Strinati, D. (2000) *An Introduction to Studying Popular Culture*. London: Routledge.

Strossen, N. (2000) *Defending Pornography: Free speech, sex, and the fight for women's rights*. New York: New York University Press. (1st edition, 1995.)

Suler, J. (1996) *The Psychology of Cyberspace*. (Available online at: http://users.rider.edu/~suler/psycyber/psycyber.html)

Swingewood, A. (1998) *Cultural Theory and the Problem of Modernity*. Houndmills, Basingstoke: Macmillan.

Taylor, P. and Harris, J. (2008) *Critical Theories of Mass Media: Then and now*. Maidenhead, Buckingham and New York: McGraw-Hill/Open University Press.

Taylor, P., Richardson, J., Yeo, A., Marsh, I., Trobe, K. and Pilkington, A. (1995) *Sociology in Focus*. Ormskirk: Causeway.

Thompson, D. (1939) *Between the Lines: Or, how to read a newspaper*. London: Frederick Muller.

Thompson, J.B. (1990) *Ideology and Modern Culture*. Stanford: Stanford University Press.

Thompson, J.B. (1995) *The Media and Modernity: A social theory of the media*. Stanford, CA: Stanford University Press.

Thompson, K. (ed.) (1997) *Media and Cultural Regulation*. London and Buckingham: Sage and Open University Press.

Thompson, K. (1998) *Moral Panics*. Abingdon: Routledge.

Thussu, D.K. (2007) *News as Entertainment: The rise of global infotainment*. London: Sage.

Tiffen, R. (1989) *News and Power*. Sydney: Allen & Unwin.

Todorov, T. (1981) *Introduction to Poetics*. Brighton: Harvester. (1st French edition, 1968.)

Tuchman, G. (1972) 'Objectivity as strategic ritual: an examination of newsmen's notions of objectivity', *The American Journal of Sociology*, 77 (4): 660–79.

Tuchman, G. (1978) *Making News: A study in the construction of reality*. New York: The Free Press.

Turkle, S. (1995) *Life on the Screen: Identity in the age of the Internet*. New York: Simon & Schuster.

Turner, G. (2001) 'Sold out: recent shifts in news and current affairs in Australia', in M. Bromley (ed.), *No News is Bad News: Radio, television, and the public*. Harlow: Pearson. pp. 46–58.

Turner, G. (2003) *British Cultural Studies: An introduction*. Abingdon: Routledge. (1st edition, 1990.)

Urry, J. (2007) *Mobilities*. Cambridge: Polity Press.

van Dijk, T. (1991) *Racism and the Press*. Abingdon: Routledge.

van Dijk, T. (1998) *Ideology: A multidisciplinary approach*. London: Sage.

van Dijk, J. (1999a) *The Network Society*. London: Sage.

van Dijk, J. (1999b) 'The one-dimensional network society of Manuel Castells', *New Media and Society*, 1 (1): 127–38.

Virilio, P. (1997) 'The overexposed city', in N. Leach (ed.), *Rethinking Architecture*. London: Routledge. pp. 381–90.

Vološinov, V. (1973) *Marxism and the Philosophy of Language*. New York: Seminar. (1st edition, 1930.)

Wajcman, J. (1991) *Feminism Confronts Technology*. Sydney: Allen & Unwin.

Wajcman, J. (1994) 'Technological a/genders: technology, culture and class', in L. Green and R. Guinery (eds.), *Framing Technology: Society, choice and change*. Sydney: Allen & Unwin. pp. 3–14.

Wajcman, J. (2004) *TechnoFeminism*. Cambridge: Polity Press.

Wajcman, J., Bittman, M., Jones, P., Johnstone, L. and Brown, J. (2007) *The Impact of the Mobile Phone on Work/Life Balance: Phase 1 final report*. Australian Research Council Linkage Project. Canberra: ANU/AMTA.

Wallerstein, I. (1999) *The End of the World as We Know It: Social science for the twenty-first century*. Minneapolis, MN and London: University of Minnesota Press.

Ward, D. (ed.) (2008) *Television and Public Policy: Change and continuity in an era of global liberalization*. New York: Lawrence Erlbaum.

Waterman, D. (1992) '"Narrowcasting" and "broadcasting" on nonbroadcast media', *Communication Research*, 19 (1): 3–28.

Webster, F. (1995) *Theories of the Information Society*. London: Routledge.

Webster, F. (ed.) (2004) *The Information Society Reader*. Abingdon: Routledge.

Webster, F. (2007) *Theories of the Information Society* (online edn). Hoboken, NJ: Taylor & Francis. (1st edition, 1995.)

Weiner, N. (1961) *Cybernetics or Control and Communication in the Animal and the Machine*. Cambridge, MA: MIT Press. (1st edition, 1948.)

Whitty, M. (2002) 'Liar, Liar! An examination of how open, supportive and honest people are in chat rooms', *Computers in Human Behaviour*, 18: 343–52.

Whitty, M. and Gavin, J. (2001) 'Age/sex/location: uncovering the social cues in the development of online relationships', *CyberPsychology and Behaviour*, 4 (5): 623–30.

Williams, R. (1957) 'Fiction and the writing public', *Essays in Criticism*, 7: 422–8.

Williams, R. (1961) *The Long Revolution*. London: Chatto & Windus.

Williams, R. (1969) 'On reading Marcuse', *Cambridge Review*, May 30: 366–8.

Williams, R. (1970) 'Radical and/or respectable', in R. Boston (ed.), *The Press We Deserve*. London: Routledge & Kegan Paul. pp. 14–26.

Williams, R. (1973) *The Country and the City*. London: Chatto & Windus.

Williams, R. (1974a) *Television: Technology and cultural form*. London: Fontana.

Williams, R. (1974b) 'Communications as cultural science', *Journal of Communication*, 24: 17–24.

Williams, R. (1976a) *Keywords: A vocabulary of culture and society*. London: Fontana.

Williams, R. (1976b) *Communications*. Harmondsworth: Penguin. (1st edition, 1962.)

Williams, R. (1977a) *Marxism and Literature*. Oxford: Oxford University Press.

Williams, R. (1977b) 'Realism, naturalism and their alternatives', *Cine-tracts*, 1 (3): 1–6.

Williams, R. (1978) 'The press and popular culture: an historical perspective', in G. Boyce, J. Curran and P. Wingate (eds.), *Newspaper History: From the seventeenth century to the present day*. London: Constable. pp. 41–50.

Williams, R. (1979) *Modern Tragedy*. London: Verso. (1st edition, 1966.)

Williams, R. (1980a) 'Means of communication as means of production', in R. Williams, *Problems in Materialism and Culture*. London: Verso. pp. 50–66.

Williams, R. (1980b) 'Base and superstructure in Marxist cultural theory', in R. Williams, *Problems in Materialism and Culture*. London: Verso. pp. 31–49.

Williams, R. (ed.) (1981) *Contact: Human communication and its history*. London: Thames & Hudson.

Williams, R. (1983a) *Towards 2000*. London: Chatto & Windus.

Williams, R. (1983b) *Keywords: A vocabulary of culture and society*. London: Flamingo. (1st edition, 1976.)

Williams, R. (1986) 'The uses of cultural theory', *New Left Review*, 158: 19–31.

Williams, R. (1989a) 'Problems of the coming period', in R. Williams, R. Gable (ed.), *Resources of Hope: Culture, democracy, socialism*. London: Verso. pp. 161–74. (1st edition, 1983.)

Williams, R. (1989b) 'Brecht', in N. Belton, F. Mulhern and J. Taylor (eds.), *What I Came To Say*. London: Hutchinson-Radius. pp. 261–6. (1st edition, 1981.)

Williams, R. (1989c) 'Communications technologies and social institutions', in F. Mulhern (ed.), *What I Came to Say*. pp. 172–92. (1st edition, 1981.)

Williams, R. (1989d) 'Culture is ordinary', in R. Williams, R. Gable (ed.), *Resources of Hope*. London: Verso. pp. 3–18. (1st edition, 1958.)

Williams, R. (1990) *Culture and Society*. London: Hogarth. (1st edition, 1958.)

Williams, R. (1995) *The Sociology of Culture*. Chicago, IL: University of Chicago Press and Shocken Books. (1st edition, 1981.)

Willmott, G. (1996) *McLuhan, or Modernism in Reverse*. Toronto: University of Toronto Press.

Winston, B. (1998) *Media, Technology and Society: A history from the telegraph to the Internet*. Abingdon: Routledge.

Winston, B. (2005) *Messages: Free expression, media and the West from Gutenberg to Google*. Abingdon: Routledge.

Wolfreys, J. (1998) *Deconstruction – Derrida*. New York: St Martins Press.

Woo-Young, C. (2009) 'OhmyNews: citizen journalism in South Korea', in S. Allan and E. Thorsen (eds.), *Citizen Journalism: Global perspectives*. New York: Peter Lang. pp. 143–52.

Zayani, M. (ed.) (2005) *The Al Jazeera Phenomenon*. Boulder, CO: Paradigm.

Zelizer, B. (2004) *Taking Journalism Seriously: News and the academy*. Thousand Oaks, CA: Sage.

Zelizer, B. (ed.) (2009) *The Changing Faces of Journalism: Tabloidization, technology and truthiness*. New York: Routledge.

Made in the USA
Lexington, KY
19 January 2017